Cities around the World

Cities around the World

Struggles and Solutions to Urban Life

VOLUME 2

Jing Luo, Editor

An Imprint of ABC-CLIO, LLC
Santa Barbara, California • Denver, Colorado

Copyright © 2019 by ABC-CLIO, LLC

All rights reserved. No part of this publication may be reproduced, stored in a retrieval system, or transmitted, in any form or by any means, electronic, mechanical, photocopying, recording, or otherwise, except for the inclusion of brief quotations in a review, without prior permission in writing from the publisher.

Library of Congress Cataloging-in-Publication Data

Names: Luo, Jing, editor.
Title: Cities around the world : struggles and solutions to urban life / Jing Luo, Editor.
Description: First edition. | Santa Barbara, CA : ABC-CLIO, An Imprint of ABC-CLIO,
   LLC, [2019]– | Includes bibliographical references and index.
Identifiers: LCCN 2018051701 (print) | LCCN 2018052097 (ebook) |
   ISBN 9781440853869 (ebook) | ISBN 9781440853852 (hard copy (set) : alk. paper) |
   ISBN 9781440853876 (hard copy (vol. 1) : alk. paper) | ISBN 9781440853883
   (hard copy (vol. 2) : alk. paper)
Subjects: LCSH: City planning. | Policy sciences.
Classification: LCC HT166 (ebook) | LCC HT166 .C473 2019 (print) |
   DDC 307.1/216—dc23
LC record available at https://lccn.loc.gov/2018051701

ISBN: 978-1-4408-5385-2 (set)
      978-1-4408-5387-6 (vol. 1)
      978-1-4408-5388-3 (vol. 2)
      978-1-4408-5386-9 (ebook)

23 22 21 20 19   1 2 3 4 5

This book is also available as an eBook.

ABC-CLIO
An Imprint of ABC-CLIO, LLC

ABC-CLIO, LLC
147 Castilian Drive
Santa Barbara, California 93117
www.abc-clio.com

This book is printed on acid-free paper

Manufactured in the United States of America

Contents

VOLUME 1

Preface ix

Acknowledgments xi

Introduction xiii

Employment and Jobs 1
    Overview 1
    Lagos, Nigeria: Government Reform Is Key to Job Creation 6
    London, United Kingdom: Brexit, the Known Unknown 12
    Mumbai, India: Exploring Employment Solutions in Temporary Jobs 19
    New York City, United States: Economically and Environmentally Friendly 24
    Paris, France: A Locomotive of Job Creation 31
    Riyadh, Saudi Arabia: Creating Jobs in the Post–Oil-Boom Era 36
    San Juan, Puerto Rico, United States: A Stronger Local Government Is Key to Job Creation 41
    Seattle, United States: Have Job, Going Homeless 48
    Shenzhen, China: Struggle to Leave Shanzhai Behind 52
    Stockholm, Sweden: Employers Stress Educational Credentials 58

Energy and Sustainability 65
    Overview 65
    Beijing, China: Battling Water Shortage 70
    Copenhagen, Denmark: Striving to Be Carbon-Neutral by 2025 74
    Frankfurt, Germany: Protecting the City from Climate Changes 79
    London, United Kingdom: Improving Mobility Can Save Energy 86
    Melbourne, Australia: Toward a Greater Reliance on Alternative Energy 92
    Mumbai, India: Providing Energy for a City of 21 Million 97
    Pittsburgh, United States: Air Quality Is a Work in Progress 106
    Rio de Janeiro, Brazil: A City with a Passion for Conservation and Renewable Energy 111

Singapore City, Singapore: Go Solar! 116
Toronto, Canada: A City with a Passion for Energy Conservation 120

Green Spaces 127
  Overview 127
  Abu Dhabi, United Arab Emirates (UAE): Building a Greener City with a More Open Culture 131
  Aguascalientes, Mexico: Returning Industrial Ruin to Green Space 135
  Halifax, Canada: Near-Urban Wilderness Protection 140
  Hong Kong, China: Adding Green Spaces to Densely Populated Neighborhoods 147
  Moscow, Russia: Planting 1 Million Trees 154
  New York City, United States: Pursuit of More Green 159
  Paris, France: Returning to Nature 164
  Rotterdam, The Netherlands: Building an Edible City 169
  Tel Aviv, Israel: Community Gardening 173
  Tokyo, Japan: Making the City More Livable 178

Housing and Infrastructure 185
  Overview 185
  Almaty, Kazakhstan: Housing Reform 189
  Caracas, Venezuela: Will Informal Settlement Be Forever? 195
  Chongqing, China: Chongqing's Ingenuity in Providing Public Housing for a City of 33 Million 200
  Dandong, China: One Bridge, Two Islands 206
  Detroit, United States: Housing and Infrastructure after the Auto Boom 213
  Havana, Cuba: Facing Challenges of Housing and Infrastructure in Economic Transition 220
  Munich, Germany: The Munich Wall 226
  Sydney, Australia: Struggle for Affordable Housing 233
  Touba, Senegal: A Spiritual Solution to Affordable Housing 239
  Vienna, Austria: Making Access to Public Housing Equitable 244

Migration and Demographic Changes 249
  Overview 249
  Buenos Aires, Argentina: Impact of European Migration 254
  Guangzhou, China: Foreign Communities Facing Challenges of Adaptation 259
  Kinshasa, Democratic Republic of the Congo (DRC): Reaching for Demographic Dividend 264
  Lima, Peru: Migration and Demographic Changes Driven by Climate Changes 269
  London, United Kingdom: Facing the Challenges of Population Growth 274
  Los Angeles, United States: A Dynamic Demographic Mix 279
  Tehran, Iran: Toward a More Open and Tolerant Society 283
  Tokyo, Japan: Sustainable Growth Calls for Immigration Reform 289

Vancouver, Canada: The Most Asian City in the Western World   294
Williamsport, United States: A Quiet Town in Deep Pennsylvania   299

Index   305

VOLUME 2

Pollution   1
  Overview   1
  Baku, Azerbaijan: A Tainted Reputation   6
  Boston, United States: Cleaning Boston's Waterways—An Overview   11
  Flint, United States: National and Local Politics in the Creation of a Public Health Emergency   16
  Karachi, Pakistan: How Pollution Gets Out of Control   23
  Krakow, Poland: Old Furniture, New Fuel Source   28
  New Delhi, India: Success of Pollution Control Depends on Effective Collaboration   33
  Rome, Italy: Reducing Spatial Segregation Contributes to Pollution Control   39
  Sao Paulo, Brazil: Fighting the Deadly Air Pollution   45
  Seoul, South Korea: When Every Citizen Takes It to Heart   50
  Shiprock, United States: Radioactive from the Inside Out   55

Schools   61
  Overview   61
  Bamako, Mali: Private and Public Sectors of Education   67
  Berlin, Germany: Making the City a Center of Learning   72
  Boston, United States: A Model City of STEM Education   78
  Ouagadougou, Burkina Faso: Investing in Higher Education for the Country's Future   83
  Seoul, South Korea: "Education Fever"   87
  Sydney, Australia: Making International Education a Thriving Sector of the Economy   91
  Taipei, Taiwan: Taipei's K–12 Education and Special Education   96
  Tokyo, Japan: The *Yutori* Educational Reforms   100
  Vologda, Russia: Education in the Russian Federation—A City's Solutions   105
  Xi'an, China: Where China's Private Education Debuts   111

Traffic and Transportation   119
  Overview   119
  Beijing, China: Beijing's War on Traffic Congestion   124
  Casablanca, Morocco: Will a Change in Lunch Habit Improve the Town's Traffic?   130
  Istanbul, Turkey: Building More Tunnels and Bridges Won't Make Congestion Go Away   134
  Kolkata, India: When More People Drive Their Own Cars   140
  Mexico City, Mexico: Improving Governance Is Key to Solving Traffic Challenges   145

New York City, United States: The New York Subway   150
Osaka, Japan: Attracting Private Investments to Public Transportation   154
Saint Petersburg, Russia: Swamped with Traffic   160
Stuttgart, Germany: A City with the Best Mass Transit   165
Zurich, Switzerland: Improving Traffic and Transportation through All Possible Venues   170

Violence, Corruption, and Organized Crime   177
Overview   177
Aleppo, Syria: Drought, Global Warming, and Civil War   182
Baghdad, Iraq: Restitching a Torn Society Isn't Easy   187
Beijing, China: Tight Surveillance and Harsh Punishment   193
Brussels, Belgium: Facing Safety Challenges in the 21st Century   197
Chicago, United States: Stop the Crimes before They Spread   202
Kabul, Afghanistan: What Went Wrong?   207
Mexico City, Mexico: Crime, Corruption, and Violence Have Deep Roots   213
Seoul, South Korea: The Continuing Public Fight for Democracy   220
Sicily, Italy: Fighting Organized Crime in the New Era   226
Tokyo, Japan: Violence, Corruption, and Organized Crime   230

Waste Management   237
Overview   237
Baghdad, Iraq: Hauling Garbage in Hell on Earth   241
Cairo, Egypt: The Zabaleen   246
Calgary, Canada: Waste Management Is a National Effort and Calgary's Priority   251
Dakar, Senegal: Peri-Urban/Urban Agriculture and Urban Waste Management   257
Delhi, India: Current Problems and Opportunities for the Future of the National Capital Territory   262
Kobe, Japan: The Cleanest City in the World   267
Naples, Italy: Coping with a Rubbish Crisis   272
Oslo, Norway: Prevention and Reduction, What Makes Oslo Clean   276
Port-au-Prince, Haiti: Challenges of Waste Management under Poor Governance   281
San Francisco, United States: Becoming a "Zero-Waste City"   288
Singapore City, Singapore: Managing Food Waste   293

Selected Bibliography   299

About the Editor and Contributors   309

Index   315

Pollution

OVERVIEW

The 21st century has seen a number of terms that used to circulate within the scientific communities become part of the popular lexicon: carbon dioxide, carbon monoxide, nitrogen dioxide, sulfur dioxide, particulate matter (PM), $PM_{2.5}$, PM_{10}, and ozone. The list goes on. The linguistic changes reflect a dire reality. According to the data of the United Nations Environmental Program (UNEP), this is what happens to the world population every year: 6.5 million people die prematurely because of poor air quality, 600,000 children develop intellectual disabilities because of exposure to lead, 1.8 billion people are exposed to contaminated drinking water, 25 million agricultural workers experience unintentional pesticide poisoning, 8 million tons of plastic waste enter the world's oceans, and the world produces 50 million metric tons of e-waste (electronic hardware) every year (equivalent to 125,000 jumbo jets). The list goes on. Additionally, pollution results in climate changes that claim tens of thousands of lives each year, and financial losses in the billions of dollars. In this section, 10 articles are included to share successful experiences as well as failures of 10 world cities in their struggle for sustainable development.

Pollution Can Be Reversed, If There Is a Will

The experience of successful cities shows that sustaining a healthy environment depends on the strong will of every citizen. When citizens are involved in the decision-making process, and when they are committed to adopting environment-friendly lifestyles, they can achieve their environmental goals.

Boston, Massachusetts, is known for top educational institutions and a clean urban environment. What is less known is that Boston's water pollution was once notorious. As Cumo explains, the history of the treatment of the Charles River reflects a persistent effort by the city's residents to make the water clear. Historically, the Charles River not only provided drinking water to the city, but also carried its waste into Boston Harbor. Since the 17th century, as migration and farming activities intensified, the river was slowed down, resulting in a piling up of waste. Industrialization in the 19th century added its share of pollutants. As bacteria multiplied in the sewage-filled flow, the Charles River had become a source of stench by the 1960s. In the early 1970s, scientists and policymakers founded the Charles River Watershed Association to address the problem. They raised money to fund water treatment projects; their dream was to return the river to its original condition where people could swim and the water would be safe to drink. They received massive support from Bostonians who volunteered time, and eventually significant funding from the U.S. Environmental Protection Agency (EPA). By 2015, the river's water quality was raised to B+ from the D mark of four decades earlier. The success prompted the City to invest even more in the cleaning of the Boston Bay. The treatment work eventually succeeded. The message of Boston's water treatment story, as Cumo indicates, is that "clean water is not luxury, but a right of Bostonians and of Americans in general."

Similar to Boston, Seoul, the capital of South Korea, has cleaned up its pollution to become the seventh most sustainable city in the world. Seoul's struggle is arguably more impressive in that the city's scale is much larger. Its 25 million residents represent more than 25 times Boston's. Imagine the work needed to recycle 35,000 tons of waste per day or 85 percent of the total daily waste, not including the landfill. Compared to its recycling rate at barely 15 percent in 1995, Seoul's achievement is indeed impressive. Like Boston, Seoul has a river to treat. The Hangang River that runs across the city was polluted by industrial waste in the 1960s–70s to the extent that swimming was banned. Since the 1980s, a series of projects, with the latest being under way in 2017, have purified the water, revamped riverside parks, and built sidewalks on both banks. Seoul further established the Arisu program that monitors water quality in people's homes. Air quality, however, appears to be a challenge, not because the city lacks clean public transit, but because of pollutants wind-blown from China. The Air Quality Index shows that Seoul's AQI reading ranks just after those of New Delhi and Beijing. What the city can do is set up sophisticated AQI warning systems. So, what has made Seoul succeed in most of its environmental plans? Chung argues that it is because the challenges are so great that they invigorate government and people to constantly watch out for ecological issues and address them in a timely manner.

The story of Baku, the capital city of Azerbaijan, is one of a polluted environment on its way to recovery. Baku is endowed with oil, and residents were already extracting oil back in Marco Polo's time. In certain locations, the fossil fuel flows out of the ground without drilling needed. Historically, local people used oil for lighting and treating skin disorders. When kerosene became industrial fuel in the 19th century, Baku became an oil production center, attracting migrant populations to the city. During the era when Azerbaijan was part of the Soviet Union, production was further intensified. The industry used a crude production method, known as "gushers," to pump oil mixed with sand and gases into oil ponds. A consequence of the method was that it polluted nearby soil, rivers, and the Caspian Sea. As Kovalyuk notes, during the Soviet era, the motto was "Break the record at any price," with no concern for the environment. Oil refineries likewise dumped by-product chemicals into the environment. In addition, unregulated waste disposal, unmanaged waste incineration, and exhaust from motor vehicles contributed to heavy air pollution. In 2007, Baku was ranked as the filthiest city in the world according to one report. Baku started to aggressively treat its environment under the leadership of the Ministry of Ecology and Natural Resources. Projects included detoxification, reforestation, sewage purification, emission control, and building pipelines to supply residents with clean underground water. Universities and research centers also stepped up educational efforts. Apparently, Baku is repeating much of what Boston went through, except that the scale of damage is much larger and the results are yet to be seen.

Krakow is the second-largest city in Poland with a population of 765,000. Like Baku, Krakow was once under Soviet influence. Part of the economy remains state-owned today, and coal mining is part of it. Discarding outdated production methods is a solution in itself for most of the city's pollution problems, according to Polyuha. The primary environmental problem for Krakow is air pollution from coal burning. In the worst times of the year, the particulate density of PM_{10} and $PM_{2.5}$ could reach more than 50 percent above the WHO-recommended safety limit. The sources of the smog are surrounding steel plants, including factories as far as in the Czech Republic. Another source is Soviet-era coal-burning stoves that people continue to use in their homes. The geolocation of the city being in a basin does not help dissipate smog quickly. With regard to solutions, in Krakow's case, many solutions seem to be coming along with the progression of economic liberalization. As Soviet-era plants are gradually closed, coal burning will stop. The municipality assists environmental cleaning by creating laws and regulations to reduce reliance on coal, by financially helping households replace old stoves, and by building central heating for the city. Being historically a center of modern science, Krakow is getting serious with its environment issues now.

With 19 million inhabitants in its metropolitan region, Sao Paulo, Brazil, is the largest industrial and business hub in Latin America. Its manufacturing sector is diverse, producing everything from fuel-energy products and motor vehicles, to clothing and daily appliances. As a result, the Paulistanos typically live a fast-paced life and spend a lot of time on the road. "Earn in Sao Paulo, so you can spend in Rio" is a Brazilian aphorism reflecting a popular perception that one could strike it rich by working hard in Sao Paulo. However, to meet the daily mobility requirement, the Paulistanos prefer driving their own cars. There are 6.3 million cars in the metropolitan region, not counting the public transit vehicles that carry 30 percent of the residents. In terms of the impact on people's health, residents of Sao Paulo are constantly breathing in the smoggy air, 90 percent of which comes from car exhaust. Polluted air kills more people than breast cancer and six times more than AIDS, Giraldo writes. To address this problem, the municipality is trying to reduce the number of cars. Sao Paulo has adopted Beijing's method of restricting car use by assigning driving days according to plate numbers. However, that only leads to a reduction by 20 percent. The city further added new bus lines and metro lines, and is constantly working to improve connectivity and efficiency. These efforts appear to be on the right track. The challenge remains, as Giraldo indicates, convincing the majority to use the mass transit. Before that happens, the problem is only partially resolved.

Mismanagement and Lack of Management Can Exacerbate Pollution

While every citizen shares the responsibility of protecting the environment, the government plays a more important role. Because sources of pollution are complex, only the government is in a position to organize efforts coming from all sectors of the society. The government can inform and inspire people, set policies, monitor flaws, and enforce regulations. Boston and Seoul's stories attest to the importance of a strong urban government. On the other hand, when the governance makes wrong decisions, the impact can be widespread. Likewise, when the governance is inefficient or corrupt, there is little hope for the city to tackle pollution.

Some cities apparently face much tougher struggles than others. Karachi, Pakistan, is one of them. Being the most populous urban center in Pakistan and a city with robust industrial growth, Karachi's pollution is one of the worst. A major cause, as Cumo reveals, is that "neither Karachi's government, nor the private sector appear to rate the diminution of pollution a priority. Without the commitment of the government and the private sector, there seems to be little chance of making headway against pollution." One noticeable problem that hurts the urban scene, as Cumo points out, is the absence of functional waste management. Garbage is piled up on the streets; some of it is burned, sending smoke into the air; some finds its way to the beaches. Additionally, traffic congestion accounts for more air pollution. Due to a lack of public transit, private cars abound, filling Karachi's air with exhaust and all sorts of lung-damaging particles. By 2030, there will be 2 million cars and 3 million motorcycles on the road. To improve transportation, Karachi is providing funds to build a fleet of buses. In the meantime, the city is also reaching out for China's support.

New Delhi, India, with a population of close to 17 million, suffers from some of the world's worst air pollution. As a result, cardiovascular and respiratory ailments are the city's leading causes of death. The sources of the pollution, as Haney notes, are varied, including motor vehicle traffic, road dust, indoor cooking stoves, construction dust, brick kilns, coal-fired power generation, factories, and open burning of waste materials. But behind all these is a broader problem that appears to be plaguing both Indian and Pakistani pollution control—a lack of management. For example, while air-monitoring stations exist across Indian cities, sampling methodologies vary, resulting in inconsistent interpretation of toxicity levels. Deficiencies like these make detailed identification, such as the sizes of particulate matters and chemical compounds, impossible. As a result, enforcement of regulations is lacking. As such, in areas such as emission control, traffic regulation, and waste disposal, there exists a lack of standards. An important step, according to Haney, is to bring together scientists who work in different areas of the pollution control process and policymakers, because understanding the complex interconnections among pollution sources is key to creating effective measures to reduce air pollution levels and mitigate the impacts associated with climate changes.

Flint, Michigan, is different from Karachi in many aspects. There is, however, one thing in common: when the management breaks down, disasters are bound to happen, and with no less severity. The story of the water pollution crisis in Flint reflects a problem on a different scale: when city administrators are blinded by their political divide, they can make the city's water undrinkable. What Evans presents are pieces of a puzzle that, when put together, show the picture of an environmental nightmare: thousands of children testing positive for lead poisoning, mistakes made with regard to water supply options, racial bias given the majority of the citizens affected were African Americans, administrators sticking to party lines, and finally, ignoring a simple solution costing just $100 per day for the right anti-corrosion treatment. Evans shows that policymaking in the United States can be affected by political divisions, which is reflected in the adamant denials. He argues that the Flint water crisis demonstrates "differing approaches of the country's two main political parties." The story of Flint also attests to the fact that sustainable development must include the monitoring of policy implementation as an integral element.

Shiprock, New Mexico, is one of the sites funded by the EPA's Superfund to clean up radioactive waste. Cleaning and testing continue to this day. The majority of the population of Shiprock is Native American, its government being represented by the Navajo Nation. From 1944 to 1986, nearly 30 million tons of uranium ore were extracted from Navajo lands under leases with the Navajo Nation where Shiprock is located. Johansen's article explores a horrific environmental disaster involving Native Americans working in uranium mines for decades, hauling thousands of barrels of uranium ore also known as "yellowcake." Hundreds of workers died of lung cancer and other types of diseases believed to have been caused by inhaling airborne radioactive dust, drinking and bathing in contaminated water, and living in dwellings built with radioactive building materials made of rocks of the tailings. Johansen indicates that the health hazards were not communicated to the miners in a timely way. Some neighborhoods near tailing piles "were not told of the danger until 1990, 22 years after the mill that produced the pile had closed, and 12 years after Congress authorized the cleanup of uranium mill tailings in Navajo country." Johansen stresses that even though the mining has stopped, the history of its deadly toll has yet to be completely understood or told.

Fostering the Social Capital Is Key to Sustainability

Urban sprawl tends to go hand in hand with pollution. The 21st century is seeing more migrations to metropolises than ever before. Migrant populations often find themselves neglected. Their economic conditions eventually affect the social fabric of society. Creatively handling new problems is integral to municipalities' responsibilities today.

Rome, Italy, is one of the oldest and largest cities in the world. The city's historical urban design features a large number of green spaces and road systems. The greenery contributes to better air quality and decorative appeal. High population density in modern Rome carries visible socio-environmental impact, as Ard notes, left by urban sprawl. Urban sprawl is associated with land fragmentation, increased car use, air pollution, biodiversity loss, and class segregation. With the increase in the number of journeys made in private cars, 60 percent of all journeys currently,

Rome's air pollution has worsened. Spatial inequality is becoming increasingly noticeable. In the 1990s, refugees fleeing from the Balkan conflicts built small clusters of dwellings forming shantytowns. Marginalization resulted in low education rate, the spread of infectious diseases, high infant mortality, and widespread poverty. These dwellings were later removed, and the residents were relocated to government housing. Ard argues that spatial inequality, however, will likely be a continuous challenge for Rome due to the recent humanitarian crisis in which hundreds of thousands of political and economic refugees have flooded into Europe. As a result, improving social capital will ensure the rights and participation of the vulnerable population. The struggle to foster social capital in conjunction with pollution control sets forth a new frontline for Rome and many European countries.

Further Reading
Sifferlin, Alexandra. 2017. "Here's How Many People Die from Pollution around the World." *Time—Health,* October 19. http://time.com/4989641/water-air-pollution-deaths.
United Nations Environment Assembly. n.d. "Air." http://web.unep.org/environmentassembly/air.

Baku, Azerbaijan: A Tainted Reputation

In 2007, Baku, the capital city of Azerbaijan, was ranked the filthiest of the world's 215 cities by Mercer's Human Resource Consulting. At that time, the assessment seemed very fair—after all, the city had most aspects of pollution on the checklist—dense smog in the air, poisoned waters, oil spills in the Caspian Sea, eroding soil. The sadly ironic fact is that for the most part the main resource of the country's wellness is the source of its dire ecological situation—the Baku oil industry.

LAYERS OF DISASTER

The History of Blackening Gold. Baku oil fields have been there, discovered and used, for ages—the first mentions date back as far as to the time of Marco Polo, the 13th century. However, it should be noted that in the preindustrial period, it never hurt the ecology much. The oil was only used for burning and as a salve for skin diseases, so it sufficed to use what seeped to the surface, with no heavy drilling required. As time passed and the Russian Empire grew, the true potential of the oil fields was inevitably to be unlocked.

In the beginning of the 19th century, Baku Khanate became a part of the Russian Empire. The state monopoly for oil extraction was purchased by individual industrialists from Russia and Armenia. Given the primitive methods of that time—shallow wells dug manually and the absence of incentive to enhance them—the initial volumes were not at all impressive. The demand remained moderate, still revolving around using the oil for lighting and traditional remedies.

By the end of the 19th century, however, kerosene and paraffin factories started to appear as the answer to the approaching technological era. The drilling became increasingly commercial, with Western investments pouring in. Soon enough, the oil industry became the pivot point for the whole city of Baku. The cityscape was dependent on the financial influx, which in turn was attracted by the oil.

At that time the main source and an imminent consequence of the oil production were oil gushers. A large amount of oil, gas, highly mineralized rock, and water would be gushed out from the well under high pressure in the process of the drilling. Without the appropriate technology, which was not introduced fast enough, this was a quick but dangerous and ecologically harmful way of producing the black gold.

In the 20th century, which was full of wars and revolutions, Azerbaijan's oil industry was a rollercoaster of overproduction at one moment and multiple oil crises at other times. Ups or downs, one thing remained unchanged—no one had the time or the money to care about the harm to the environment when the motto was "Break the record at any price," To make ecological conditions worse, a new potential area for offshore exploration was introduced, and the quest for oil moved into the Caspian Sea. The total oil production of Azerbaijan (Baku being one of the major sources) by the middle of the 20th century was a record 23.5 million tons, but the price might have been too high.

To sum up this short historical introduction, since the dawn of industrial exploration, oil-related pollution sources of Baku included both oil gushers and oil refinery waste. The gushers, spontaneously initiated by drilling, as a combination of gas, oil, and oil-field water, contaminated the air, the soil, and the water around and inside Baku. The oil refinery waste, instead of being properly utilized, has been

A decommissioned oil derrick decorates a park in Baku, Azerbaijan, 2017. Baku's oil industry brought wealth to the city, but sloppy, Soviet-style extraction methods led to massive pollution. Since 2007, the city has embarked on an aggressive campaign to improve the quality of its land, air, and water. (Aquatarkus/iStockphoto.com)

dumped in the area for years. All this means that it is small wonder the ecological state of the city was critical and called for large-scale actions and considerable investment.

Poison in the Air. It is, however, not only the oil industry impact that should be of concern. Any large industrial city full of people working in factories—and in the case of Baku, oil fields—is bound to produce trash in enormous quantities. These millions of tons of garbage must be disposed of properly to avoid harming the environment. Unfortunately, that is exactly what Baku municipality did not consider for many years.

Since 1963, the garbage has been uncontrollably piling up in the Balakhani landfill, the total area of which is approximately 120 hectares. No precise records of waste amounts are available. The preferred way of garbage disposal used to be through incineration. Every now and then, a giant cloud of thick smog from the burning waste would enshroud the city of Baku, rendering the atmosphere hardly breathable.

Big industrial city also means high transport density, and factories mean harmful fume releases into the air. According to the statistics for the country, in the year 2000 the emissions release to the atmosphere amounted to 908.1 thousand tons of CO_2 including 392.7 thousand tons from transport, while in 2011 the indices grew to 970 thousand tons and 750 thousand tons correspondingly. This means the growth rate for the emissions release from transport for 2000–2011 is 190.8 percent, a number that must be particularly true for the capital city (Huseynov 2012).

Poison in the Water. The capital of Azerbaijan has had a shortage of potable water starting in the late 19th century, even though Baku's territory is surrounded by lakes—Boyukshor, Khodasan, Binagadi, Bulbulya, and so on. All of them are filled with salty water, and all of them are becoming increasingly polluted.

The lakes of Absheron peninsula used to be outstanding sources of therapeutic muds and salts before the golden age of industrial oil production. Both oil and oil field waters eventually ending up in the lakes, ruining the chemical composition of the water. Phenols, detergents, and petrochemicals can be found in most of the lakes. Meanwhile, some of them, namely Boyukshor, also suffer from other industrial facilities' discharges (Azerelektroterm, Baku iodine plant, etc.), with environmental levels of lead (300 times over the norm), copper (200 times over the norm), and zinc (150 times over the norm) going off the charts. The surface of Boyukshor is covered with an oil slick, while heavy oil residue has permeated the lake mud as deep as one meter (Kahramanova 2012).

An underdeveloped sewage system has made matters even worse. Uncontrolled industrial and residential water release also led to a rising of the water level and the consequential increase of the area covered by the lakes. Absheron lakes constitute a closed system with no significant outflow, so the waste continues to accumulate, adding to the city's dire ecological situation.

CITY SPRING CLEANING

In recent decades as the dust of getting independence from the USSR finally settled (Azerbaijan became independent in 1991), the country realized the extent of the ecological disaster it was facing. Large-scale programs, aimed at the improvement of polluted air, water, and soil, have been hastily introduced. This started in 2001 with the establishment of the Ministry of Ecology and Natural Resources; continued through 2003–4 as the president of Azerbaijan Republic launched several programs on reforestation, rational use of pastures, and development of a hydro-meteorological service; and was pushed into action with what was presented as the crucial step: "The Plan of complex measures on Azerbaijan Republic ecological situation improvement for 2006–2010." The oil industry, as much as it has proved to be a curse for the environment, supplied the financial resources for implementation of the latter. In 2008, Azerbaijan also became a part of the World Bank Global Gas Flaring Reduction Partnership, taking part in international scientific seminars and conferences and introducing a number of contemporary measures to the oil and gas production processes.

Battling the major enemy—irresponsible oil production and refinery—the plan imposed the task of environment protection on the companies dealing in oil drilling. In 2006, the State Oil Company of Azerbaijan Republic (SOCAR) and a foreign investor, Lancer Services S.A., established a company working solely with detoxification and disposal of harmful substances released into the water, soil, and atmosphere. Ekol Engineering Services has kept itself busy with disposal of industrial waste, cleansing of groundwaters, oil sludge treatment, and ecological monitoring activities. There was so much to do that as long as the companies, bound by governmental regulations, hired specialists, they can get contracts.

As a solution to the problems of garbage incineration, smog, and the growing landfill, the plan introduced a waste-to-energy incineration and recycling plant in Balakhani, supposedly the largest in Eastern Europe. Covering the area of 20 hectares with a capacity of 500,000 tons of municipal solid waste per year, it receives approximately 350 tons of solid waste daily with 25 percent of it recycled and reused. According to the ecological norms of the European Union, the ash residue after incineration is to be filtered, with heavy ashes used in road construction. The very same plant also functions as an alternative energy source, along with wind power plants in Absheron peninsula, Ganja-Dahskesen, Sharur-Julfa, and the Caspian seashore.

The Absheron lake pollution problem also calls for immediate attention. So far, the steps taken in that direction include the improvement of sewage system filters, residential sewage purification, allowing for reuse of the water, and oil-field waters' volume contraction. The latter is achieved through the return of water to clean levels, with the improvement in drilling and filtering technologies. Much work is also required to clean the lake system of oil and chemical waste, with eventual restoration of therapeutic mud layers and salt levels to normal.

A set of measures has also been taken to provide Baku citizens with much-needed freshwater. Water purification units installed in 2007–8 and the Oguz-Gabala-Baku water pipeline project can be considered major successes in this critical task. The potable water is delivered at the rate of 5 kiloliters per second from underground springs of the Oguz-Gabala region of the country to Baku, which gives a life-saving resource to 75 percent of its population.

Another crucial resource ecologically disrupted by oil production in the Baku region is the Caspian Sea. With offshore oil exploration and continuous industrial water releases, in recent years the Azerbaijan government decided to deal with the matter at hand. As part of the plan implementation, the Ministry of Ecology and Natural Resources has been cleaning the Baku bay of shipwreck and bulk waste.

According to the latest annual report found on the official Azerbaijan Ministry of Ecology and Natural Resources site and filed in 2014, a certain amount of work is being done to raise citizens' awareness. Apparently, the ministry widely uses fines and warnings as a countermeasure for various violations in the fields of water resources; air, soil, and flora protection; as well as infringements of state regulation in the field of industrial waste management.

The ministry also has cooperated with higher education institutions, establishing a university organization called "Ecoclub" with the laudable purpose of promoting the idea of natural resources conservation among young people.

Established as a part of the ministry, the Azerbaijan National Monitoring Department of Environment continues its monitoring activity in atmospheric pollution, chemical composition of atmospheric rainfalls, surface water and soil pollution with oil products, pesticides, and heavy metals. According to the report, the data comes to the department at an impressive rate of every half hour.

Finally, in addition to environmental remediation procedures mentioned earlier, some restoration steps are also reported to be under way, such as reforestation (10,125 hectares in 2014) and some attempts to recover endangered fish species in the Caspian Sea, rivers, and inner-water basins of the region.

Taking into consideration all the measures that the city municipality and the country as a whole implemented over the years since its dishonorable mention in the ranking of 2007, Baku must really be on its way to clearing both its name and the surrounding area.

Anastasia Kovalyuk

See also: Green Spaces: Moscow, Russia: Planting 1 Million Trees; *Pollution:* Krakow, Poland: Old Furniture, New Fuel Source

Further Reading

Alakbarov, Farid. 2002. "Baku: City That Oil Built." *Azerbaijan International*, Summer. http://azer.com/aiweb/categories/magazine/ai102_folder/102_articles/102_overview_alakbarov.html.

Huseynov, Arif. 2012. "Ecological Situation in Azerbaijan and Ways of Its Management" (in Russian). *Kazan Technological University Journal Scholar* 15, 22. http://cyberleninka.ru/article/n/ekologicheskaya-obstanovka-v-azerbaydzhane-i-puti-eyo-ozdorovleniya.

Kahramanova, Shakhla. 2012. "The Basic Sources of Lake Pollution on the Territory of Baku" (in Russian). *Academic Journal UralNIIproektRAASN*. February. http://cyberleninka.ru/article/n/osnovnye-istochniki-zagryazneniya-ozer-na-territorii-goroda-baku.

Mir-Ismail, Alman. 2011. "Azerbaijan Opens New Water Pipeline." *Eurasia Daily Monitor*, January. https://jamestown.org/program/azerbaijan-opens-new-water-pipeline/#sthash.GkqCL4lR.dpuf.

UN. 2011. "Environmental Performance Reviews—Azerbaijan." http://www.unece.org/fileadmin/DAM/env/epr/epr_studies/Synopsis/Azerbaijan%20ECE.CEP.158.synopsis%20english.pdf.

World Bank Group. 2013. "In Azerbaijan: Managing Waste Safely." *World Bank,* August. http://www.worldbank.org/en/results/2013/08/21/in-azerbaijan-managing-waste-safely.

Boston, United States: Cleaning Boston's Waterways—An Overview

Pollution has besieged Boston as it has every other city. In a metropolis in which water is so important, the story of pollution in Boston is in part the saga of waterborne pollution and its effects on the city. An important aspect of this story is Boston's residents. They have not been complacent about pollution but have fought it, notably in the Charles River and Boston Harbor. Success has crowned these efforts, so that Boston has emerged as a hallmark of what is possible to achieve through gritty environmental action.

ORIGINS OF THE PROBLEM OF POLLUTION

Geography has made water a central feature of Boston, Massachusetts, a port along the Atlantic Ocean and with the Charles River running through the city. The centrality of water has led the literature to focus on aquatic pollution in the city to include the harbor and its estuary and the Charles River. Ecologists have been keen to identify estuaries, the intersection between the briny ocean and the freshwater river, as regions of rich biodiversity and as places sensitive to the deleterious effects of pollution. In this context, one may think of pollution as any human-made element that degrades the environment. As humans have grown more numerous, they have become prodigal polluters, and one need not reflect long to think of multiple ways that people, through the ordinary discharge of wastes, through agriculture and industry, and through transportation, pollute their environs. This scenario has unfolded in Boston as elsewhere.

Pollution must not always have been a concern in Boston. In pre-Columbian times, human settlements along the Charles River and near the Atlantic Ocean must have been sparse and transient, as even with the advent of agriculture, many Native American groups were slow to give up hunting and gathering and become sedentary. Because human populations were small and settlements temporary, people did not befoul their environment to any great degree. In any case, nature could cope with human waste in two ways in what is today Boston. First, people who discharged their waste into the Charles River allowed its natural flow to transport that waste downstream to the ocean, moving waste from an area of greater to lesser concentration, a process known as diffusion. A second force and one that complemented the first was the tide. Recall that the moon exerts a gravitational attraction upon earth, including its bodies of water. As the moon revolves around earth, it causes water to bulge as gravity draws it toward the moon. The bulging of the Atlantic Ocean in Boston Harbor pushes water up the Charles River, causing the ocean and river to rise. Twice daily this rising of the ocean and river reaches an apex, known as high tide, and twice it ebbs to its lowest point, known as low tide. The movement of water from high to low tide causes a kind of flushing of pollution. The water gathers pollutants at high tide and puts them out to sea at low tide. All this is prelude to announcing the fact that left to itself, Boston could cope with pollution from small bands of nomads or semi-nomads who discharged their wastes into the Charles River.

Problems only arose with the migration of Europeans, at first the English, into what would become Boston beginning in the 17th century. These Europeans were entirely sedentary, having adopted agriculture millennia earlier in the Old World. Even so, their numbers were at first small, and pollution became a problem only around the turn of the 19th century as populations began to grow, and perhaps more importantly, people began to modify their environment, weakening the effects of the Charles River and the tide. By the 1820s, Bostonians had begun to dam parts of the Charles River, impeding its natural flow toward the ocean. These dams were meant to provide a source of falling water to turn the waterwheels that would in turn power the new mills of the Industrial Revolution. But water that could not flow toward the ocean could not carry wastes with it, allowing pollution to build to hazardous levels. In the 1830s, the railroad, an English invention, made its debut in Boston, an early adapter of this technology. The locomotive, burning coal, was an obvious polluter as the burning of coal liberated innumerable pollutants. The release of carbon dioxide, carbon monoxide, and sulfur dioxide alone polluted the atmosphere and has led to global warming and various modifications of the climate including the production of acid rain. In short order a green slime began to cover aquatic environments and produce a horrible stench as bacteria began to feast on sewage and multiply. These bacteria, as part of their life cycle, released the gases, themselves a type of pollution, that caused the stench; and by about the mid-19th-century, parts of Boston were cesspools of filth. Sewage from homes and factories continued to pour into these cesspools, exacerbating the problems of pollution.

BOSTON SEEKS TO REMEDY THE PROBLEMS OF POLLUTION

Apart from the ethos of conservation during the Progressive Era, the 19th century was not a period of environmental activism. Pollution had damaged the estuary of Boston's harbor, the estuary being known as the Back Bay. In the 19th century, Boston's authorities gave no thought to trying to restore the estuary to something of its former biodiversity. Rather, more human activity was in the offing. The first attempt in the late 19th century was simply to remake this former estuary into a neighborhood. By filling the formerly aquatic environment with gravel and soil, the authorities of Boston could create a kind of landfill. This new land was to be an exclusive, pricey neighborhood. It had to be an expensive area to keep out the poor, immigrants, and other undesirables who would likely only exacerbate the problems of pollution. With private and public capital, Boston's authorities transformed the Back Bay into a posh region for the city's elites. This tactic did not solve the problem of pollution but only confined filth to other, less attractive areas of Boston. Nineteenth-century Boston did not tackle the twin problems of poverty and pollution that made the slums so repugnant.

A view of Boston across the Charles River. Once heavily polluted, the Charles River is now a popular destination for sailing, kayaking, and other watersports. (Luna Marina /Dreamstime.com)

The pollution of the Charles River was not entirely Boston's fault. Upriver farms discharged agrochemicals like fertilizers, herbicides, and insecticides into the Charles River. The use of these chemicals and their runoff had begun after about 1840 but had become serious only after World War II because of advances in agricultural chemistry. For example, an increase in the use of nitrogenous fertilizers, notably anhydrous ammonium, led to the river's pollution with nitrates. Pollution grew as farmers near Boston saw synthetic fertilizers as the answer to the long-standing problem of infertile soils, at least in comparison to lands farther west. Boston's industries added to this pollution, so that by the 1960s, the Charles River was arguably among the dirtiest waterways in the United States.

Boston's residents were not satisfied with the status quo. Benefiting from the incipient environmental movement, Boston's forward-looking scientists and policy-makers formed in the early 1970s the Charles River Watershed Association (CRWA). Not content to work on the margins, the CRWA has the ambitious agenda of restoring the Charles River to as pristine a condition as possible. From the outset the organization wanted to restore the river to such a state that Bostonians could boat and swim in it and even drink from it. This ambitious goal could not be achieved without the commitment of massive resources, and the CRWA early looked for partners who could finance a cleanup campaign. Alliances followed with the State of Massachusetts and the federal government, namely the U.S. Environmental Protection Agency (EPA). By 1991, the EPA alone contributed $1.5 million annually to clean up the Charles River. The CRWA makes the most of these resources by relying on the talents of thousands of volunteers who sample water quality at 37 sites along the river. With its money, the CRWA has hired scientists and engineers to plan policy and guide the efforts to clean the Charles River. Buoyed by this talent, the CRWA announced in 2005 the goal of making water from the river safe enough to drink within a decade. The achievement of this goal was not meant by 2015, but the CRWA is nearing its objectives. When the CRWA began work some four decades ago, it graded water quality in the Charles River a D. Today steady, workmanlike progress has raised this mark to a B+. Of course, machinations in Washington, D.C., threaten to undermine progress as the new Trump administration appears hostile to efforts to clean up the nation's bodies of water or at least hostile to the idea of committing federal dollars to accomplish this task. The CRWA may need to rely more on local and state funds rather than on assistance from the EPA. Whatever the outcome in Washington, D.C., the CRWA maintains a commitment to the ideal that a pollution-free Charles River is a public good that benefits all Bostonians. Clean water is not a luxury, but a right of Bostonians and of Americans in general.

The desire to purify Boston's water spread beyond the confines of the Charles River to Boston Harbor. As with the river, pollution reached a dismal state in the harbor before Boston acted. This state of affairs is not surprising given the intimate connection between river and harbor. It is axiomatic that whatever pollution lurked in the river inevitably reached the harbor because of the inexorable flow of the Charles River downstream toward the harbor. To pollute the Charles River was at the same time a decision to pollute the adjacent harbor into which the river emptied. In many ways, then, the history of Boston Harbor mirrored that of the Charles River. Almost from Boston's founding in 1630, its residents built sewers that discharged wastes into the harbor. Over time, the stench that had characterized conditions in the river stretched over the harbor as well. In brief but intense intervals at the end of the 18th and the beginning of the 19th century, in the late 19th century, and after 1980, discontent bubbled to the surface. The first episode in the late 18th and early 19th centuries stemmed from what was surmised about the transmission of diseases, then not a science. In this period, the old miasma theory recrudesced. The miasma theory stipulated that pollution—in this case decaying sewage and the microbial action associated it (though microbes were then only poorly understood)—corrupted the air, causing it somehow to carry contagion. As a result, disease descended on the hapless residents of Boston, causing epidemics, illness, and death. To fight disease was thus to fight pollution. In the late 19th century, as part of the Progressive Era, an interest arose in sanitation as a way to combat pollution and by combating pollution to keep diseases at bay. The sanitation movement decried conditions in Boston Harbor and demanded the creation of a cleanup campaign. After 1980, the modern environmental movement, a creation of the 1960s and the dissatisfaction with the agrochemical industry and its discontents, demanded action to cleanse the harbor of pollutants. Citizens mobilized, lawsuits proliferated, and ultimately Boston spent several billions of dollars to reduce pollution in the harbor. Once one of the most polluted parts of the United States, Boston Harbor emerged in the 21st century as among the cleanest bodies of water. Bostonians had taken back their harbor and their city, minimized pollution, and restored something of the pristine beauty of the metropolis and the water that graced it. The success of the cleanup campaign demonstrated that in unity the residents of Boston could

Charles River

Massachusetts's longest river to have its source (Hopkinton in Middlesex County) within the state, the 80-mile (130-kilometer) Charles River empties into the Atlantic Ocean at Boston Harbor. As such, the river, draining some 300 square miles, is central to the geography, economy, recreation, and ecology of Boston and Massachusetts at large. The river's economic importance was evident early because it yielded fish and shellfish to the pre-Columbian peoples—Mohican, Nauset, Wampanoag, Pocomtuc, Pequot, Nipmuc, and Massachusetts—who settled the area. These groups inhabited lands near the river perhaps 4,000 years before Europeans' arrival in the 17th century. In 1615, English explorer John Smith (1580–1631) named the river after the future King Charles I (1600–1649). Boston's founding a few years later demonstrated England's intention to settle Massachusetts and control the river. In the 1630s, the English established businesses, schools, a college, and a park near the Charles River. Occupying and conducting business in these lands, the English and other Europeans who settled the watershed disturbed the river's ecology. Notable were projects to dam the river and fill the estuary. Inhabiting the watershed in dense populations, Europeans polluted the Charles River more than American Indians had in pre-contact times. Pollution endangered aquatic animals, including the uncommon blue-spotted salamander and spotted turtle, and plants, among them the laurel rhododendron, river bulrush, and Dragon's-mouth orchid. Although the Charles River cannot be returned to pristine condition, environmentalists have done much to rehabilitate it.

achieve notable victories and bring a body of water back to nearly pristine condition. The success of Boston Harbor became a hallmark of success for the environmental movement and the desire to rid the United States of pollution and its many deleterious effects.

Success in fighting pollution in the Charles River and Boston Harbor has not banished pollution from Boston. Today the battlefield appears to have shifted to the air, where pollution remains a menace. By one estimate, Bostonians, by breathing in pollution from the air, inhale the equivalent of five cigarettes per year. Although this number may not seem perilous, it is enough to give pause. Automobiles, spewing a kind of airborne sewage of pollutants into the atmosphere, are the bane of Boston and other cities. Many of these airborne particles are incredibly small, with a diameter less than one-tenth the width of a human hair. Being so small, these particles penetrate deep into the body, causing great mischief. Boston has yet another battle to wage against pollution.

Christopher Cumo

See also: Waste Management: San Francisco, United States: Becoming a "Zero-Waste City"

Further Reading

Dolin, Eric Jay. *Political Waters: The Long, Dirty, Contentious, Incredibly Expensive but Eventually Triumphant History of Boston Harbor—A Unique Environmental Success Story.* Amherst and Boston: University of Massachusetts Press, 2004.

Kemp, Roger L., ed. *Cities and Water: A Handbook for Planning.* Jefferson, NC, and London: McFarland, 2009.

Newman, William A., and Wilfred E. Holton. *Boston's Back Bay: The Story of America's Greatest Nineteenth-Century Landfill Project.* Boston: Northeastern University Press, 2006.

Flint, United States: National and Local Politics in the Creation of a Public Health Emergency

In April 2014, the city of Flint, Michigan, switched to a new source for its water system and began receiving water from the Flint River instead of Lake Huron. A year and a half later, after most of the city's residents had been exposed to high lead levels and a host of other health problems, Flint switched back. Originally aimed at saving money, the poor decision making and bad policies wound up endangering the health of the city's 100,000 residents and costing hundreds of millions of dollars.

FLINT, MICHIGAN: BACKGROUND

Flint's history is similar to that of many other industrial cities in America's Midwest. Like Detroit, approximately 70 miles (110 km) to the southeast, and other cities in the state of Michigan, beginning in the early 20th century, Flint's economy was driven by the automotive industry. By the mid-20th century, it was home to one of the nation's biggest car-manufacturing plants. Flint's population peaked in 1963 at almost 200,000.

However, as factories began to close in Michigan and throughout the Midwest, unemployment increased and people began to leave. Between 2000 and 2015, Michigan was the only state[1] in the country whose population remained stagnant. While the population nationwide grew approximately 10 percent, Michigan lost about 0.5 percent of its population. During that same period, Flint's population loss was far greater than the state average, with the city shedding approximately one-fifth of its population. Today Flint's population stands at approximately 98,000, less than half that of its peak.

Flint is an impoverished city, with approximately 40 percent of its population below the poverty line, more than twice the statewide and nationwide rates. Flint's median household income is less than half the state or national median income. The city has a black majority in a state that is 80 percent white. Thus, leading up to the water crisis, the city was already poorer and demographically different than the rest of the state of Michigan.

POLITICAL FRAMEWORK

In 2011, Michigan's newly elected Republican governor, Rick Snyder, replaced Flint's elected government with an appointed city manager following a state treasury audit that showed the city with a growing deficit. A significant share of Flint's budget deficit was found to have accrued from the city's water fund. A few months prior, one of Snyder's first acts as governor was to split the Department of Natural Resources and Environment into two different state agencies, the Department of Natural Resources (DNR) and the Department of Environmental Quality (DEQ).

---

1. Not including the territory of Puerto Rico, which also experienced a population loss.

This reversed a decision by the governor's predecessor, Democratic Governor Jennifer Granholm, to combine the departments. Following the establishment of the two agencies, Governor Snyder appointed Dan Wyant as head of DEQ.

In April 2013, Flint's appointed emergency manager, Ed Kurtz, informed the state treasurer that the city would reduce its water expenditures by building its own pipeline to connect to the Karegnondi Water Authority (KWA). Although the decision was supported by the mayor and city council, they had already been stripped of power by the governor with the appointment of the city manager.

THE FLINT RIVER

Until that point, Flint had received water from Lake Huron delivered via the Detroit municipal system. With the decision, Detroit informed Flint that it would terminate service a year later in April 2014. However, the city would not be connected with the new pipeline until 2017. As a stopgap measure, until the new pipeline was completed, it was decided to use water from the Flint River.

The river, from which the city originally got its name, was not known as a particularly clean water source. As early as the 1930s, fish were observed to be disappearing due to the constant discharge of industrial waste and municipal sewage. However, the Flint River supplied drinking water to the city until 1967, when Flint switched to Lake Huron from Detroit's water system.

HEALTH PROBLEMS BEGIN

Four months after the city switched to the Flint River, on August 14, the city warned that fecal coliform bacteria had been detected in the water and advised citizens on the city's west side to boil their water. Six days later, the advisory was lifted. However, on September 5, another bacteria discovery led to a second advisory being issued. Four days later, residents were told that they could safely drink the water.

The next month, General Motors (GM) announced that it would no longer use the city's water supply because high chloride levels in the water were corroding its machinery. The switch by GM, which uses an average of 75,000 gallons (300,000 liters) per day, meant an additional financial loss of hundreds of thousands of dollars for the struggling city. However, it also raised further questions about the safety of the water, which was still drawing complaints from residents about its smell and color. However, the Michigan Department of Environmental Quality (MDEQ) assured the public that chloride levels were within health guidelines.

Two months later, in January 2015, the city of Flint issued a warning of chemicals in the water that comprise health risks, including increased likelihood of cancer. However, residents were told the water was still safe to drink, though the elderly and parents of children were advised to consult their physician. That same month, with increasing press accounts of rashes and illness due to the strangely colored water, the Detroit water system offered to reconnect Flint. Despite Detroit's offer to waive the $4 million reconnection fee, Flint officials thought the restored service was more than they could afford.

The next month MDEQ reported to the governor that while there were "some initial hiccups" in Flint's water system development, that included "a couple of 'boil water' notices." MDEQ minimalized the water problems, including the presence of TTHM in the water. MDEQ's letter states, "Put in context, the EPA (which established the standard and the rule) estimates the existence of the TTHM standard prevents an estimated 280 bladder cancer cases each year . . . out of more than 330 million people who use public water supplies around the country." Put in this context, most health standards appear meaningless, and the letter states explicitly, "But it's not like an eminent threat to public health" (Flintwaterstudy.org 2016).

The MDEQ letter to the governor then puts it in the context of the emerging political debate and public protests, stating, "The key to the conversation is that TTHM is not a top health concern. That's key because residents need to understand TTHM in context, and it is key because it appears the mayor has seized on the public panic (sparked, frankly, by their poor communication of the violation notice) to ask the state for loan forgiveness and more money for their infrastructure improvement."

A FIGHT TO RECOGNIZE THE PROBLEM

At the end of February 2015, the U.S. Environmental Protection Agency (EPA) notified MDEQ that it had detected dangerous lead levels in Flint's water. Testing showed the water in one Flint home at 104 parts per billion (ppb), nearly seven times the EPA's maximum safe level of 15 ppb. Three weeks later, a follow-up in the same home showed lead levels at 397 ppb.

A few weeks later, in March 2015, Flint's City council voted 7 to 1 to return to purchasing water from the Detroit Water and Sewage Department. However, the council was overruled by the governor's appointed city manager, Jerry Ambrose. Ambrose, the second to hold the position, said it would be a waste of money and stated, "Flint water today is safe by all (U.S. Environmental Protection Agency) and (Michigan Department of Environmental Quality) standards, and the city is working daily to improve its quality."

Three months after that, in June 2015, the EPA warned that the city was not providing corrosion control treatment to mitigate the presence of lead in drinking water. New tests in one home found lead levels exceeding 13,000 ppb, almost three times the level classified as hazardous waste. MDEQ continued to assure the public that the water was safe to drink.

In September 2015, a team from Virginia Tech reported that preliminary tests showed that 40 percent of Flint homes had water with lead levels above the recommended standard, with several homes 20 times higher than the standard and one home at 200 times the maximum safe level. An MDEQ spokesperson said the city had long-term infrastructure issues and cast doubt on Virginia Tech's testing, warning it "could be seen as fanning political flames irresponsibly." Two days later the Virginia Tech team responded that Flint's water was not safe for cooking or drinking. Two weeks later, a medical research team found several children with elevated lead levels in their bloodstream.

Two weeks later, the lead pediatric researcher from Flint's Hurley Medical Center issued a health warning after finding high lead levels in children's blood. MDEQ dismissed the report and said the water controversy was "near-hysteria."

RECOGNITION OF THE PROBLEM

In October 2015, a year and a half after the city began using water from the Flint River, the state finally began to recognize the problem. The Michigan Department of Health and Human Services (MDHHS) reviewed and verified the Hurley Center's findings. As a result, the state began testing schools' drinking water and distributing free water filters. Less than a week later, on October 8, MDEQ reported that three schools were found to have dangerous lead levels in their water. Michigan Governor Snyder announced that the city would stop using Flint River water and signed a bill appropriating $9.35 million to aid Flint's reconnection with the Detroit water system. That month the EPA established a Safe Drinking Water Task Force for the city.

Two months later, in December 2015, the mayor of Flint declared a state of emergency, "in response to a man-made disaster caused by the City switching to the Flint River as a water source in 2014." The governor followed suit in January 2016, declaring a state of emergency and sending the state's National Guard to distribute water and filters in Flint.

The governor's decision followed the EPA Task Force's report placing primary responsibility for the Flint water crisis on MDEQ, which was the primary agency responsible for enforcing the Safe Drinking Water Act, and criticized MDEQ's "minimalist approach." MDEQ director Dan Wyant resigned immediately after the report's release. Eleven days after the governor's announcement, U.S. President Barack Obama declared a state of emergency in Flint and authorized the Federal Emergency Management Agency (FEMA) to coordinate responses and provide three-fourths of the funding for water, filters, and other items.

The following month, in February 2016, the U.S. House of Representatives Committee on Oversight and Government Reform began holding hearings on Flint's water crisis. Governor Snyder testified before the committee in March.

HEALTH CONSEQUENCES

Residents of Flint suffered from a number of health problems following the decision to switch water sources. Almost immediately after the city started drawing from the Flint River there were reports of high levels of coliform and E. coli in the water. In addition to advising residents to boil water, city authorities increased the amount of chlorine in the water. This resulted in elevated levels of total trihalomethanes (TTHM), which are chemical compounds formed when organic matter combines with chlorine. The health hazards of TTHMs include increased cancer risk and can be potentially fatal. In addition, Flint residents complained of rashes, burning skin, and hair falling out after showering.

Immediately after switching to the Flint River, testing showed Flint's drinking water to have very high bacteria and trihalomethane levels. A Legionnaire's disease outbreak in the Flint area also coincided with the switch, sickening about 90 and leaving 10 people dead. Because of the nature of the disease, it is difficult to prove a direct link, and MDEQ denied there was one. However, health experts surmised that when the river water corroded the city's pipes it left spaces that enabled the bacteria that causes the disease to grow.

The acidic water corroded old lead pipes, allowing lead and other heavy metals to seep into Flint's drinking water and cause serious and widespread lead poisoning. Children exposed to the lead-poisoned water for prolonged periods suffered a range of incurable developmental issues. The source of the lead was not the Flint River but the city's pipes. As a result of a failure to inject the required anti-corrosive additive, the river water corroded the old pipes and caused dangerously high lead levels to enter the water.

It was estimated that all 9,000 of Flint's children were exposed to elevated lead levels in the water. However, since lead does not stay in the bloodstream more than a month and testing was limited, it is difficult to measure the full effects of this problem. Yet the possible long-term effects of ingestion of lead at this level can include high blood pressure and other cardiovascular problems, kidney damage, anemia, hearing loss, memory and neurological problems, learning disorders, ADHD, developmental delays, and reduced IQ.

POLITICAL FRAMEWORK AND PUBLIC POLICY ACTORS

The water crisis in Flint is revealing in terms of the different types of actors who affect policymaking in the United States and the ways in which decision making is divided. The crisis also exposed demographic differences and the differing approaches of the country's two main political parties.

On the local level, the Democratic mayor and city council were stripped of power by the Republican governor, who replaced them with appointed emergency mangers. State authorities initially claimed that this move would efficiently reduce the city's debts and bring financial stability. However, critics asserted that the problems were due to demographic shifts that were not the city's fault. They also pointed out that the Michigan cities in which the governor replaced elected leaders were primarily Democrat-run cities with black-majority populations.

There were also conflicts between national and local administrative authorities: between the U.S. EPA and the state MDEP, with the former headed by an appointee of the Democratic U.S. president and the latter appointed by the Republican governor of Michigan.

Total Trihalomethanes (TTHM)

TTHM is a group of chemical compounds resulting from water being treated with a disinfectant chemical, chlorine. In the United States, chlorination treatment of municipal water was started in 1908 in New Jersey. Before the routine chlorination treatment, waterborne diseases were common causes of illnesses and deaths. Chlorination has been hailed as a giant technological breakthrough of the 20th century in making water safe for drinking. The treatment, however, also produces disinfectant by-products that carry health risks. The federal TTHM limit is 80 parts per billion. According to the EPA, potential health effects of TTHM at higher levels include liver, kidney, and central nervous system problems, as well as an increased risk of cancer. To reduce TTHM level, it is recommended to reduce organics from water prior to chlorination.

The conflicts between state and national authorities and between Democrats and Republicans were further revealed in hearings held by the U.S. Congress in February 2016. During the hearings, Democratic Congress members focused their criticism on the Republican governor, while Republican members aimed primarily at the EPA administrator.

In addition to the formal institutional bodies, there were a number of other actors who affected the decision-making process. Among these were private citizens and community groups who called attention to growing health concerns, and researchers from Virginia Tech, as well as the American Civil Liberties Union, which filed a lawsuit against the school district for exposing children to lead-tainted water and publicized the state's inaction. Finally, there was the media, which exposed citizens' grievances and experts' reports.

CONCLUSION: ADMINISTRATIVE FAILURE

It is clear that the water crisis could have been avoided. While the Flint River water was not as clean a source as the Lake Huron water from the Detroit system, it was not the main problem. When the switch was made to using the Flint River as the city's water source, those in charge failed to use a standard anti-corrosion additive that would have cost approximately $100 per day. Without this additive, the river water, which was more corrosive than Lake Huron water, wore away at the city's old lead pipes, which then polluted the drinking water. Thus, most of the water problems, which have subsequently added up to tens of millions of dollars in damages and health problems, could have been prevented for less than $100,000 over a three-year period. However, political and ideological divisions prevented pragmatic decision making and led to inefficient decision making that hurt people and wasted money.

Matt Evans

See also: Pollution: Shiprock, United States: Radioactive from the Inside Out

Further Reading

Associated Press (AP). 2015. "Doctors Urge Flint to Stop Using Water from Flint River." *Crains Detroit Business*, September 28. http://www.crainsdetroit.com/article/20150928/NEWS01/150929872/doctors-urge-flint-to-stop-using-water-from-flint-river.

Bosman, Julie. 2016. "E.P.A. Waited Too Long to Warn of Flint Water Danger, Report Says." *New York Times*, October 20. https://www.nytimes.com/2016/10/21/us/epa-waited-too-long-to-warn-of-flint-water-danger-report-says.html.

Carmody, Tim. 2016. "How the Flint River Got So Toxic." *The Verge*, February 26. http://www.theverge.com/2016/2/26/11117022/flint-michigan-water-crisis-lead-pollution-history.

CNN (CNN1). 2017. "Flint Water Crisis Fast Facts" February 22. http://www.cnn.com/2016/03/04/us/flint-water-crisis-fast-facts.

Davey, Monica, and Mitch Smith. 2016. "2 Former Flint Emergency Managers Charged over Tainted Water." *New York Times*, December 20. https://www.nytimes.com/2016/12/20/us/flint-water-charges.html.

Edwards, Marc. 2015. "Our Sampling of 252 Homes Demonstrates a High Lead in Water Risk: Flint Should Be Failing to Meet the EPA Lead and Copper Rule."

September 8. http://flintwaterstudy.org/2015/09/our-sampling-of-252-homes-demonstrates-a-high-lead-in-water-risk-flint-should-be-failing-to-meet-the-epa-lead-and-copper-rule.

Energy and Environmental Affairs. 2004. "Current Regulatory Limit: Total Trihalomethanes (TTHMs)." https://www.mass.gov/guides/drinking-water-standards-and-guidelines#guidelines.

Flintwaterstudy.org. 2016. "Gov. Rick Snyder—Flint Water Study." http://flintwaterstudy.org/wp-content/uploads/2016/01/snyder-emails.pdf.

Fonger, Ron. 2015a. "Emergency Manager Calls City Council's Flint River Vote 'Incomprehensible.'" *mlive*, March 24. http://www.mlive.com/news/flint/index.ssf/2015/03/flint_emergency_manager_calls.html.

Fonger, Ron. 2015b. "Feds Sending in Experts to Help Flint Keep Lead out of Water." *mlive*, September 10. http://www.mlive.com/news/flint/index.ssf/2015/09/university_researchers_dont_dr.html.

Fonger, Ron. 2015c. "General Motors Shutting Off Flint River Water at Engine Plant over Corrosion Worries." *mlive*, October 13. https://www.mlive.com/news/flint/index.ssf/2014/10/general_motors_wont_use_flint.html.

Ganim, Sara, and Linh Tran. 2016. "How Tap Water Became Toxic in Flint, Michigan." CNN.com, January 13. http://www.cnn.com/2016/01/11/health/toxic-tap-water-flint-michigan.

Goodnough, Abby. 2016. "Michigan Governor Tells Congress He Was Misled on Flint Water." *New York Times*, March 17. https://www.nytimes.com/2016/03/18/us/michigan-governor-tells-congress-he-was-misled-on-flint-water.html.

Goodnough, Abby, Monica Davey, and Mitch Smith. 2016. "When the Water Turned Brown." *New York Times*, January 23. https://www.nytimes.com/2016/01/24/us/when-the-water-turned-brown.html.

Ingraham, Christopher. 2016. "This Is How Toxic Flint's Water Really Is." *Washington Post*, January 15. https://www.washingtonpost.com/news/wonk/wp/2016/01/15/this-is-how-toxic-flints-water-really-is.

Kennedy, Merrit. 2016. "Lead-Laced Water in Flint: A Step-By-Step Look at the Makings of a Crisis." National Public Radio, April 20. http://www.npr.org/sections/thetwo-way/2016/04/20/465545378/lead-laced-water-in-flint-a-step-by-step-look-at-the-makings-of-a-crisis.

Lasher, Geralyn. 2011. "Governor Snyder Signs First Executive Order, Creates Separate Departments of Natural Resources and Environmental Quality." Michigan Governor's Website, January 4. http://www.michigan.gov/snyder/0,4668,7-277-57577_57657-248895--,00.html.

Michigan Treasury Department. 2011. "Report of the Flint Financial Review Team." State of Michigan, November 7. https://www.michigan.gov/documents/treasury/Flint-ReviewTeamReport-11-7-11_417437_7.pdf.

Population, US. "Population of Flint, MI." https://population.us/mi/flint/.

Rodrick, Stephen. 2016. "Who Poisoned Flint, Michigan?" *Rolling Stone*, January 22. http://www.rollingstone.com/politics/news/who-poisoned-flint-michigan-20160122.

Rose, Joan B. 2015. "TTHM in Drinking Water: The Flint, Michigan Story, a Lesson for Us All." Water Quality & Health Council. https://waterandhealth.org/newsletter/Flint.pdf.

U.S. Census Bureau. "Flint, Michigan." http://www.infoplease.com/us/census/data/michigan/flint.

Wisely, John. 2016. "Was Flint River Water Good Enough to Drink?" *Detroit Free Press*, January 30. http://www.freep.com/story/news/local/michigan/flint-water-crisis/2016/01/30/flint-river-water/79396268/.

Karachi, Pakistan: How Pollution Gets Out of Control

The most populous city in Pakistan, Karachi, is the capital of Sindh province. Because of its dense population and robust industrial growth, Karachi is badly polluted. Pollution circulates in the air, infests the ground, and enters what should be potable groundwater. This pollution causes health problems and contributes to the early deaths of some residents. Because of Karachi's size and the scale of pollution, the government is not always able to remedy what ails the city. Karachi's struggle against pollution does not mean that solutions do not exist. One promising avenue of action is the planting of trees to absorb air pollution. Another is the development of a more robust mass transit system to encourage people to take buses, trams, and railways rather than rely on the automobile, a notorious polluter. Both government and the private sector must cooperate to lessen pollution in Karachi. In some cases, foreign companies and governments may be able to provide loans and other sources of funds to aid Karachi in reducing pollution through a variety of approaches.

THE PROBLEMS AND MAGNITUDE OF POLLUTION

The financial and industrial engine of Pakistan, Karachi, partly due to rapid industrialization, is one of the world's five most polluted cities according to a conference, "Mission: Save and Rehabilitate Karachi." The article "Karachi among the Five Most Polluted Cities in the World" (*The Express Tribune*, 10 July 2017) offers some detailed descriptions. One anecdote holds that it was once possible to toss a coin into the Arabian Sea near Karachi and see it on the bottom. Now pollution obscures the waters to such an extent that this is no longer possible. The World Health Organization (WHO) blames pollution for some 29,000 deaths per year in Karachi. In addition, pollution may cost Karachi's economy roughly 4.5 billion rupees per year. Waste and sewage treatment plants appear to be unable to keep pace with the pollution the city generates. The Pakistan Chambers of Commerce, the National Forum for Environmental Health, and the Sindh Environmental Protection Agency worry that conditions, poor as they are, may worsen before they improve. Neither Karachi's government nor the private sector appears to rate the reduction of pollution a priority. Without the commitment of the government and the private sector, there seems to be little chance of making headway against pollution.

In Karachi, pollution takes a variety of forms. Air pollution is severe, and the metals chromium, cadmium and lead pollute groundwater, making much of it unsafe to drink. Industrial discharges and exhaust fumes from automobiles have sullied the coastline of Karachi. Lead has contaminated aquatic life and in turn the people in Karachi who consume it. Already lead poisoning causes anemia, brain damage, and kidney ailments in Karachi's citizens. Pollution endangers the

Burns Road in Karachi, Pakistan. Karachi's large population and industrial economy has made it one of Pakistan's most polluted cities. (Akash Chawla/Dreamstime.com)

mangrove ecosystems along the coast that are an important source of biodiversity. Factories disgorge pollutants into the Arabian Sea. Air pollution threatens the ozone layer, which protects people from the sun's ultraviolet light that causes skin cancer. The problem is insidious because ultraviolet light is invisible to the human eye, so that citizens may not be mindful of the danger it poses. Air pollution includes carbon monoxide, a gas that can suffocate humans because it binds so tightly to the hemoglobin in the blood, depriving it of the ability to carry oxygen to the body's cells. Other contaminants in the air include sulfur dioxide, a contributor to acid rain; nitrogen oxide; and the chlorofluorocarbons that appear to be carcinogens. Consequently, smog is a serious threat to Karachi's residents.

The WHO has cataloged the state of pollution in Karachi, rating air pollution very high. In addition, the agency warns of the dangers to health of water pollution. Pollution contributes to the conviction among residents that Karachi is dismal and dirty. Consequently, people prefer not to live in the city or travel to it. Residents also decry the lack of trees, a subject of the next section.

Karachi's dense population contributes to pollution because they produce large amounts of garbage. The city, unable to dispose of all this garbage, allows it to aggregate throughout Karachi in large heaps. Enterprising residents collect the garbage and sell it to others to burn as fuel. Yet the burning of garbage in Karachi adds pollutants to the air, exacerbating the problem.

Dire as the situation may be, Karachi's government may not have the money to combat pollution. In fact, Karachi has trouble even assessing the scope and magnitude of the problem. Part of the problem lies in the government's inability since 2011 to fund research stations that monitor the amount and kind of pollutants in Karachi. Three of the city's stations, often known as environmental monitoring stations and created by the Pakistan Environmental Protection Agency, are in disrepair. These three stations were once at the forefront of monitoring air pollution near Karachi's factories. Without monitoring, it is difficult to know the scope and magnitude of industrial pollution in the city. The Pakistan Environmental Protection Agency no longer funds these stations, and Karachi's government seems unable to afford the cost of their operation. Even were these stations functional, it is difficult to know how effective they would be given that Karachi has no air quality index against which to measure the severity of air pollution. In this regard, Karachi lags behind many of the world's cities in the ability to quantify pollution. It seems axiomatic that Karachi will have difficulty combating pollution if it cannot measure what it hopes to curtail.

URBAN FORESTRY

The magnitude of these problems demands solutions. Not every solution need involve an overhaul in technology. Low-tech solutions exist and in some cases are simple. Among the most prominent is the planting of trees in Karachi, a practice known as urban forestry. One can think of trees as air cleansers. According to one study, a single hectare of trees may remove some 15 tons of pollution from the atmosphere (Illyas 2016). Trees serve this function because of their anatomy and physiology. During transpiration, the stomata, tiny structures on the underside of leaves, open to absorb carbon dioxide. The stomata do not absorb the constituents in the air selectively. Rather, they absorb all particles in the air, including contaminants. That is, the stomata of leaves absorb pollution. At the same time, trees, and all plants for that matter, emit oxygen into the atmosphere, a gas without which the aerobic respiration of humans and other animals would be impossible. A diversity of tree species seems to work best in cleansing the air. Under consideration in Karachi are trees known as neem, peepal, and gulmohar. Already Karachi is planting conocarpus trees, but opinion is divided about their efficacy in removing pollutants from Karachi's air. The problem with conocarpus is their production of large quantities of pollen, contributors to asthma. Neem, peepal, and gulmohar may be better candidates because they are native to this region of Pakistan and so are easy to propagate and maintain. A city of Karachi's size may need at least 140 million trees to cleanse the air of pollutants ("Karachi among the Most Polluted Cities in the World"). Such a proliferation of trees appears to be difficult to achieve because of population density.

The best strategy involves planting trees near the sources of pollution in Karachi: roads, especially highways and heavy traveled streets, and factories. As a rule, Karachi should plant trees most densely where pollution is greatest. Although difficulties will abound in the competition for scarce land, trees should be planted where humans are most crowded. Not blessed with abundant rainfall, Karachi needs trees that require little water. Trees are most vulnerable to shortages of water when they are young and the roots comparatively shallow, so irrigation of seedlings and young trees will be necessary. Protection of trees at all stages of development is important, especially because as a tree grows large, so does its capacity to absorb pollutants. Evergreen species appear to be particularly valuable because of their ability to absorb pollutants year-round. Deciduous trees, by contrast, in losing their leaves in autumn, cease to be active and so can remove pollutants from the air during only part of the year. Karachi's authorities and urban planners should avoid planting trees that emit volatile organic compounds during transpiration because under certain conditions such chemicals may combine with others in the air to form pollutants. Such trees may emit chemicals that form ozone. Their utility is debatable. In a city like Karachi where pollutants are depleting ozone, the production of ozone may seem desirable, but too much of it will in turn be a pollutant, especially if this ozone is in the lower atmosphere where humans and other animals can inhale it. In concert with planting trees, Karachi must launch an educational campaign to alert its citizens to the benefits of trees and to teach them to care for those near them. Karachi's urbanites must become stewards of the biota.

MASS TRANSIT

Because automobiles are a major source of pollution, Karachi should promote mass transit as an alternative. In the 1960s, the city took an important step in this direction by building a system of above-ground trams. Electricity powers these trams. The use of electricity does not mean the trams are free from pollution. The generation of this electricity occurs at utilities that burn fossil fuels to spin a turbine to generate electricity. The burning of fossil fuels, of course, causes pollution. Trams, however, pollute Karachi less than does the automobile because they can carry more people per unit of energy and thereby reduce the emission of pollutants.

Another form of mass transit is the railroad, but Karachi shortsightedly abandoned this option in 1975. As a result, the city does not have sufficient mass transit for all its residents. The shortage of mass transit has reinforced the reliance on the automobile. By 2030, Karachi may have 2 million cars and more than 3 million motorcycles. A report titled "A Look at Karachi's Mass Transit Problems" published by *The Express Tribune* in 2017 provides an account of this problem. The automobile is well known as an insidious polluter. It emits a variety of pollutants including small particles, some much smaller than the diameter of a human hair. These particles include toxic metals and soot that contribute to smog. They can penetrate deep into the lungs, causing respiratory ailments. Automobiles also emit

---

Conocarpus erectus

Also known as buttonwood or button mangrove, *Conocarpus erectus* is a species of mangrove tree often classified as a shrub because it seldom grows taller than 20 feet (6 meters). As a mangrove, the shrub has evolved to tolerate brackish and even saline soils, an adaptation uncommon among plants and one that allows it to grow along shores. Unable to tolerate frost, the species grows in the tropics and subtropics. Karachi's planting of the shrub to absorb air pollutants is controversial. Critics charge that city authorities are cutting down formerly diverse tree species to make space for *Conocarpus erectus*. This monoculture may leave the shrub vulnerable to epidemics because a pathogen that kills one tree is likely to be dangerous to its neighbors. Had Karachi retained a diversity of species, the danger would lessen because a pathogen that targeted one species might not harm others. Moreover, birds that had nested in the previous plantings are leaving Karachi because *Conocarpus* shrubs are alien to them. But being a shrub, *Conocarpus erectus* is a compact tree that needs less pruning than larger trees, a benefit to cost-conscious urban planners. Moreover, able to tolerate salinity, the shrub is hardier than many other species.

hydrocarbons, long chains of carbon atoms bonded to one another. These hydrocarbons can react with nitrogen oxide, another automobile pollutant, to form ozone, another cause of respiratory problems. Nitrogen oxide itself irritates the lungs. Automobiles, furthermore, emit poisonous carbon monoxide. Moreover, automobiles emit sulfur dioxide, a component of acid rain. The greenhouse gases, like carbon dioxide, that automobiles emit are pollutants in their own right. In short, a reliance on the automobile has exacerbated air pollution in Karachi. Karachi's motorcycles also emit these same pollutants, but in a smaller amount per mile than do cars.

Karachi has not been idle in the face of air pollution from automobiles and motorcycles. The Karachi Infrastructure Development Company is using government money to create a fleet of buses and a grid of roads on which they will operate. To be sure, buses emit the same pollutants as do automobiles and motorcycles, but their capacity to carry many people means that they emit fewer pollutants per mile and per person than do cars.

Another option lies in the projected Karachi Circular Railway. In its construction, the railway relies for funding from Karachi's government and the Japan International Cooperation Agency. Yet each organization expects the other to contribute more money than it has and is reluctant to commit more money unless the other loosens its purse strings. According to plans, the railroad is to span nearly 30 kilometers from the Karachi City Station, the old railroad hub, and Drigh Road Station (Azam 2017). The project may cost nearly 250 million rupees. Because cost overruns are common in such endeavors, the real cost is likely to be higher. The difficulty in receiving sufficient funds has led Karachi to consider other suitors, including China. China is funding other transportation projects, notably a railroad to run north and south through Pakistan.

Christopher Cumo

See also: Traffic and Transportation: Beijing, China: Beijing's War on Traffic Congestion; Istanbul, Turkey: Building More Tunnels and Bridges Won't Make Congestion Go Away; Mexico City, Mexico: Improving Governance Is Key to Solving Traffic Challenges

Further Reading

Azam, Oonib. 2017. "In Transport-Starved Karachi, Fate of KCR Hangs in Balance." *The Evening Tribune*, November 8. https://tribune.com.pk/story/1224747/hitting-snags-transport-starved-karachi-fate-kcr-hangs-balance.

Illyas, Ferya. 2016. "Greener City: Urban Forestry to Counter Air Pollution in Karachi." *The Express Tribune*, March 21. https://tribune.com.pk/story/1069565/greener-city-urban-forestry-to-counter-air-pollution-in-karachi.

"Karachi among the Five Most Polluted Cities in the World." 2017. *The Express Tribune*, June 5. https://tribune.com.pk/story/1116509/lets-clear-air-karachi-among-five-polluted-cities-world.

"A Look at Karachi's Mass Transit Problems." 2017. *The Express Tribune*, December 11. https://tribune.com.pk/story/1260545/going-around-city-look-karachi-mass-transit-problems.

Numbeo.com. 2019. "Pollution in Karachi, Pakistan." http://www.numbeo.com/pollution/in/karachi.

Krakow, Poland: Old Furniture, New Fuel Source

With a population of approximately 765,000 (2015), Krakow (or Cracow) is the second-largest city in Poland. Until 1596, the city was the capital of Poland, and from 1846 to 1918, it was the capital of the Grand Duchy of Krakow. For centuries, Krakow was a place where coronations of Polish monarchs took place. Jagiellonian University, one of the oldest universities in the world (founded in 1364), makes the city an important cultural and educational hub. Prominent figures such as astronomer Nicholaus Copernicus, Pope John Paul II, writer Stanislaw Lem, and Nobel laureate in literature Wislawa Szymborska are listed among the university alumni. The city is also famous for its Jewish quarter, Kazimierz, which was turned into a ghetto during the Second World War and, more recently, was featured in Steven Spielberg's historical drama *Schindler's List*. In 1978, UNESCO added Krakow to the World Heritage List, and in 2013, the former capital became a UNESCO City of Literature. With millions of visitors every year, Krakow is one of the most popular tourist destinations in Europe.

POLLUTION IN KRAKOW

Since early medieval times, Krakow has been associated with a *smok* (Polish for "dragon") that, according to legend, devoured the city's residents. The dragon held the entire region in terror until, one day, a shrewd and brave lad named Krakus killed it and thus liberated the city from the monster. Many centuries have passed since then, but the danger has reappeared. Nowadays, Krakow faces a new deadly and virtually homophonic enemy—smog. The former capital of Poland, one of the most important academic and economic centers, and an official European Capital of Culture (2000), Krakow has also become known for its alarmingly high levels of air pollution. Rich in particulate matters, sulfur dioxide, benzo(a)pyrene, and nitrogen dioxide, the city's smog poses a serious threat to human health and life. When the Cracovians go to work, their bags frequently contain a respirator and their smart phones are tuned to indicate smog levels. It is also not rare to see the local newspapers advising the inhabitants not to spend too much time in the "fresh" air.

CURRENT SITUATION

According to the World Health Organization (2014), Krakow's air is the sixth worst in Europe (after the Bulgarian cities of Pernik, Sofia, and Plovdiv; Serbian Nis; and Polish Sosnowiec). Krakow's annual average of PM_{10} (inhalable coarse particulate matters with a diameter between 2.5 and 10 microns) is 59 micrograms per cubic meter ($\mu g/m^3$), while $PM_{2.5}$ (particulate matters with a diameter less than 2.5 microns) is 40 $\mu g/m^3$ (2014). Those numbers are significantly higher than in Essen, Germany's dirtiest city (30 $\mu g/m^3$ and 19 $\mu g/m^3$ correspondingly), or France's Marseille (35 $\mu g/m^3$ and 17 $\mu g/m^3$). While there are really no safe limits of particulates, the European emission standards recommend that annual average PM_{10} not exceed 40 $\mu g/m^3$ and $PM_{2.5}$ be no more than 25 $\mu g/m^3$. Krakow's air, therefore, exceeds the standard limits by about 50 percent (for PM_{10}) or 60 percent (for $PM_{2.5}$).

Krakowski Alarm Smogowy, a nongovernmental organization that advocates for clean air in Krakow, has recently published a disturbing slogan: "You breathe Krakow's air? You smoke 2,500 cigarettes a year!" Similar to tobacco, air contamination may cause not only respiratory diseases (e.g., asthma, lung cancer), but also cardiovascular diseases (e.g., atherosclerosis), premature delivery, and birth defects. In fact, according to the European Study of Cohorts for Air Pollution Effects (ESCAPE) (2013), with an increase of PM_{10} and $PM_{2.5}$ by just 10 μg/m³, lung cancer rates rise by 22 percent and 36 percent respectively. It is thus not accidental that Poland leads among the European countries in numbers of death associated with air pollution—5,358 people annually, according to the Greenpeace International (Myllyvirta 2013, 24). In comparison, Germany recorded 3,128 deaths related to air pollution, France 928, and Italy 499.

POLLUTION SOURCES

What are the reasons for such a high level of air pollution? Just two words: geography and coal. While such factors as local industry and traffic do contribute (23 percent and 16 percent respectively for PM_{10}; and 17 percent and 13 percent for $PM_{2.5}$) to air contamination, it is inflow from outside Krakow (19 percent for PM_{10} and 36 percent for $PM_{2.5}$) and the city's solid-fuel stoves (42 percent for PM_{10} and 34 percent for $PM_{2.5}$) that largely make the situation so dire.

Smog over Krakow, Poland, 2017. Krakow's air pollution is caused primarily by the burning of coal. The city is attempting to address the problem by creating laws and regulations to reduce reliance on coal, among other initiatives. (Beezeephoto /iStockphoto.com)

Geographically, Krakow sits in a valley at the foot of the Carpathian Mountains, between the Jurassic Rock Upland in the north and the Tatra Mountains in the south. Architecturally, the city has a number of relatively tall buildings and many narrow streets that tend to trap the air, thus preventing proper ventilation. In addition, Krakow has not been lucky with winds—on average, 30 percent of days annually have practically no wind at all. But when there is a wind, the situation often becomes even worse: "The west wind blows in tons of toxic dust laden with heavy metal, sulfur, and nitrous oxide from Upper Silesia; when the east wind blows, the filth comes in even greater concentrations from Nowa Huta, the enormous steel complex in the eastern part of the city" (Gökay 2001).

Nowadays, the Nowa Huta steel plant is part of the international steel giant ArcelorMittal S.A., but it is not by far the biggest pollutant. Most of the contaminants come from Upper Silesia located in the heavy industrialized coal-producing region, as well as different factories around Skawina (Poland) and Ostrava (the Czech Republic).

Krakow's coal-burning heating stoves are also an enormous concern. The city with a population of 759,131 (2012) had 30,000 coal-burning stoves and a number of coal-fired boiler houses (in the beginning of the millennium, the situation was even worse—130,000 stoves and 1,300 coal-fired boiler houses). Old stoves, the legacy of the Communist era, are generally not every efficient and do not have filters. The situation is worsened by the fact that many Cracovians burn cheap, poor-quality coal and sometimes even dangerous materials (such as plastic, waste, or old furniture).

Furthermore, coal lobbies are very strong in Poland. They are afraid of losing a massive domestic market share (90 percent of Polish electricity is generated by coal, and 76 percent of Poles in villages use coal and wood to heat their houses). Without the domestic market share, the coal-mining companies will not be able to count on governmental subsidies (the Polish coal industry has long been subsidized due to its expensive-to-extract coal). Politicians are also cautious with the coal industry (the majority of which is state-owned), since it employs 120,296 miners and constitutes a sizable share in the national economy.

SOLUTIONS

For almost two decades, there was virtually no solution to the issue. Nonetheless, even without any visible measures, the situation has been gradually improving due to external economic factors. Many factories that polluted the air during the Communist times have run out of business and closed down. Upon privatization, the Nowa Huta steel factory became more efficient, and it currently presents a lesser threat to the environment. The coal industry has lost more than 330,000 jobs, and its annual production levels have decreased from more than 200 million tons (early 1980s) to 140 million tons (2013).

Nowadays, the city is searching for solutions in a comprehensive manner. Not only must the new legal framework be created, but also new systems of heating have to be installed, finances for those installations should be found, traffic issues have to be addressed, and the citizens must be properly informed and educated about the environmental problems.

The best practices in the prevention of air pollution are widely discussed among city residents. Polish environmental scientists closely studied the Clean Air Act adopted in the United Kingdom in 1956, the Irish Air Pollution Act 1987, as well as other related legislation. Comparing the situation in Krakow with London's Great Smog of 1952 would perhaps be an exaggeration, since the latter, according to some estimates, registered 14,000 µg/m³ level of PM_{10} and caused many instant deaths; but nonetheless, some activists do see the parallels. Even though the scale of the problem is different, the reasons are similar. In both cases, the air pollution was primarily instigated by coal-burning habits. The governments' initial denial of the problem was also similar, as economic factors often take priority over ecological concerns. Since the ban on coal appears to be the only viable solution, coal lobbies naturally try to downplay the danger. Thus, it took four years for the British Parliament to act on the very hazardous situation. Similarly, although the ban on coal burning was widely discussed in Krakow, there was little progress, as the Supreme Administrative Court often blocked the prohibition initiatives of the Lesser Poland Regional Assembly (Krakow is the capital of the Lesser Poland region).

However, common sense ultimately prevailed. With the introduction of the Clean Air Act, smoke-control areas in London were created. Those areas allowed usage of only smokeless fuels. Londoners were also encouraged to switch from coal to electric and natural gas heating. In the end, the measures did bring the desired result, and the tragedy of 1952 was left in the past.

Having this telling example in front of them, Polish authorities decided to act in a similar way. In October 2015, Polish President Andrzej Duda signed a so-called "anti-smog" law, which lets the municipalities decide which measures should be implemented to stop burning environmentally hazardous materials in privately owned houses. Immediately following the law's implementation, Krakow introduced a ban on coal-burning stoves and developed plans to replace all the outdated heating facilities by 2019. According to these plans, the municipality offers 100 percent reimbursement on the cost of installation of natural gas heaters or connecting the house to the centralized heating system. The reaction of many Cracovians was positive—in 2016, 4,500 residents applied for the rebate, a significant increase from the previous year (2,600 applications). As of today, however, it remains unclear how the city will find funding and enforce the ban.

The government has also started to control the industry in a more rigorous way. Thus, previously untouched large industrial companies are closely monitored by environmental activists. In 2015, for example, there were 15 minor accidents in ArcelorMittal Factory in the Nowa Huta district of Krakow. As a result of those accidents, approximately five tons of pollutants were emitted into the atmosphere. The most dangerous of them were benzo(a)pyrene, nitrogen, and heavy metals. Even though the factory administration denied that the accidents posed any threat to the population, the city government launched an investigation, and the company faces hefty fines, which will be in addition to the amount it pays annually for the environmental cleaning-related usage (almost $700,000). ArcelorMittal also invests in the modernization of its equipment. In accordance with the company's plans, one of the largest furnaces will be replaced in the near future, and this investment will cost more than US$4 million.

Yet, despite the encouraging first results in air quality improvement, not everyone is optimistic. There are small businesses that earn money on smog or materials that may contribute to the pollution. Companies that sell respirators or warning apps have been flourishing in Krakow. While their success is predictable, the city has also seen the rise of an unusual type of business—small firms and individuals who sell old furniture pieces to the poor. Operations of this sort are illegal and are possible only in the black market. Despite the fact that city authorities managed to virtually stop such clandestine activities, new violations are reported from time to time.

Critics also complain that for many years, Krakow has had a program that encourages Cracovians to replace their solid-fuel furnaces. The program, however, has not been enthusiastically embraced by the residents, as they quickly learned that their new heating systems, despite being installed with municipal financial assistance, result in significantly higher monthly bills. Krakowski Alarm Smogowy sees the solution in promoting district heating. A rapid expansion of the district heating network is required before a ban of solid fuels can be instituted in Krakow. This system offers a way to heat homes that is both affordable and good for air quality in the city. Local authorities should make investments that quickly connect citizens to this ecologically clean heating system a top priority. Although the district heating system does burn some coal, this usage is thought to be better for the city's air than the burning of coal in domestic heating systems. Unlike household furnaces, power plants are equipped with filters, and controlling one emitter is easier than controlling furnaces in 30,000 homes.

In addition, Krakowski Alarm Smogowy offers educational programs for the Cracovians and informs them about the sources of money (municipal subsidies for boiler replacements and financial assistance "for the poorest people who will receive bills after switching from coal to friendly air source heating systems"). Due to the ubiquitous presence of the external warnings and the environment-centered mass media campaign, the majority of the inhabitants are knowledgeable about the situation and follow smog alerts daily.

These measures will hopefully help to eliminate the smog and, thus, the noble image of the city will be restored.

Mykola Polyuha

See also: *Pollution:* Baku, Azerbaijan: A Tainted Reputation

Further Reading

Gökay, Bülent. 2001. *Eastern Europe since 1970: Decline of Socialism to Post-Communist Transition.* London: Taylor & Francis.

Krakowski Alarm Smogowy. https://krakowskialarmsmogowy.pl/en.

LaMontagne, Jerome, and Barbara Pierce. 1992. "How Much Will Pollution Reduction in Krakow Cost?" Proceedings of the American Council for an Energy-Efficient Economy (ACEEE) Conference. http://aceee.org/files/proceedings/1992/data/papers/SS92_Panel9_Paper13.pdf.

Myllyvirta, Lauri. 2013. *Silent Killers: Why Europe Must Replace Coal Power with Green Energy.* Green Peace International. https://www.greenpeace.org/slovenia/Global/international/publications/climate/2013/Silent-Killers.pdf.

Stokes, Jamie. 2015. "Krakow's Air Quality among the Worst in the World." *Krakow Post*, November 6. http://www.krakowpost.com/6285/2015/11/krakows-air-quality-among-the-worst-in-the-world.

Wilczynska-Michalik, Wanda. 2003. "Air Pollution and Damage to the Cultural Heritage in Cities: The Decay of the Cultural Heritage of Krakow." In *Sustainable Urban Patterns around the Baltic Sea: Case Studies*. Vol. 4. Uppsala: Baltic University Press, 42–53.

New Delhi, India: Success of Pollution Control Depends on Effective Collaboration

Air pollution refers to those substances that are released into the air that pose a danger to people or the environment. According to the World Health Organization (WHO), the types of air pollutants that pose the greatest threat to public health include carbon monoxide, nitrogen dioxide, particulate matter (PM), ozone, and sulfur dioxide. As population growth occurs in areas around the globe and locations become more urbanized, environmental issues like air pollution and water pollution place an increasingly large burden on the quality of life for residents. A total of 37 cities in India are among the top 100 world cities with the worst levels of PM_{10} pollution, or those inhalable particles with a diameter of 10 micrometers and smaller in size; the Indian cities of Delhi, Lucknow, and Gwalior are listed in the top 10 (WHO 2014). $PM_{2.5}$ or those inhalable particles with a diameter of 2.5 micrometers or less, also pose a risk to populations in South Asia. According to the National Ambient Air Quality (NAAQM) Monitoring Report, concentrations of PM in numerous Indian cities frequently exceed the air quality standards set forth by the WHO (Central Pollution Control Board 2012). Delhi is one of the world's most polluted cities, and as a result, respiratory ailments and cardiovascular disease are among the leading causes of death in the country. In New Delhi the air pollution problem is complicated by the geographic context, numerous sources of pollution, lack of data on emission sources, and limited awareness of and communication of the problem between scientists and the general public. However, solutions are available that involve opportunities for both the Indian population and government officials to strengthen existing pollution reduction measures to sustain a growing population.

New Delhi, the administrative capital of India, is located within the Delhi metropolitan area. The 2011 Census estimates that Delhi has a population of 16.79 million (Maji et al. 2017). Air pollution in New Delhi is a complex issue with many sources contributing to the problem including but not limited to the following: motor vehicle traffic, road dust, indoor cooking stoves, construction activities, brick kilns, power generation and manufacturing industries, and open burning of waste materials. Although the role of individual sources must be considered in order to propose solutions for improving air quality in New Delhi and other Indian cities, both geographical and meteorological factors greatly influence the severity of this environmental problem. Unlike megacities that are along the coasts and thus have access to sea breezes, landlocked cities like Mexico City, Mexico, and Cairo, Egypt, typically suffer from the transfer of and accumulation of air pollutants from outside

Table 1 Select Cities and Associated Levels of Pollution from Particulate Matter

City and Country	Population (2016)	PM_{10} Annual Mean, µg/m³	Year	Number of and Type of Monitoring Stations	$PM_{2.5}$ Annual Mean, µg/m³	Year	Number and Type of Monitoring Stations	Source
Bamenda, Cameroon	500,000	141	2012	1 station, residential/commercial	132	2012	1 station, residential/commercial	J. Antonel, Z. Chowdhury (2014), Atmospheric Environment 95, 344–54
Beijing, China	21.7 million	108	2013	NA	85	2014	14 stations; NA	China National Environmental Monitoring Center
Xingtai, China	6.7 million	193	2014	NA	128	2014	4 stations; NA	China National Environmental Monitoring Center
(Greater) Cairo, Egypt	18.7 million	179	2013	47 stations	76	2013	NA	Annual report on air quality in Egypt 2012/2013
Delhi, India	16.79 million	229	2012	12 stations	122	2013	10 stations; residential and others	Open Government Data (OGD) Platform India
Gwalior, India	1 million	329	2012	2 stations; NA	176	2012	NA	Open Government Data (OGD) Platform India
Lucknow, India	2.8 million	211	2012	5 stations; NA	113	2012	NA	Open Government Data (OGD) Platform India
Tehran, Iran	8.3 million	77	2014	21 stations: 16 urban stations, 3 traffic stations, 2 pre-urban stations	32	2014	21 stations: 16 urban stations, 3 traffic stations, 2 pre-urban stations	Hosseini V., Head of Tehran Air Quality Control, Presentation for FOCUS Event, Zurich, June 2015
Zabol, Iran	374,143	527	2012	1 station; NA	217	2012	NA	Department of Environment
Mexico City, Mexico	8.9 million	42	2014	9 stations; NA	20	2014	7 stations; NA	CDMX ciudad de Mexico, SEDEMA
Riyadh, Saudi Arabia	6.1 million	368	2014	1 station; NA	156	2014	NA	Official communication from Saudi Arabia

their city centers, which are exacerbated by the lack of air circulation that may break up and ultimately disperse hazardous pollutants (Kumar et al. 2015).

The factors related to the geographic context and regional meteorology are compounded by the changing building heights in the Delhi metropolitan region that interfere with ventilation and the dispersal of air pollutants; this was established upon examination of the residential living spaces in Delhi (3.31 m_2) and Beijing (21.85 m_2), respectively (Kennedy et al. 2015). Seasonal factors also influence air pollution concentrations in New Delhi, with levels reportedly being significantly higher during the winter (December–February) compared to the summer (March–May). These higher air pollution concentrations in the winter can be attributed to both the meteorological conditions and the strength of the sources. In the summer months, increased wind speeds can improve the breakup and distribution of pollutants, whereas the winter months are typically marked by low wind speeds and less solar radiation, which may lead to increased concentrations of pollutants. Findings also suggest that additional pollution sources contribute to the problem, largely the combustion of waste, which is more common during the winter months due to its use as a heating source in Indian homes (Pant et al. 2015).

Compared to other world cities, those in India have higher levels of both PM_{10} and $PM_{2.5}$, respectively (as shown in Table 1). However, the collection methodology of air pollution sampling data via monitoring stations set up across Indian cities varies considerably and calls into question the validity of the estimates provided. Experts agree that the sampling data on air pollution in New Delhi and other Indian cities are inconsistent and require improvements in both the number of monitoring stations available and the outlets for dissemination of results to the general public. Interestingly, while one may assume that cities with the highest populations tend to have more problems with air pollution, this is not necessarily true. For example, Zabol, Iran, an eastern city with a population well below 500,000, represents a disproportionate burden of the air pollution problem for both PM_{10} and $PM_{2.5}$ levels. This problem has been exacerbated by both poverty and the loss of wetlands, which contributes to more frequent and intense dust storms during the summer months. Further, Beijing, China, which is often cited by media outlets as being the world's most polluted city, tells a different story when examining the contributions from PM. However, to be clear, it is important to recognize that these data only provide a snapshot of one primary type of air pollution; it does not shed light on other toxic pollutant levels such as sulfur dioxide (SO_2) and nitrogen dioxide (NO_2).

Delhi is home to 29 industrial complexes and 5 factories that encompass a range of activities including the production of metals, leather, chemicals, and food and beverages. Delhi also boasts two coal power plants and four natural gas power plants in addition to numerous brick kilns that operate in and around the metropolitan region (Guttikunda and Calori 2013). As mentioned previously, the sources of air pollution in New Delhi are multiple and will be discussed in detail below.

Motor vehicles and their respective emissions, fuel emission standards, and urban travel behaviors play a significant role in the air pollution problem in Delhi. In 2010, there were an estimated 4.74 million motor vehicles on the roads in Delhi, and that number is expected to reach nearly 26 million by 2030 (Kumar et al. 2011). Given that India's fuel emission standards lag behind global benchmarks, higher standards must be implemented to offset the increasing emissions and energy requirements in the country. In recent years, there has been a push for converting public transport vehicles like buses, taxis, and auto rickshaws (partially enclosed three-wheeled vehicles that provide little protection from emissions) to run on compressed natural gas (CNG). Similarly, monetary measures like congestion pricing programs and restrictive parking policies have been developed to increase the likelihood of public transport use among urban residents. Congestion pricing programs, which have been successfully employed in London and Singapore, charge drivers to use road networks during times of peak traffic use. The goal of these initiatives is to minimize motor vehicle use during heavy traffic periods, thus decreasing congestion and promoting the use of alternative forms of transport (bus, rail, bicycle, walking). An additional measure that may serve to encourage commuters to use public transport is increased costs of parking; when combined with increasing fuel and maintenance costs of private vehicle ownership, this may prove to be an effective option. Other countries like China have taken a different approach and instead introduced government measures to minimize the expansion of private vehicles in cities such as Beijing and Shanghai by effectively reducing the number of driver's licenses issued annually (Nagpure et al. 2016). Given the growing contribution of mobile sources of pollution in New Delhi and the multitude of public health risks from cancer, birth defects, and reduced pulmonary functioning, solutions like those identified above should be considered in the Indian context.

Emissions from coal-fired power plants play a role in the degradation of air quality in New Delhi. As of 2012, there were an estimated 111 coal-fired facilities operating in India, and findings from pollution reports revealed that these power plants were responsible for approximately 80,000–115,000 premature deaths and over 20 million cases of asthma associated with $PM_{2.5}$ (Pant and Harrison 2012). Given the low sulfur composition of Indian coal compared to other types, this results in a higher ash content, which may help explain the PM levels. The Indian government has insufficient regulations in place to tackle these environmental and health problems; the emission standard for PM falls behind those implemented in other countries like China, the United States, and the European Union (EU). In order to combat the growing emissions from the power-generation sector, stricter regulations should be introduced for major pollutants, and flue-gas desulfurization (FGD) technologies, commonly referred to as scrubbers, should be required. FGD systems have the ability to reduce concentrations of $PM_{2.5}$ by up to 40 percent and thereby remove highly toxic gases like sulfur dioxide (SO_2) and hydrogen chloride (HCl) (Guttikunda and Jawahar 2014).

Diesel generators associated with telecommunication towers also contribute to the air pollution problem in New Delhi. The Telecom Regularity Authority of India (TRAI) estimated that over 300,000 towers used more than 2 billion liters of diesel in 2010 alone (Guttikunda and Calori 2013). This is worrisome considering that the number of mobile supporters is expected to rise in growing cities like New Delhi. One alternative to consider may be to encourage the use of renewable energy sources that would not have detrimental impacts on public health and the environment, although this is not simple in countries like India with its intermittent power outages due to increased stresses on the poor quality of electric infrastructure. A significant overhaul of infrastructure would be required, which could serve to reduce both air pollution and greenhouse gas emissions contributing to global climate change.

Another pollution source in New Delhi is directly related to traditional building construction practices in Indian cities: brick kilns. There are currently over 100,000 brick kilns operating in India generating between 150 and 200 billion bricks per year, utilizing 25 million tons of coal, and employing 10 million workers (Maithel et al. 2012). Given their widespread geographic distribution, brick kilns have a negative impact on air quality in other cities in India like Chennai, Kolkata, and Hyderabad.

Construction activities like excavation and demolition are also to blame for PM generation; vehicles constantly moving around the numerous sites allow for particles to be picked up and deposited greater distances along road networks. Similarly, dust from the roads is a major problem responsible for up to 40 percent of PM_{10} pollution in urban areas throughout India (Guttikunda and Jawahar 2012). Improved methods of dust collection and street sweeping could dramatically reduce this pollutant in New Delhi and are among the least costly in terms of accessible solutions to improve air quality.

The burning of waste in open areas in Indian cities poses a threat to both public health and the environment; toxic substances like dioxins and volatile organic chemicals (VOCs) are among those released when garbage is burned. Expansion of solid waste disposal and collection services in urban areas to include landfills and other efficient measures that will discourage open waste burning are greatly needed.

Given the multiple sources contributing to the degradation of air quality over the last decade, the Government of National Capital Territory (NCT) of Delhi has taken steps to decrease levels of air pollution and improve the quality of life for its residents. Some solutions that have been implemented include the conversion of public transportation to CNG, more restrictive vehicle emission standards, increased penalties for open waste burning, decommissioning of old motor vehicles, and scrubbing devices for minimizing emissions from diesel generators which have shown to reduce sulfur dioxide, carbon monoxide, and lead emissions (Maji et al., 2015). However, these measures have not been as effective at curbing the pollution from PM. While New Delhi has done more to address air pollution than other Indian cities, existing efforts must be strengthened, and support of both the communities and government officials is a must if progress is to be made. Public health experts and scholars recommend the expansion of pollution monitoring stations throughout all cities and the creation of outlets for the dissemination of that information to the general public. Collectively, these measures will increase public awareness of air pollution in New Delhi and help to situate this environmental problem in the context of broader economic and social issues. Currently there is a lack of data on emission sources and their respective characteristics that take into account the contributions from local, peripheral, and regional influences; in other words, inventories must be established that consider the range of geographic sources that may fall outside New Delhi's city limits (Kumar et al. 2015).

> **Air Quality Impacts Associated with Diwali**
>
> While pollution in New Delhi comes from numerous sources, one that is often overlooked has to do with ancient cultural traditions associated with this region. Diwali, the five-day Hindu Festival of Lights, is India's most important national holiday and is typically celebrated in October or November. Sunday, October 30, 2016, marked a recent gala and was characterized by chains of electric lights, large family gatherings, dazzling clay lamps, firework displays, and bonfires, all of which pay worship to Lakshmi, the Hindi goddess of wealth and fortune. According to India's Central Pollution Control Board (CPCB), due to the thousands of firecrackers set off throughout Delhi, the 2016 festival generated dangerous levels of $PM_{2.5}$, the pollution threat that poses a significant danger to public health. Moreover, in a northern suburb of Delhi, $PM_{2.5}$ concentrations were nearly double those of the previous year's festival. In the days that followed, the Indian government issued an emergency declaration urging residents to stay indoors and ordering a temporary halt on construction activities and coal-fired facilities in an effort to improve the situation.

According to scientists, perhaps the greatest challenge that India faces in terms of reducing air pollution levels is the clear separation of policies that aim to target climate change and air pollution, respectively (Chatterjee 2008). It will be necessary to bring together those working to address climate change with those working to improve air pollution in order to design policies and initiatives that provide clear benefits to both. For example, policies that curb emissions from PM_{10} and sulfur dioxide will likely reduce emissions of greenhouse gases contributing to climate change. Understanding the complex interconnections among pollution sources is necessary and will ultimately determine the long-term success of measures created to reduce air pollution levels and mitigate the impacts associated with climate change in New Delhi and elsewhere.

Jennifer Haney

See also: Employment and Jobs: Mumbai, India: Exploring Employment Solutions in Temporary Jobs; *Waste Management:* Delhi, India: Current Problems and Opportunities for the Future of the National Capital Territory

Further Reading

Central Pollution Control Board (CPCB). 2012. "National Ambient Air Quality Status and Trends in India, 2010." *National Ambient Air Quality Monitoring Series (NAAQMS)* 35: 2011–12.

Chatterjee, Rhitu. 2008. "New Delhi: Integrating Air and Climate Policies." *Environmental Science & Technology* 42, 16: 5835.

Guttikunda, Sarath K., and Giuseppe Calori. 2013. "A GIS Based Emissions Inventory at 1 km × 1 km Spatial Resolution for Air Pollution Analysis in Delhi, India." *Atmospheric Environment* 67: 101–11.

Guttikunda, Sarath K., and Puji Jawahar. 2012. "Application of SIM-Air Modeling Tools to Assess Air Quality in Indian Cities." *Atmospheric Environment* 62: 551–61.

Guttikunda, Sarath K., and Puji Jawahar. 2014. "Atmospheric Emissions and Pollution from the Coal-Fired Thermal Power Plants in India." *Atmospheric Environment* 92: 449–60.

Guttikunda, Sarath K., Rahul Goel, and Pallavi Pant. 2014. "Nature of Air Pollution, Emission Sources, and Management in the Indian Cities." *Atmospheric Environment* 95: 501–10.

Kennedy, Christopher A., et al. 2015. "Energy and Material Flows of Megacities." *Proceedings of the National Academy of Sciences* 112, 19: 5985–90.

Kumar, Prashant, B. R. Gurjar, Ajay Singh Nagpure, and Roy M. Harrison. 2011. "Preliminary Estimates of Nanoparticle Number Emissions from Road Vehicles in Megacity Delhi and Associated Health Impacts." *Environmental Science and Technology* 45: 5514–21.

Kumar, Prashant, Mukesh Khare, Roy M. Harrison, William J. Bloss, Alastair C. Lewis, Hugh Coe, and Lidia Morawska. 2015. "New Directions: Air Pollution Challenges for Developing Megacities Like Delhi." *Atmospheric Environment* 122: 657–61.

Maithel, Sameer, R. Uma, Tami Bond, Ellen Baum, and Vu Thi Kim Thoa. 2012. "Brick Kilns Performance Assessment, Emissions Measurements, and a Roadmap for Cleaner Brick Production in India." Report prepared by Green Knowledge Solutions, New Delhi, India.

Maji, Sanjoy, Sirajuddin Ahmed, and Weqar Ahmad Siddiqui. 2015. "Air Quality Assessment and Its Relation to Potential Health Impacts in Delhi, India." *Current Science* 109, 5: 902–9.

Maji, Sanjoy, Sirajuddin Ahmed, Weqar Ahmad Siddiqui, and Santu Ghosh. 2017. "Short Term Effects of Criteria Air Pollutants on Daily Mortality in Delhi, India." *Atmospheric Environment* 150: 210–19.

Nagpure, Ajay Singh, B. R. Gurjar, Vivek Kumar, and Prashant Kumar. 2016. "Estimation of Exhaust and Non-Exhaust Gaseous, Particulate Matter and Air Toxics Emissions from On-Road Vehicles in Delhi." *Atmospheric Environment* 127: 118–24.

Pant, Pallavi, and Roy M. Harrison. 2012. "Critical Review of Receptor Modelling for Particulate Matter: A Case Study of India." *Atmospheric Environment* 49: 1–12.

Pant, Pallavi, Anuradha Shukla, Steven D. Kohl, Judith C. Chow, John G. Watson, and Roy M. Harrison. 2015. "Characterization of Ambient PM2.5 at a Pollution Hotspot in New Delhi, India and Inference of Sources." *Atmospheric Environment* 109: 178–89.

World Health Organization (WHO). 2014. "Burden of Disease from Ambient Air Pollution for 2012." World Health Organization.

Rome, Italy: Reducing Spatial Segregation Contributes to Pollution Control

The capital city of Italy, Rome has been termed "the first megacity" (Kotkin 2006). As one of the oldest and largest cities in the world, Rome's inhabitants have been dealing with the environmental and social effects associated with a high-density population for centuries. Many of the solutions developed to ameliorate the problems arising from these high-density populations are applicable to other cities, while other solutions provide lessons of what not to do. The following paragraphs outline the varying systems and social processes that have provided environmental benefits and disadvantages in the city of Rome over time.

Rome was one of the first cities to develop municipal infrastructure by way of the aqueduct. As early as the 3rd century CE, the capital of the Roman Empire was providing clean water to their citizens and removing waste. The importance of infrastructure in supporting human health cannot be overstated. Throughout history, living in a high-density, unsanitary, urban environment has been the cause of widespread epidemics like cholera and yellow fever (Taylor 2009). Although Roman waste was stored in dangerously close proximity to the city's water supply (Koloski-Ostrow 2015), the large-scale use of both public and private toilets in ancient Rome likely went far to alleviate much of the risk from water polluted with human waste. This put the city of Rome earlier in line to experience what public health scholars call the epidemiological transition, a phase of development when a society moves from high rates of mortality from infectious disease toward one characterized by degenerative diseases.

While the benefits from a public water system are many, Romans historically were susceptible to technocratic promises provided by metallurgy that ultimately undermined this protective infrastructure (Hodge 1981)—specifically the use of lead pipes to transport their water. Despite the fact that ancient Romans knew of the major health hazard caused by lead, they continued to use it in their water system because it was inexpensive and convenient (Hodge 1981). Some scholars have argued that the widespread use of lead in ancient Rome led to the downfall of the Roman Empire (Nriagu 1983). However, recent work has found the effect of lead in water pipes alone was not enough to bring down the population (Delile et al. 2014). Nevertheless, the fact that ancient water had lead levels 100 times greater than local spring waters still posed a major public health issue (Delile et al. 2014). It was not the last time cheapness and convenience outweighed public health issues. Lead was used in public water systems across the developed world until the 1920s, as evidenced, for example, by the highly publicized 2014 water crisis in Flint, Michigan, in the United States. This story, as well as others, highlights the fact that many of the developed world's lead-lined water systems are still in use today.

The Roman transportation system provides a similar story of successful infrastructure with latent unintended consequences. The extensive road system of ancient Rome was unparalleled. It was made up of 80,000 kilometers of hard-covered roads originating from the city center, prompting the proverb "all roads lead to Rome" (Rodrigue et al. 2016). This network of roads was essential to the development of the economic and political power of ancient Rome and formed the base of building projects in contemporary Rome (Rodrigue et al. 2016; Higgins 2014; Fusch 1994). The fact that these pathways are still in use today through adaptive reuse of this ancient transportation infrastructure means these networks are a fundamental organizing feature of present-day Italy. They continue to efficiently transport people across the city of Rome. In addition, this road system is at the foundation of one of contemporary Rome's major economic activities, tourism. Rome hosts an annual average of 30 million visitors whose tourist activities are centered on the historic center of the ancient Roman road system (Higgins 2014).

Whereas these ancient roads used to be lined with horse-drawn buggies and carts, they are now lined with automobiles. The public transportation is not sufficient to reduce the number of vehicles on the road (Battista et al. 2016). This creates issues of pollution and congestion that are "now more urgent than ever" (Higgins 2014). In 2015, at least 60 percent of journeys started in Rome were with private vehicles (Roma Capitale 2015). Traffic has been shown to be the main source of the harmful pollutants: benzene, carbon monoxide, and PM_{10} (Battista et al. 2016). The air pollution emitted from these automobiles has been shown to be responsible for the degradation of the relics the tourist economy relies on (Ghedini et al. 2000). In addition, analysis of PM_{10} concentrations in Rome in the winter of 2015 showed that over the 31-day observation period, PM_{10} levels only dipped below the EU limit (50 mg/m^3) three days (Renzi et al. 2016). Over the three days, these levels of toxins were associated with an additional 26 natural deaths, 20 hospitalizations, and 30 emergency room visits (Renzi et al. 2016). These results reflect those from the World Health Organization, which found that across the 13 largest cities in Italy (i.e., Turin, Genoa, Milan, Trieste, Padua, Venice-Mestre, Verona, Bologna, Florence, Rome, Naples, Catania, Palermo), 9 percent of all-cause mortality (excluding accidents) in the population over 30 years of age were due to PM_{10} concentrations of 20 mg/m^3 or higher (WHO 2017).

While it is true that Roman success in infrastructure has had unintended harmful consequences for human health, the historically planned areas of the city were organized in a way that has been shown to mitigate the harmful impacts of urban life. Specifically, the historic protection of areas from development—i.e., the maintenance of historic green spaces and piazzas—has been shown to positively impact both the environment and human health. The large green spaces throughout central Rome have been largely traced back to Napoleon's investment in the city in the early 1800s (Taylor et al. 2016). One of Napoleon's policies of social justice was to ensure all Romans had equal access to green space for fresh air and socialization (Taylor et al. 2016). Today we know that environmentally these green spaces work as pollution sinks, which absorb carbon from the atmosphere and help to filter out air toxins that otherwise might contribute to climate change and harm human health (Gratani and Varone 2014). In addition, these areas foster biodiversity. Areas with greater levels of biodiversity are also more likely to exert restorative effects on their visitors (Carrus et al. 2015), and greater access to pedestrian-only areas increases the likelihood of healthful behaviors like exercise. Socially, piazzas are integral to Italian society (Fusch 1994). These are spaces that have continuously been used throughout Rome's history as places for religious practices, politics, commerce, and recreation (Fusch 1994). The social interaction facilitated by these spaces helps to develop social capital in the Roman populace. Social capital is conceptualized as resources held in the density of the social network and patterns of civic engagement and is a key concept in the public health literature used to explain how "place" influences health. A 2013 meta-analysis found that social capital increased the odds of good health by 27 percent (Gilbert et al. 2013). There are multiple mechanisms through which the social capital held within these social networks positively influences health, such as increased flow of health information and greater social support (Ard et al. 2016; Gilbert et al. 2013). The integration of these areas into the city design and culture is likely to bolster social capital and the resulting positive health effects for Romans.

While the historic center of the city has well-established, planned green space, this planning has not kept up with changing population demands. From 1990 to 2008, roughly 1,000 hectares of largely agricultural land surrounding the city was overtaken by urban sprawl—that is, low-density built-up areas (Quatrini et al. 2015).

Urban sprawl has been found to be associated with several negative environmental and social characteristics. Environmentally, urban sprawl is associated with "higher environmental impacts" (Camagni et al. 2002), such as increased commuter numbers, distances and car use that increase air pollution (García-Palomares 2010), and land fragmentation and biodiversity loss (Irwin and Bockstael 2004; Dupras et al. 2016). Socially, urban sprawl is associated with class segregation, of which Rome already has a history (Lemanski 2007; Maloutas 2007).

The history of class segregation in Rome goes back to the 1500s when the city's Jewish population, the largest in Italy, was spatially segregated into ghettos (Taylor et al. 2016). Jews were forced there from sunset to sunrise, subjecting them to overcrowding, poor hygienic facilities, and virtual imprisonment (Taylor et al. 2016; Clough Marinaro 2015). This area of the city was modernized during unification and is a lively, predominately Jewish area today. When Italy unified in 1861, and the city was designated as Italy's capital in 1871, the overall population of Rome increased through internal migration. Unable to penetrate the well-established central city, many individuals of the lower class began settling on the fringes of the city (Forgacs 2014). In fact, from 1873 all urban plans of Rome placed lower-class housing on the rim of the city (Forgacs 2014). This spatially separated the poorest groups away from central transportation lines, as well as basic amenities like water and sewage services, exacerbating the problems of poverty (Forgacs 2014). The placement of the poor into periphery communities continued through Mussolini's fascist regime and extended as rent control in the city was eliminated in 1966, further forcing out those who could not afford the higher rents (Taylor et al. 2016). The settlement of the less wealthy away from the central city, into the growing suburbs—for example, Casale San Nicola—has had profound social, environmental, and health consequences (Kirchgaessner 2015).

As new waves of immigrants from the Balkans conflict in the 1990s fled to Rome, they entered into a context of spatial inequality, one that preserved wealthy residents in the central city and pushed those with less wealth to the periphery. Rome has traditionally been an "immigrant city," attracting populations from diverse cultural heritages and "since the 1970s has recorded net positive immigration from foreign countries" (Mudu 2013, 426). One of the major ethnic minority groups that entered Rome from the Balkan conflict was the Roma population (Clough Marinaro 2015). This population built hundreds of borghetti, small clusters of jerry-built dwellings, and baracche, single shacks (Taylor et al. 2016). In 2009, the Italian government enacted a new housing policy that shut down these shantytowns and moved this population into government-built containers at the city's periphery (Clough Marinaro 2015; Forgacs 2014). In 2014, the Roma population in the capital was made up of roughly 12,000 to 15,000 individuals, most of whom lived in eight state-built "nomad camps" that were originally constructed to house only 6,000 people (Marinaro and Daniele 2014). These spatially segregated areas are described as having leaking roofs and overflowing toilets, as well as being highly overcrowded, with high fences and constant policing (Clough Marinaro 2015).

The spatial separation and concentration of this marginalized population has long-term health and social consequences for its members. For example, children living in these areas are susceptible to growth retardation and low vaccination rates

(Ercoli et al. 2015; Zeman et al. 2003); while the overall population suffers from a lack of adequate health coverage, higher infant mortality rates, infectious diseases like hepatitis A, and other issues associated with conditions of long-term poverty (Zeman et al. 2003). Current demands for living space have only increased in recent years as hundreds of thousands of political and economic refugees flood into Europe; "87,000 arrived in Italy between January and July 2014 alone" (Taylor et al. 2016). Without a sound solution for this spatial inequality, these impoverished areas will only grow with Rome's new inhabitants. This pattern of spatial segregation of socio-economic groups has been highlighted as a hindrance to sustainable, healthy, economically viable communities (Amnesty International 2012). Scholars looking into these issues suggest improving social capital can boost political participation of these vulnerable populations (Nguyen Long 2016) in order to ensure their concerns are being addressed.

As urban centers like Rome are predicted to have continued growth over the next few decades, policymakers are well advised to review the lessons provided by Rome's long history of urban development.

Kerry Ard

See also: Waste Management: Naples, Italy: Coping with a Rubbish Crisis

Further Reading

Amnesty International. 2012. "Italy: Briefing to the UN Committee on the Elimination of Racial Discrimination." https://www.amnesty.org/en/documents/eur30/001/2012/en/.

Ard, Kerry, Cynthia Colen, Marisol Becerra, and Thelma Velez. 2016. "Two Mechanisms: The Role of Social Capital and Industrial Pollution Exposure in Explaining Racial Disparities in Self-Rated Health." *International Journal of Environmental Research and Public Health* 13, 10.

Battista, Gabriele et al. 2016. "Assessment of the Air Pollution Level in the City of Rome (Italy)." *Sustainability* 8, 9: 838.

Camagni, R., M. C. Gibelli, and P. Rigamonti. 2002. "Urban Mobility and Urban Form: The Social and Environmental Costs of Different Patterns of Urban Expansion." *Ecological Economics* 40, 2: 199–216.

Carrus, Giuseppe et al. 2015. "Go Greener, Feel Better? The Positive Effects of Biodiversity on the Well-Being of Individuals Visiting Urban and Peri-Urban Green Areas." *Landscape and Urban Planning* 134:221–28.

Clough Marinaro, I. 2015. "The Rise of Italy's Neo-Ghettos." *Journal of Urban History* 41, 3: 368–87.

Committee on the Elimination of Racial Discrimination. 2012. "Review of Italy. Open Society Justice Initiative." http://www2.ohchr.org.proxy.lib.ohio-state.edu/english/bodies/cerd/docs/ngos/OSJI_ASGI_Italy80.pdf.

Delile, Hugo et al. 2014. "Lead in Ancient Rome's City Waters." *Proceedings of the National Academy of Sciences of the United States of America* 111, 18: 6594–99.

Dupras, J., J. Marull, L. Parcerisas, F. Coll, A. Gonzalez, M. Girard, and E. Tello. 2016. "The Impacts of Urban Sprawl on Ecological Connectivity in the Montreal Metropolitan Region." *Environmental Science and Policy* 58: 61–73.

Ercoli, L. et al. 2015. "Unequal Access, Low Vaccination Coverage, Growth Retardation Rates among Immigrants' Children in Italy Exacerbated in Roma Immigrants." *Minerva Pediatrica* 67, 1: 11-8.

Forgacs, D. 2014. *Italy's Margins: Social Exclusion and Nation Formation since 1861*. Cambridge: Cambridge University Press.

Fusch, Richard. 1994. "The Piazza in Italian Urban Morphology." *Geographical Review* 84, 4: 424–38.

García-Palomares, J. C. 2010. "Urban Sprawl and Travel to Work: The Case of the Metropolitan Area of Madrid." *Journal of Transport Geography* 18, 2: 197–213.

Ghedini, N., G. Gobbi, C. Sabbioni, and G. Zappia. 2000. "Determination of Elemental and Organic Carbon on Damaged Stone Monuments." *Atmospheric Environment* 34: 4383–91.

Gilbert, Keon L., et al. 2013. "A Meta-Analysis of Social Capital and Health: A Case for Needed Research." *Journal of Health Psychology* 18, 11: 1385–99.

Gratani, Loretta, and Laura Varone. 2014. "Atmospheric Carbon Dioxide Concentration Variations in Rome: Relationship with Traffic Level and Urban Park Size." *Urban Ecosystems* 17, 2: 501–11.

Higgins, Valerie. 2014. "Rome's Contemporary Past." In Isabella Clough Marinaro and Bjørn Thomassen, eds. *Global Rome: Changing Faces of the Eternal City*. Bloomington: Indiana University Press.

Hodge, A. Trevor. 1981. "Vitruvius, Lead Pipes and Lead Poisoning." *American Journal of Archaeology* 85, 4: 486–91.

Irwin, E. G., and N. E. Bockstael. 2004. "Land Use Externalities, Open Space Preservation, and Urban Sprawl." *Regional Science and Urban Economics* 34, 6: 705–25.

Kirchgaessner, S. 2015. "Tensions Run High in Rome's Suburbs as Italy Struggles with Migration Crisis." *Guardian*, July. https://www.theguardian.com/world/2015/jul/26/italy-migrant-crisis-rome-protests-tensions-casale-san-nicola.

Koloski-Ostrow, Ann Olga. 2015. *The Archaeology of Sanitation in Roman Italy: Toilets, Sewers, and Water Systems*. Chapel Hill: University of North Carolina Press.

Kotkin, J. 2006. *The City: A Global History*. New York: Random House.

Lemanski, C. 2007. "Global Cities in the South: Deepening Social and Spatial Polarisation in Cape Town." *Cities* 24, 6: 448–61.

Maloutas, T. 2007. "Segregation, Social Polarization and Immigration in Athens during the 1990s: Theoretical Expectations and Contextual Difference." *International Journal of Urban and Regional Research* 31, 4: 733–58.

Marinaro, I., and Daniele, U. 2014. "A Failed Roma Revolution: Conflict, Fragmentation and Status Quo Maintenance in Rome". *Ethnicities* 14, 6: 775–792.

Mudu, P. (2013). "Patterns of Segregation in Contemporary Rome." *Urban Geography* 27, 5: 422–40.

Nguyen Long, L. A. 2016. "Does Social Capital Affect Immigrant Political Participation? Lessons from a Small-N Study of Migrant Political Participation in Rome." *Journal of International Migration and Integration* 17, 3: 819–37. http://doi.org/10.1007/s12134-015-0434-0.

Nriagu, Jerome O. 1983. *Lead and Lead Poisoning in Antiquity*. New York: John Wiley.

Quatrini, Valerio et al. 2015. "Monitoring Land Take by Point Sampling: Pace and Dynamics of Urban Expansion in the Metropolitan City of Rome." *Landscape and Urban Planning* 143: 126–33.

Rabun Taylor, Katherine, and R. S. Wentworth. 2016. *Rome: An Urban History from Antiquity to the Present*. New York: Cambridge University Press.

Renzi, Matteo, et al. 2016. "Health Effects of Air Pollution in Rome in December 2015." *Epidemiologia e prevenzione* 40, 1: 29–32.

Rodrigue, Jean-Paul, Claude Comtois, and Brian Slack. 2016. *The Geography of Transport Systems*. London: Routledge.

Roma Capitale, Piano Generale del Traffico Urbano (City Urban Traffic General Plan) (in Italian). 2015. April. https://www.comune.roma.it/pcr/it/dip_mob_delibere.page.

Shammin, M. R., R. A. Herendeen, M. J. Hanson, and E. J. H. Wilson. 2010. "A Multivariate Analysis of the Energy Intensity of Sprawl Versus Compact Living in the U.S. for 2003." *Ecological Economics* 69, 12: 2363–73.

Taylor, Dorceta E. 2009. *The Environment and the People in American Cities, 1600s-1900s: Disorder, Inequality and Social Change*. Durham, NC: Duke University Press.

World Health Organization (WHO). 2017. "HIA of Air Pollution in Italian Cities." *Health Impact Assessment (HIA)*. http://www.euro.who.int/__data/assets/pdf_file/0012/91110/E88700.pdf.

Zeman, C. L., D. E. Depken, and D. S. Senchina. 2003. "Roma Health Issues: A Review of the Literature and Discussion." *Ethnicity & Health* 8 (March): 223–49.

Sao Paulo, Brazil: Fighting the Deadly Air Pollution

"Earn in Sao Paulo, so you can spend in Rio (de Janeiro)" is a Brazilian aphorism that for decades has summarized a widespread perception of the difference between the two cities, where a superior quality of life is awaiting in Rio de Janeiro to those middle class that can find success and prosperity in the workaholic and fast-paced environment of urban life in Sao Paulo (Schneider et al. 2016). When the local newspaper reported to the world that in 2011 "traffic pollution kills more people than traffic accidents" (G1.Globo 2013) in Sao Paulo, it was clear that the aphorism also suggest a major challenge for the average Paulista (resident of Sao Paulo) trying to achieve his dreams of prosperity. They need to add to the problems of daily life a potential high risk to their health caused by environmental problems of great magnitude beyond those of the colloquial rivalry of the two cities.

A study by Evangelina da Motta Pacheco de Araujo Vormittag, a medical doctor specializing in pathology, reported that in 2011, 4,655 Sao Paulo residents died from causes produced by traffic pollution, a figure that is three times more than those killed by breast cancer and six times more than those killed by HIV. This study was presented to the local municipal Camera (of Commerce). A follow-up report produced by the Institute for Sustainability led by Dr. de Araujo Vormittag found that the environmental cost of air pollution for local residents of Sao Paulo will decrease their life expectancy by 1.5 years, with a financial loss for the country estimated in the millions of dollars a year (Da M. P. A. de Araujo Vormittag et al. 2013).

Sao Paulo's environmental problems are the consequence of great economic success. The city's expansive economy, based on diversified industrial sector growths, expanded faster than the local awareness of the environmental risk and damage to residents' health. The economic prosperity brought by the coffee industry made Sao Paolo grow as an agricultural and financial center but always in the shadow of Rio de Janeiro. However, the misfortunes during the first half of the 20th century made Sao Paolo the favorite of wealthy Brazilians who sought an alternative to the corruption and gang violence of Rio (*Economist* 2011).

Today, the state of Sao Paulo and the city are the largest industrial hub in the Southern Hemisphere, the largest business center in Latin America, and the fourth-largest metropolis in the world receiving foreign investment in 2011, according to the government of the state of Sao Paulo (Governo do Estato Sao Paulo 2016). Sao Paulo is indeed a large metropolis and a world leader economy with a manufacturing sector that includes motor vehicles, electric appliances, automobile components, textiles, chemical and pharmaceutical plants, oil refineries, transportation, heavy equipment, and thousands of other industries. Nevertheless, it is the large workforce participating in the economy that is the root cause of the problem of air pollution in the city.

The main means of transportation in Sao Paulo includes privately owned cars, city buses, taxis, and a metro system that transports 3 million out of the 11 million residents (*Economist*, 2014). Also, the city has the second-largest helicopter fleet in the world, used by wealthy businesspeople to avoid the congested streets (*Economist* 2011). But private cars are the preferred means of transportation, with almost 6.2 million cars in the metropolitan area, and 4.2 million in the municipality of Sao Paulo providing transportation (Biderman 2008). While public transportation accounts for 55 percent of the trips in the city, privately owned vehicles account for the remaining 45 percent according to a report of the Brazilian Institute of Integrated Analysis of environmental risk (Do Globo 2012).

While they are a transportation solution for some, private cars, motorcycles, and trucks are the largest source of Sao Paulo's air pollution today, contributing 90 percent of the pollutants. Traffic pollution, exacerbated by traffic congestion, is responsible for the deaths of 12 people per day and more than 200 people sick, according to a study from the pollution lab at the University of Sao Paulo. This figure is higher than the rate of deaths by violence for the same year, according to writer Gilberto Dimenstein (Dimenstein 2008).

The great impact of the environmental stresses of Sao Pablo on its residents, and the great magnitude of its environmental problems, are not new and are common in other world-class industrialized cities. In fact, urbanization and industrial development often have been associated with poor air quality, a by-product of economic development and the improved urban life. Cities like London, Delhi, Los Angeles, and Mexico City suffered and still suffer the consequences of their industrial success in the poor quality of air breathed by their residents. In the 1940s and 1950s, the cities of Donora in Pennsylvania in the United States and London in Great Britain, important industrial centers, served as the "canary in the coal mine" (an analogy suggesting an alarm system) to indicate the enormous risk to humans and to society of unregulated and uncontrolled air pollution within urban areas.

In late October of 1948, Donora was covered by a dense fog that obscured the city during daylight, filling residents' lungs with a mix of pollution produced by the local steel and zinc factories (Murray 2009). Lest than a week later, after a children's fog-enshrouded Halloween parade, 20 people were dead, forcing local doctors to recommend residents leave the city. Changes in weather conditions finally cleaned the air, and a new sense of environmental awareness was born in the local residents but also in the whole United States. Less than five years later in 1953, during the celebrations of the golden jubilee (the anniversary of the queen), 4,000 residents of London were killed initially by a smog filled with dark fumes that remained in the air for a week due to local weather conditions. The consequences of inhaling this air lingered for weeks. Months after the air returned to normal, 12,000 deaths were attributed to this event (Devis 2002).

In both the United States and England, these disasters brought a new environmental awareness and a legacy of strong environmental legislation that served as a model to the world to regulate industries and car emissions. A Clean Air Act was approved in England in 1956 and implemented in 1964, and six year later in 1970 in the United States (Rogers 1990).

In Sao Paulo, early incidents of air pollution in the 1960s forced local municipalities to create a local commission to control air and water pollution (CETESB) with the objective of starting the first monitoring program for air quality in 1972. Fourteen stations were established to monitor sulfur dioxide, collecting readings twice a day and their results were made public using print bulletins. During those early days of air monitoring, efforts concentrated on industrial pollutants. However, in the 1980s and for the first time, studies started looking at assessing smog produced by vehicles in the streets. These studies coincided with the first attempts to mix gasoline with ethanol, finding that the pollution resulting from their combustion was lower than from gasoline alone (CETESB 2016). Not until then did the government of Brazil start looking at legislation to guarantee air quality. The National Environment Council (CONAMA), a government agency in charge of setting guidelines that states and local municipalities must follow, established the National Program for Air Quality (PRONAR) in 1989 and the CONAMA Resolution 3 in 1990, establishing a list of pollutants and their allowed limit in the air. This resolution became a landmark in regulating air quality in the country (CONAMA 1990).

Despite the fact that air pollution has been a well-known problem for over 25 years, strategies and actions to control or minimize its impact have progressed slowly. In 2013, a new set of goals were introduced into local policy to guide short- and long-term strategies to clean the city's air. These goals adopted as a reference point the value of 10 µg/m^3 of particulate matter (pollutants in the air) of a diameter of less than 2.5 micrometers, or $PM_{2.5}$ (a micrometer is a thousandth of a millimeter) established by the World Health Organization (WHO) (Osseiran and Chriscaden 2016). Historical data from Sao Paulo and adjacent municipalities showed all the stations with more than double the pollution of the WHO index. In fact, the problem extends beyond the city of Sao Paulo since 11 municipalities in its metropolitan area were found with values similar or larger than those from the city (Da M. P. A. de Araujo Vormittag et al. 2013).

Looking to decrease traffic congestion and air pollution, the city of Sao Paulo has established a system of traffic management using plate restriction to decrease 20 percent of the cars on the streets. Under this system, certain plate numbers are not allowed to circulate during weekdays between 7 a.m. and 10 a.m. and 5 p.m. and 8 p.m. However, it is clear that this system is insufficient, and a larger effort is necessary to have residents opting for public transportation instead of their private vehicles (Biderman 2008). The solution seems pretty obvious; while a new highway lane can transport 5,450 passengers per hour, a new metro line has the potential to transport up to 60,000 passengers (Do Globo 2012). The

> **Carbon Tax**
>
> The carbon tax is a relatively new concept that gained popularity in the past 10 years. The purpose of applying a carbon tax on hydrocarbon products—such as coal, oil, and natural gas that emit CO_2 into the atmosphere in the energy conversion process—is to recuperate costs that will be incurred in pollution treatment. The tax also serves to curb consumption through the market mechanism of supply and demand. The tax is often expressed as a value per ton of CO_2 equivalent (per tCO2e). According to the World Bank, 15 countries and regions currently impose carbon taxes: British Columbia (Canada), Chile, Costa Rica, Denmark, Finland, France, Iceland, Ireland, Japan, Mexico, Norway, South Africa, Sweden, Switzerland, and United Kingdom. Tax levels vary, as do the ways of redistribution. For example, British Columbia implements a revenue-neutral scheme by returning the revenue to citizens through a reduction in other taxes. Costa Rica uses it to pay for environmental services and incentives for forest conservation. In Switzerland, the tax is imposed on all fossil fuels, unless they are used for energy—companies that participate in the country's Energy Trading System are exempt from the carbon tax. As of this writing, no U.S. state has a carbon tax. In the state of Washington, citizens put a carbon tax proposal known as Initiative 732 before voters. The initiative failed to secure the majority of votes.

effect of the metro system in improving the air quality of the city is also dramatic. When comparing days when metro service was reduced due to strikes with days with normal operation for 2003 and 2006, the levels of air pollution in the city almost doubled, according to researchers of the Federal University of Sao Paulo (UniFeSP).

With 313 kilometers of combined metro and train, Sao Paulo's rail system has great potential for expansion. Cities like New York and London currently have double the kilometers in metro lines that the metro in Sao Paulo has, and they occupy metropolitan areas much smaller (Biderman 2008). Also, local authorities and municipalities are eager to promote an already well-established culture of using public transportation in the city, particularly among the poor, with actions such as the single-ticket system, where metro users pay a single fare regardless of distance or number of transfers.

Unfortunately, immediate solutions are unlikely to come from metro systems, considering the great economic cost associated with large infrastructure projects and their effect on the political and economic forces in the country. Recognizing the problem, local Sao Paulo authorities are taking actions to improve local infrastructure with projects that increase the efficiency, connectivity, and accessibility of bus rides. In this initiative, more than 500 kilometers of bus corridors are planned to be added by 2025, as well as new stations and terminals (Biderman 2008). At this point, the big challenge for Sao Paulo to solve air pollution and transportation problems seems to depend on finding a balance between the needs of the poor and the needs of those with the economic means to own a car.

Mario A. Giraldo

See also: Pollution: New Delhi, India: Success of Pollution Control Depends on Effective Collaboration; *Traffic and Transportation:* Mexico City, Mexico: Improving Governance Is Key to Solving Traffic Challenges

Further Reading

Biderman, Ciro. 2008. Sao Paulo's Urban Transport Infrastructure (in Portuguese). LSECities. https://lsecities.net/media/objects/articles/sao-paulo-urban-transport-infrastructure/en-gb.

CETESB. 2016. Qualidade do Ar Historico. Companhia Ambiental do Estado de Sao Paulo CETESB (in Portuguese). http://ar.cetesb.sp.gov.br.

CONAMA. 1990. Conselho Nacional Do Meio Ambient (in Portuguese). Resolução CONAMA no. 3, de 28 de Junho de 1990. August 22. Seção 1, páginas 15937–39. http://www.mma.gov.br/port/conama/legiabre.cfm?codlegi=100.

Da M. P. A. de Araujo Vormittag, E., C. Guimarães-Rodrigues, J. Affonso-Cavalcante, R. Rodrigues-da-Costa, C. Acosta-Camargo, and P.H. Nascimento-Saldiva. 2013. Avaliacao do impacto da poluicao atmosferica no estado de Sao Paulo sob as visao da saude. Instituto Saude e Sustentabilidade (in Portuguese). September 16: 83. http://www.saudeesustentabilidade.org.br/site/wp-content/uploads/2013/09/Documentofinaldapesquisapadrao_2409-FINAL-sitev1.pdf.

Devis, Debra. 2002. "The Great Smog: Devra Devis Look at the London Smog Disaster of 1952–1953." *History Today* 52, 12 (December). http://www.historytoday.com/devra-davis/great-smog.

Dimenstein, Gilberto. 2008. Pior do que assassinato. Folha Online (in Portuguese). October 3. http://www1.folha.uol.com.br/folha/pensata/gilbertodimenstein/ult508u380368.shtml.

Do Globo Naturaleza. 2012. São Paulo teria poluição 75% maior se metrô parasse um ano, diz estudo (in Portuguese). *Do Globo*, June 26. http://g1.globo.com/natureza/noticia/2012/06/sao-paulo-teria-poluicao-75-maior-se-metro-parasse-por-um-ano-diz-estudo.html.

Economist. 2014. "The Americas View. Brazil before the World Cup: Traffic and Tempers." *Economist* blog, June 10. http://www.economist.com/blogs/americasview/2014/06/brazil-world-cup.

Economist. 2011. "Doing Business in Brazil: Rio or Sao Paolo." *The Economist blog*, September 3rd, 2011. http://www.economist.com/node/21528267.

G1.Globo. 2013. 24/09/2013 00h12—Estudo aponta que poluição mata mais que o trânsito em São Paulo. September 24.

Governo do Estado Sao Paulo. 2016. http://www.saopauloglobal.sp.gov.br/eng-index.aspx.

Haddad, Ricardo. 1963. La contaminacion atmosferica en Sao Paulo Metropolitano, Brasil: Análisis previo del problema. World Health Organization. *Boletín de la Oficina Sanitaria Panamericana* (OSP) 56, 3 (March).

Lavelle, Marianne. 2016. "Washington State Voters Reject Nation's First Carbon Tax." *Inside Climate News*, November 9. https://insideclimatenews.org/news/09112016/washington-state-carbon-tax-i-732-ballot-measure.

Mosley, Stephen. 2014. Air Pollution: The Impact of the 1956 Clean Air Act. Friends of the Earth, January 14. https://www.foe.co.uk/blog/air-pollution-impact-1956-clean-air-act.

Murray, Ann. 2009. "Smog Deaths in 1948 Led to Clean Air Laws." United States, National Public Radio, *All Things Considered*, April 22. http://www.npr.org/templates/story/story.php?storyId=103359330.

Osseiran, Nada, and Kimberly Chriscaden. 2016. WHO Releases Country Estimates on Air Pollution Exposure and Health Impact. World Health Organization News Release 2016. http://www.who.int/mediacentre/news/releases/2016/air-pollution-estimates/en.

Rogers, Paul G. 1991990 "The Clean Air Act of 1970." *EPA Journal.* (January/February): 21–23. https://nepis.epa.gov/Exe/ZyPDF.cgi/40000CB9.PDF?Dockey=40000CB9.PDF.

Schneider, R. M., A. Leite, and C. W. Minkel. 2013. "Sao Paulo, Brazil." Encyclopaedia Britannica, June, 16, 2016. https://www.britannica.com/place/Sao-Paulo-Brazil

The World Bank. "Putting a Price on Carbon with a Tax." https://www.worldbank.org/content/dam/Worldbank/document/SDN/background-note_carbon-tax.pdf.

Seoul, South Korea: When Every Citizen Takes It to Heart

Seoul, the capital and largest metropolis of the Republic of Korea with 10 million inhabitants, has served as a cultural, economic, and political center for more than 2,000 years. Due to a growing number of people migrating into Seoul, the government has constructed satellite cities near Seoul, resulting in the creation of the Seoul Capital Area with 25 million residents, half of the country's population, who mostly commute to the inner city. Seoul and its neighboring cities' dense population is tied to various industrial complexes, concentrated dwelling types, and heavy traffic which become major sources of pollution. The city has strived to reduce levels of water and air pollution, and to promote waste recycling. The city's continuing effort made Seoul the seventh most sustainable city in the world in 2016 (Arcadis 2016).

WATER POLLUTION

The Han River (Hangang) that runs through the middle of Seoul had been an important source of water supply and a major locus of leisurely activities like swimming and fishing until the early 1960s. With rapid industrialization and urbanization in the 1960s and 1970s under the Five-Year Plans for the development of the national economy in South Korea, the Han River's water quality worsened due to the constant inflow of polluted water from industrial complexes and residential areas. Without proper wastewater treatment facilities, water pollution of the Han River reached a point where the city had to ban swimming in 1967, boating in 1973, and fishing in 1981. The river's high biochemical oxygen demand (BOD) level in 1979 resulted in a complete shutdown of its water supply system, transporting clean water from Paldang Reservoir outside Seoul. Fifty species of fish disappeared during this period, with only 30 species currently found in the Han River (Kwon 1986).

To restore the dying urban river, the Seoul Metropolitan Government embarked on the Hangang Comprehensive Development Project from 1982 to 1986. The project involved creating proper sewage systems, four wastewater treatment facilities, and public riverside parks. Costing $900 million, the project also focused on reconfiguration of the 36-kilometer section of the river. The meandering Han River's original flow was artificially straightened with construction of underwater dams and concrete levees along the riverbanks. Excavating riverbeds was part of the project, which aimed to deepen the river's water level for river cruises and arguably to improve water quality. After the completion of the project, the Han River became

Seoul, South Korea, from the Han River, 2015. Cleaning up this polluted urban river took decades. (In Sung Choi/Dreamstime.com)

one-kilometer wide and 2.5 meters deep on average, with two highways on both its sides. The highlight of the project is 11 riverside parks that encompass a 39.9-square-kilometer area along the river. These public parks have pedestrian walkways, two-way cycle tracks, swimming pools, basketball courts, soccer fields, and picnic areas. With its cleaner water and recreational facilities, the Han River has reclaimed its fame. Despite the project's apparent success, a few environmentalists have criticized its concrete levees and underwater dams that disrupted the river's ecosystem. Responding to this reproach, the city administered the Hangang Renaissance Project from 2006 to 2010, adding three ecological parks and renovating the aging riverside parks. The city continues its effort to return the Han River back to its natural state with a newly commenced Hangang Restoration Project of 2017, according to the Seoul Municipality.

There has been a systematic approach to improving drinkable water quality. In February 2004, the city named its public water "Arisu," which was the Han River's previous name. With the new branding, the city adopted the Seoul Water-Now System in the same year. This is an automatized surveillance system with 156 branches for water quality control and responses throughout the entire water supply chain. The city also provided free Arisu quality testing from 2008 to 2010 by sending testing personnel to 26 million households and checking levels of free chlorine, pH, turbidity, iron, and copper in the public water of each domestic unit. The Seoul Water-Now System and Arisu Quality Check System won the United Nations Public Service Awards in 2009. The city further obtained ISO 22000 (the International Organization for Standardization's Food Safety Management

System) Certification in 2016, and ISO 14001 (Environmental Management System) Certification since 2000 for its public water. These certifications prove that Arisu and its system are concerned about environmental obligations.

AIR POLLUTION

The most troublesome pollution in Seoul is fine particulate matter ($PM_{2.5}$), which is a mixture of solid particles and liquid droplets found in the air. With diameters that are generally 2.5 micrometers and smaller, almost 1/30th the width of a single human hair, fine particulate matter is small enough to be inhaled directly into the lungs, causing serious health issues. According to the 2016 OECD's Better Life Index, South Korea's average fine particulate matter was 29.1 micrograms per cubic meter, which was twice as much as OECD's average (14.05 $\mu g/m^3$) and three times worse than the guideline of the World Health Organization (10 $\mu g/m^3$). An Air Quality Index (AQI) record in March 2017 reported that Seoul was ranked one of the three most polluted cities after New Delhi and Beijing (*Financial Times* 2017).

The root causes of toxic smog and fine particulate matter in Seoul are still under investigation and debated, while several studies find long-range transport of air pollutants originating in China as a possible contributor. A 2017 article published in *Nature* argues that "local air quality can be affected by atmospheric transport of pollution from distant sources," linking $PM_{2.5}$ pollution produced in China in 2007 to 30,900 premature deaths in South Korea and Japan (Oh et al. 2015). This result reveals that the transboundary health impacts of $PM_{2.5}$ pollution are substantial, and international collaboration is needed to reduce global air pollution. As OECD warns that increasing concentration of $PM_{2.5}$ and ground-level ozone will lead to 6 to 9 million premature deaths in the world and cost 1 percent GDP by 2060, the Seoul Metropolitan Government endeavors to reduce emissions of air pollutants and establish an adequate warning system (OECD 2016).

Recognizing chemicals such as sulfur dioxide, nitrogen oxides, and carbon dioxide as major pollutants emitted from power plants and automobiles in Seoul, the government modernized its public transport system in 2004 and has enforced a summertime electricity conservation policy. The public transport reform included construction of express lanes for buses in the inner city, better coordination of bus and metro services, and conversion of the bus fleets to compressed natural gas (Allen 2013). In order to make public transportation more accessible and affordable, the city also implemented a fully integrated fare structure and ticketing system across modes, offering free transfers between bus and subway, free rides for those who are 65 years or older, and 50 percent discount for students, along with a heavily regulated basic fare (Pucher et al. 2005). To decrease emissions from automobile exhaust and advocate walkable urbanism, bus stops and subways stations are located within walking distance of every part of the city, and walkable streets accentuated by public art programs are constructed. The city also implemented a bicycle-sharing system in 2015, first only available in the riverside parks and later expanded with 300 bike stations in the inner city with 3,000 bicycles available. Charging only a dollar per hour, the city plans to add more bike stations and increase the number of bicycles up to 20,000 (Bikeseoul.com).

Each summer, campaigns on energy conservation are led by Korea Energy Agency and the Ministry of Trade, Industry and Energy, mainly promoting 26 to 28 degrees Celsius (78 to 82 degrees Fahrenheit) as adequate room temperatures. Korea's hot and humid summers invite a spike in energy consumption for air conditioning and cause a few power outages due to the overloading of mains electricity. Public buildings like schools and courts and commercial high-rise buildings are under scrutiny for their room temperatures. While the government guideline does not affect residential buildings, saving electricity becomes a main motto advocated in mass media that encourages residents to self-ration their electric energy consumption.

The Seoul Metropolitan Government along with the National Institute of Environmental Research under the Environment Ministry has established a real-time warning system on air pollution. It provides hourly updates on the levels of coarse particles (PM_{10}), fine particulate matter ($PM_{2.5}$), ozone, carbon dioxide, carbon monoxide, and sulfur dioxide in 25 districts of the city and major boulevards. Its alert levels include preliminary advisory stage, advisory, and warning. Its action plan instructions for residents are specified, detailing when sensitive groups of children, the elderly, and people with respiratory or cardiovascular conditions should remain indoors, wear protective masks, or refrain from going to areas with heavy traffic. The warning system also educates its residents on the importance of daily routines like drinking water, closing windows, and using mass transit. The updated information on air quality can be accessed online and via text messaging service.

CHEONGGYECHEON STREAM RESTORATION PROJECT

One of the most successful eco-friendly projects that Seoul initiated is the Cheonggyecheon Stream Restoration Project, which transformed a ghetto just off the busiest boulevards in the inner city into a beloved public park. The area had been notorious for its impoverished residents living in makeshift houses, accompanied by trash and waste along the polluted stream. Due to its odor, contamination, and unpleasant appearance, the stream was covered up with concrete in the late 1950s. The site became a symbol of Seoul's urban planning in the 1970s when its elevated Cheonggye Expressway allowed an uninterrupted traffic flow to the center of Seoul. Its lack of greenery reflected the country's focus on industrial development and disregard for nature and ecology. As a result, the stream dried up under the pavement.

In 2003, the project to revitalize Cheonggyecheon and its ecosystem began. Removing overpasses and rehabilitating the stream with 120,000 tons of water pumped in daily from the Han River, the project created a pedestrian-only public space with vegetation and biodiversity in the center of Seoul (Marshall 2016). Yonhap News reported that between the pre-restoration period in 2003 and the end of 2008, there occurred a drastic increase in biodiversity by 639 percent, with the number of fish species increasing from 4 to 25, bird species from 6 to 36, insect species from 15 to 192, and plant species from 62 to 308. More positive environmental effects of the project on air quality have been reported over the years. Thanks to the removal of the paved expressway, reduction in automobile trips, and increased vegetation, fine particles were reduced by 35 percent and nitrogen dioxide by

29 percent. The urban heat island effect was noticeably weakened, with temperatures along the stream 3.3 to 5.9 degrees Celsius cooler than on a parallel road four to seven blocks away, per Yonhap News reports.

Inspired by this ecological improvement along the Cheonggyecheon Stream, the Seoul Metropolitan Government has organized a collaborative program to construct multiple carbon offset forests in various districts since 2014.

"Working jointly with a handful of corporations and thousands of residents, the city has hosted 11 tree-planting events with a hope that 600,000 trees newly planted in these forests would reduce 2,095 tons of carbon dioxide for the next 30 years and improve general air quality" (Song 2016).

WASTE AND RECYCLING

Seoul has embraced a zero-waste recycling strategy, achieving a recycling rate of 85 percent in 2015 with 35,000 tons of materials per day diverted from landfill to recycling. Twenty years ago, the city's recycling rate was only 15 percent. This drastic change was enabled by a strict national volume-rate garbage disposal system that began in 1995. The government has mandated its residents to purchase official garbage bags for small fees. These garbage bags are only for nonrecyclable materials. Any recyclable item is not allowed in a garbage bag. Recyclable materials including plastic bottles, tin cans, metal, Styrofoam, glass, and paper are collected without charge. Food waste is also collected separately, with 100 percent recycling rate turning 3,000 tons of food scraps per day into compost. In order to save fees that are based on garbage volumes, residents have actively participated in recycling and reducing waste. According to the 2015 Ministry of Environment's report, the amount of garbage was 43 percent reduced compared to that of 1994, the year before the volume-rate garbage disposal system was adopted (Ministry of Environment 2015).

CONCLUSION

Being the most populous city in South Korea, Seoul continuously faces environmental challenges like water and air pollution and waste minimization. The municipal and local district governments and citizens need to come together for concerted efforts to reduce greenhouse gas emissions and other pollutants. Only with constant attention to ecological issues and eco-friendly projects and practices can Seoul remain sustainable.

Nogin Chung

See also: Waste Management: Kobe, Japan: The Cleanest City in the World; Singapore City, Singapore: Managing Food Waste

Further Reading
Air Quality Information (in Korean). http://cleanair.seoul.go.kr.
Allen, Heather. 2013. "Bus Reform in Seoul, Republic of Korea." In *Global Report on Human Settlements.* Nairobi: UN Habitat.

Bikeseoul.com (in Korean). http://www.bikeseoul.com.

E-Arisu (in Korean). http://e-arisu.seoul.go.kr.

Financial Times. 2017. "South Korea Joins Ranks of World's Most Polluted Countries." https://www.ft.com/content/b49a9878-141b-11e7-80f4-13e067d5072c. Real-time Air Quality Index can be found in http://aqicn.org/map/southkorea.

Korea Energy Agency. http://www.energy.or.kr.

Korea Landscape Architecture Newspaper. 2017. "The City of Seoul Created the 11th Carbon Offset Forest in Jongro." April 5.

Kwon, Sookpyo. 1986. "Effects of the Hangang Comprehensive Development Project on Water Quality." *Environment Information* 8, 17: 2–9.

Marshall, Colin. 2016. *Guardian*. "Story of Cities #50: The Reclaimed Stream Bringing Life to the Heart of Seoul." The Ministry of Environment. August 6. *Waste and Recycling Report*.

Ministry of Environment, 2015 White Paper of Environment, 2015. http://webbook.me.go.kr/DLi-File/091/020/009/5592862.pdf.

OECD. n.d. Better Life Index. http://www.oecdbetterlifeindex.org.

OECD. 2016. *The Economic Consequences of Outdoor Air Pollution*. Paris: OECD Publishing.

Oh, Hye-Ryun, et al. 2015. "Long-Range Transport of Air Pollutants Originating in China: A Possible Major Cause of Multi-Day High-PM_{10} Episodes during Cold Season in Seoul, Korea." *Atmospheric Environment* 109 (May): 23–30.

Pucher, John, et al. 2005. "Public Transport Reforms in Seoul: Innovations Motivated by Funding Crisis." *Journal of Public Transportation* 8, 5: 41–62.

Qiang Zhang, et al. 2017. "Transboundary Health Impacts of Transported Global Air Pollution and International Trade." *Nature* 543, 7647 (March 30): 705–9.

Seoul Metropolitan Government Website. http://english.seoul.go.kr/life-information/natural-attractions-parks/hangang/00-parks-hangang-river/.

Song, Chanyoung. "Seoul Creates Anti-Carbon Dioxide Forests." *Energy Economy News*, April 3, 2016. http://www.ekn.kr/news/article_print.html?no=210879.

Sustainable Cities Index 2016: Putting People at the Heart of City Sustainability. Amsterdam: Arcadis, 2016, 9.

Yonhap News. 2005. "Weakening Urban Heat Island Effect after the Remodeling of Cheongyecheon." October 24.

Yonhap News. 2006. "Improvements of Air Quality and Noise after the Remodeling of Cheongyecheon." June 5.

Yonhap News. 2009. "Increase of Biological Species in Cheonggyecheon." February 23.

Shiprock, United States: Radioactive from the Inside Out

The toxic legacy of Native North America is pervasive, but largely invisible to most of us. Many toxic sites are located in out-of-the-way rural areas largely forgotten by majority America, such as Shiprock, New Mexico. Today, one-third of Environmental Protection Agency Superfund sites in the United States are on Indian reservations, one of which is Shiprock (Hansen 2014). From the (now-closed) uranium mines of Navajo country to the PCB-laced turtles on the Akwesasne Mohawks' homeland in upstate New York, Native American peoples are resisting energy and resource colonization to survive.

Uranium mined from Native American lands supplied a substantial proportion of the fuel for early nuclear power plants as well as the U.S. nuclear arsenal. The Navajos succeeded in stopping uranium mining and milling on their homeland after several hundred people had died of its effects and many more had suffered the tortures of cancers that once were nearly unknown in their country. Following several decades of death in the mines, by about 2010 uranium mining and milling was outlawed on the Navajo Nation, as the people there heeded what tradition calls their "original instructions" to leave the soft, radioactive yellow rocks in the ground. Shiprock is full of uranium widows whose husbands died in the mines.

NAVAJO CANCERS ACCELERATE

About half the recoverable uranium in the United States lies in New Mexico—and about half of that is beneath the Navajo Nation. There is no word for "radioactivity" in the Navajo language. And the miners had no idea that many of them would die of cancers caused by radiation within the next 20–30 years. In the early years of mining, when the emphasis was on quick profits, few companies placed ventilation systems in their mines. Many miners spent 20 hours a day in mines filled with silica dust thrown up by the blasting of sandstone. Often, mine owners would not even provide the miners with toilet paper, causing them to wipe themselves with fists caked with radioactive "yellowcake"—uranium ore.

By 2014, 350 to 400 former Navajo underground uranium miners had died from maladies caused in large part by exposure to radiation, according to Chris Shuey, an environmental health researcher with the Southwest Research and Information Center (Knight 2013). Many more Native people also have died of a wide variety of malignant cancers, often not from mining uranium themselves, but because they lived with the "yellow dirt" in windswept waste (tailings) piles that have now blown into every crack and crevice, indoors and outdoors, for decades, in Navajo communities such as Shiprock.

In addition to the mining and milling of nuclear fuel, New Mexico also supplied the United States with its first test site for the atomic bomb, detonated on July 16, 1945, on a 100-foot tower. The Trinity site on today's U.S. Army's White Sands Missile Range is surrounded by two Apache tribes, several Navajo communities, and 19 American Indian pueblos. Reports at the time by American Indians and government witnesses in places such as Shiprock described a light ash that fell for days after the explosion, the effects of which were not investigated until 2014, when the National Cancer Institute started a study of radiation levels in New Mexico from that first test blast. With no prior evidence of effects, no one has been eligible for compensation under the Radiation Exposure Compensation Act, which covers other nuclear and uranium workers as well as "down-winders" who were exposed to radiation from later atomic tests (Lee 2014).

Uranium mine dust left silicosis deposited in the miners' lungs. Lung cancer and other problems associated with exposure to radioactivity were on the rise. By the 1960s, nearly 200 miners had died of causes related to uranium. By 1990, the number of deaths doubled. In addition to the work environment, drinking water was also contaminated in parts of the Navajo reservation. Cases of birth defects and Down syndrome emerged. Such cases were previously rare among the Navajo.

The government knew of the risk at least by 1978, when the Department of Energy released a Nuclear Waste Management Task Force report disclosing that people living near the tailings piles ran at least twice the risk of lung cancer as the general population. The Coalition for Navajo Liberation (CNL), an activist group, had been aware that a number of miners were dying of lung cancer. They had no power to change government policy. As a result, Navajo miners continued to sicken and die. Children who played in water flowing from abandoned mines and tailings piles were found to suffer from burning sores. Windblown dust from yellowcake uranium processed at the mills could spread to the surrounding landscape. Contaminated areas could stretch as far as half a mile away.

RADIATION PERVADES NAVAJO LIFE

In much the same way coal miners hauled coal, Navajo uranium miners hauled radioactive uranium ore out of the earth. They ate their lunches in the mines and drank water from the mines. Their family homes may be built with blocks containing radioactive material. The food chain was contaminated as domestic animals may have watered in small ponds filled with water from the mines. Winds could carry radioactive dust far and wide, resulting in widespread contamination.

Kerr-McGee was the first corporation to mine uranium on Navajo Nation lands (beginning in 1948). The company found the reservation location extremely lucrative. The cost of mining uranium was low at the time, as there were no taxes nor insurance for miners' health or safety to pay. There were barely any pollution regulations. Moreover, the many Navajos who had recently arrived home from service in World War II had few other opportunities. On the other hand, the profit was good due to high demand for uranium for armament.

The first uranium miners in the area were almost all Navajos. They remember being sent into shallow tunnels within minutes after blasting. They loaded the uranium ore into wheelbarrows, and as they worked they had to inhale the dust. Many remember coughing so hard that they experienced headaches. The working conditions exposed the miners to between 100 and 1,000 times the level of radon gas later considered safe. Officials for the U.S. Public Health Service (PHS) estimated these levels of exposure after the fact; in the earliest days, no one was monitoring the Navajo miners' health.

Carrie Arnold (2014) wrote in Environmental Health Perspectives, published by the National Institutes of Health, that the miners and their families "were not told that the men who worked in the mines were breathing carcinogenic radon gas and showering in radioactive water, nor that the women washing their husbands' work clothes could spread radionuclides to the rest of the family's laundry" after they had worked in the 521 now-abandoned uranium mines on the reservation ranging in size from "dog holes" that could accommodate only a single man to large mines from which radioactive ore was extracted in carts on rails.

Arnold wrote that health workers were allowed to interview uranium miners only after they "had to strike a Faustian bargain with the mining companies: They could not inform the miners of the potential health hazards of their work. Seeing it as the only way to convince government regulators to improve safety in the mines, the researchers accepted. The PHS monitored the health of more than 4,000 miners between 1954 and 1960 without telling them of the threat to their health. By 1965, the investigators reported an association between cumulative exposure to uranium and lung cancer among white miners and had definitively identified the cause as radiation exposure." The effects had been no secret, even early as 1950, when government workers monitored radiation levels in the mines that were as much as 750 times the limits deemed acceptable at that time.

THE WIND IS RADIOACTIVE

Only less than 1 percent of the rocks were useful. The rest were cast as tailings near mine sites after the uranium had been extracted. Some lines of tailings near Shiprock grew to be a mile long and 70 feet high. On windy days, dust from the tailings blew into homes, filling the air and landing in water supplies. At the time, in the 1950s, the Atomic Energy Commission (AEC) assured worried local residents that the dust was harmless.

During the early years of uranium mining, little attention was paid to proper disposal of tailings. Handling tailings, however, is a staggering challenge, because even buried underground the radioactive material could contaminate water sources. The EPA reported radioactive contamination in drinking water in 1976 on the Navajo Reservation in Grants, New Mexico, near the mines.

Arnold (2014) wrote of the mine tailings' legacy:

> In a low, windswept rise at the southeastern edge of the Navajo Nation, Jackie Bell-Jefferson prepares to move her family from their home for a temporary stay that could last up to seven years. A mound of uranium-laden waste the size of several football fields, covered with a thin veneer of gravel, dominates the view from her front door. After many years of living next to the contamination and a litany of health problems she believes it caused, Bell-Jefferson and several other local families will have to vacate their homes for a third round of cleanup efforts by the U.S. Environmental Protection Agency. Members of Bell-Jefferson's family had used radioactive water for years, "splashing and swimming in pools of radioactive water that had been pumped out of the mines and then collected on their property. The contaminated water looked and tasted perfectly clean. Families used it for cooking, drinking, and cleaning. Hogans and corrals were built with mine wastes, as were roads." (Arnold 2014)

RADIOACTIVE DUST EVERYWHERE

When dry winds blew dust from tailings piles through the streets of many Navajo communities, including Shiprock, there was no way to avoid it. Locals recall playing on the tailing piles. Some residents learned about the radioactivity facts of the tailing piles only in 1990, more than two decades after the processing mills had closed and 12 years after Congress authorized the cleanup of uranium mill tailings in Navajo country. Contamination continued, however, as domestic animals were found sheltered in abandoned mines.

Peter Eichstaedt reported on the horrendous sufferings of miners due to radiation poisoning that permeated their entire lives. Some miners were put to work packing thousand-pound barrels of yellowcake. Some of the miners ingested so

> ### "Original Instructions," Uranium Mining, and Navajo Cultural Values
>
> The mining of uranium became a major political and cultural issue among the Navajo during the 1970s as the cancer death toll mounted. Lung cancer became so widespread that it had major cultural implications, provoking many Navajo to reexamine traditional teachings about the need for harmony with regard to the Earth. Following debate centered on this examination, uranium mining and milling henceforth became illegal in the Navajo Nation.
>
> In this cultural interpretation, the commercial use of the yellow dirt turned it into *Leetso*, a powerful monster that inflicted punishment on the Navajo people in the form of disease and suffering. The only way to restore harmony with nature (a very important attribute in Navajo culture) is *hozho nashaadoo* ("to walk in harmony"). The only proper response was to restore harmony by banning the mining and milling of uranium. The yellow dirt is a poison that disrupts the gathering of sacred herbs in contaminated areas. The Navajo seek to balance elements of land, water, and sunlight (fire). Some of the elders blamed themselves for allowing disruption of *hozho nashaadoo*.

much of the dust that it was "making the workers radioactive from the inside out" (Eichstaedt 1994, 11).

Radioactive contamination has been fueling deep concerns over health risks, particularly over longtime exposure to low-level radiation. These concerns were voiced by both Indian and non-Indian groups. Protests by Indian and white groups in the 1970s demanded the halt of mining until tailings could be properly treated. Several non-Navajo groups provided evidence of contamination reaching as far as the Colorado River basin that supplies water to much of the southwestern United States. Thus, even though the mining and milling of uranium has stopped in Navajo country, the history of its deadly toll has yet to be completely experienced, or told.

Bruce E. Johansen

See also: *Energy and Sustainability:* Pittsburgh, United States: Air Quality Is a Work in Progress; *Pollution*: Flint, United States: National and Local Politics in the Creation of a Public Health Emergency

Further Reading

Arnold, Carrie. 2014. "Once upon a Mine: The Legacy of Uranium on the Navajo Nation." Environmental Health Perspectives. http://ehp.niehs.nih.gov/122-A44.

Eichstaedt, Peter. 1994. *If You Poison Us: Uranium and American Indians*. Santa Fe, NM: Red Crane Books.

Hansen, Terri. 2014. "532 Superfund Sites in Indian Country." Indian Country Today Media Network, June 17. https://newsmaven.io/indiancountrytoday/archive/h-bomb-guinea-pigs-natives-suffering-decades-after-new-mexico-tests-jpZAFe1gFEmRCGfiq42BDg/.

Knight, Danielle. 2013. "Native Americans Denounce Toxic Legacy." TWN: Third World Network, June 14. https://www.revolvy.com/page/Anaconda%2C-New-Mexico.

Lee, Tanya H. 2014. "H-Bomb Guinea Pigs! Natives Suffering Decades after New Mexico Tests." Indian Country Today Media Network, March 5. https://newsmaven.io/indiancountrytoday/archive/h-bomb-guinea-pigs-natives-suffering-decades-after-new-mexico-tests-jpZAFe1gFEmRCGfiq42BDg/.

Schools

OVERVIEW

Providing education is one of the fundamental reasons why cities exist. Today, offering quality education is more important than at any time in the past. A better-educated workforce produces optimal economic growth; this correlation has been proven by countless studies. In the real world, however, investment in education is not always translatable into immediate benefits. This is not only due to socioeconomic conditions; different levels of education are a contributing factor to inequality as well. The best option is to make education more accessible to every member of the society. In the Global Education 2030 Agenda adopted by the General Assembly in 2015, the United Nations endeavors to achieve seven outcome targets:

1. By 2030, ensure that all girls and boys complete free, equitable, and quality primary and secondary education leading to relevant and effective learning outcomes.
2. By 2030, ensure that all girls and boys have access to quality early childhood development, care, and pre-primary education so that they are ready for primary education.
3. By 2030, ensure equal access for all women and men to affordable and quality technical, vocational, and tertiary education, including university.
4. By 2030, substantially increase the number of youth and adults who have relevant skills, including technical and vocational skills, for employment, decent jobs, and entrepreneurship.
5. By 2030, eliminate gender disparities in education and ensure equal access to all levels of education and vocational training for the vulnerable, including persons with disabilities, indigenous peoples, and children in vulnerable situations.
6. By 2030, ensure that all youth and a substantial proportion of adults, both men and women, achieve literacy and numeracy.
7. By 2030, ensure that all learners acquire the knowledge and skills needed to promote sustainable development, including, among others, through education

for sustainable development and sustainable lifestyles, human rights, gender equality, promotion of a culture of peace and non-violence, global citizenship and appreciation of cultural diversity and of culture's contribution to sustainable development (United Nations 2015).

Articles in this section reflect progress that 10 world cities have made toward these goals.

Broadening Educational Provision

In the 21st century, making education accessible to citizens remains a challenge. Bamako of Mali, Ouagadougou of Burkina Faso, Vologda of Russia, and Xi'an of China have made admirable progress in addressing the challenge.

Compared to the country's economic growth, China's higher education reform could have gone at a faster pace, according to Chen. The sector of education remains predominantly state controlled in China. As such, it bears the hallmarks of state-owned enterprises—well funded, but lacks sensitivity to market demand. As such, the supply of educational opportunities is not able to meet the demand. Tens of thousands of students are left out of provincial or national universities, and struggle to get into a four-year college of good quality. The city of Xi'an wants to address the shortage through developing private education and takes the lead in building private universities. Many private universities have grown out of their background as vocational schools. Private universities offer a range of two-, three-, or four-year college education. Some are for profit, others are nonprofit; some are affiliated with brand-name public schools, while others are independent. Educators and entrepreneurs find ways to raise funding and gingerly navigate the Party's policies. As Chen shows, the success of private institutions has been phenomenal. Xi'an International University, for example, is currently a four-year university accredited by the Ministry of Higher Education, with a faculty of 2,000 members and 23,000 students. It was a vocational school with only 3,000 students in the 1990s. A number of advantages have allowed private institutions to get ahead—less government intervention, less bureaucracy, better cost control, and more flexible personnel management. The headwind is also strong—private institutions are not preferred recipients of government funding. They must compete in the market as a group, and often among themselves as well. They work harder to develop academic strengths to win recognition by the society and are more competitive in seeking opportunities to expand, compared to public institutions.

A comparable scenario is seen in Bamako, Mali. As a next-door neighbor of Burkina Faso, Mali is plagued by the ubiquitous social-political instability in the African region. Since the country's independence in 1960, the government that runs its public education has done little for education. Public funding for educational purposes has been diverted to other uses. In Bamako, the capital city, government-sponsored primary and secondary schools are venues of education for most children, as public schools are free. However, public schools only enroll a third of the students due to a shortage of teachers and run-down facilities. Day-to-day teaching can be interrupted by social unrest and protests, and educational quality can't be guaranteed. The passing rate for the baccalaureate examination is less than 25 percent today, compared to 68.7 percent in the 1980s. As such, more parents are willing to pay tuition to send their children to private schools. The flourish of private education appears to be Bamako's solution to the failure of public education, as Roy points out. Private schools typically include Catholic schools and Islamic schools, the latter further divided into Islamic madrassas, Franco-Arab madrassas, and Quranic schools. Madrassas are under the supervision of a division of the Ministry of Education. They abide by the non-religious discrimination policy, and their graduates continue on to college education. Quranic schools, however, are taught by *cheikhs* (masters), and their goal is to form good Muslims or theologians. In a Quranic school, the curriculum is exclusively centered on the Quran, and the pedagogy is constituted primarily of tablet reading and memorization of the verses.

The city of Ouagadougou, the capital of Burkina Faso, serves as a good example of how an African city braves adverse economic and social conditions and achieves advances in higher education. Burkina Faso suffers from an unemployment rate of over 70 percent and an illiteracy rate of over 40 percent. Political instability is a major source of the crisis. Ouagadougou sees the future for prosperity and peace in promoting higher education. The city has transformed itself into one of Africa's best-known centers of higher education. Ouagadougou is home to a variety of public and private universities offering a broad range of science and humanities programs. The University of Ouagadougou, for example, enrolls 45,000 students, or 83 percent of the country's public university population. To achieve its goal, Ouagadougou maintains an active collaboration with universities in France, the United States, and other Western countries for academic and financial support. However, Ouagadougou understands that a stable socioeconomic environment is critical for higher education to take hold, and for graduates to want to stay and put knowledge to work. This, however, is a more broadly encompassing challenge than what educational institutions alone could resolve.

In Russia, education is provided by the government through the Ministry of Education and Science. There is a great shortage of funding for education. The government enforces an 11-year compulsory general education to all citizens including preschool, primary school, middle school, and high school for youths until age 18. Middle and high schools offer a set of standard subjects that include Russian language and literature, algebra, geometry, physics, chemistry, biology, history, geography, social sciences, foreign languages, information technologies, music, art, and physical education. The grading system is rigorous—tests are graded with plus-minus letter grades. Russian schools pay attention to identifying talented students at an early stage of schooling, and make extra support available to them. Students are divided into a science track and a humanities track by the time they apply for college. They take the Unified State Examination and get enrolled according to demonstrated performance. The city of Vologda offers education at all levels to its 320,000 citizens. The challenge is to compete with large cities nearby, such as Moscow and St. Petersburg that are within 400 miles and well funded. In post-reform Russia, in particular, after 1990, state sponsorship has trickled to partial funding, and scholarships are becoming rare. To face the challenge, Vologda has been successful in making higher education more affordable. Institutions such as Vologda State University are not only successful locally, but also attracting students from nearby cities, such as Totma, Sokol, and Cherepovets.

Struggle for Offering Equal Educational Opportunities

Cities in developed economies are progressing in making education more accessible by overcoming barriers based on race, age, gender, and physical conditions. In this area, Berlin, Germany, and Taipei, Taiwan, in China have demonstrated strengths. Sydney, Australia, stands out as a model city for making international students feel more at home.

In Berlin, early education in the form of day-care centers, nurseries, and kindergartens is mostly run by private or nonprofit organizations. "Kindergarten" is a German invention dating back to the 18th century. While the goal of every institution is to offer a first-rate education, for schools that lack public funding a major challenge is a shortage of teachers. An influx of immigrants in recent years has only made the shortage more pressing. Parents' financial contributions are typically of nominal help, insufficient for hiring more teachers. This is an area where solutions are urgently needed, as Polyuha indicates. In Germany, primary education and secondary education are free of charge, and homeschooling at these levels is illegal. The system traditionally sorts out students according to their academic performance at an early age, and places them in a track of either humanities or science. This is typically done during grades 5 to 13. Top-performing students are recruited by Gymnasiums and given elite training. For these students, enrollment to universities is guaranteed. As of the early 2000s, most students went to *Hauptschule* and *Realschule,* both secondary schools, with the latter being more selective. To better equalize educational opportunities, Berlin educational authorities combined *Hauptschule* and *Realschule* to create *Sekundarschule*, or general secondary school. Gymnasium is left out of this reform and remains a stand-alone track. The combination, however, has drawn criticism that the change was for cost-saving purposes, with an adverse effect on educational quality. A more recent challenge at the pre-college level is to find ways to properly educate immigrant students, so that they will not be severed from their linguistic and cultural heritage. At the level of college education, Berlin is unquestionably a leader in offering free college education to all students. The city's goal is to provide excellent education for all and be an outstanding location for academics, science, and research.

Taiwan has had sustained economic growth during the past 30 years. The capital city of Taipei has grown into a center of education in Asia and worldwide. Taipei gives education the top priority as it has historically done. One area that demonstrates the city's dedication is its tremendous efforts in supporting special education, as Pang indicates. The municipality is directly involved in improving accessibility and in establishing accommodative guidelines. In K–12 education, the city government dedicates ample budget to hiring additional teachers and to opening after-school programs. There is funding even for small groups of less than 10 students. The government is keen on maintaining academic rigor by implementing various evaluation procedures. Moreover, the Taipei government understands that education is not all about delivering content; students' physical health is of greater importance. In special education, Taipei issues detailed guidelines to regulate accommodative services, curricular designs, and teacher training. It ensures that students with disabilities enjoy equal learning opportunities in every aspect. Likewise, major efforts are made to accommodate gifted students. Overall, Taipei does everything in its power to provide an all-around education.

For the city of Sydney, international education occupies a central place. The city's higher education system is so successful that it attracts tens of thousands of international students every year, particularly from China and India. Sydney enjoys the reputation of being the gateway of Australia's global influence. In return, international education contributes to the city's cultural "super diversity," as well as economic benefits. International education brings in billions of dollars in revenue and funds thousands of jobs. There is probably not another city in the world where higher education counts as a dependable sector of export, as Luo argues. A big challenge, however, has been about how to create and maintain a welcoming environment where international students could easily adapt. High rents and cost of living are one of the major barriers. Helping international students learn English, providing them with training on an individual's rights, racial equality, tips on safety and security, cultural etiquette, and necessary academic skills are tasks that every university takes seriously. Helping international students deal with racial discrimination is at the top of every institution's agenda. Provision of job opportunities and health-care services surpasses the ability of educational institutions. However, the municipality and universities work together to get problems resolved. Sydney's continued success in keeping its international education programs strong proves that it has much to share with developed cities worldwide.

Charting New Directions

How to train a workforce for solving problems of the 21st century? Cities such as Seoul, Tokyo, and Boston ponder this question to find ways to develop curricula and methodology around it. Much of their pioneering work offers new insights.

South Korea has achieved nearly universal enrollment in primary and secondary education. The country's quality of education is one of the highest in the world. Korean students achieve high test scores in the Program for International Student Assessment (PISA), ranking consistently in the top 10 countries in math, science, and reading literacy. Moreover, the performance is broad-based in relevant age groups. The country has caught an "education fever" during the past 60 years in pursuing educational excellence, as Long remarks. Seoul has become a preferred destination for students of Asian countries to seek higher education. Korea's achievement comes from a rich heritage. The Confucian legacy of selecting civil servants from the best-educated circle constitutes its traditional foundation. On the other hand, South Korea has integrated elements of management and mass education drawn from Japanese and American practices. Behind the success, however, there is a hidden challenge that educators in Seoul are trying to tackle—schools are overloading students with hours of additional courses in after-school time. Seventy-four percent of all students receive "shadow" instructions in the hope of getting into the most prestigious universities. The mental and physical toll on the youth is worrisome. Additionally, such competition contributes to wider economic gaps. While many Koreans believe the educational fever is justified by the country's economic and academic success, many more are finding ways to lighten students' burden.

Japan's modern education dates back to the Meiji Reforms in the 1870s when the Japanese government introduced Western-style education including centralized and compulsory education. Western learning has yielded many benefits, noticeably improving Japan's economy in a short time. As the Japanese economy peaked in the 1990s, however, educators began to reflect on the next phase of reforms, as Long explains. In the centralized system, college entrance examination became a critical juncture in a student's life. Frequent testing and after-school courses made learning a burdensome experience. While the system had contributed to a phenomenal economic growth in the 1970s and 1980s, its impact on students' physical and mental health is immense and worries parents. Since the 1990s, Japan's Ministry of Education has been working to meet this challenge by implementing a new reform known as "Yutori," or pressure-free education. It aims to encourage learning desire, lessen the burden of schoolwork, and meanwhile enhance the quality of learning. In practice, this involves reducing classroom time for certain subjects, improving lifelong learning skills, and getting the community involved in education. For the city of Tokyo, the new challenge is to create a society in which people of all ages, from children to adults, can learn and apply their found skills anytime, anywhere.

Boston, Massachusetts, is home to some of the top universities in the world. It is also a city that most forcefully promotes science, technology, engineering, and math (STEM). As Cumo explains, to spark interest among students, Boston public schools explore multiple forms. One of the avenues is to partner with the Massachusetts Institute of Technology (MIT), which involves letting MIT design STEM courses, train teachers at all levels, and offer jointly hosted workshops, such as Boston STEM Week, to provide immersion STEM experience. During this week, participating schools integrate STEM contents in all subjects, including humanities and social sciences. The message is clear: STEM knowledge can be integrated throughout the curriculum. Another form is demonstrated by the Dearborn STEM Academy. This public school offers hands-on experience allowing students to take college courses and one internship before graduation. Guest lectures introduce career experiences to help students understand STEM applications in life. Private schools seem to push STEM even more aggressively. Roxbury Latin School, for example, adopts an integrated curriculum that embeds STEM in every subject. Its intensive lab workshops encourage participants to solve real-world problems. Another pathway is to utilize the Boston Museum of Science, one of the world's top science museums, to reach out to younger students and those in poor communities. The Eye Opener Program, for example, attract students as young as the second grade. The museum's curriculum, "Engineering Is Elementary," targets students from grade one through five. Through these efforts Boston prepares students for solving the world's most challenging problems.

Further Reading
United Nations Educational, Scientific and Cultural Organization. 2015. *Unpacking Sustainable Development Goal 4 Education 2030*. http://unesdoc.unesco.org/images/0024/002463/246300E.pdf.

Bamako, Mali: Private and Public Sectors of Education

Schooling issues in Bamako reflect the wider economic, social, and political difficulty of providing quality education in Mali, where the public finances do not allow for adequate spending on schools. Education in Mali has been in a state of profound crisis since the independence of the country in 1960, due to poor funding, lack of qualified teachers, and poor infrastructure. In the 1980s, the Malian state made significant cuts in education because of the pressures on the national budget imposed by the International Monetary Fund and the World Bank's Structural Adjustment Plans. The public schooling system of Mali has limited resources that are overstretched, leading to a lack of investment in the system. Therefore, in Bamako as in the rest of Mali, quality education is a rare commodity, and various options for private schooling have become increasingly popular with Malian parents.

As an imperfect measure of the shortages and limitations of the Malian educational system, success rates at the Diplôme d'Études Fondamentales (DEF) and *baccalauréat* national examinations are telling. At the national level, the success rates at the national *baccalauréat* examination went from 68.7 percent in 1988–89 to 39.7 percent in 1996–97 and 26 percent in 1999–2000 (Diakité 2009). In 2016, the success rate at the *baccalauréat* was of 24.28 percent in Mali (Magassa 2016). At the local level, in the district of Bamako, in the schooling division of the neighborhood of Torokorobougou, the success rates of students for the DEF standardized text was 58.2 percent for the *médersas* (modern Islamic schools), 30.8 percent for community schools, 29.5 percent for private (secular, French-speaking) schools, and 12.6 percent for public schools (Torokorobougou 2010). These statistics, at the national level and in in Bamako, highlight the overall issues of quality in the Malian educational system and the differences that exist among the various types of schools found in the capital city.

The educational field was made increasingly diverse through social innovation seeking to fill the gaps left by the state and the poor quality of public education. The educational sector of the 1990s—in Mali in general but even more so in Bamako, where much of the country's wealth and social actions are concentrated—was a result of this diversification, where private and community schools flourished outside of the state's control. If public schools remain the biggest provider of fundamental and secondary education, other options include secular private schools, community schools, and various forms of Islamic education. For the 2015–2016 school year, the partial statistics available suggest that in Mali, 69.6 percent of children are enrolled in the primary cycle of fundamental education and 49.6 percent are enrolled in the secondary cycle. That same year, the numbers for the district of Bamako are clearly superior to the national average: 81.2 percent at the primary cycle and 95.2 percent at the secondary cycle (Synthèse des données provisoires 2015–2016). Despite these encouraging enrollment numbers for the district of

Bamako's fundamental education, success rates at the DEF and *baccalauréat* examinations demonstrate that accessing quality education remains a challenge.

ORGANIZATION

Primary and secondary schooling in Mali is under the supervision of the Ministère de l'Education Nationale (MEN). The Decree n° 2015—0633 /P-RM of October 15, 2015, states that the MEN prepares and implements the national policy for preschool and special education, primary and secondary schooling, technical and professional schooling, and of nonformal education and literacy. In order to do so, the MEN is divided into several offices in charge of these various types of education. The Direction Nationale de l'Enseignement Fondamental is responsible for overseeing the fundamental education, that is, grade one through nine. Fundamental education is further divided into two cycles: the primary cycle, from grade one to six, and the secondary cycle, from grade seven to nine. At the end of their fundamental education, students are administered a national standardized test that, if passed, will grant them the diplôme d'études fondamentales (DEF). The Direction Nationale de l'Enseignement Secondaire Général supervises the "lycées," which cover the grades 10 through 12. At the end of secondary school, students must again pass a national standardized test called the *baccalauréat* that will grant them access to higher education. The MEN also oversees efforts in technical and professional education (vocational education), nonformal education, and national languages education.

Fundamental and secondary education's supervision is further decentralized by being administered locally through an académie d'enseignement (AE) in each region of Mali (and two for the district of Bamako), itself divided into numerous centres d'animation pédagogiques (CAP) that directly help schools with training and inspects them regularly. The supervision of fundamental and secondary schooling in the district of Bamako is done by the Académie d'Enseignement de la Rive-Gauche (with eight CAPs: Djélibougou, Banconi, Bozola, Hippodrome, Centre commercial, Bamako coura, Lafiabougou, and Sébénicoro) and the Académie d'Enseignement de la Rive-Droite (with seven CAPs: Baco Djicoroni, Banankabougou, Faladié, Kalabancoura, Senou, Sogoniko, and Torokorobougou).

This organization of the Malian educational system applies first and foremost to Bamako's public schools, which are at its core, but also to all private schools registered with the MEN. The MEN also regularly revisits the curricula for fundamental and secondary education to be applied primarily in public schools but that must also be followed by private schools wishing to have their diplomas validated. The last revision of the curriculum for fundamental education took place and was implemented in 2010 (Programme d'Investissement 2010).

PUBLIC SCHOOLS

During the school year 2013–14, the public schooling system in the district of Bamako educated 130,384 students in 329 primary-cycle fundamental schools and

80,641 students in 199 secondary-cycle fundamental schools (Annuaire Succinct National 2014). In both cases, this represents about a third of the children schooled in the district. Thus, the Malian State remains the main provider of fundamental and secondary education in Bamako but does not educate most children. Public schools use French as the language of instruction for all classes and sometimes integrate local languages (convergent pedagogy) in the first years of schooling as a transition for young pupils. Public schools are entirely secular, as mandated by the Malian Constitution, free of tuition charges, and open to all Malian children that qualify.

One reason for the low enrollment in public schools is that although public schools are officially free in Mali, and any form of private school requires tuition fees, corruption within the public system (bribes to teachers for better grades are common occurrences, for example) increases the cost of education there. Since the independence of Mali, political issues have also plagued the public schooling system with endemic crises such as student revolts and "white years" (time wasted) that could not be validated. Conflicts between the state and the teachers as well as between the students and the state have stopped the delivery of classes in public schools temporarily.

Other issues have been with the implementation of the official curriculum and the poor quality of education due to the student/teacher ratio and "double or even triple-shift schooling." This last practice is a cost-efficiency measure put in place since the 1980s to maximize the use of buildings and teachers with two or three groups of children rotating in classrooms. In the district of Bamako, the student/teacher ratio for primary-cycle fundamental public school is 50 students per teacher (the second-highest ratio in the country after the region of Kayes) and 66 students per classroom (the highest in the country). For the secondary cycle of fundamental schools, there are 79 students per classroom, by far the highest ratio in the country (Annuaire Succinct National 2014). The poor quality of the infrastructure has also contributed to the dismal situation of public education. These issues stem from the lack of funding for public schools in Mali and encourage the development of varied educational opportunities in the private sector.

PRIVATE SCHOOLS

The private schooling offered in Bamako is highly diverse. Being the capital city of a centralized state where much of the wealth is concentrated, innovations in terms of education often start and develop rapidly in Bamako. Two broad categories of private schools emerge: the secular or Catholic, French-speaking private schools; and the Islamic schools, where French and Arabic are used.

The majority of private schools in Bamako are registered with the government and follow the official curriculum of the state. The language of instruction is French, and there is no religious component. There are about 900 such primary-cycle and 580 secondary-cycle fundamental private schools in the district of Bamako (Annuaire Succinct National 2014). Promoters using private funds are the engine of private schools, and the running costs are covered through tuition fees, which can vary greatly depending on the reputation of the school. The Catholic diocese of Bamako

An Islamic school in Bamako, Mali, 2010. Private, Islamic schools offer parents an alternative to public schools, which are often poorly funded. (Godong/Universal Images Group via Getty Images)

also runs private Catholic educational institutions that are registered with the MEN and follow the national program while including religious education. Like Islamic schools, Catholic schools cannot discriminate on the basis of religion for enrollment. There are 14 Catholic fundamental institutions and three secondary institutions. They present students for the national standardized examination of the DEF and *baccalauréat*. Community schools are private schools following the program of the MEN. Like all other private schools, community schools are registered with the state and are subject to all governmental legislation; they can also receive funds from the state. However, community schools differ from other private school insofar as they stem from the local community's effort, which also finances most of its running costs. The last available data for the district of Bamako list 55 fundamental and 26 secondary community schools (Annuaire Succinct National 2014).

Islamic-centered education has been present for centuries in Mali, and the current educational system recognizes two forms of it: the Islamic *médersa* and the Franco-Arabe *médersas*. Like Catholic schools, Islamic schools that are registered with the MEN cannot discriminate on the basis of religion for enrollment. The first Islamic médersas were created in the 1940s and 1950s in Mali, including one in Bamako in 1949. The aim of the founders of those first médersas was to combine the Islamic sciences in which they specialized with the content and pedagogy of modern schooling provided by colonial schools and later secular, French-speaking, public schools. Until the 1980s, médersas developed as grassroots innovations outside of all government control and independently of each other. A decree in 1985 integrated the Islamic médersas into the educational system as private schools. Médersas function similarly to public schools with a fundamental education with two levels and a secondary education, following the program of the MEN but where the language of instruction is Arabic and religious classes are allowed at the discretion of the school. Médersas are under the authority of the MEN through its Division de Contrôle et d'Animation du Système des Médersas (DCASM). For the school year 2013–14, 13.3 percent of children attending the primary cycle of the fundamental education in the district of Bamako did so in a médersa; at the secondary cycle, it was 7.6 percent of enrolled students in the district (Annuaire Succinct National 2014). Some Islamic médersas in Bamako started with Arabic as the language of instruction but progressively moved to the Franco-Arabe médersa model to give students better mastery of French if they were to integrate into Malian higher education or work in the formal sector. As such, the Franco-Arabe médersas follow the program developed for the médersas which includes Islamic education in Arabic, but offer the secular classes in French, the official national language.

Quranic schools are not part of the formal educational system in Mali and are not regulated in any way by the MEN. They are traditional Islamic schools usually set in mosques or in private houses where young pupils are taught individually by a *cheikh* (master) and progress through the curriculum based on the personal spiritual development of the child. The curriculum is composed exclusively of Islamic sciences and starts with the memorization of verses of the Quran written by the master on wooden tablets and repeated by the student. The pedagogy also follows Islamic tradition where the aim is to socialize a good Muslim at the basic level and to form an Islamic theologian at a higher level. Although there are no statistics available, a significant number of children in Bamako pass through a Quranic school, often before starting their educational careers in formal educational structures, but some will stay until they obtain the *ijaza,* an acknowledgment of their mastery of a discipline of Islamic sciences.

Émilie Roy

See also: *Schools:* Ouagadougou, Burkina Faso: Investing in Higher Education for the Country's Future; Xi'an, China: Where China's Private Education Debuts

Further Reading

Annuaire Succinct National des Statistiques Scolaires de l'Enseignement Fondamental 2013–2014. 2014. Edited by Cellule de Planification et de Statistique. Bamako: Ministère de l'Éducation Nationale, République du Mali.

Bleck, Jaimie. 2015. *Education and Empowered Citizenship in Mali.* Baltimore: Johns Hopkins University Press.

Brenner, Louis. 2001. *Controlling Knowledge: Religion, Power and Schooling in a West African Muslim Society.* Bloomington: Indiana University Press.

Diakité, Drissa. 2009. "La crise scolaire au Mali." *Nordic Journal of African Studies* 9, 3: 6–28.

Magassa, Moussa. 2016. "BAC 2016: 24,28% d'admis." *Journal du Mali.* January 8. http://www.journaldumali.com/2016/08/02/bac-2016-2428-dadmis.

Pearce, Caroline, Sébastien Fourmy, and Hetty Kovach. 2009. "Delivering Education for All in Mali." June 15. *Oxfam Research Report.* https://policy-practice.oxfam.org.uk/publications/delivering-education-for-all-in-mali-112413.

Programme d'Investissement pour le Secteur de l'Education: Descriptif de la Troisième Phase (2010–2012). 2010. Edited by Ministère de l'Éducation de l'Alphabétisation et des Langues Nationales. Bamako: Ministère de l'Enseignement Supérieur et de la Recherche Scientifique, République du Mali.

Synthèse des données provisoires 2015–2016, Statistiques scolaires de l'enseignement fondamental. 2016. Edited by Cellule de Planification et de Statistique. Bamako: Ministère de l'Éducation Nationale, République du Mali.

Torokorobougou, C. A. P. 2010. Rapport de Fin d'Année. 2009–2010. Edited by Centre d'Animation Pédagogique de Torokorobougou. Bamako.

Berlin, Germany: Making the City a Center of Learning

The capital of Germany, Berlin is one of the largest and most multicultural cities in Europe. In 2015, the city had 3,610,156 residents representing more than 180 nations. For almost 600 years, Berlin served as a capital of various political entities: Brandenburg Principality, the Kingdom of Prussia, the German Empire, the Weimar Republic, the Third Reich, the German Democratic Republic, and, finally, the Federal Republic of Germany. With its rich history, thriving economy, and lively cultural scene, the city continuously attracts a plethora of different people, both Germans and foreigners. Given the fact that the population constantly increases (only in the last couple of years, Berlin became home to approximately 90,000 refugees), the municipal government faces numerous challenges, the establishment of effective and efficient educational system being one of them.

RESPONSIBILITY AND EFFICIENCY

For a long time, Germany enjoyed its reputation as a country with very high standards of education. In the year 2000, however, the Program for International Student Assessment (PISA) published a report that shocked the entire country—it revealed that 15-year-old German high school students were significantly underprepared in the areas of reading, mathematics, and sciences, and they performed well below their counterparts in other developed countries. The German educational authorities immediately developed the measures necessary for analyzing and improving the situation. As a result, the 2012 PISA report indicated significant progress, and Germany continues to be one of the successful countries for education.

This quick reaction of the government to the problem shows that in German society, the educational sector is high priority. Public schooling is considered particularly important and, since most teaching institutions provide services free of charge, much federal, provincial, and municipal funding is directed toward education. Of all the cities in Germany, Berlin comes second only to Hamburg in terms of spending on schools (1,515 euros per capita) (The Governing Mayor of Berlin and Senate Chancellery 2014).

EARLY EDUCATION IS A FOCUS

With its first kindergartens being established as early as in 1780, Germany is credited with inventing the concept. Nowadays, German federal states vary as to the types of kindergartens they have. In Berlin, the most common are the following:

1. ***Nurseries*** (*Kinderkrippe*)—for children between eight weeks and three years old;
2. **Day-care centers** (*Kindertagesstätte* or *KiTa*)—for children between three and six years old. *KiTas* are normally open until midnight;
3. **Kindergarten**s (*Kindergarten* or *KiGa*)—also for children between three and six years old, but, unlike *KiTas*, they are typically open until midday.

According to Amt für Statistik Berlin-Brandenburg (Berlin-Brandenburg Bureau of Statistics), in 2012, the city of Berlin had 2,052 preschool institutions that accommodated 142,498 children. Since Germans generally attach much value to communal experiences, it is not surprising that by the age of three, the vast majority (76.7 percent) of Berlin children attend the kindergartens.

As kindergartens are not part of public education, most of them are run by nonprofit organizations. Even though there are free-of-charge kindergartens, parents typically contribute some payments. Only during the last year of kindergarten, before the child starts attending elementary school, child care is completely free of charge.

Despite the fact that the German government takes measures to create first-rate child care, there are simply not enough trained professionals in the field. Most kindergarten teachers work part-time and must supervise many children at once. The existing facilities have a limited number of spots, and, as a result, parents have difficulty securing a place for their kids.

With the influx of immigrants, a new problem arises—foreign-born parents send their children to kindergartens, so that the latter can become proficient in the language. Those parents, however, often want to preserve the cultural heritage of their homeland, which becomes a hard-to-achieve goal. Indeed, despite their multicultural, all-inclusive tendencies, German preschool institutions can prepare children only for life in Germany. Thus, fearing that children might grow up alienated from the culture of their ancestors, migrant parents have frequently ambiguous attitudes toward preschool education.

PRIMARY AND SECONDARY EDUCATION ARE COMPULSORY

All German children ages 6–14 attend primary school (*Grundschule*). According to law, school attendance is compulsory. Homeschooling is illegal, as parents are not considered to be qualified to teach their children all the school subjects.

As in the United States, the majority of children attend primary school in their neighborhood. However, there are noticeable differences between the two countries. For example, in Germany there are no school buses, and students often use regular public transportation to get to their schools. Furthermore, even though German students have to study more days per year compared to their American counterparts, they enjoy more frequent breaks. During the breaks and holidays, students often undertake longer trips (e.g., to Paris or London). The grading system is also different, as the grades range from "1" to "6" (with "1" being the highest and

Second-graders attend class at an elementary school in Berlin, Germany. Berlin struggles to maintain the quality of its educational system as tens of thousands of immigrants arrive in the city each year. (Sean Gallup/Getty Images)

"6" the lowest grades). Until recently, German students were required to repeat the year if they failed several subjects, but this custom has been discontinued.

Currently, Berlin has 361 primary schools, which accommodate 157,669 students (2015–16 academic year). Upon finishing the seventh grade, students and their parents must select a type of secondary school. Formerly, this selection was done by the teachers. The new regulations, however, give priority to parents. Selection is based on parent surveys (the first one is done in the primary school), teachers' recommendations, achievement tests, teachers' surveys, student survey, and principal survey.

Traditionally, the German system offered the following main options for secondary education:

1. *Hauptschule* (grades 5–10): This type of school is considered the least demanding, appropriate for students who would like to enter the trades. Along with studying general educational subjects, pupils typically work part-time as apprentices, an experience that prepares them for a vocational career. When they graduate from the *Hauptschule*, they can opt either to try passing the graduation exams at a more academically challenging school (*Realschule*) or go to a vocational school (*Berufschule*), where they will master certain blue-collar professions.

2. *Realschule* (grades 5–10): The most popular type of school is *Realschule*, appropriate for future mid-level managers and supervisors (approximately 40 percent of students attend this type of school). The *Realschule* academic

standards are high, and graduates obtain a *Realschule* diploma, which allows them to either apply to *Berufschule* or enroll in classes that would prepare them for college.

3. ***Gymnasium*** (grades 5–12 or 5–13).

Finally, the most rigorous type of secondary school is called *Gymnasium*. Along with advanced calculus and science courses, *Gymnasium* offers a number of honors courses, and studying at least two foreign languages is typically required. Graduates receive *das Abitur* (a diploma that certifies passing the statewide matriculation examinations). This diploma serves as an entry requirement to university. Thus, graduates of *Gymnasium* are essentially guaranteed a university admission (even though admission to a major of their choice is not assured). Nowadays, approximately 90 percent of German university students are *Gymnasium* alumni.

Unlike in the United States, place of residence does not determine the school district, and German students may attend any school they want. Students are grouped into classes or homerooms. Each class typically stays in the same classroom (exceptions might be for classes of music or physical training), and teachers move between the classes. Each class has a homeroom teacher called *Klassenlehrer*. In grades 10 through 13, the grading system is different from in the primary and lower secondary schools—students are awarded grades from "0" (the lowest) to "15" (the highest).

Even though it dates back to the Middle Ages and has withstood the test of time, this educational system has been heavily criticized, as many scholars believe that it promotes inequality. The existing school structure essentially sorts students to be intellectuals, skilled personnel, and unskilled workers. Students who come from underprivileged backgrounds suffer the most, since they and their parents often do not understand how the educational system works and thus cannot make informed choices. While students of *Gymnasium* show consistently high results, graduates of *Hauptschule* have difficulty working through the social hierarchy. According to Jan-Martin Wiarda, "Conservatives prized the success of the Gymnasium, for them the finest school form in the world—indeed, it is by far the number one in the PISA league table. But what they prefer to forget is that this success came at the cost of a catastrophe in the *Hauptschulen*."

The 2003 PISA report in particular pointed out the inequality in educational experiences. The 2007 Organization for Economic Cooperation and Development (OECD) report on education in Germany also stated the problem by indicating that the country had "the least permeable of all school systems (despite being free of charge) in respect to social preconditions" (qtd. in Baez et al.).

The Berlin education authorities decided to tackle the educational issues in the following way:

1. pay more attention to the linguistic competence of children who attend kindergartens;
2. strengthen the links between primary and secondary education;
3. improve reading skills and understanding of basic mathematic and scientific concepts;

4. provide more support for students with underprivileged or international background as well as to students with special needs;
5. link educational standards and the result-oriented evaluation;
6. eliminate segregation at schools.

As a result of implementation of those principles, *Haupschule* and *Realschule* have been combined into a single *Sekundarschule*, while *Gymnasium* has been left practically intact. The graduates of the *Sekundarschule* obtained a chance to pass *das Abitur*.

In theory, these measures look great. In practice, however, there are a number of problems. Not all the parents want to send their children to a school with students of different abilities. Dr. Raiser describes that there is "difficulty in convincing the parents of a child who is excelling academically to enroll their student into a partnership school instead of *Gymnasium*, given that they might perceive this experimental school to be of lower quality than the Gymnasium" (Baez et al.). He adds that there is the even more "difficult task of convincing the general public that *Gemeinschaftsschulen* [the new integrated schools] are indeed a step in the right direction towards creating a more supportive environment for the students to achieve academically at higher levels" (Baez et al.).

Like the kindergartens discussed earlier, the recent inflow of refugees and increasing numbers of *Kinder mit Migrationshintergrund* ("children with the migratory background" as they are called in Germany) also present a challenge. Students whose parents do not speak German are less likely to succeed in school since they have no one at home who can check their home assignments, correct their grammar, or explain the intricacies of the three-tier school structure. With German spoken during the classes and a native language during the breaks and at home, children commonly have insufficient knowledge of both languages. At the same time, German teachers, whose shortage is very palpable, do not have enough contact hours to alleviate the situation. Thus, frequently, not only children, but also their parents must make a point of learning about the German educational system.

Funding of the newly integrated schools presents another problem. Despite the fact that *Haupschule* and *Realschule* have been relatively easily amalgamated, not all of the new conglomerates have the personnel or facilities to properly conduct the *Abitur* examination. The less-funded *Gemeinschaftsschulen* (community schools) have to establish alliances with other schools to compensate for their lack of resources. For this reason, some Berliners say that without advanced university preparatory classes, many new integrated schools are unofficially the *Hauptschule* in disguise.

Currently, Berlin has 2,959 public secondary schools that accommodate 75,679 students (2015). In addition, the city has 1,634 *Gymnasiums*, in which 68,709 students study (2015). Besides, there are a number of private schools, bilingual schools, and vocational schools.

TERTIARY EDUCATION IS FREE FOR ALL

Tertiary education is represented by universities and colleges. The Berlin region leads Germany in terms of the number of postsecondary institutions. In the 2013–14 winter semester, a total of 165,923 students were enrolled in Berlin's 42 institutions of higher education.

There are four big public research universities and 27 colleges. The following Berlin-based universities are the largest in Germany:

- Freie Universität Berlin (FU Berlin)—34,518 students (2014);
- Technical University of Berlin (TU Berlin)—33,933 (2016);
- Humboldt University of Berlin (HU Berlin)—33,540 (2015);
- Berlin University of the Arts (UdK)—3,779 (2015).

Three universities in Berlin feature in the QS World University Rankings 2015/16. The highest ranked of these is Freie Universität Berlin at 119th in the world, followed by Humboldt-Universität zu Berlin at 126th, and by Technical University of Berlin at 178th. With approximately 16 percent foreign students, Berlin universities are also among the most international.

German and American universities differ in many ways. In Germany, the university consists of classrooms, libraries, and, in some cases, modest dormitories. There are no varsity sport teams, expensive common areas, or fraternities. Academic advisement is virtually absent—students have to decide themselves what classes to take and in what order. There are also no general education classes—everyone goes directly into their major, chosen at the moment of application to the university. Classes typically do not require attendance, and the final grade is often based on single final examination.

The virtual absence of tuition is, however, the most unusual feature of the German university system. Even though there were attempts to introduce a very minimal tuition (approximately 500 s), most of the universities dropped their tuition requirements after massive student protests. Unlike their American counterparts, German students enjoy a relatively cheap cost of textbooks, inexpensive meals at eateries (*Mensa*), discounts on public transportation and on tickets to theatrical performances.

Even though many challenges still exist, Berlin has become one of the most progressive educational centers in Europe. And Klaus Wowereit, the city's mayor, has rightly declared that "excellent education for all, an outstanding location for academics, science, and research, high-quality child care, affordable housing, a unique range of cultural offerings, creative development potential, and a sense of community and solidarity—all of that goes hand in hand in Berlin" (*Berlin: A Success Story*).

Mykola Polyuha

See also: Schools: Boston, United States: A Model City of STEM Education; Tokyo, Japan: The *Yutori* Educational Reforms

Further Reading

Baez, Oscar, Anton Guhl, and Samson Lim. 2008. "Why Not? A Critical Look at Upward Mobility within Berlin's Impermeable Education System." Humanity in Action. http://www.humanityinaction.org/knowledgebase/105-why-not-a-critical-look-at-upward-mobility-within-berlin-s-impermeable-education-system.

Blickpunkt Schule: Schuljahr 2015/2016. 2015. https://www.berlin.de/sen/bildung/schule / . . . /blickpunkt_schule_2015_16.pdf.

Carey, David. 2008. "Improving Education Outcomes in Germany." *OECD Economics Department Working Papers*, No. 611, OECD Publishing. http://www.oecd-ilibrary.org/docserver/download/241675712618.pdf.

The Governing Mayor of Berlin and Senate Chancellery. 2014. *Berlin: A Success Story. Facts. Figures. Statistics.* https://www.berlin.de/rbmskzl/_assets/aktuelles/2014/oktober/140911_berlin_erfolgsgeschichte_2014_engl.pdf.

Wiarda, Jan-Martin. 2009. "A New Class of Education." *Guardian*, September 21. https://www.theguardian.com/commentisfree/2009/sep/21/germany-now-education.

Boston, United States: A Model City of STEM Education

In Boston, Massachusetts, as elsewhere, schools face the challenge of preparing students for the 21st century. Part of this challenge involves training students for careers in science, technology, engineering, and mathematics, the so-called STEM subjects. In an economy driven by technological change and innovation, employers need graduates trained in STEM subjects. Yet these are the graduates that employers are having difficulty recruiting. It thus falls to schools to improve instruction in science, technology, engineering, and mathematics to provide employers with a suitably skilled workforce. The rewards of such training may be distilled in economic terms given that because STEM graduates are in demand, they command a higher salary than do graduates in other fields.

EARLY INTERVENTION

Schools in Boston are not waiting until students reach high school, the traditional period during which college and career plans are made, to promote STEM subjects on the theory that too many students lose interest in the four subjects by middle school if not earlier. It follows that teachers must spark interest and proficiency in STEM subjects in elementary and middle schools.

The effort to reach students early takes many forms. One promising avenue is to pair Boston elementary students with college graduates who work in the STEM subjects. These graduates serve as mentors after school and on weekends to introduce students to STEM careers. Such a program teaches young students the value of a STEM education while they are impressionable enough to benefit from such experiences.

This partnership with STEM graduates is part of a larger effort that extends to a partnership between Boston public schools and the Massachusetts Institute of Technology (MIT), a university with a long tradition of fostering excellence in science, technology, engineering, and mathematics. This partnership leans on MIT in three ways. First, the university has designed STEM courses for the Boston public schools. Second, MIT faculty mentor and train Boston teachers at all levels e to strengthen their ability to teach STEM subjects. Third, MIT and the Boston public schools collaborate in immersing students in these subjects for a week. In 2016, Boston STEM Week occurred in October and focused on middle school students. The initial course offerings targeted roughly 6,500 students at 36 Boston middle schools. MIT tailored courses to this week in a variety of STEM outlets that included creating a garden, building robots, extracting deoxyribose nucleic acid (DNA), and performing surgery. Boston STEM Week required all subjects, even those traditionally seen as part of the humanities and social sciences, to focus on science, technology, engineering, and mathematics. This integrative approach confirms the interdisciplinary character of all knowledge and emphasizes the ways that STEM subject can be integrated throughout the curriculum. The program seems poised to spread to more students and grades in the future.

BOSTON'S DEARBORN STEM ACADEMY

The Dearborn STEM Academy is at the leading edge of STEM education in the Boston public schools. It targets students in grades 6 through 12, extending education in science, technology, education, and mathematics to a broad group of young people. The academy focuses on translating an education in the STEM subjects to success in college and career. The individualized nature of instruction enables faculty to tailor the STEM curriculum to each student. In keeping with the career and college focus, students articulate their goals early in their tenure at the academy.

To promote awareness of options, the academy schedules college visits and aids students in exploring and preparing for careers in science, technology, engineering, and mathematics. Central to this mission are internships and a mentoring program that pairs students with adults who work in these areas. The academy expects that before graduation each student will hold at least one internship and take at least

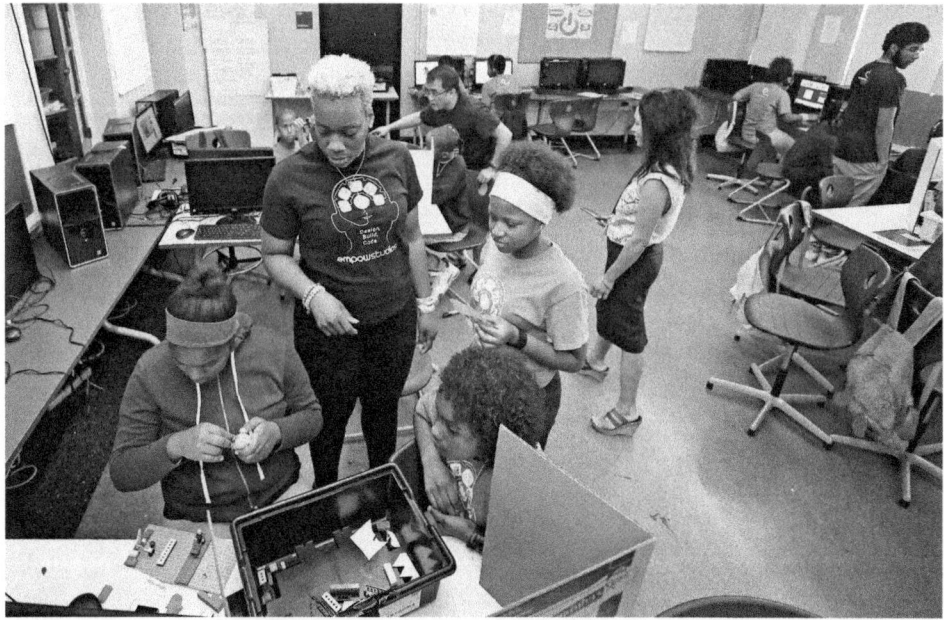

A teacher helps her students use a 3-D printer during a summer learning program run by the Dearborn STEM Academy, at the Jeremiah Burke High School in Boston, 2017. (David L. Ryan/The Boston Globe via Getty Images)

one course for college credit. Ten colleges and universities partner with the academy in welcoming students to tour their campus to learn about STEM majors and careers. In addition, the academy hosts an annual college fair at the Boston Convention Center to acquaint students with the STEM offerings of a diversity of colleges and universities in Boston and elsewhere in Massachusetts and the United States. In partnership with the Wentworth Institute of Technology, the academy offers weekly meetings in which students learn about the diversity of careers open to STEM graduates. The result is intensive immersion in a variety of pathways to a career in STEM subjects. Thanks to these initiatives, the academy boasts high attendance and a high rate of acceptance to a college or university.

The experience at the Dearborn STEM Academy mirrors a kind of 21st-century apprenticeship in science, technology, engineering, and mathematics. Close coordination with the community of STEM practitioners helps students cement ties with important people in these fields. The focus on careers is pragmatic and helps students understand the practical applications of what they learn in the classroom and in the community. In these ways the academy seeks to bridge the divide between the classroom and industry by preparing students to leverage their STEM training into remunerative and satisfying work.

ROXBURY LATIN SCHOOL

If new initiatives like the Dearborn STEM Academy represent the future of education in the Boston public schools, then older institutions merit mention for retooling in the direction of STEM. Roxbury Latin School bills itself not only as the first school in Boston but also as the oldest school in the United States. An early emphasis on languages and preparation for service to religious life was once the school's focus, but it now embraces the 21st century's desire for a more modern curriculum anchored in STEM.

Roxbury Latin School, in the West Roxbury neighborhood in Boston, educates roughly 300 boys in grades 7 through 12. Unlike Boston's public schools, Roxbury is a private school with a large endowment. This endowment enables the school to subsidize tuition for boys whose families cannot afford the cost of attendance. Despite its orientation as a private school, Roxbury partners with the Boston public schools to further education in STEM subjects. In summer, it trains teachers to teach the latest findings in STEM subjects. In addition, Roxbury extends this regimen into October during Boston STEM Week, when it focuses on training those who teach STEM subjects in grades six through eight. This focus comports with the emphasis on reaching students early, before their interest in STEM subjects declines. Roxbury trains not only STEM teachers but teachers across a variety of disciplines to integrate STEM subjects into areas traditionally emphasizing the humanities and social sciences. The result is a curriculum that integrates knowledge in science, technology, engineering, and mathematics into a diversity of settings. This vision of an integrated curriculum dates to 2012, when Roxbury Latin School alumnus Ethan Berman encouraged both Roxbury and the Boston public schools to collaborate in improving instruction in STEM subjects for both teachers and students. The emphasis at Roxbury and the Boston public schools is on learning by doing. STEM subjects are ideal for this approach because of the emphasis on experimentation and problem solving. This approach has an antecedent in the efforts of educational reformers who promoted the hands-on study of nature in the early 20th century. The approach makes sense because people acquire knowledge of STEM subjects by observing and doing.

Among state-of-the-art offerings at Roxbury Latin School is an advanced course in biotechnology. This subject is frequently in the headlines and at the forefront of learning at the school. Biotechnology has such widespread applications in agriculture and medicine that it seems perfectly adapted to an emphasis on practical and career-focused education in Boston's schools. In 2017, Roxbury offered the course to students in grades 9 through 12 as a June elective in its summer session. The course is not inexpensive, with tuition near $3,000. Tuition funds an intensive laboratory experience coupled with trips to leading biotechnological and pharmaceutical companies. The course also includes study at the prestigious Woods Hole Oceanographic Institution in Woods Hole, Massachusetts. At Roxbury, state-of-the-art computer labs intensify the immersion in technology. As part of its mission, Roxbury hosts STEM camps during summers for students aged 9 through 13. Many of the courses at these camps have emerged as part of a partnership between Roxbury Latin School and MIT. These courses focus on applications in computer science, medicine, and chemical engineering among other branches of STEM subjects. In one medical course, for example, students focus on the potential role of antibodies in targeting and killing cancer cells, work that is at the forefront of cancer research. Computer courses teach students not only how to use applications but to design them.

COLLABORATION WITH THE MUSEUM OF SCIENCE, BOSTON

The partnership with MIT is not the only fruitful avenue of cooperation between Boston's schools and outside interests. The city's Museum of Science, one of the world's largest centers for the promotion and exhibition of science, has many initiatives that promote STEM subjects. In its Eye Opener Program, for example the museum hosts an annual event for 2,500 to 3,000 second graders from the Boston public schools. The program introduces STEM subjects to those students who, because they come from poor communities, might not otherwise have access to cutting-edge research and pedagogy. The attempt to reach second graders represents a commitment to promoting STEM subjects to youths at an age when their enthusiasm for these subjects is still robust. The Eye Opener Program, which began in 1986, is a partnership among the museum, the Boston public schools, and the Germeshausen Family Foundation. Financial support from the foundation ensures that disadvantaged second graders can attend the program at no cost. In addition, the program relies on volunteers to curb the cost of hiring staff. The program includes not only study of the museum's exhibits but experimentation and the cultivation of the critical thinking skills that are central to success in science, technology, engineering, and mathematics.

> **STEM Subjects**
>
> The STEM subjects position schools to tout their relevance because many experts believe that technical knowledge is basic to careers in the 21st century. This line of thinking holds that technical knowledge is essential to innovation and improvements in all facets of life. Accordingly, employers value those who possess such knowledge above people with a general education. The U.S. Department of Education internalizes this logic by predicting double-digit growth in the percentage of jobs in various technical fields by 2020. STEM advocates value more than employability. They argue that scientific and technical literacy is essential in a world governed by science and technology. Such knowledge is necessary if students are to understand and function in society. STEM proponents call for the United States and other nations to increase production of scientists, engineers, and mathematicians. Anecdotes suggest, however, that some science, engineering, and mathematics graduates, especially PhD holders, struggle to find work.

Like MIT, Boston's Museum of Science designs curriculum for use in the city's schools. An example is the Engineering is Elementary (EiE) curriculum, which targets students in grades one through five. Again, the emphasis is on solidifying students' interest and aptitude in engineering at a formative stage in their lives. The emphasis on a practical approach to formulating and solving problems is at the core of engineering. Such skills prepare young Bostonians for the world of work. Where EiE ends, the museum's Engineering Everywhere begins. It targets students in grades six through eight, building on the concepts and habits of inquiry that they learned in the EiE curriculum.

THE IMPORTANCE OF STEM SUBJECTS IN BOSTON'S SCHOOLS

The focus on STEM subjects is shaping education in Boston's schools. Worthy of note is the teaching of science, technology, engineering, and mathematics across the curriculum. This integrative approach challenges the tendency to pigeonhole knowledge into discrete compartments because these subjects are relevant to all facets of life. The focus in Boston is on using STEM subjects to propel young people toward college and careers. This emphasis counters the criticism that schools are producing graduates ill-suited for the world of work. Boston's schools are using STEM subjects to address this traditional mismatch between graduates and jobs. Moreover, the emphasis in STEM subjects on critical thinking and careful evaluation of evidence are skills that employers prize in a variety of occupations.

Christopher Cumo

See also: *Schools:* Berlin, Germany: Making the City a Center of Learning; Seoul, South Korea: "Education Fever"; Tokyo, Japan: The *Yutori* Educational Reforms

Further Reading

"Boston Public Schools Pioneer STEM Immersion Program with Boston STEM Week." https://www.bostonpublicschools.org/site/default.aspx?pagetype=38domainid =48moduleinstanceid=148viewid=047e6be3-6d87-4130-8424.

"Dearborn STEM Academy." https://www.bpe.org/dearborn-stem-academy.

"Museum of Science, Boston." https://www.mos.org.

"Science Opportunities—BLS-BLSA." https://www.bls.org/apps/pages/index.jsp?urec_id=191782&type=d&termrec_id=&prec_id=408276.

Ouagadougou, Burkina Faso: Investing in Higher Education for the Country's Future

Burkina Faso is a young West African country with a territory of 274,000 square kilometers, slightly larger than Colorado, and a population of approximately 19.5 million. The country's official language is French. Burkina Faso gained independence from France in 1960, and replaced its original country name, Haulte Volta, in 1984 with the current name. Ouagadougou is the capital city with a population of 1.47 million (Ministère 2012). The majority of the population are Muslims, and approximately one-third are Christians. The colonial history has left Burkina Faso's educational system with a deep and continuing influence of the French system.

Since its founding, Burkina Faso has survived frequent economic turmoil and social insecurity, including multiple military coups. Economically, Burkina Faso suffers from widespread poverty; most of its economy depends on subsistence farming, which is often devastated by recurring droughts. The country has relatively few natural resources. As such, its industrial base is rather limited. Cotton and gold are primary export products; gold contributes three-fourths of the country's total export revenues. Political instability, resulting from both governmental corruption and poor management, and conflicts with surrounding countries such as Mali, Togo, Ivory Coast, Benin, Ghana, and Niger, negatively impact the country's economy. The unemployment rate reached 77 percent in 2004, and 40 percent of the population is under the country's poverty line in 2009 (CIA 2018). Economic depression has apparently taken a toll on the job market: Millions of Burkinabes migrate to Ivory Coast, Togo, Benin, and Ghana to look for jobs (Ministère 2012). The country's population is young; according to statistics from 2016, 45 percent are 0–14 years of age and 21 percent are ages 15–24 (CIA 2018). However, while the high fertility rate accelerates population growth, it puts increasing pressure on the country's employment capacity. The mayor of Ouagadougou, Armand Beouinde, stresses the strength of the country's dynamic labor force and recognizes the challenges the city is faced with: "Ouagadougou has primarily a young population. With everyone's contribution, the city strives to meet many new challenges. To implement an effective governance, we will implement the Program of mandate in all fronts of urban life and in which all citizens participate" (Mairie de Ouaga).

EDUCATIONAL INFRASTRUCTURE

For Burkina Faso, high population growth and low literacy rate are a major source of instability. The literacy rate, defined as the ability to read and write by age 15, stood at 36 percent in 2015 (CIA 2018). To meet this challenge, the Burkinabe government is taking advantage of historical connections with France and other western countries, including the United States, to establish multiple higher education institutions in Ouagadougou. By 2011, Burkina Faso's higher education had been provided by several institutions. The University of Ouagadougou, Polytechnic University of Bobo-Dioulasso, and the University of Koudougou are the three major public universities enrolling the majority of students. The remaining student population are enrolled by two local university centers—the University Center of Fada, and University Center of Ouahigouya—and two private universities—the University of St. Thomas d'Aquin at Ouagadougou and Catholic University of West Africa. All campuses are located in the capital city.

Public Institutions. In general, the Burkinabe higher education adopts the French curricula framework that stresses the importance of preparing students for employment. Courses focus on applied knowledge and skills that the workforce is expected to need in the workplace. Assessment is conducted by West-African Higher Education Excellence of Teaching Network (REESAO in its French abbreviation). There is an active and continuing collaboration between Burkinabe institutions and their French counterparts through which French universities provide scholarships, faculty training, and funding for research. Universities in cities such as Paris, Bordeaux, Lyon, and Toulouse maintain a wide range of networks with Burkinabe universities. For example, out of the 13 autonomous universities in Paris, 7 have been active sponsors for decades.

The University of Ouagadougou (UO) was created in 1974. The enrollment was fewer than 400 students at the beginning. Today, UO is the largest university in the country. In 2011, enrollment reached 45,000, or 83 percent of the country's public university population. A restructuring in 2000 made the university a comprehensive institution covering science, technology, and humanities in seven colleges. Language, Arts and Communication, Social Sciences, and Science of Politics and Law are the areas that attract the majority of students; followed by Economics and Management Science, and Basic and Applied Sciences. The colleges of Health Science and Science of Life and Earth have seen an increasing enrollment due to drastic climate changes and the rapid spread of epidemic diseases in the past decade. Additionally, the university runs Burkinabe Institute of Arts and Professions, which has become popular in Africa's higher education system.

Polytechnic University of Bobo-Dioulasso (UPB) was founded in 1995 to be a standard university for training teachers. The school was later converted to a polytechnic university in 2011 and enrolls 2,600 students. The university runs three colleges: Computer Science, Rural Development, and Technology. The school of technology offers seven programs including electrical engineering, mechanical engineering, electronic engineering, industrial maintenance, mechanical production, commercial-financial management, and secretary training.

The University of Koudougou (UK) was created in 2005 as an expansion from the base of the Normal University of Koudougou, and enrolled 5,400 students by 2011. UK runs four institutes: Teacher Training, Economics and Management, Social Sciences and Literatures, and Technology.

University centers of Fada and Ouahigouya enroll fewer students than regular universities. The Fada center offers programs in mining, civil engineering, and social sciences. The Ouahigouya center offers programs in medicine and finance. Logistics and management at the university centers appear to be underdeveloped and underfunded. During a student protest in 2016 at the University Center of Ouhigouya, students voiced concerns over missed scholarship payment, run-down dining facilities, and poor food quality. In particular, protesters expressed frustration with the failure of management for many years to address these issues. Faculty members also complained about the school's inefficient management that had resulted in weeks without courses properly scheduled in medical studies (Ouedraogo 2016).

Private Institutions. There are more than 30 private institutions in Ouagadougou and Bobo-Dioulasso specializing in a variety of vocational training. The more comprehensive institutions are University of St. Thomas d'Aquin at Ouagadougou (USTA) and Catholic University of West Africa (CUWA). USTA offers programs in economics, management, political science, law, and medicine. It also operates a School for Career Training. UCWA offers similar programs as USTA, with additional programs in biology and computer science.

EDUCATIONAL RELATIONSHIP WITH THE UNITED STATES

The United States runs several educational programs in Burkina Faso through Fulbright Exchange Programs. The Hubert H. Humphrey Fellowship Program, for example, supports Burkinabe mid-level professionals to take graduate-level training in U.S.-based universities for a period of nine months. The Fulbright Visiting Student Program sponsors qualified senior Burkinabe students to study in U.S. universities under the guidance of American faculty for up to a year. The Fulbright Senior Specialists Program sponsors U.S. faculty and professionals to conduct teaching and research in Burkina Faso (U.S. Embassy). Additionally, many American universities have study abroad programs with Burkina Faso, one of which is Georgetown University. The Education and Social Justice Project at Georgetown University supports students to travel to Burkina Faso and other developing countries to conduct in-depth examinations of innovative educational initiatives, with a focus on the work of Jesuit institutions (Berkley Center for Religion 2015). The United States also funds the International School of Ouagadougou, a K–12 institution established in 1976, with an enrollment of more than 200 students and a 41-person teaching staff as of 2016–17.

CHALLENGES IN HIGHER EDUCATION

As with most developing countries, education in Burkina Faso is typically underfunded. Students' living and learning conditions are directly affected by economic stresses. Furthermore, a shortage of teaching resources compromises the quality of instruction. This is best reflected in the remarks of Sibalo Mamadou, a student at the University of Ouagadougou, on the state of education in Burkina Faso:

> The system of education in Burkina Faso is chaotic. We cannot know what is really going on. There are some who benefit from scholarships, scholarships to study abroad in France or the United States. But these are very limited, and practically, the

government is in the process of privatizing the system of education. There are more private schools in Ouagadougou than public schools. The population does not believe in the system of education. On the campus of the University of Ouagadougou, one school year can take more than thirteen months. Because of this academic mess, there are a lot of challenges for those seeking master's or doctoral degrees. There is a lack of professors. And the social condition of students is not secure. (Berkley Center for Religion 2014)

While reviving the economy through investing in higher education is an ideal solution, it typically takes long-term efforts before palpable benefits are seen. Will the educational institutions be able to deliver specialized job skills to the masses of students coming from disadvantaged economic backgrounds? Will graduates be able to find jobs? Will the country's social stability be improved, so that entrepreneurs and people with college-level training will stay? These are some of the questions the Burkinabe government struggles to resolve. In 2017, the Burkinabe government revamped its education sector plan and developed a new plan for the period of 2017–30. The new education sector plan stresses five goals: 1) ensuring harmonious, equitable, and inclusive early childhood development; 2) ensuring universal completion of the primary cycle and establishing equitable and quality basic education for all; 3) resolving the lack of trainers in technical and vocational high schools; 4) adjusting higher education to the needs of the economy; and 5) fostering efficient management, so that resources can produce optimal educational outcomes (Global Partnership).

The long-term plan appears to be comprehensive and focused, reflecting the government's determination to bring changes. On the other hand, it is essential for the educational communities in developed countries to support the plan's implementation. Helping Burkina Faso strengthen its higher education is critical in ensuring the country's future. To that end, the value of educational support may last longer than any form of economic aid.

Jing Luo

See also: Schools: Bamako, Mali: Private and Public Sectors of Education; Xi'an, China: Where China's Private Education Debuts

Further Reading

Berkley Center for Religion, Peace & World Affairs, Georgetown University. 2014. "A Discussion with Mamadou Sibalo, Student, University Of Ouagadougou, Ouagadougou, Burkina Faso." https://berkleycenter.georgetown.edu/interviews/a-discussion-with-mamadou-sibalo-student-university-of-ouagadougou-ouagadougou-burkina-faso.

Berkley Center for Religion, Peace & World Affairs, Georgetown University. 2015. "The Education and Social Justice Project: International Summer Research Fellowships." https://berkleycenter.georgetown.edu/publications/the-education-and-social-justice-project-international-summer-research-fellowships-2014.

Burkina Faso Government. "Programme Sectoriel Education/Formation du Burkina Faso (PSEF:2012–2021)." http://www.globalpartnership.org/fr/download/file/fid/45867.

CIA. 2018. "The World Factbook—Burkina Faso." https://www.cia.gov/library/publications/the-world-factbook/geos/uv.html.

Global Partnership for Education. "Education in Burkina Faso." http://www.globalpartnership.org/country/burkina-faso.

Mairie de Ouaga (Mayor's Office). www.mairie-ouaga.bf/.

Ministère des affaires étrangères et de la coopération régionale. 2012. "Guide du Burkinabe de l' étranger" (in French). https://burkinausa.files.wordpress.com/2017/08/guide-du-burkinabe-de-etranger.pdf.

Ministère des affaires etrangères et Européennes, Ambassade de France au Burkina Faso. n.d. "Fiche Burkina Faso" (in French). http://www.diplomatie.gouv.fr/fr/IMG/pdf/BURKINA_18-5-11__2_.pdf.

National Institute of Statistics and Demographics. "Education." http://www.insd.bf/n/index.php/indicateurs?id=73 (in French).

Ouedraogo, Emery Albert. 2016. "Centre Universitaire Polytechnique de Ouahigouya: les étudiants marchent sur le gouvernora" (in French). https://fr.allafrica.com/stories/201603231025.html.

Université d'Ouagadougou. Official Website. http://www.univ-ouaga.bf/spip.php?rubrique39.

University World News—African Edition. 2008. "Burkina Faso: Ouagadougou University Reopens," September 14. http://www.universityworldnews.com/article.php?story=20080911164127977.

U.S. Embassy in Burkina Faso. "Exchanges Programs." https://bf.usembassy.gov/education-culture/exchanges-programs.

U.S. State Department. "Burkina Faso, Ouagadougou: International School of Ouagadougou—2017–2018 Fact Sheet." https://www.state.gov/m/a/os/1286.htm.

William, Jerome. 2016. "Insider's Guide to Ouagadougou: Signed Chicken, Potholes, but No Plastic Bags." *Guardian*, November 28. https://www.theguardian.com/cities/2016/nov/28/insiders-guide-ouagadougou-tropical-drinks-colourful-fabrics-burkina-faso.

Seoul, South Korea: "Education Fever"

Ravaged after three bloody years of back-and-forth warfare between 1950 and 1953, Seoul's economic revival in the late 20th century was nothing short of miraculous. It was and still is a miracle based on Seoul's greatest resource: its people. South Korea lies at the end of a relatively small peninsula where the mineral resources are largely in the North and the agricultural resources are mainly in the South. To make the most of its human resources, the government established its central control over the education system and developed an academic model that has produced astonishing results. Over the last 60 years, the government has achieved nearly universal enrollment in its primary and secondary schools, and South Korean students today continue to excel on international achievement tests like the Program for International Student Assessment (PISA). Yet, as scholars, journalists, and others who have lived and worked in South Korea during the last few years have also noted, the price of Seoul's "education fever" on the emotional well-being of its young people has been high.

"EDUCATION FEVER:" A CONDENSED HISTORY

As Michael Seth highlighted in his research on the South Korean obsession with education, most everyone starts with the traditional Korean cultural heritage to explain the origins of what Koreans call their "education fever" (Seth 2002, 9). What Seth is referring to is the important role that Confucianism has played in shaping traditional Korean attitudes toward education through most of its history. Confucianism introduced from China to traditional Korea in the seventh century emphasized the selection of the most educated men to participate in ruling the country. How did you recruit such men? You held government exams regularly to choose the best and the brightest minds to serve in the government and advise the king on policy decisions. Thus, a number of formal and informal schools developed over time to prepare students to take the highly competitive civil service exams. These exams, in turn, became the primary means of raising one's social status in Korean society, bettering one's family name, and gaining access to the halls of political power on the peninsula. So the central place of the entrance examination in Korean educational life extends from the Koryŏ period (918–1392) through the long Chosŏn or Yi dynasty (1392–1910) and continues in South Korea to this very day (Seth 2002, 9–14).

Koreans often liken their geopolitical location in East Asia to the proverbial shrimp caught in the battering waves of its larger neighbors, China, Japan, and eventually Russia. From the late 19th to the mid-20th century, Chosŏn Korea was thrown into the emerging global economy as a host of foreign countries intervened in Korean affairs and forced a number of changes upon Koreans. The introduction of Western-style educational systems through interaction with the Japanese model of education had the greatest impact on the peninsula. From the Japanese education system, Koreans adopted its centralized model with a Ministry of Education that determined the curriculum, the approval of textbooks, teacher certification, and the detailed regulations for managing the schools (Seth 2002, 16). This focus on centralized administration of the educational system later became a defining feature of the South Korean school system during the late 20th century. However, as Japanese influence on the peninsula grew to direct colonial rule from 1910 to 1945, the Japanese educational policy came to infuriate the Korean people. It left an unsavory legacy of limiting Korean access to education beyond elementary school and of employing education as a means to indoctrinate and then assimilate the Korean populace from the 1930s to 1945. Ultimately, the Japanese inheritance on the peninsula came to include "the use of education as a political instrument by a powerful centralized state . . . that was followed by the governments of both North and South Korea" (Seth 2002, 19).

With the American occupation of the Korean peninsula's southern half, between 1945 and 1948, Koreans were introduced to the American model of mass education that sought to "democratize" Koreans. At first the promised educational reforms of the "New Education Movement" appealed to many Korean educators, but over time, it became clear that the U.S. military government overseeing the occupation did not have the time, the resources, nor the inclination to put these ideas into practice. Maintaining political stability on the southern end of the peninsula and keeping it out of Communist hands was the mission for the American occupation officials. As a result, the centralized educational model from the colonial period remained the norm with adjustments like the 6-3-3-4-year educational model from the American system added onto the Japanese template (Seth 2002, 34–50).

What this experience did set in motion was a continuing debate among South Korean educators. The issue was how best to meld the progressive concern for the individual introduced by the Americans with the traditional Confucian focus on moral training, and the preferred centralized educational administration that was part of the colonial Japanese education model (Seth 2002, 50–59). During the second half of the 20th century, another important and pressing question became how this educational system should work to serve the needs of the newly created nation-state, the Republic of Korea in the south? These were questions that persisted through the devastating war between North and South, the autocratic regimes that governed the South until 1987, and that are still considered in different guises even today.

With the promulgation of the Basic Education Law on December 31, 1949, the first priority became establishing a system of compulsory universal education. This was accomplished in the primary schools by the 1960s and then in middle school education by 1979, and in high school education by 1985 (Kim and Cho 2014, 784). Under the military regime of General Park Chung-hee in the 1970s, the need for economic growth led the Park government to support vocational education and technical training as the main objectives of its educational development plan. By the mid-1990s, however, the Korean government began developing a new educational model that "allow[ed] more autonomy and accountability to schools" to encourage schools to strive for academic excellence and educational quality beyond the initial push for universal education (Kim and Cho 2014, 784). This became the driving impetus for the Seventh Curriculum that the Ministry of Education began implementing in March 2000 and that was updated in 2007 and again in 2009 (National Curriculum Information Center).

A WORLD-CLASS EDUCATION AND SEOUL'S "SHADOW EDUCATION" SYSTEM

On the bright side, Korean students perform extraordinarily well on international achievement tests. On both the TIMSS (Trends in International Mathematics and Science Study) and the PISA tests in the 2000s, Korean students ranked consistently among the top 10 countries in the world in math, science, and reading literacy. What's more, studies show that the difference between high and low achievers among Korean students on these exams is much less than other OECD (Organization for Economic Co-operation and Development) countries, meaning that even Korean students who do not do as well on these tests are still outperforming students from other countries. These are remarkable achievements that are the envy of many other countries. Moreover, South Korea's reputation for educational success has also begun to attract increasingly growing numbers of international students—over 63,000 students by 2011—traveling to Seoul for their higher education. In particular, students across Asia are flocking to the urban campuses at one of the SKY (Seoul National University, Korea University, and Yonsei University) universities (Collins 2014, 246). They are simply following in the footsteps of earlier Korean students who moved to Seoul with their families in hopes of realizing their dreams (Seth 2002, 144). Their goal was to pass the entrance exam for a prestigious university and then obtain a degree that would set them for life, since the name of the university they graduated from counted for more in the workplace than what they actually studied at the university. In the eyes of many foreign and domestic politicians, in the 21st century South Koreans have reached the goal of establishing a world-class educational system with Seoul at the center of that success.

Still beneath the public image of equal educational opportunities for all in South Korea, the "shadow education" system, which is most prominent in Seoul, reveals the socioeconomic divide that persists in South Korea today. Shadow education refers to the private tutoring academies known as *hagwon* in Korean. At the end of the school day at public or private schools, Korean students return home for a quick dinner and then, for those who can afford it, they head out to the *hagwon* for another several hours of test preparation classes. Traditionally, those classes ended anywhere from 10 p.m. to 1 a.m. depending on your school year and on your level of educational ambition. Scholars have noted that the number of students attending these private academies in Seoul is almost double the numbers in small towns. Moreover, those students who come from wealthier families are better able to pay for time in a *hagwon*, creating a disparity in educational opportunities even in Seoul (Kim and Cho 2014, 787). As journalist Amanda Ripley noted, "In 2010, 74% of all students engaged in some kind of private after-school instruction . . . at an average cost of $2,600 per student for the year" (Ripley 2011). In her article she follows several officers who are in charge of enforcing a 2008 government curfew on the *hagwon* who must finish classes at 10 p.m. How do the *hagwon* get around this curfew? They become an "after-hours self-study library" for students after 10 p.m. and move more of their curriculum online so that students purchase these lessons and continue their studies at home late into the night (Ripley 2011). More recent articles from the *New York Times*, *BBC News*, and National Public Radio confirm that the emphasis on educational achievement to enter a prestigious university has not lessened. Each article follows the stories of individual Korean students and the long hours they put in to prepare for the college entrance exams. In the end, these articles acknowledge the academic achievement of the South Korean educational system overall, but question the validity of this model for the United States and express concern over the immense physical and mental toll of this system on Korean students. Thus, despite some scholars and journalists pointing out the difficult burden placed on its youth, South Korea's "education fever" remains a driving force behind the academic and economic success of Seoul in the 21st century.

Jeff E. Long

See also: Schools: Boston, United States: A Model City of STEM Education; Toyko, Japan: The *Yutori* Educational Reforms

Further Reading

Asia Society. "South Korean Education Reforms." http://asiasociety.org/global-cities-education-network/south-korean-education-reforms.

Chakrabarti, Reeta. 2013. "South Korea's Schools: Long Days, High Results." *BBC News*, December 2. http://www.bbc.com/news/education-25187993.

Collins, Francis. 2014. "Globalising Higher Education in and through Urban Spaces: Higher Education Projects, International Student Mobilities and Trans-Local Connections in Seoul." *Asia Pacific Viewpoint* 55: 242–57.

Diem, Richard, Tedd Levy, and Ronald VanSickle. "South Korean Education." Asia Society. http://asiasociety.org/global-cities-education-network/south-korean-education.

Hu, Elise. 2015. "The All-Work, No-Play Culture of South Korean Education." *npr*, April 15. http://www.npr.org/sections/parallels/2015/04/15/393939759/the-all-work-no-play-culture-of-south-korean-education.

Kim, Yong, and Young Hoan Cho. 2014. "The Second Leap toward 'World Class' Education in Korea." *Asia-Pacific Education Researcher* 23: 783–94.

Koo, Se-Woong. 2014. "An Assault upon Our Children: South Korea's Education System Hurts Students." *New York Times*, August 1. http://www.nytimes.com/2014/08/02/opinion/sunday/south-koreas-education-system-hurts-students.html.

National Curriculum Information Center. "Education System of Korea." http://ncic.kice.re.kr/english.inf.ivi.index.do.

Park, Hyunjoon. 2013. *Re-evaluating Education in Japan and Korea: Demystifying Stereotypes*. Routledge Studies in Education and Society in Asia. New York: Routledge.

Ripley, Amanda. 2011. "Teacher, Leave Those Kids Alone." *Time Asia*, September 25. http://content.time.com/printout/0,8816,2094427,00.html.

Seth, Michael J. 2002. *Education Fever: Society, Politics, and the Pursuit of Schooling in South Korea*. Honolulu: University of Hawai'i Press.

Sydney, Australia: Making International Education a Thriving Sector of the Economy

SYDNEY—AUSTRALIA'S HUB OF INTERNATIONAL EDUCATION

Sydney is the capital city of the state of New South Wales, which is located on the east coast of Australia. Historically, Sydney was a former British colony. Today, it is the largest portal city of Australia and home to 5 million people. Population growth has accelerated in the past 15 years, adding 1 million to the city's population. A driving force is the city's growing fame in international education. Sydney was ranked "the most popular international study destination worldwide" and "the best student city" in 2015 and 2016 by the London-based Best Student Cities Index. Sydney embraces international students as an integral part of the community that contributes to the city's "superdiversity." Moreover, international education has become a resource for economic prosperity (Spoonley 2014). As such, offering the best learning and living environment to international students has been high on the city's agenda.

There are multiple reasons why international students, particularly from Asian countries, attend schools in Sydney. The top reason appears to be that Sydney has the most choices to offer: it is the hub of campuses of five major universities of Australia—the University of Sydney, the University of Technology of Sydney, the University of New South Wales, Macquarie University, and Western Sydney

University. A student interested in any academic field or coming from any economic background would most likely be able to find a place to study. Second, the multicultural environment is welcoming to international students. Those from China, India, and other Asian countries find it easy to adapt, and many say that they embrace the high degree of freedom. In Australia, universities put a great emphasis on equity, diversity, and inclusion, which is often highlighted in student handbooks. The University of New South Wales, for example, states in its grand plan, UNSW 2025, as follows:

Accepted for who you are

UNSW understands that everyone is different, and we value the perspectives and life experiences that all of our employees bring to the workplace. Our desire is for all employees and students to reach their full potential and to feel they can be themselves regardless of their gender, disability, cultural background, sexual orientation or gender identity. Our aim is by having Diversity Champions, network and advisory groups and diversity training, we create an environment where people feel supported to have the learning experience or can build the career they truly want. (UNSW Web)

Third, the atmosphere of teaching/learning, as many students reflect, is one of "laid-back" and "relaxed-vibe." "Lecturers genuinely seem to be chill, and at my uni shoes seem to be optional," as one student says (Thomson 2015). Students who run away from the Chinese killer *Gaokao* (considered one of the toughest college entrance exams in the world) obviously adore this environment. In fact, Chinese students make up the largest student group in the system. Fourth, there are jobs for students to subsidize living in one of the world's most expensive cities. The University of South Wales charges AUD$375 per week for living on campus; an average arts degree costs AUD$19,000. One of the job sources is government services. The New South Wales state government invests millions in innovation, construction, and technology. In 2014–15, 50,000 new jobs were created, and the government promised 150,000 new jobs over the following four years. That being said, for new arrivals finding jobs remains a major challenge. Finally, Sydney offers convenient health-care plans for international students. In Australia, students are required to carry medical insurance during their study period. They can access health care through the Overseas Student Health Cover (OSHC) Scheme, which reduces medical expenses. Insurance and care providers are well networked—the patient can pay out of pocket and get reimbursed by OSHC later or let the provider bill OSHC first. Sydney's universities provide information and convenience to link students to the network.

THE ECONOMIC PICTURE

There are currently 4.5 million international students globally, and the number is expected to double by 2025, according to a report by the *Economist*. More and more students from emerging economies will be heading to countries with developed economies, as incomes will grow globally and more scholarships will become available as well. Most notably, Japan will continue to be one of the top destinations in Asia. Germany's influence will expand as it will offer an increasing number of postgraduate courses in the English language. Germany has abolished all tuition and fees even for foreign students. Nevertheless, the United States remains the most attractive country for foreign students, with 975,000 foreign students in academic year 2014–15, compared to Australia's 348,000, Britain's 312,000, and Canada's 195,000 (*Economist* 2016). Quality education and generous scholarships make the world's brightest minds want to study in American schools.

Economically, there are good reasons why the Australian government stresses international education. According to a study commissioned by the Australian government, international education was valued at $18.8 billion in 2014–15, making it the third-largest export sector of the country. An additional $935 million was generated in four kinds of related economic activities: 1) learning of English as a second language by nonstudents; 2) tourism by visiting friends and family members; 3) operation of offshore campuses; and 4) study tours conducted by institutions abroad to Australian schools. These revenues were estimated to be able to support 130,700 full-time equivalent (FTE) jobs in 2014–15, which would account for 1.3 percent of Australia's total employment. States that created the most jobs from international education opportunities include New South Wales, where 1.5 percent of employment (46,903 jobs) was supported by revenues from international education, and Victoria, where 1.6 percent of employment (39,169 jobs) was created. Metropolitan Sydney hosts 50,000 international university students and an equal number of English learners of nonstudent status. They contribute $1.6 billion to the city's economy, creating 4,000 jobs, according to the city's statistics (City of Sydney 2015).

However, a far more important contribution by international education is that it adds 130,000 skilled migrants, with college degrees, representing a 3 percent increase, to the Australian workforce. While migrant workers contribute an estimated $8.7 billion to Australia's GDP (Deloitte Access Economics 2015, 3), their potential contribution is far greater when considering the international network that the migrants carry with them. For example, knowledge exchange, cultural capital, and expansion of Australia's international influence constitute a favorable background for greater economic development.

ACCOMMODATIVE CAMPUSES

To accommodate new international students, Sydney promises to do more. For newcomers, adapting to the new environment is a challenging process. Lack of English-language proficiency, difficulties in finding affordable housing, insecure employment conditions, financial pressures, underperformance due to unfamiliar academic requirements, social isolation from the host community, loneliness, homesickness, racism and discrimination—these can all potentially affect international students' well-being (Augoustinos et al. 2011). Academic institutions in Sydney proactively dedicate resources to help international students deal with difficulties they may encounter.

Academic. Universities in Sydney strive to offer the best learning and living environment to international students. At the University of New South Wales (UNSW), for example, a dedicated Careers and Employment team is available to assist international students. New students are paired with peer mentors who offer tips about faculty, courses, and campus life. New students can also pick a "cultural mentor," a senior student of the same ethnic/cultural background, for consultation about cultural adaptation. The university provides free English training programs, such as weekly conversation classes, to those who wish to improve their language skills. Students can also make appointments with peer writing assistants, who typically provide help with language and style for writing essays and reports. UNSW provides a great deal of information and training online. In the area of academic skills, for example, students learn about academic integrity through an online module. They also get advice on writing skills, critical thinking, reading and note-taking, oral presentation skills, and exam preparation. Workshops, such as Thesis Writing for Art & Design and Study Smart: Techniques for Less Stressful Exam Preparation, are freely available and announced on an events calendar.

Living. While students can apply for on-campus housing as part of the standard application, they can also apply online for a broad range of options for living off-campus. One popular option is to live in the suburbs and take the transit. Some locations are within easy walking distance. Living off-campus offers the flexibility of sharing to reduce costs. Students can also find job opportunities in the neighborhood. Efforts by the Sydney municipality, local community, and private businesses have jointly made suburban student housing safe, convenient, and culturally attractive.

There are more than 20 suburban residential villages where students find places to live. Chippendale, Glebe, Newtown, and Redfern are some of the popular ones. Chippendale is known for its unique architecture, cafés, restaurants, and its location next to the Victoria Park and Central Railway Station, which is the city's main transit hub. Chippendale has become the city's newest hotspot of creativity and cultural diversity, as well as a preferred residential area for international students. Glebe is a residential village for students. Bus lines can get students into the city in less than 20 minutes. Its abundant cafés, bookstores, and great view from Jubilee Park make the suburb a quiet living and studying environment. Newtown is known for its great display of Asian cultures through arts and dining. Redfern is characterized by aboriginal and migrant traditions.

THE WELL-BEING OF INTERNATIONAL STUDENTS IN SYDNEY

In 2016, the City of Sydney commissioned the University of Technology's Sydney (UTS) Institute for Public Policy and Governance to conduct a survey on the well-being of international students in Sydney in the areas of social, physical, and mental health. The following are some of the key findings.

On the positive side, students enjoy their experience studying in Sydney and find the city a great place to live and study in. They would willingly recommend the city to friends. More students found getting a job less difficult than anticipated; they also found local Australians more welcoming than anticipated. The survey showed that finding suitable housing was difficult, particularly for new arrivals from Asian countries. High rents were among the most troubling problems. However, most found it from easy to moderately difficult to get the problem resolved. The majority did receive support from friends, relatives, or their educational institution in finding a place to live. They also found living in the downtown an expensive but cool experience. Students found the city's festivities and other cultural events highly enjoyable.

On the negative side, students found adaptation a difficult period for several reasons. Homesickness could be worsened due to lack of information support, and would make them feel isolated. Some found that international students were not treated equally or teachers were not able to really understand their issues. Additionally, many students found academic challenges greater than they had anticipated. English proficiency was a high barrier felt by both students and the locals. Most students depended on part-time work to buy food and pay for school costs; however, the success rate was mixed, which contributed to emotional stress.

In general, these results echoed the findings by earlier studies. However, the study suggested that the city may find a solution in addressing the students' issues and improving information delivery. With older students tending to be better problem solvers than younger ones, the city could make information more accessible to the latter, helping them find accommodative services and work opportunities. Moreover, the city could do better in providing training on safety rules, individuals' rights and responsibilities, and cultural etiquette. Additionally, the study recommended that the city more broadly involve international students in its events and planning processes, which would create an environment where they can meet, network, gain information, and share knowledge.

Jing Luo

See also: Housing and Infrastructure: Sydney, Australia: Struggle for Affordable Housing; *Schools*: Berlin, Germany: Making the City a Center of Learning

Further Reading

Augoustinos, M., C. Beasley, and S. Hanson-Easey. 2011. *Overseas Students Health Lens Project: Improving the Health and Wellbeing of Overseas Students Undertaking Post-Secondary Study in SA in the VET Sector.* http://www.sahealth.sa.gov.au/wps/wcm/connect/ccafe2804ecc8b14ae85eedcceff86b3/International+Students+Research+Report-PH%26CS-HiAP-20130213.pdf?MOD=AJPERES&CACHEID=ROOTWORKSPACE-ccafe2804ecc8b14ae85eedcceff86b3-lqr.WUS.

Australian Bureau of Statistics. 2017. "Sydney Population Hits 5 Million." http://www.abs.gov.au/ausstats/abs@.nsf/lookup/3218.0Media%20Release12015-16.

City of Sydney Website. 2015. *International Education.* http://www.sydneymedia.com.au/archives.

Deloitte Access Economics (commissioned by the Australian Government). 2015. "The Value of International Education to Australia." https://internationaleducation.gov.au/research/research-papers/Documents/ValueInternationalEd.pdf.

"Overseas Student Health Cover." *Studies in Australia—The International Students' Guide.* https://www.studiesinaustralia.com/studying-in-australia/how-to-study-in-australia/student-visas/overseas-student-health-cover.

QS. 2016. *Best Student Cities Index 2016.* London: Quacquarelli Symonds.

Spoonley, P. 2014. "Superdiversity, Social Cohesion, and Economic Benefits." *IZA World of Labor Website.* https://wol.iza.org/articles/superdiversity-social-cohesion-and-economic-benefits/long.

Staff Writer. 2016. "Brains without Borders." *Economist*. http://www.economist.com/news/international/21689540-australia-and-canada-seek-attract-more-foreign-students-america-and-britain-could.

Thomson, Keegan. 2015. "What Makes Sydney Such a Great City for Students?" *Guardian*. https://www.theguardian.com/education/2015/dec/02/what-makes-sydney-great-city-for-students.

University of New South Wales. https://www.unsw.edu.au.

University of Sydney. http://sydney.edu.au.

UTS (Commissioned by the City of Sydney). 2016. "Wellbeing of International Students in the City of Sydney." https://www.uts.edu.au/sites/default/files/Research%2Binto%2Bthe%2BWellbeing%2Bof%2BInternational%2BStudents%2Bin%2Bthe%2BCity%2Bof%2BSydney_Final_27%2BJuly%2B2016.pdf.

Taipei, Taiwan: Taipei's K–12 Education and Special Education

Taipei, the capital of Taiwan, occupies an area of 272 square kilometers. It is located at the bottom of the Taipei Basin, sitting on three rivers flowing through Taipei City and into the Taiwan Strait. In 1990, Taipei revised its administrative subdivision and changed from 16 districts to 13 districts by combining some districts. Approximately one-eighth of Taiwan's population live in Taipei. It is the second-largest city in Taiwan, next to Xinbei City. Taipei is one of six municipalities in Taiwan that are directly controlled by the government.

Taipei has a long history of playing a dominant role in the area's geopolitics. In 1875, Shen Baozhen, an imperial envoy from Mainland China, built Taipei Prefecture to supervise Taiwan's military and civil affairs. Taipei has since gradually evolved into the political and economic center of Taiwan, with offices of the largest national and international companies. The city also serves as the center of cultural tourism.

One of the top items on Taipei municipality's agenda is to maintain its educational system. Quality education is on the mind of every citizen and administrator. The Ministry of Education of the Republic of China implements an education system of "6-3-3-4," which includes six years of elementary school, three years of middle school, three years of senior high school, and four years of higher education. In 2014, the compulsory education was extended from 9 years to 12 years to cover senior high school education. The preschool education is not mandatory, but financial support is provided to preschoolers from a low socioeconomic background.

EARLY EDUCATION AND PRIMARY EDUCATION

According to the *Taipei 2014–2015 Education Year Book*, the number of public preschools in Taipei has increased in recent years. The Taipei government provides funding to these preschools in order to make preschool education more accessible and affordable to the public. In 2014, there were 148 preschools that provided early education services to 18,062 preschoolers ranging from two to four years of age.

Over 80 percent of the students were four years old. The ratio of preschoolers attending public and private preschools today is 37 to 60.

In order to monitor preschool quality, the government sets up an evaluation system and requires all preschools to be evaluated in terms of its management, sanitation, personnel training, and safety. The student/teacher ratio is set to be 8 to 1 in the two-year-old preschoolers, different from the 15 to 1 in three- to five-year-old preschoolers. After-school programs are available that can provide child care till as late as 6:30 p.m. If there are fewer than 15 children signing up for after-school programs, the city government will subsidize the program instead of collecting more tuition from the participating families (Taipei Board of Education).

Primary school students are required to participate in an annual assessment that includes testing on phonetic knowledge, reading, writing, math, and English. Tests include both multiple choice and open-ended questions. The data is used to monitor individual and group academic performance. In some areas, such as the Chinese-language arts, the entire student body's test results are evaluated from the perspective of learning effectiveness; while for other tests such as English reading and writing, results are selectively evaluated as a way to follow individual students' progress. In recent years, the government made plans to add ancient Chinese calligraphy to the primary and secondary curriculum. For example, calligraphy classes will be made available as part of the curriculum of higher classes every semester. The government provides funds to train primary and secondary education teachers to teach lessons such as traditional calligraphy and classical Chinese art appreciation. Another area of educational spending is in strengthening English instruction by hiring native English speakers as English-language teachers. The teachers are assigned to after-school English programs that are available to students who struggle with English. The city government also provide funding for public primary schools to hire reading specialists; the funding is available to 29 schools in Taipei who have qualified for it. Tutorial services are provided to primary school students who demonstrate inadequate performance, and retired teachers and college students are encouraged to serve as tutors (Taipei Board of Education).

SECONDARY EDUCATION IN TAIPEI

According to its *2014–2015 Annual Year Book*, the Taipei government promotes 12-year compulsory education for the school-age population. The government, together with the higher education institutions, provide information about college programs to high school students, such as information about major and minor programs. The goal of this operation is to help students select areas of study at an early stage, so as to smoothly transition to higher education. For specialized disciplines such as arts, music, and sports, alternative criteria are used to select students. Additionally, the municipality has allocated money to encourage higher education institutions to offer vocational training to students with disabilities. Even for private middle and high schools, if they agree to adopt a competitive quality curriculum, they can receive special funding from the government to support the implementation of the curriculum. However, schools must submit documents to demonstrate student learning effectiveness and program quality in order to continue receiving subsidies from the government.

SPECIAL EDUCATION

According to the Cathay Glory Association, the first special education institute was established in 1956, funded by the Christian Children Fund. In 1962, special education programs were piloted in public schools. In 1968, the Nine-Year Education Plan was initiated, requiring special education and services be provided to school-age children with physical or intellectual disabilities, and those who are gifted. The special education reached a milestone in 1984 with the first special education law. This law supports the establishment of special education schools and advocates for the right of education for students with exceptionalities. In 1993, the Special Education Development Plan was created, and two years later a national conference on the education of students with intellectual disabilities and mental or emotional problems was held. Also in the same year, the first white paper on education and services for school-age population with physical and intellectual disabilities was issued.

According to the Cathay Glory Association, in recent years, special education has witnessed rapid development. For example, in 1997, the number of special education categories was expanded to 12. In 1998, a five-year special education improvement plan was created. According to this plan, preschool special education and services should be provided to children as young as three and cover educational, medical, and social welfare services. The government must provide special assistance to young children with disabilities, enroll them into schools close to home, and provide a variety of academic placement options. In 2001, a policy was issued to safeguard 12-year education for children with disabilities, and those students can choose to enroll in public senior high schools located close to the neighborhoods where they reside (Cathay Glory Association). The government aims to create more opportunities for students with disabilities to access a general education curriculum and interact with their peers (Cathay Glory Association). Since 2007, special criteria have been adopted at the national college entrance exam for high school graduates with disabilities, thus increasing the enrollment rate for these students to postsecondary education. The new Five-Year Special Education Development plan, created in 2008, requires quality education and accommodation be provided to school-age children with exceptionalities.

The Mental and Physical Disability White Paper, issued in 2012, further specifies guidelines on service provision for students with disabilities (Taipei Board of Education). It requires the provision of 12-year public education to students with disabilities, assigning early-intervention professionals with high credentials to every early-intervention program in Taipei. The white paper contributed to the improvement of public awareness of disabilities, and to the provision of social and emotional support to students with disabilities. It also promoted exchange programs for special education teachers and for students with disabilities.

In order to promote physical education for students with disabilities, the Taipei government also issued a four-year Physical Education Plan for students with disabilities in 2015 (Taipei Board of Education). The plan provides guidelines for physical education delivery in elementary, middle, and high schools. It serves as a guideline for collaboration between special education and physical education teachers. It provides guidance for maximizing the involvement of students with disabilities in physical activities and competitive sports; and it also promotes interaction between students with and without disabilities. Guidelines have also been created with respect to reforming the special education curriculum, implementing individualized education, and providing intensive instruction to students with disabilities. Additionally, the government sponsors regular scholarly seminars and conferences for discussions on special education curriculum.

The Taipei government seeks ways to involve the society's support. It creates plans to modify both physical and social environments in regular schools to maximally accommodate the special needs of students with disabilities (Taipei Board of Education). Examples of a modified physical environment include a barrier-free campus with wider elevators and sidewalks for wheelchair users. In order to create an accommodative social environment, the Taipei government encourages schools to post accommodative services on the school website and update that information periodically. The government provides on-site evaluation for Taipei's special education schools, including evaluations of students' academic performance, school curriculum, and administrative support systems. Wenshan, Qizhi, Qiming, and Qicong Special Education Schools in Taipei are receiving such evaluations. Between 2016 and 2017, the Taiwan government designed the Tianxin Plan aimed at assisting students with disabilities with their adaptation to the inclusive classrooms. The plan requires Taipei's schools to provide social, emotional, and academic assistance to facilitate adjustment to an inclusive general education curriculum and environment.

According to the Golden Decade report released in 2011 (Ministry of Education Republic of China), the programs provided by the Taipei government to K–12 students with disabilities can be categorized as follows according to their functions:

1. Establishing guidelines for special education to promote inclusion.
2. Enhancing quality and quantity of special education classes and services.
3. Increasing special education services for preschoolers and establishing early intervention services.
4. Improving special education services for K–12 students and offering more special education resources.
5. Modifying special education curriculum to better suit children's special needs.
6. Training high-quality special education teachers.
7. Accommodating children who demonstrate gifted special needs in the general education classroom.

EDUCATION FOR THE GIFTED

In 2015, the Taipei government also created the Guideline on Education for the Gifted White Paper (2016–2020), which increased funding for the gifted. The document encourages innovation on curriculum for the gifted, and increases in-service training for teachers and professionals working with students who are gifted. Schools are required to provide intensive instruction and assistance to gifted students before referring them to special education services (Taipei Board of Education).

NUTRITION, HEALTH SCREENING, AND OTHER EXPECTATIONS

According to the *Taipei 2014–2015 Education Year Book*, starting on February 24, 2015, all elementary school students in Taipei receive free dairy or soy products. A total of 157 schools receive these products. Among the elementary students who receive them, 59.6 percent received milk, 9.7 percent soy milk, and 30.7 percent yogurt. Together with the free dairy/soy drink initiative, the government also promotes physical education and nutrition education. Free health screening including dental and vision tests is offered to first graders twice a year. This initiative aims to reduce the rate of myopia and dental cavities.

Additionally, the Taipei government has special requirements for swimming lessons for all K–12 students. Swimming lessons are offered to all Taipei elementary students starting in fourth grade as part of their physical education. Moreover, students in Taipei are required to demonstrate a certain level of swimming ability in order to graduate. Special graduation requirements have been set up for all of Taipei's K–12 students. For example, elementary school students must be able to complete a 50-meter swim; middle school students must be able to swim 75 meters, and high school students 150 meters. K–12 students in Taipei rank at the top in competitive swimming contests among students from across Taiwan.

Yanhui Pang

See also: Schools: Boston, United States: A Model City of STEM Education; Tokyo, Japan: The *Yutori* Educational Reforms

Further Reading

Cathay Glory Association (in Chinese). http://www.cathayglory.org.

Long Weiwen. 2010. "Taiwan's Special Education" (in Chinese). Cathay Glory Association. http://www.cathayglory.org/index.php?option=com_content&view=article&id=61:2010-12-07-17-57-00&catid=34:todaystopics&Itemid=59.

Ministry of Education Republic of China. 2015–2016 Education in Taiwan—Study in Taiwan. https://stats.moe.gov.tw/files/ebook/Education_in_Taiwan/2015-2016_Education_in_Taiwan.pdf.

Ministry of Education Republic of China (Taiwan). 2009. Key Measures for Special Education. http://english.moe.gov.tw/ct.asp?xItem=11659&ctNode=783&mp=1.

Taipei Bureau of Education. *Taipei 2014–2015 Education Year Book* (in Chinese). http://online.fliphtml5.com/ukeo/uzgu/.

Tokyo, Japan: The *Yutori* Educational Reforms

Modern Japan has undergone several rounds of adjustments to its educational system since 1867 and its initial encounters with the foreign instructional models from the West. However, in Tokyo today, the Japanese government is attempting to do what no previous Japanese administration has done: develop a functional, home-grown educational model for elementary, middle, and secondary schools that will serve the needs of Tokyoites in the 21st century. The *yutori* ("pressure-free") educational reforms presented in the 1990s by the Ministry of Education, Sports, Culture and Technology (MEXT) and that the ministry strengthened in the early 2000s is still a work in process. Yet, as officials work to balance the goal of cultivating a genuine desire to learn in Japanese students with public expectations of academic excellence in schools, MEXT in its own words seeks to "creat[e] a society in which people of all ages, from children to adults, can learn and apply their newfound skills anytime, anywhere" (MEXT).

JAPAN'S MODERN HISTORY OF EDUCATION REFORMS: THE MEIJI YEARS

As Mark Lincicome observed in his research on the development of the Japanese educational system during the Meiji (1867–1912) years, Meiji reformers usually grumbled about the Tokugawa (1600–1867) government's Neo-Confucian education of the samurai ruling class as uninspiring, and ultimately leading to the political stagnation that sparked the Meiji Restoration (Lincicome 1995, 4–9). Lincicome points to a number of other educational alternatives like the Ancient Studies (*kogaku*) scholars, the home instruction that samurai and commoners alike pursued to fulfill their needs that provide a more varied picture of the Tokugawa legacy for the Japanese education system. What Lincicome also makes clear is the Neo-Confucian educational model's stress on the moral development of the individual as its primary goal. This emphasis on educating virtuous men would survive into the Meiji years along with the differing instructional models that emerged during the later period of Tokugawa rule (Lincicome 1995, 4–9).

For the Meiji leaders, education reform became a top priority and an important means to an end: the development of a strong and stable modern state that could resist Western imperialism in Asia and the Pacific. From the onset of the Meiji period in 1867 to around 1875 the Meiji government sent young Japanese students overseas to obtain an education in Europe or the United States. Many of these students were from the former samurai class, but students from the wealthier merchant and landlord classes also took advantage of these opportunities to study abroad. While these students were being trained, the state employed foreign experts in educational reform to start the process of establishing a Western-style education system in Japan. Finally, the Meiji leaders also adopted and then adapted those parts of foreign educational models that they considered most appropriate for Japan. It was an eclectic mix. As a historian of the Japanese education system, Edward Beauchamp, has written:

> As a result, a highly centralized administrative structure with an emphasis on state-run normal schools was borrowed from France; a system of higher education rooted in a handful of elite public universities was the German contribution; the English model of Spartan-like, character-building preparatory schools stressing moral discipline fit nicely in the Japanese context: and from the United States came the model

for elementary education, a number of practical pedagogical approaches, and an interest in vocational education. (Beauchamp 1987, 300)

Through the first decade of rule, the Meiji leaders viewed this blend as a perfect recipe to successfully modernize the Japanese education system. If the ultimate goal was to build national strength and a wealthy country, then Meiji Japan needed an education system that could arm its youth with the latest knowledge and skills to compete in the world economy. Thus, in 1872 the Meiji state announced plans to create a group of national universities, and it introduced compulsory education for all children through the fourth grade. This was part of the government's goal of establishing a nationwide elementary and middle school system. To prepare teachers for these schools, the government also created a system of normal schools the same year. With the founding of the cabinet system in 1885, Japan's first Ministry of Education worked to build a variety of vocational and professional schools to give students chances to learn a trade or an occupation. By 1907, the ministry made elementary school education through the sixth grade mandatory. To prepare its best students for the national universities, the government also developed a set of higher schools (*kōtō gakkō*) between 1886 and 1901 that became feeder schools for the national universities (Gordon 2003, 106). Both middle schools and higher schools required the passage of difficult entrance exams that fostered a sense of eliteness among their graduates. Succeeding on these exams and attending top universities became their credentials for life, which separated them from others in Japanese society and created what Japanese refer to as a *gakureki shakai*, or a society based on one's academic training.

However, by the 1880s, many Japanese elites worried that this new education system sacrificed the traditional Neo-Confucian emphasis on loyalty to national authority for the immediate gain of national wealth. To correct this perceived imbalance, the Meiji state developed and promulgated the 1890 Imperial Rescript on Education. This document placed loyalty to the state as symbolized and embodied by the Japanese emperor as the subject's first priority. This became the educational doctrine that carried Japan through the dark years of militarism during the 1930s and early 1940s (Beauchamp 1987, 300–302). It would be bolstered later by the Ministry of Education's promulgation of "The Cardinal Principles of the National Polity" (*Kokutai no hongi*) in 1937, which reaffirmed loyalty to national authority as a Japanese subject's main duty in life.

THE AMERICAN EXPERIMENT AND THE POST-OCCUPATION YEARS

Japan's defeat in the Pacific War left Tokyo in shambles and led to the Japanese state's experiment with the American education system during the occupation years from 1945 to 1952. As part of its democratization and decentralization goals for Japanese society at large, the First United States Education Mission arrived in 1946 and soon began making recommendations for the wholesale transformation of the prewar Japanese educational system to the American model. Beauchamp notes that "many of these reforms, such a coeducation, comprehensive schools, and local control, were deeply rooted in the American democratic model but were dysfunctional when transported to the Japanese context" (Beauchamp 1987, 304). Despite these incongruities, Japanese officials from the Ministry of Education turned these recommendations into a number of educational laws that were passed in 1947 and 1949 that attempted to recreate the American model of education in Japan.

Again, as we observed in the Meiji period, once the occupation authorities left Japan in 1952, the officials at the Ministry of Education began to rescind and modify these laws. Several concepts from the prewar Japanese education system re-entered the education model: for example, the centralization of the school system under the direction of local administrations, the reintroduction of moral education in the curriculum, and the reversion to a society where one's social status was based on one's academic background, which in turn, revitalized the significance of the university entrance exams in determining one's future employment (Beauchamp 1987, 306–8). Additionally, members of Japan's business community put pressure on the Ministry of Education in the 1950s to develop a curriculum that would give more weight to the study of mathematics, science, and technical skills in the classroom. As these changes were made to the educational model, they would help fuel Japan's phenomenal economic growth in the 1960s, '70s, and '80s.

EDUCATION REFORMS AND JAPAN'S LOST DECADE

However, the country's tremendous economic growth reached its limit in the mid-1990s, and the Japanese government again began to rethink its educational model. This time, as Edward Beauchamp has observed, the Ministry of Education argued that "educational expansion had run its course, and there was now a need to move in the direction of improving the quality of education" (Beauchamp 1987, 319). Of course, how to define and then develop "the quality of education" had been subject to much debate since the 1970s. External entities like the Organization for Economic Co-operation and Development (OECD) stressed that Japanese schools needed to relieve the pressure on students to excel on entrance examinations so that they could assert their own personalities and develop their own creative talents and unique viewpoints. Domestic critics contended that the over-centralization and the standardization of the education system reduced social mobility and was contributing to both the problem of *ijime* or school "bullying" and the increasing number of dropouts in Japanese schools (Beauchamp 1987, 320–4). The solution, then, was to provide a more "relaxed or pressure-free" educational experience that took shape in the *yutori kyōiku* reforms the government began to implement in the 1990s.

Japan entered a long period of incremental economic growth in the so-called "lost decade" of the 1990s that has extended into the 21st century. This period of economic difficulties also framed government attempts to strengthen the *yutori* education reforms. Following the merging of the Ministry of Education with Science, Sports, and Culture and the Science and Technology Agency to create MEXT in 2001, the ministry produced a new Handbook for Education (*Gakushū Shidō Yōryō*), which it distributed in 2002. Its goal was to develop a sincere desire to learn among students (Fish 2016). To that end, MEXT lessened the total number of hours that students spent in school, eliminating Saturday morning classes. It reduced the

Students take the national achievement examination in Tokyo, Japan, 2015. Japan is working to develop educational reforms that balance the goal of cultivating a genuine desire to learn with public expectations of academic excellence in schools. (The Asahi Shimbun via Getty Images)

time spent on certain academic subjects during classes, and it sponsored the creation of an "integrated studies" curriculum to foster lifelong learning along with other reforms. As Robert Fish, a historian of Japanese education, has noted, these changes had a negative impact on Japanese students' results on international achievement tests like the TMMS (Trends in International Mathematics and Science Study) and the PISA (Program for International Student Assessment) (Fish 2016). In Tokyo and elsewhere, MEXT responded by gradually increasing the number of hours spent on key subjects in the classroom, and by 2007 had introduced standardizing testing in the sixth and ninth grades. Based on the information gained from the student and teacher surveys that accompanied this testing, MEXT continues to revise the *yutori* educational reforms (Fish 2016).

Additional changes were made in 2012, and another update is planned for 2017 following the latest PISA results announced in December 2016. Yet MEXT has already been working on new ways of dealing with the social problems of bullying and truancy that have continued to grow since the 1980s in Japanese schools. During the years leading up to educational reforms in 2007, MEXT began drawing on the "community school model" from the United Kingdom. The goal was to decentralize control of the schools in some areas of Japan and to integrate local people's ideas and their direct participation into the education model. With parents and local people taking part in the management of the schools, the government hopes that this renewed sense of community will mean that fewer children slip through the cracks, while local people hope that more of the children will stay home and contribute to maintaining local traditions (*Japan Times* 2005). In 2016, the government introduced in certain Tokyo schools a compulsory nine-year school system. This system combines elementary and middle school to ease the difficult transition for students during the first year of middle school when much of the bullying occurs. There are challenges to this system, such as teachers and principals obtaining certification to teach at both the elementary and middle school levels. Yet MEXT has already started the process of launching this compulsory nine-year school system nationwide (*Japan Times* 2016). In this way, the Japanese government and its people continue to renovate and increasingly innovate their education system to meet the challenges of the 21st century.

Jeff E. Long

See also: Schools: Boston, United States: A Model City of STEM Education; Seoul, South Korea: "Education Fever"

Further Reading

Beauchamp, Edward R. 1987. "The Development of Japanese Educational Policy, 1945–85." *History of Education Quarterly*, 27, 3 (Autumn): 299–324.

Berlatsky, Noah. 2013. "Japan's Cutthroat School System: A Cautionary Tale for the U.S." *Atlantic*, November 22. https://www.theatlantic.com/education/archive/2013/11/japans-cutthroat-school-system-a-cautionary-tale-for-the-us/281612/.education/archive/2013/11/japans-cutthroat-school-system-a-cautionary-tale-for-the-us/281612/.

"Compulsory Nine-Year School System Kicks Off in Japan." 2016. *Japan Times*, June 10.

Fish, Robert. 2016. "Japan: Recent Trends in Education Reform." Asia Society. https://asiasociety.org/global-cities-education-network/japan-recent-trends-education-reform.

Gordon, Andrew. 2003. *A Modern History of Japan: From Tokugawa Times to the Present*. New York: Oxford University Press.

Lincicome, Mark E. 1993. *Principle, Praxis, and the Politics of Educational Reform in Meiji Japan*. Honolulu: University of Hawai'i Press.

MEXT, Ministry of Education, Culture, Sports, Science and Technology Japan. http://www.mext.go.jp/en/.

Yokota, Minora. 2005. "Kyoto's Community Schools Let Locals Call the Shots." *Japan Times*, September 20.

Vologda, Russia: Education in the Russian Federation—A City's Solutions

The city of Vologda is the capital of the Vologda region, which is situated in the northwestern part of Russia and is one of the 85 subjects of the Russian Federation. The city is approximately 300 miles from Moscow, the capital of Russia, and about 340 miles from St. Petersburg, the second-largest city in Russia and its cultural capital. Vologda is a typical ancient Russian city, founded—according to the official history—in 1147 and thus a contemporary of Moscow. According to a legend, Vologda had a chance to become a capital of Russia in the 16th century, when the tsar, Ivan the Great (also called Ivan the Terrible) intended to move the capital from Moscow to Vologda. Nevertheless, it did not happen, and in the course of history, Vologda became the capital of the Vologda region. The population of the city of Vologda is about 320,600 (2016), according to Vologda Municipality. Vologda is an important economic center, one of the largest transportation hubs in northwest Russia, with a well-developed public transportation system, represented by buses and trolleys. The cultural landscape is also quite impressive, with many museums, galleries, theatres, cinemas, concert halls, and so on.

Like other cities in the Russian Federation, Vologda presents a diversified system of educational institutions, from kindergartens, comprehensive primary and secondary schools, colleges and universities to postdoctoral programs. Vologda can be viewed as an example of national educational traditions, established before the revolution and developed during the Soviet times. Nowadays, however, Russia is going through a reform process and encounters numerous challenges.

In the Russian Federation, education is mainly provided by the state, and educational practices are regulated through the Law of Education and controlled by the Ministry of Education and Science. According to the law, the 11-year general education in Russia is compulsory for all the citizens of the Russian Federation who are under 18 years old (Lenta.ru. News Agency) and may be provided by educational institutions or in the form of homeschooling (Article 63, point 2). Regions, however, differ in terms of number and types of educational institutions. These differences are stipulated by the population, geography, climate, and dominant industry.

According to the Law of Education, the educational system in Russia is divided into general education, professional education, additional (or supplementary) education, and vocational training.

General education includes the following four levels: preschool education, primary (or elementary) school (grades 1–4), basic general education (middle school, grades 5–9), and high school (secondary) education (grades 10–11).

All these levels are presented in various ways in Vologda.

PRESCHOOL EDUCATION

The preschool education is provided by the kindergartens, established in Russia in the 1860s. Nowadays, the kindergartens in Russia are mainly run by the state, and this system is well developed. The most common types of kindergartens are:

- Nurseries, for children between 1.5 and 3 years old;
- Public (municipal) kindergartens, accommodating children between 3 and 7 years old.

The relatively low fees of kindergartens (since February 1, 2017, in the Vologda region, it is 92.87 rubles per day or US$1.50) ("Fee increase for kindergarten") and hours of operation (from 7 a.m. till 7 p.m.) make them a desirable option for working parents. Nevertheless, due to the rise in birth rate, kindergartens lack capacity, which necessitates the enrollment of kids very early, almost right after the birth. This situation has resulted in the establishment of private kindergartens that often provide better services, but are significantly more expensive, which makes them inaccessible for many parents.

ELEMENTARY SCHOOL

Elementary education lasts four years and covers grades one through four. The school year begins on September 1 all over Russia. Children start attending the school between 6 and 7 years (i.e., by September 1 a child must be at least 6.5 years old). Traditionally, in elementary school, there is one teacher for all subjects except foreign languages, music, and exercise sciences. This person usually acts as a homeroom teacher and communicates with parents, organizes meetings with parents, as well as extracurricular activities for students. Beginning from the second grade, children start learning a foreign language (English in most schools). School in Russia is basically free, but, in most cases, parents have to contribute money for additional learning materials, renovation of the school building, or expenses for extracurricular activities.

Elementary school children are usually separated from upper-grade students, occupying either a dedicated floor or a side wing of a school building. Only in rare cases would an elementary school occupy a separate building. Usually, children go to the school according to place of residence, usually the closest school to their home. To have their child enrolled, parents have to submit an application. School access is guaranteed to every child. Vologda has 721 daycare centers and nursery schools and 538 secondary schools, with over 120,000 pupils enrolled (Vologda Oblast).

Nevertheless, in every city, there are prestigious, higher-ranked schools (gymnasiums or lyceums), or those that specialize in certain subjects (e.g., foreign languages, sciences, natural sciences, etc.). To enroll into such a specialized school, it is necessary to attend preparatory courses and pass entrance examinations. This approach offers certain advantages—such schools admit children who are intellectually and psychologically better prepared for the academic workload and amount of homework and are more motivated. Furthermore, these schools give gifted children a better chance to develop their abilities and study at a faster pace than their counterparts in regular schools. However, many parents believe that all schools (at least at the elementary level) provide equal education. They are more concerned with the psychological comfort of their children, enrolling them in schools located close to their home.

SECONDARY EDUCATION

Secondary education in Russia embraces grades from 5 through 11 and lasts seven years. This level is divided into incomplete secondary education (grades 5–9) and high school (or complete secondary education) (grades 10–11). In a standard school, students have a unified schedule and do not choose elective subjects.

In a secondary school, unlike the elementary school, students move from one classroom to another, and classrooms are allotted for certain disciplines, especially those that need special equipment (e.g., physics, chemistry, biology).

The main standard subjects are Russian language and literature, algebra, geometry, physics, chemistry, biology, history, geography, social sciences, foreign languages, information technologies, music, art, and physical education (sports). Classes usually last 40–45 minutes, and there are on average six classes per day.

The grading scale is officially from 1 to 5, with 5 (or excellent) as the highest grade, 4 is good, 3 is "satisfactory, and 2 is unsatisfactory. Since 1 is almost never assigned to students, the grading system consists of only four grades. In practice, teachers may also add + or − to students' grade. Therefore, the best answer or written assignment may be graded as 5+. This gives the teacher an opportunity to distinguish between different levels of knowledge: 4+ is somewhat better than 4, and 3− may be given to enable a student with the unsatisfactory grade in a certain subject to pass the examination and move into the next grade. Nevertheless, such grades may not be given in official exams and are never seen in school certificates.

After the ninth grade, students have two options: they go either to a high school or to a vocational school (now called "college"). Unlike in the United States, colleges in Russia are not institutions of higher education, instead representing a type of school providing professional training. This is the result of a renaming process in Russia that has been going since the 2000s. Earlier, in the Soviet time, colleges were called *Professionalno-technicheskoe uchilishche* (technical vocational school) and *technikums* (higher technical vocational school). Students may enter colleges after the 9th grade or after the 11th.

In Vologda, there are 10 colleges and 4 technical schools (technikums) ("Colleges in Vologda 2017"). Among the most popular are Teacher Training College, Vologda Regional Medical College, Vologda Construction College, and others. After graduation from a college, students may start working or apply to a university.

Along with standard secondary schools, there are specialized schools with advanced study of one or several subjects—this may be a foreign language (English or German being the most popular), mathematics and sciences, or liberal arts.

According to new federal state academic standards, bifurcation of general education in Russia takes place in high school (grades 10–11). However, in certain educational institutions, bifurcation starts much earlier, after elementary school (i.e., from the fifth grade). Schools usually offer the following areas of high school education: liberal arts, sciences, or natural sciences. In some cases, they may also specialize in social sciences or information technologies.

In the Vologda Multidisciplinary Lyceum, for instance, specialization starts early. Established in 1992, the lyceum is currently among the top 25 schools in Russia. The institution excels in placement of its students into prestigious universities, achievements in national and international academic competitions (Academic Olympics), and results of the Unified State Examination.

Lyceum applicants have to take several entrance examinations and pass interviews with members of the selection committee. The applicants' results are converted into rankings, and it is the ranking that determines the future specialization—those with better results typically opt for sciences, while the rest are directed toward the liberal arts. Both streams have a rigorous program of advanced study of either sciences or liberal arts as well as a number of additional disciplines. For example, in a liberal arts class, there is an increased number of academic hours for such subjects as literature, Russian language, history, and foreign languages. The lyceum provides each student with an individually tailored learning program. According to this program, students have additional classes in the afternoon—mostly specialized courses in their major subjects, tutorial sessions intended to prepare the learners for the Academic Olympics or help them with their research projects.

Like everywhere in Russia, lyceum works according to the class-and-lesson system. Classes consist of 20–24 students (a regular school typically has 30–35 students in a class), and every class has lessons according to the schedule. Lyceum students have six to seven classes per day (from 8:00 a.m. to 2:30–3:30 p.m.) six days a week, and they stay for one or two additional lessons until 4:30 or 5:30 p.m. Teachers in the lyceum usually have rich teaching experience. Among the teachers, there are sometimes university professors with PhD degrees.

At the end of the 11th grade, all students take the Unified State Examination in several subjects, with Russian language and mathematics as mandatory subjects and several electives (reflecting students' interests). At this stage, the secondary education is considered completed, and young people may go to a university or other type of tertiary educational institution (academies, conservatories, etc.), acquire professional education in a college (vocational school), or start working. In fact, upon graduation from the lyceum, an overwhelming majority of alumni become students at prestigious universities in Moscow or St. Petersburg (the two largest cities in Russia), or apply for study abroad.

UNIVERSITY LEVEL OF EDUCATION

University education in Russia consists of several levels: bachelor's (four years) and master's (two years) degrees. Some universities provide five-year education, with a specialist degree. Universities also provide opportunities to obtain graduate and postgraduate degrees.

In Vologda, after graduating from a school, students get access to a wide variety of educational opportunities. There are basically three options: some students with better results in the State Unified Examination try to enter universities in bigger cities like Moscow and St. Petersburg. Relatively fewer students go to study abroad. And those students who decide to stay in Vologda may choose among several universities. The universities in Vologda face strong competition in the educational market. The appeal of studying in a city like Vologda is the relatively low cost of both education and living in comparison with the capitals and other bigger cities. Another point specific to Russian culture is that many students prefer to stay with their parents until they graduate, and many choose not to move out of the city immediately after graduation. That is why the majority of students of Vologda universities come from the city of Vologda, from other cities and villages of the Vologda region such as Cherepovets, Totma, Sokol, etc. Many also come from the northern regions of Russia, such as the Archangelsk, Murmansk, and Komi regions where climate conditions are harsh.

The largest university in the city of Vologda is Vologda State University, with currently over 13,000 students. It is the largest educational and research center among Vologda's universities and offers the most varied educational and training programs. According to its official website, the university offers degree programs at the bachelor's, master's, and doctoral levels in a wide range of professional fields.

During its history, the university has experienced several changes in status and title: initially, it was established in 1966 as a branch of North-Western Polytechnic Institute. In 1975, it was reorganized into the Vologda Polytechnical Institute. In 1999, the institute was given the rank of a university and the name of Vologda State Technical University. In 2013, it was renamed Vologda State University. In June 2014, another university, Vologda State Pedagogical University (then the second largest), was attached to it ("University"). Now, the university consists of 15 departments and machine-building training college and provides bachelor's, specialist's, and master's degree programs.

Until the 1990s, the institutions of higher education were funded by the state and education was free. Now, the universities are only partly financed by the state and have a limited number of tuition waivers (universities and departments determine that number on a yearly basis). The main tendency all over Russia, as well as in Vologda, is that technical and engineering departments offer more tuition waivers in comparison with liberal arts or economic or law departments. Thus, only applicants with top scores in the Unified State Examination have a chance to study free of charge.

Along with Vologda State University, there are three other universities: Vologda State Agricultural Academy, Vologda Institute of Law and Economics, and Vologda Business Institute. There are also branch campuses of school of Moscow and St. Petersburg, including Moscow State Law Academy, St. Petersburg State University of Engineering and Economics, North-West Academy of Public Service, University of International Law and Economics named after A. Griboedov, Modern Humanitarian Academy, and Moscow University of Business and Modern Technologies ("Students").

After graduating from the university with a bachelor's degree, students may enter the master's program, which lasts two years. Those who are interested in research and scientific work may enter the postgraduate program, which lasts three years. After the successful defense of their dissertation, postgraduates obtain a degree of candidate of sciences, which is the Russian equivalent to PhD. The next step is a postdoctoral fellowship with the Dr. Habil degree. Overall, Vologda strives to be competitive in the northwest region of Russia in offering the best education at every level.

Elena Krasilnikova

See also: Schools: Xi'an, China: Where China's Private Education Debuts

Further Reading

"Colleges in Vologda 2017." *Vsekolledzhi.ru* (in Russian). http://www.vsekolledzhi.ru/kolledzh/city/vologda.

"Fee Increase for Kindergarten in Vologda" ("V Vologde uvelichitsia plata za detskiy sad") (in Russian). *MK RU*, January 19, 2017. http://vologda.mk.ru/articles/2017/01/19/v-vologde-uvelichitsya-plata-za-detskiy-sad.html.

"Law of Education in RF." http://zakon-ob-obrazovanii.ru/10.html.

Lenta.ru. News Agency. 2007. "State Duma Introduced Mandatory 11-Year Education" (in Russian). "Gosduma vvela obyazatelnoe 11-letnee obrazovanie." *Lenta.ru*. July 6. https://lenta.ru/news/2007/07/06/education.

Official Portal of the Government of the Vologda Region. http://www.vologda-oblast.ru/vlast/pravitelstvo_oblasti.

"Students." http://tour.vologda-portal.ru/students.

"University." *Official site of the Vologda State University.* 2017. https://vogu35.ru/home/istoriya-universiteta.

Vologda Municipality. https://vologda-oblast.ru/en/municipalities/vologda/ .

Vologda Municipality. "Schools in Russia" ("Rossiiskie shkoly"). http://russianschools.ru/vologda.

Vologda Oblast Official Website. https://vologda-oblast.ru/en/about_the_region/education/secondary_education/.

Xi'an, China: Where China's Private Education Debuts

Xi'an is the capital city of Shaanxi Province and the largest metropolis in China's northwest with a population of 8.7 million. The greater Xi'an area covers more than 10,000 square kilometers. The city is an important national base for industrial development, scientific research, education, and tourism, and its key industries include manufacturing, advanced technology, tourism, culture, and modern services. Being an important "one belt one road" city in the nation, Xi'an aims to become an international metropolis, and according to the urban development plan approved by China's central government, will by 2020 have an urban population of more than 10 million and an urban area of more than 800 square kilometers.

A HISTORICAL CAPITAL CITY

Known as "Changan" (eternal peace) in ancient times, Xi'an has 3,100 years of urban culture establishment and 1,100 years of being the capital of 13 dynasties. It was once the starting point of the ancient Silk Road. The city prides itself for being one of the four civilized ancient capitals along with Athens, Rome, and Cairo. It is a world-famous tourist city, and an inexhaustible treasure house of historical relics. Tourists flock to Xi'an all year round; ceremonies are commonly held in the city to welcome heads of states. In Xi'an, not only have the Terra-Cotta Warriors been the most visited historical and cultural site in the country, but also the average citizen can tell stories of eminent figures from ancient dynasties. The saying goes that in Xi'an, a random piece of brick may turn out to be a valuable antique from ancient times.

In Xi'an, modern development and prosperity exist in the middle of the traditional environment, which includes the narrower streets, the ancient city wall, the modern commercial buildings in the ancient empire style, the site of the starting place of the ancient Silk Road on a busy commercial street, and so on. The city wall is one of the largest ancient military defense systems, and the most complete extant ancient city wall in China. It was built in the early Ming Dynasty (1368–1644) and renovated in recent years. Outside the city wall is a moat, and a circular park has now been built along the high wall and the deep moat. When dust falls and the haze vanishes in the darkness, one enjoys beautiful lights that sketch the contours of the stately buildings, modern city structures, and ancient sites. Travelers are impressed by the city's night life, blended-in historical and cultural features, and the variety of cultural events.

COULD TRADITION BE A CHALLENGE TO DEVELOPMENT?

An ancient civilization may become a challenge to development in that it generates complacency and fear of those who wish to make changes. China's success in ancient times had nurtured a great resistance to change. As a result, China was surpassed by Western civilization in the era of the industrial revolution. The reforms and opening that started about 40 years ago finally made China realize how far it had fallen behind economically and socially, as well as the urgency to get back on the track of continued development.

A good example is the city of Xi'an, and the Shaanxi Province it governs. Comparatively and in terms of economic development (measured by GDP), Shaanxi has been lagging behind not only the four province-equivalent municipalities of Beijing, Shanghai, Tianjin, and Chongqing, but also behind the coastal provinces of Zhejiang, Jiangsu, Guangdong, Shandong. Moreover, it fails to measure up to some inland provinces such as Hubei and Sichuan. Likewise, Xi'an's economic development ranks lower in the list of major metropolises. Outward mobility of human resources, especially highly educated talent, has been an adverse factor in the development of both the province and the city. In addition to the brain drain, the geographical and historical context may have contributed to a complacency and a mindset that is unwilling to dynamically improve.

Geographically, Xi'an shares with other inland cities the problems of higher logistical cost, underdeveloped infrastructure for transnational corporations to locate their headquarters, difficulties in attracting talent, and lack of exposure for the common people to the outside world.

As a result, there is a reluctance to change. Forward thinking, seeking improvement and new ways of development to become a world-class metropolis, appear to be thwarted by an inertial force. This mindset is reflected in what people in Xi'an describe as "city wall thinking"—too good to change. Compared to coastal cities as well as neighboring cities of Chengdu and Chongqing that have similar inland city conditions, Xi'an's pace of life is much more relaxed; people seem less interested in the outside world, bureaucracy tends to be more prevalent, and market services are less customer-friendly.

Xi'an is one of the cities where the legacy of a state-owned economy is deeply rooted. Being a leader in heavy industry, the defense industry, and state enterprises, sectors that were the core of the central planning era, Xi'an inherits a tremendous inertia with respect to reform. In the recent Provincial Conference on Technological Innovation, it was reported that Shaanxi's economy faces several problems of intra-provincial imbalance in regional development. This is reflected in heavy reliance on energy industries and an underdeveloped service sector. Businesses' lack of innovation further exacerbates the problems.

PRIVATE HIGHER EDUCATION

Shaanxi has sustained its status in the nation as a province with the most abundant resources in higher education, although its relative ranking has been declining. In 2012, there were 109 higher education institutions and 1.442 million enrolled students in the province, amounting to more than 6 percent of all students nationwide. Within the province, Xi'an houses more than 80 percent of public and private universities and colleges and 100 percent of the highly ranked research universities, according to the *Shaanxi Education Yearbook*. This is not uncommon, considering that allocating key resources such as higher education institutions to provincial capital cities is a typical feature of planning in China. In that sense, Xi'an qualifies as an educational powerhouse on the same footing with Beijing and Shanghai, Guangzhou, Wuhan, and Nanjing, although it is far from being a strong economic competitor.

Worth noting are the private higher education institutions in Xi'an that consist of nine four-year and nine two- to-three-year private colleges and universities, and 12 four-year "independent colleges" (out of 322 in 2015 nationwide) that are semi-private in nature. The semiprivate nature of the 12 independent colleges stems from their partnership with their affiliated public universities. The latter are typically able to granting PhDs. As such, independent colleges benefit from the established reputation and faculty resources of their affiliated public universities. For example, independent colleges may take advantage of the reputation of their affiliated universities to secure student enrollment. In return, however, they must submit an affiliation fee that may range from 10 to 30 percent of the tuition revenues to the universities. At the level of management, the supervising universities typically send representatives to assume top administrative positions at their affiliated colleges. Since most independent colleges are only semiprivate, our discussion here of private higher education institutions will focus on the four-year colleges and universities in Xi'an that are fully privately owned.

The nine private four-year colleges and universities in Shaanxi and Xi'an are shown in Table 1, all located in the Greater Xi'an metropolis of which Xianyang

Table 1   4-Year Colleges/Universities in Shaanxi and Xi'an

Name	Year Founded	City Located	Student Scale 2010	Student Scale 2015
Xi'an Peihua Univ.	1984	Xi'an	21184	21983
Xijing Univ.	1994	Xi'an	22058	22171
Eurasia Univ.	1995	Xi'an	18654	21807
Xi'an Intl Univ.	1992	Xi'an	19814	24993
Xi'an Fanyi Univ.	1987	Xi'an	17559	22395
Xi'an Siyuan Univ.	1998	Xi'an	13362	18733
Shaanxi Institute of Intl. Trade & Commerce	1997	Xianyang	9069	15127
Shaanxi Fashion Engineering Univ.	1995	Xianyang	7556	10438
Xi'an Traffic Engineering Institute	1994	Xi'an	7036	6746

Source: Research on the Development of Quality Private Higher Education in Shaanxi Province, by Li Weimin and Yin Bingbing, Shaanxi People's Publishing House, December 2016.

City is considered a part. Together with the aforementioned nine two- to three-year private colleges, the 18 of them comprise about 5.5 percent of the 330 private colleges in the nation. More impressive are the leading positions of the four-year colleges. According to the rankings by China's Alumni Association, on average four private colleges and universities in Xi'an would take the top 15 spots nationwide, and they are most often Xi'an International University (XAIU hereafter), Eurasia University, Xijing University, and Xi'an Fanyi University or Xi'an Peihua University. In 2015, for example, Xi'an International University was ranked no. 1 in enrollment size; Eurasia University ranked no. 4; Xi'an Fanyi University no. 13, and Xijing University, no. 15. In other words, about 30 percent of China's top 15 private four-year universities are located in Xi'an. No wonder a top Chinese official famously said, "Shaanxi possesses three No. 1's in the nation: converting farming land to forestry, record yield of apples, and private higher education." Private universities have become hot tourist spots as well—when visiting Xi'an, the recommendation goes, one must see two things: the Terra-Cotta Warriors and private universities.

CONTRIBUTING FACTORS TO PRIVATE HIGHER EDUCATION DEVELOPMENT

Opening and Reforms. Before 1978 when economic reforms were launched in China, central planning and public ownership were dominant concepts. Being an area that is especially ideologically sensitive, higher education reforms had prohibited private ownership of educational facilities until the 1990s (see Table 1). This was much later than the entry of private entrepreneurs in economic sectors that started in late 1970s. At their early stages, many of the owners, including the founder (Mr. Huang Teng) of XAIU (Xi'an International University), ran the risk of breaking the rule against private ownership of higher education and were prepared for the worst. It was the extremely strong demand for higher education and the shortage in supply of public universities that gave rise to the development of the private higher education institutions. Many started as training agencies. As the reforms and opening deepened and the private economy grew, private higher education institutions gradually evolved to degree-granting and accreditation by China's Education Ministry. However, it takes longer for discriminative policies and adversary attitudes against private higher education to gradually diminish. Even today, while government policies advocate equal treatment of public and private higher education institutions, the public and those who work at public colleges and universities still deem their counterparts at private institutions as "system outsiders," making it more difficult for private institutions in recruiting and retention.

Nonetheless, private higher education survived, and most of the schools have become medium-scaled universities of more than 20,000 students (see Table 1), with beautiful campuses, and decent academic quality. Take XAIU as an example. Although it has a history of only 25 years, it is not only accredited by China's Education Ministry for four-year baccalaureate programs, but also enrolls more than 23,000 students. The school employs about 2,000 faculty and staff, and has a beautiful campus. XAIU places its emphasis on quality education and aims to become a world-class university.

Systemic Advantages. The systemic advantages of China's private higher education, compared with public colleges and universities, can be summarized thus: 1) as system outsiders with little government support to rely on, they are much more sensitive to social and market demand, which allows them to quickly react and make necessary changes; 2) as a result of much shorter chain of command and much less bureaucracy, private institutions are efficient in decision making and implementation; 3) private institutions are more effective in controlling costs, and maintain clear property rights; whereas their public counterparts are struggling with soft budget constraints; 4) the faculty have a clear sense of responsibility. Rules of hiring and firing are more effectively implemented commensurate with performance.

In the global picture, China's private higher education is gaining momentum. Its efficiency surpasses that of public universities, much like the private sector in the Chinese economy that outruns the state-owned sector in growth and expansion. As an example, XAIU recently set up a Research Institute on Shaanxi's Free Trade Zone, less than four months after the Free Trade Zone was approved by the central government. The institute provides a platform to gather scholars and resources nationwide and internationally. XAIU aims to become a think tank for the economic development of the province, especially for the one belt one road plan. This agile action caught the academic community and policy circle by surprise and has considerably narrowed the gap in the area of research between XAIU and public universities that are relatively more resource abundant. As another example, XAIU established the College of Entrepreneurship Education in 2009, long before the launch of Massive Innovative and Entrepreneurship Practices by the central government in 2015. Being far ahead, the College of Entrepreneurship Education at XAIU has been visited by followers from all over the country, and the university has been designated one of the 2016 National Top 50 Universities and Colleges of Outstanding Experiences in Creativity and Entrepreneurship Education by China's Education Ministry.

Tourism. As mentioned earlier, Xi'an has been a top tourist destination in China, which has created high demand for foreign-language interpreting services. The demand has continuously been met by private entrepreneurs who initially set up language training agencies. This was the model of early development of many private universities in Xi'an, such as Xi'an International University and Xi'an Fanyi University. They later grew into degree-granting full-fledged colleges and universities thanks to the overall strong demand for higher education. As Chairman Huang Teng of XAIU stated, "I had expected that it would be quite ambitious to expand my training school into one with 3,000 students, but never imagined I could turn it into a university of more than 20,000 students."

Challenges Ahead. At the early stage of private higher education, it was relatively easy for schools to survive. The agglomeration effect results primarily from schools learning from and helping one another other to develop and expand. As the scales of the schools stabilized, they have continued to benefit from mutual support. This includes reaching out to the society as a group raising awareness, seeking fairness of policy, and sharing teaching resources. The agglomeration effect has been the most important contributing factor to Xi'an's leading position in

> ### One Belt One Road
>
> Launched in 2013 by President Xi Jinping, the "one belt one road" (OBOR) initiative is aimed at expanding trade relationships globally. The "belt" and "road" refer to the Silk Road Economic Belt and the 21st-centry Maritime Silk Road. Under the OBOR initiative, China plans to spend billions of dollars in infrastructure construction in countries in Central Asia, Russia, European Union countries, and South Asia. Infrastructure projects include high-speed rails, roads, bridges, and ports. It is speculated that through OBOR, China will create markets for its excess capacities in cement, steel, and other materials. At the geopolitical level, experts believe that China under President Xi Jinping appears to be breaking away from former leader Deng Xiaoping's policy of keeping a low profile and never taking the lead in the international arena. Per Chinese government's reports, as of 2016, several projects have started, including the Hungary-Siberia Railway, the Jakarta-Bandung High-Speed Rail, the China-Laos Railway, and the China-Thailand Railway. The China-Russia-Mongolia economic corridor, the Eurasian Land Bridge economic corridor, and the Bangladesh-China-India-Myanmar economic corridor are reportedly progressing. However, OBOR faces strong headwinds. Concerns have been raised on China's new expansionary policy by countries in the South China Sea where territorial tensions are on the rise. Additionally, developments along the westward land route traversing through territories influenced by extremist religious groups are bound to face many challenges. President Xi Jinping has assured the world that the OBOR initiative is based on three principles: 1) projects must result from extensive consultation, joint contribution, and yield shared benefits; 2) OBOR is open and inclusive rather than exclusive; and 3) OBOR will not be a solo venture by China, but rather a chorus of all countries along the routes.

private higher education. Such an effect has kept the private schools continuously expanding, made the provincial government take the lead in designing supportive policies, and initiated a new era in which private and public higher education institutions start to mingle and to ignore the ownership labeling.

At the current stage, however, as China's higher education enters the stage of intensive development with a focus on quality, the "learning from each other" stage is being gradually replaced by fierce competition. Institutions compete for scarce resources to solidify and enhance the quality of fields of specialty, for winning fiscal support and better enrollment. While competition could mean pressure on college owners and administrators at every level, it is obvious that competition is a better engine for progress.

In conclusion, while most of the successful private enterprises are headquartered in coastal cities and almost none in Xi'an due to historical, cultural, and economic structural factors, Xi'an boasts a leading position in private higher education with its institutions possessing 30 percent of the top rankings in the nation. Continuing the tradition of placing great emphasis on education, expansive tourism, stronger government support, and especially in-group support are all contributing factors. The government is currently addressing an important question of how to sustain Shaanxi and Xi'an's lead in higher education. More importantly, how to synchronize higher education with economic and social development is of prime importance. Private institutions are taking the lead in the search for solutions.

Aimin Chen

See also: Schools: Bamako, Mali: Private and Public Sectors of Education; Vologda, Russia: Education in the Russian Federation—A City's Solutions

Further Reading

About Xi'an (The official website of Xi'an Municipality) (in Chinese). http://www.xa.gov.cn/ptl/def/def/index_1121_6774_ci_trid_1111932.html.

Li Weimin, and Yin Bingbing. 2016. *Research on the Development of Quality Private Higher Education in Shaanxi Province.* Shaanxi People's Publishing House.

Shaanxi Education Yearbook. 2013. Shaanxi Provincial Government (in Chinese).

Xi'an International University. http://www.xaiu.edu.cn.

Traffic and Transportation

OVERVIEW

Transportation is critical to almost every function of a city. Congested transportation hampers a city's mobility and productivity. As cities are home to more than half of the world's population and produce more than half of the global GDP today, urban transportation is experiencing more pressure than ever before. According to the World Bank, cities in developing countries typically devote 15 to 25 percent of their expenditures to improving transport systems, and between 8 and 16 percent of urban households' income is typically spent on transport. For low-income households, the proportion of spending on transport could be higher. The articles included in this section reflect the struggles to improve conditions of transportation by 10 megacities in the world. Large cities tend to suffer from the highest travel times, the greatest congestion, and the most polluted environments. The World Bank's vision of sustainable transport includes these fundamentals: 1) equal accessibility; 2) safety and security; 3) efficiency and reliability; and 4) environmental friendliness (Irigoyen 2017).

Challenges Faced by Transitional Economies

Improving a city's transport is a comprehensive undertaking and primarily the obligation of the government. In former central planning economies today, because the tradition of state control fades rather slowly, the transition from production-centered and government-provided transport services can be a slow process as well. Typically, due to underdeveloped market mechanisms, many services are free or disproportionally low priced. Parking is one example. As a result, roads tend to be congested due to uncontrolled parking. Emission control is another weak area—vehicles fall behind environmental standards, causing severe air pollution.

Beijing's situation is a typical example. Residents compare the city's traffic congestion to the frequent smog attacks for which improvement is unreliable and short-lived. While the city spends billions on constructing new beltways, the reality is that roads are only getting more clogged. Experts have identified multiple sources of problems, one of which is the city's growing population reaching almost 22 million as of 2018, which means increasing pressure on the public transit. Furthermore, when the middle class drive private cars, the pressure on the road system can be great. On the other hand, being a historical and capital city, spaces for developing new service lines are rather limited. Additionally, the Beijing municipality appears to be unwilling to give up the "ring road" design. The concentrically laid-out ring road system is believed to symbolize central leadership. However, experts have found that such a design can be vulnerable to minor traffic jams in the inner rings. To deal with the traffic problems, Beijing borrows from the experiences of megacities in the West, including charging congestion fees, rotating driving days by license numbers, and charging parking fees. Improvement such as these have yielded short-term results. Experts believe that in the long run, because Beijing will remain at the forefront of rural-to-urban migration for many years to come, road congestion will not likely see significant relief anytime soon.

Similar to Beijing, the tradition of central planning remains consequential in Russia. The city of Saint Petersburg is an economic boomtown and one of the most densely populated cities in Russia. A typical phenomenon of the central planning economy is that the population distribution in a city can be severely skewed. Because services are more available in production centers, communities in these areas tend to be highly dense. This is reflected in St. Petersburg: 90 percent of the city's population is concentrated in a part of the city of just 234 square miles out of 550 square miles total. The impact on traffic is significant, according to Kovalyuk. Economic ramp-up in the past decade has generated influx and a growing number of middle-class families owning cars. However, road conditions and public transits have not caught up. As such, streets are generally congested with crawling lines of cars and trucks. Rush hours are particularly clogged. Additionally, due to insufficient safety protection for passengers on public transits and the high price of the metro fare, people prefer using personal vehicles. The temperature, dropping to below freezing as early as November, is another factor that slows the traffic. Saint Petersburg has been struggling with these problems since 2014; measures have included upgrading the capacity of subway cars, making subway stations more accessible, upgrading conditions of transit stops, and introducing penalties for illegal parking. The city also taps into tourist transport, such as waterbuses, and makes them a regular part of the public transit. Meanwhile, the city has set up a budget for building bike lanes and a transport information system.

Improving Transport Depends on Efficient Management

It is a fact that the expansion in road spaces never catches up with the growing number of cars. Experience shows that increasing transport efficiency means two things: adopting appropriate technology and changing people's travel behavior. Economically well-positioned cities tend to be able to afford rail-based mass transit. In these cities, for example, an information system allows travelers to create seamless multimodal travel. In low-income cities, however, technology is often out of reach. Another challenge is motorized two-wheelers and microbuses tend to be dominant. These inexpensive vehicles are major contributors of congestion and pollution. The contrast of traffic conditions between developing and developed cities can be astounding.

Stuttgart is the largest metropolis and the capital of the state of Baden-Wuerttemberg in Germany. Home to Mercedes-Benz and Porsche, Stuttgart takes pride in improving the daily commute. However, it was ranked Germany's worst city for congestion as recently as 2015. What turned the city around was the promotion of public transit. Trains, subways, and street railways are not only efficient, these electricity-powered vehicles are also environment-friendly. The city is creative in offering discount fares and convenient sales locations to encourage the public to use the transit system. A single ticket allows the passenger to ride on all kinds of public transit vehicles. Students enjoy free rides during certain periods on weekends and holidays by showing their student ID. The metro, known as Stadtbahn, allows passengers to bring bicycles along. Bicycles are a popular tool for commuting between city and suburbs. Stuttgart residents are mindful of the environment and willingly carpool. Technology allows people options without significant sacrifice in time and comfort. Pendlernetz Stuttgart is a website where people advertise carpool information. It is estimated that carpooling reduces cars on the road by 50 percent.

Osaka, the third-largest city in Japan, has a population of between 2.5 and 3.5 million, if one counts the daily commuters. To meet the need of moving millions of people to and from work in an orderly and spotless-clean fashion, as Karsner shows, Osaka has been creative in attracting private investments. To reduce the traffic congestion due to the city being part of a high-traffic-density region, known as the Osaka-Kobe-Kyoto region, Osaka promotes public transit. The city makes a tremendous effort in providing reliable travel information, which makes public transit more accommodative and comfortable to ride in. For example, the signage is given in various languages, and senior-friendly facilities are installed in all transits. The "No-My-Car-Day Pass" is good for unlimited rides on bus, metro, and tramlines every Friday and the 20th of each month. Experts believe that privatization of Osaka's transport system played a key role in the system's innovativeness. For example, in air transportation, limited land space and the disturbing noise of jet engines required that Osaka build its modern airport, the Kansai International Airport, offshore. The astronomical costs were funded through privatizing the airport's operation. However, while the government enthusiastically pursues private funds for building key infrastructure projects, some critics call the strategy a gamble.

Zurich, the largest city of Switzerland, has the reputation of being one of the most congested cities in the world. Experts believe the problem is related to the city's function as an important financial center in Europe. Because of traffic congestion, it is estimated that Zurich loses more than US$1 million a year in tardiness for work and delayed delivery of goods. To unclog the roads, the city taps into all kinds of public transportation, some traditional and some new. Zurich also encourages residents to ride bicycles to work. As a result, it has a convenient mix of public transit, including popular streetcars, trolleybuses, and the luxury S-Bahn. To remove the hassle of ticketing, a single-ticket system has been made available for riding all public transits. Encouraging residents to bike to work and for errands is still in its early stage. The city plans to install biker-friendly roads and parking spots by 2019. Currently, half of the trips in the city are taken on public transit.

Helping more than 8 million residents and tens of thousands of visitors get to their destinations in a timely way is the challenge of New York City's transport system. Typically, rapid transit is a powerful solution to traffic congestion in megacities. Almost every megacity in the world runs a high-speed transportation system such as a subway or light rail. In this area, New York's subway system stands out as a model of the industry. Opened in the early 20th century, the New York subway is the oldest in the world. As of this writing, the system operates 472 stations and serves a ridership of over 1.7 billion trips annually. The majority of New Yorkers and tourists ride the subway as their first choice. The subway plays a fundamental role in the city's status as one of the world's top cultural and financial centers. At the center of the subway's success are its convenience and affordability. Anyone unfamiliar with the system can quickly become a proficient rider. The subway is important in facilitating the decentralization of urban neighborhoods. It allows people to live remotely from their workplaces, which, on a broader scale, has led to the reduction of urban crowding. Experts also observe that in New York City the enhanced mobility gives rise to new commercial spaces, which in turn encourages gentrification in these areas.

Deployment of Technology Is an Effective Way to Improve Congestion

When financial resources are scarce, expensive projects, such as adding new roads or new bus lines, become unattainable. However, many improvements today can be achieved at a relatively lower cost with the help of technology. Through the adoption of traffic information apps, travelers can make optimal use of existing facilities. Likewise, modifications in daily routines, for residents with flexibility, can often significantly reduce the pressure on the transport system.

Casablanca, the largest city in Morocco and the country's economic hub, is home to 3 million people. Casablanca's metropolitan area has as many as 8 million residents, and most travel to work. As middle-class families gradually replace mopeds with cars, the roads become more congested over time. Moreover, building more roads has resulted in only limited relief. As a result, Casablanca's streets are a mix of modern tramlines, urban buses, "petit taxis," "grands taxis," mopeds, motorbikes, bikes, and pedestrians, as Ross describes. The taxi-Uber cars and the black-market taxis contribute even more to the chaos. The root of congestion in Casablanca, however, is more cultural than spatial: of the 11 million daily trips, half are made on foot by people who return home for lunch. The promise has been to develop a mass transit network. An RER network that combines rapid surface and underground service lines has been proposed since the 1970s, but has not materialized. Instead, Casablanca has phased in small-scale solutions, such as a number of tramlines constructed since 2012. It appears, however, that a modification in people's lunch routine could be worth trying.

Kolkata, India, has 14 million people and a burgeoning economy. In every aspect of modern urban life, the city is catching up with some of the most prolific megacities in Asia and Latin America. Likewise, overcrowding, traffic congestion, and vehicular pollution are plagues as well. The middle class prefer using private cars rather than the public transit for several reasons. Private cars reflect a person's well-being and social status, as Roy indicates. As in many developing cities, private cars are just beginning to replace bicycles rather than the other way around. Another reason why people are reluctant to use public transit is safety concerns—vandalism is a problem in public transit. To alleviate traffic congestion, the Kolkata government seeks every way to encourage people to take public transit. For example, the city is in the process of integrating the ticketing system by deploying smart card technology. It is expected that in the future when passengers can ride buses, light rail, subway metro, and trains using a single card, they will be more likely to give up mopeds and motor bikes. On the other hand, to improve air quality, the city sets up regulations to limit the use of motorized rickshaws and outdated gas-guzzler cars. Two strategies appear to be highly helpful for improving congestion, according to Roy: 1) putting fleets of modern public transit vehicles in service; and 2) constructing more roads, as Kolkata has one of the lowest road ratios in India. Acquiring swaths of land in a densely populated city is always an uphill battle.

Istanbul, Turkey, is home to more than 8 million people. Istanbul has also been at the top of TomTom's most congested cities list. The city's prosperous tourism and its geolocation are major causes of the problem, but they are a source of strength as well. The geo-commercial position makes Istanbul the growth engine of Turkey. Located between Asia and Europe, Istanbul benefits from commercial traffic from the two continents. However, this also means that millions of freight vehicles and passenger cars jam the roads constantly. Modifying the road system to phase in high-capacity public transit has not been successful due to the city's densely built historical environment. Politicians' solution has been to build more bridges and tunnels over and under the Bosporus Strait. These monumental constructions have been blamed for failing to bring relief to the city's internal roads. Experts believe that Istanbul will eventually have to find solutions in technology to control the traffic flow. Developing a rapid transit service is an urgent need, everyone agrees. In the meantime, however, popular and temporary solutions include "leave home early" and "buy a motorcycle."

Mexico City, Mexico, has a population of 8.8 million in the city's central districts, and 21 million if the population of the greater metropolitan region is included. Mexico City has been repeatedly ranked no. 1 on TomTom's list of the most congested cities in the world. The severe road congestion is responsible for loss of productivity, deteriorating quality of life, severe air pollution, and widened economic divide. As such, fighting traffic congestion has always been a top priority. There are multiple causes, the leading ones being inefficient urban governance, runaway housing developments, an unsafe and underused public transit system, and a fast-growing number of middle-class families owning cars. As many as 6.8 million people drive their own cars to work. Experts urge the city to promote public transit and remove subsidies for car buyers. Upgrading the public transit, however, involves building new service lines, improving security conditions, and installing a traffic information system. Moreover, regulating housing development can be a critical solution, because sprawling slums bring tremendous difficulties to transport services. These efforts require collaboration between the government and businesses. However, this is where plans fail: experts believe that weakness in policy enforcement is a major problem plaguing the municipal government. Additionally, the Mexican government is unwilling to remove subsidies for car purchases due to the impact of such a measure on the economy and employment. Furthermore, at the cultural level, there is a psychological stigma attached to the public transit. Clearly, improving transportation in Mexico City is a challenge at multiple levels.

Further Reading
Irigoyen, Joe Luis. 2017. "Transforming Transportation: Toward Sustainable Mobility for All." World Bank Blogs, January 1. http://blogs.worldbank.org/transport/transforming-transportation-toward-sustainable-mobility-all.
The United Nations. 2010. "Chapter 4. Sustainable Urban Transport." *A Guide for Sustainable Urban Development in the 21st Century.* https://sustainabledevelopment.un.org/content/documents/shanghaimanual.pdf.
The World Bank. 2002. Cities on the Move—Urban Transport Strategy Review. http://siteresources.worldbank.org/INTURBANTRANSPORT/Resources/cities_on_the_move.pdf.

Beijing, China: Beijing's War on Traffic Congestion

Ask a Beijinger what the worst inconvenience is in living in the capital city, and the answer is most likely *shoudu*. The sound of the word is homophonic to "capital city," but the words stand for "capital congestion." It's a pun. What it reveals is anguish over a worsening traffic congestion citizens find themselves trapped in every day. The Beijing Municipality has made a five-year plan, from 2016 to 2020, to resolve it. The solution, however, is expected to involve socioeconomic shifts that go far beyond traffic improvement.

"THE GREAT CRAWL"

There seems to be a good reason why many depict Beijing's traffic as a great crawl. According to the China Association of Automobile Manufacturers and the *Economist* magazine, in 2016 Beijing topped the list of megacities in China with 5.6 million vehicles in use, of which 3.6 million are privately owned (*Economist* 2016). Despite the fact that Beijing has fewer cars than Hong Kong, London, and New York City, Beijing's congestion is far worse. A 2011 *UBS* (a Swiss global financial service) traffic study shows that the average driving speed in Beijing was 7.5 miles per hour, compared to 10.1 in Shanghai, 12.4 in Hong Kong, 13.4 in Tokyo, 14 in Seoul, 15.5 in Singapore and New York City, and 18 in London (Colum 2013). During rush hours, a 30-minute drive is easily extended by 32 minutes. The Beijing Commission of Transportation cites "three highs"—high number of cars, high car usage, and high growth of car buying—underlying Beijing's traffic congestion. Additionally, 30 percent of Beijing's air pollution comes from car fumes (*Economist* 2016). In winter 2016, Beijing saw multiple "red smog alerts," which forced schools to close and construction to halt, so that people could stay indoors.

SOURCES OF CONGESTION: URBANIZATION— TOO MUCH TOO SOON

How did capital congestion come about? The answer lies in the rapid expansion that propelled China to the world's second-largest economy in just three decades. Economic expansion in China is synonymic to urbanization. In Beijing, multiple waves of urban territorial encroachment have drastically changed the city's demographics. The Sixth National Census (China's national census is conducted once every 10 years) in 2010 revealed that Beijing had added 6 million residents in a 10-year period to reach 19.6 million. The census also showed that the daily peak number of passengers taking public transit alone was 15.06 million, which is not uncommon, particularly, during tourist seasons. In 2018, Beijing's population was 21.7 million, more than London and New York combined, putting overwhelming pressure on the transportation system (Westcott 2018).

MORE RING ROADS, MORE CONGESTION

Beijing's roadway system is not adequate for handling modern traffic demands. The urban layout follows the city's traditional design, which is popularly known as a "pancake grid" where roads radiate outward from a central area. Beijing's central area, where cultural and government facilities are located, is about 40 square miles. Well-known structures include Jingshan Park, Forbidden City, Tiananmen Square, the Hall of the People's Congress, Zhongnanhai, Chairman Mao's Memorial Hall, and Qianmen. Most of these structures sit on a north-south axis line that passes under the emperor's throne in the Forbidden City, a historical urban design that stresses the emperor's power. The city's layout has not changed since the Mongol empire ruled over China from here in the 13th century. Since the 1950s, Beijing has been adding concentric expressways, known to the locals as "ring roads," that are similar to beltways in some American cities. The 7th Ring Road was just completed in 2018, connecting to Tianjin and the Hebei Province (Du 2018).

Many Beijing residents believe that instead of alleviating traffic congestion, these ring roads are making it worse. Typically, when an inner ring road is congested, the outer rings are congested as well, due to a shortage of bypasses and "micronetworks" between ring roads. Constructing bypasses has been difficult due to the presence of abundant military and governmental facilities, known by local residents as "big yards." In other areas of the city, clusters of historical sites and gated residential communities (occupied by the upper class) leave little room for roads to be built. As such, on occasions of state events—such as the National Day, the Party's anniversary, state official visits, international-level cultural and economic events

Heavy traffic in Beijing, China, 2016. The city has tried to mitigate its traffic problem by alternating driving days, charging parking fees, promoting public transit, and other measures. (Xi Zhang/Dreamstime.com)

(of which there are many)—the ring roads virtually become giant parking lots, particularly within the 5th Ring. The experience of driving on an inner ring road is likened to that of a merry-go-round—it is not easy to get on and off the road at a desired time and location.

Beijing's traffic congestion is also attributable to its underdeveloped public transportation system. Despite the fact that most residents live far away from work, only 12 to 13 percent travel by public transit, compared to 60 to 80 percent in big cities in developed countries. According to data from the Beijing Transportation Development and Research Center (BTDR), the density of road network within the 5th Ring Road is only .23 kilometers per square kilometer, or one-fifth of the network coverage in big cities of developed countries. As a result, although public bus lines have dedicated lanes, these lanes often don't connect to make a complete network. Rerouting is not uncommon and may waste much time during rush hours; the longest distance between connecting stations could be as far as 1.2 kilometers away (Cao 2013). Beijing's subway system deserves high praise as one of the cleanest and most reliable in the world. The network developed from 3 lines in 2002 to 18 lines today. It is also the most comfortable form of public transit in Beijing, with air-conditioning and plenty of room inside. However, the subway has become so overcrowded that Beijing's authorities have to selectively limit entrance to subway stations at peak times. Additionally, the subway fare system, which used to charge only 2 yuan for a one-way trip to any location in Beijing, was revamped in 2014 to charge according to the distance traveled.

Overall, taking public transit to work does not necessarily save time, according to BTDR. In fact, public transit is normally 2 to 2.5 times slower than cars (Cao 2013). This situation corroborates the finding that not only does Beijing have the highest number of private cars, but it also has the highest car usage rate. In the past, most Chinese urbanites viewed buying a car as a symbol of wealth and modernity. Today, more people drive for the sake of convenience and necessity. For someone who lives in the south suburbs and works in a north district in Beijing, it is simply quicker to drive a car and leave home earlier.

CHEAP PARKING MEANS MORE CONGESTION

There are, however, circumstances where poor management encourages people to drive instead of traveling by other means. One such situation is the extremely low parking cost. Cars are often found parked illegally on sidewalks, in alleys around apartment buildings, and in random spaces almost anywhere. Authorities often turn a blind eye to illegal parking, unless it interferes with traffic. As a result, drivers tend to avoid using legitimate parking facilities, despite the fact that they only charge a few yuan for the day. According to BTDR, 80 percent of the cars were parked without being charged in 2010—about 10 percent higher than the previous year (Cao 2013). Parking fee remains low despite increases. As of 2019, cars parked on curbside within the 3rd Ring Road is charged 15 yuan maximum (about USD$2) per hour between 7:00 a.m. and 7:00 p.m. The rate is dropped by one-third and lower outside the 3rd Ring (Bendibao.com 2019). As such, there has been little incentive to build fee-based garages. When the cost of driving is cheap, people are more inclined to own a car. The low cost of parking has been a major stimulus for car buying and directly contributes to road congestion. Experts believe that weak parking management is only one of the many areas where the government is unwilling to offend the middle class, who are sensitive to government-imposed fees and tend to raise questions and complaints. One achievement of the anti-corruption campaigns in recent years is that they have made citizens more and more inquisitive.

BEIJING FIGHTS BACK—PUT MARKET MECHANISM BEHIND THE WHEEL

Beijing's Commission of Transport understands that solutions must be created in three areas: 1) reducing the number of cars on the road, 2) improving road conditions, and 3) developing public transit. The commission has announced multiple goals to be accomplished by the year 2020, including capping the number of residents in Beijing under 23 million, and building 1,000 kilometers of transit rail and 1,000 kilometers of bus routes (Du 2016). Seventy-two percent of Beijing's employees have jobs downtown, a major source of congestion. One strategy to limit Beijing's population is to relocate some old industries. Beijing has moved some polluting and labor-intensive industries out of the city in 2015, and will continue to do so (Zheng and Cao 2015). The top priority, however, is to reduce the number of cars on the road. During the 2008 Summer Olympics Games, Beijing tested the even-odd license plate policy that allocates days of driving by the numbers on license plates, with an exception for public transit vehicles, taxis, and electric cars. The system continues to be implemented today. In recent years, to curb car buying, licenses were issued through a monthly lottery. While these measures somewhat slow car sales, they have only delayed the worsening congestion. The benefits of these programs have been gradually fading and will most likely vanish. China's car market sold 21 million passenger cars in 2015 and 22.68 million in 2016; and at the rate of 8 percent annual growth, China has surpassed the United States (*Economist* 2016).

A new measure that was to take effect in 2016 was to charge a congestion fee in Beijing's most congested locations. The announced fee schedule was 20 to 50 yuan ($3 to $8) (Ge 2016). There was an attempt to collect a congestion toll back in 2010 and 2013, and there was much propaganda work to justify to the public the necessity and success of similar programs in Stockholm, Singapore, and London. Eventually, however, Beijing had to give it up due to commuters' dissent. Moreover, for any toll to be imposable, commuters must be given alternatives—something that Beijing could not do. The year 2016 came and went. As of 2019, congestion toll remains in heated debate. Many believe that the toll will likely be implemented eventually, ironically, thanks to the worsening air pollution and related health issues that seem to put an increasing pressure on the public. Likewise, parking fees and enforcement of parking restrictions in central Beijing will also increase. Nevertheless, how effective these regulations will be remains to be seen. However, in these solutions there are likely more sticks than carrots for the commuter who depends on the private car.

SHARE WHAT YOU'VE GOT

Where there is crisis, there is opportunity. Enter Uber. Ride-hailing had been an underground business ever since taxis first appeared in Beijing and other Chinese cities in the late 1980s. At the beginning, there were simply not sufficient cabs, and some drivers of private or public cars took advantage of the opportunity to offer ride service for a fee. The government had deemed such business illegal and imposed high fines. Restrictions on ride-hailing have since loosened up, particularly in major cities, because more and more drivers who offer rides now subscribe to app-based management systems that allow access by regulating agencies. In 2013, Uber initiated trial operations in Shanghai, Guangzhou, and Shenzhen. It has recently begun operations in Beijing. Uber-China has quickly gained popularity, as demonstrated by one of its brand names: "People's Uber" (anything branded with "people's" is highly regarded). Uber has further solidified its operations through a partnership with China's search giant Baidu, which allows access to its Chinese-language mapping software. Beijing issued a set of "tough" regulations on car-hailing businesses in 2017 (Xinhuanet 2017) a year after car-hailing was legalized in China (Bloomberg News 2016).

To attract residents to ride-sharing, Uber has invested more than $1 billion in China to lower fares and provide incentives to drivers. However, Uber is not alone.

The company has quickly found itself faced with a formidable competitor in Didi Kuaidi, which is backed by domestic investors and the deep pockets of Apple. The fierce competition has overwhelmed Chinese customers with free rides and incentives. Some taxi drivers abandoned their cabs to drive private cars to earn bonuses that are twice as high as the fares (Makinen 2015). The drawback, however, is that these promotion efforts have increased rather than reduced the number of cars on the road. The national newspaper, the *People's Daily*, reported that Beijing's authorities blamed the ride-on-demand services offered by Uber and Didi Kuaidi for aggravating traffic congestion and urged development of public transit (Ma 2015; Yu 2016). Experts agree, however, that ride-sharing contributes a tremendous benefit: it satisfies the ride demand, which may play a key role in reducing the number of cars on the road in the long run. The looming technology of driverless cars is said to be able to reduce Beijing's cars significantly. Baidu is actively engaged in research and test-driving self-driving cars in Chinese cities, and expects to put driverless fleets in commercial use before 2020 (*Wall Street Journal* 2016). With regard to Uber, its operation in China has been acquired by Didi Kuaidi, as of this writing.

Jing Luo

See also: Traffic and Transportation: Istanbul, Turkey: Building More Tunnels and Bridges Won't Make Congestion Go Away; Mexico City, Mexico: Improving Governance Is Key to Solving Traffic Challenges; New York City, United States; The New York Subway

Further Reading

Anonymous. 2016. "Where Baidu Is Heading with the Driverless Car." *The Wall Street Journal (online),* June 8. http://www.wsj.com/articles/where-baidu-is-heading-with-the-driverless-car-1465421461.

Bendibao.com. 2019. "A Guide for Beijing's Curbside Parking Fees" (in Chinese). January 3. http://bj.bendibao.com/news/201913/256566.shtm.

Bloomberg News. 2016. "China Said to Legalize Uber, Didi Ride-hailing as War Rages" (in Chinese). July 28. http://www.bloomberg.com/news/articles/2016-07-28/china-said-to-legalize-uber-didi-ride-hailing-as-battle-rages.

Cao, Xiaoang. 2012. "Beijing's Traffic Congestion, How Do Experts Look at It?" (in Chinese). *Auto Review,* December 12. http://www.caam.org.cn/shiluntang/20131212/1205109086.html.

Dou, Eva, and Rick Carew. 2015. "In Big, New Market, Uber Hits a Great Wall—Company Competes with Local Startup to Woo Millions of Chinese Commuters." *Wall Street Journal, Eastern Edition,* September 3. http://search.proquest.com/docview/1709149415?accountid=26459.

Du, Juan. 2018. "Construction Completed on Beijing's 7th Ring road." *China Daily Online.* June 21. http://www.chinadaily.com.cn/a/201806/21/WS5b2addc8a3103349141dd653.html.

Du, Xiaoying. 2016. "Beijing Takes Action to Ease Its Thick Traffic Congestion." *China Daily,* January 4. http://www.chinadaily.com.cn/business/motoring/2016-01-04/content_22920572.htm.

Editorial. 2016. "The Great Crawl." *Economist,* June 18. http://www.economist.com/news/china/21700676-chinese-love-their-cars-do-not-want-pay-more-driving-them-great-crawl.

Ge, Celine. 2016. "Beijing Takes Lead from London, Singapore as It Plans Congestion Charges to Curb Capital's Huge Traffic Jams." *South China Morning Post,* May 30.

http://www.scmp.com/news/china/policies-politics/article/1959352/beijing-takes-lead-london-singapore-it-plans-congestion.

Li, Yuan. 2016. "China Circuit: Ride-Share Brawl Fuels Deal Talk." *Wall Street Journal,* June 16. http://search.proquest.com/docview/1797132657?accountid=26459.

Lu, Jingyi. 2012. "A Study on Measures of Comprehensive Treatment of Beijing's Traffic Congestion" (in Chinese). *Quoging.China.com.cn,* July 5. http://guoqing.china.com.cn/2012-07/05/content_25828672.htm.

Ma, Xiaochun. 2015. "Beijing Blames Didi Kuaidi, Uber for Causing Traffic Congestion." *People's Daily On-Line,* July 24. http://www.google.com/url?sa=t&rct=j&q=&esrc=s&source=web&cd=1&ved=0ahUKEwic8PnmpsHNAhXD1h4KHVqeB_UQFggcMAA&url=http%3A%2F%2Fusa.chinadaily.com.cn%2Fchina%2F2015-07%2F24%2Fcontent_21401809.htm&usg=AFQjCNGDQuloBT4zCbFcOVdNG4IASdB5Rw&bvm=bv.125221236,d.dmo.

Makinen, Julie. 2015. "Ride-Hailing Firm Uber Faces Big Challenges in China." *LA Times,* June 23. http://www.latimes.com/business/la-fi-uber-china-20150624-story.html.

Murphy, Colum. 2014. "China's Urban Nightmare: Gridlock." *The Wall Street Journal,* January 2. http://www.wsj.com/articles/SB10001424052702303330204579247731532836694.

Nan Chen. 2010. "Congestion Intensifies. Beijing's Traffic Problems under World's Watch" (in Chinese). *Chinanews.com,* August 30. http://www.chinanews.com/auto/2010/08-30/2500036.shtml.

Westcott, Ben. 2018. "Beijing's Population Falls for First Time in 20 Years." CNN, January 24. http://www.cnn.com/2018/01/24/asia/beijing-shanghai-population-drop-intl/index.html.

Xinhuanet. 2017. "Tough New Car-hailing Regulations in Beijing." *Xinhuanet online,* May 20. http://www.xinhuanet.com//english/2017-05/20/c_136300768.htm.

Yu, Rose. 2016. "Beijing Official Blames Traffic on Popular Ride-Hailing Apps." *Wall Street Journal,* January 26. https://blogs.wsj.com/chinarealtime/2016/01/26/beijing-official-blames-traffic-on-popular-ride-sharing-apps/.

Zheng, Jinran, and Cao Yin. 2015. "Beijing to Limit Population Growth This Year." *China Daily,* January 24. http://www.chinadaily.com.cn/china/2015-01/24/content_19394117.htm.

Casablanca, Morocco: Will a Change in Lunch Habit Improve the Town's Traffic?

Casablanca offers a range of transportation options for commuters. The choice of mode of transportation is largely determined by the income level of an individual or family. As in many emerging economies of the global South, the growth of the middle class over the past several decades has led to a marked increase in private automobile ownership, resulting in increased traffic congestion and parking issues. Municipal authorities have responded to the growing needs of Casablanca's residents, notably by promoting light rail. Yet use of collective private taxis remains the most affordable form of transportation for working-class people.

Casablanca is Morocco's largest city and its economic metropolis. According to the 2014 national census, the municipality had a population of 3.36 million, whereas the metropolitan area, which includes the city of Mohammedia (pop. 289,000), had a population of 4.27 million (Kingdom of Morocco n.d.). Furthermore, Casablanca lies at the center of Morocco's Atlantic seaboard, its most heavily urbanized region, a conurbation of about 8 million people that includes the twin cities of Rabat-Salé (Morocco's capital, pop. 1.55 million), Kénitra (607,000), Temara (518,000), El-Jadida-Azemmour (312,000), Berrechid (274,000), and Settat (218,000). Morocco's Atlantic seaboard, with less than a quarter of the country's population, accounts for approximately half of its GDP. The country's largest commercial port and international airport are located in Casablanca, which lies at the hub of the national road and rail networks as well. In terms of demography, the Casablanca agglomeration is growing at a moderate rate (1.64 percent per year). In spatial terms, however, its growth since the 1990s has been rapid, with vast new high-density middle-class housing subdivisions (consisting mainly of four-story apartment blocks) and entire satellite towns (such as Bouskoura) rising at its outskirts. Spatial growth and rising incomes explain recent developments of Casablanca's transportation systems.

Casablanca's urban transportation needs have grown consistently for decades. According to a study conducted in 2010, over 11 million individual trips are made in the agglomeration daily (Berrada et al. 2014, 15). The high number of daily trips (well over twice the agglomeration's population) is due to the fact that many people return home for lunch, meaning that they commute four times a day rather than only twice. That said, just over half of these daily trips are made on foot. High residential densities, a compact urban fabric, and mild weather throughout the year are conducive to pedestrian travel. Thirty percent of daily commutes are by automobile. These trips are about evenly split between private cars and taxis. Less than 15 percent of commuters use public transit (Berrada et al. 2014, 15).

Growth in ownership of private automobiles is a feature of Morocco's economic growth and reflects the rising number of middle-class households. The number of motor vehicles on Casablanca's streets grew from about 400,000 in 2001 to over 1.5 million in 2013 (Berrada et al. 2014, 10), a fourfold increase in just over a decade. This increase in traffic has been accompanied by much road construction, including the widening of existing urban thoroughfares, the construction of multilevel interchanges, and the opening of a new trunk expressway (the A3, completed in 2003) beyond the urban fringe south of the agglomeration. This new toll expressway replaces the first one, opened in 1987, which had become very congested and embedded in high-density residential and industrial neighborhoods.

Also using the city's road network are an undetermined number of two-wheel motor vehicles (mopeds and motorbikes), as well as three-wheeled delivery vehicles. Given Casablanca's chronic traffic problems, these light motor vehicles are increasingly popular as they can weave their way through the heaviest and slowest traffic. They are particularly efficient as delivery vehicles for the garment industry, wholesale districts, provisioning bottle drinks to stores, and so on. Until May 2015, small-motor two- and three-wheeled vehicles (less than 50 cm^3) did not need to be registered, so there is no data on their numbers.

While middle-class households aspire to ownership of a family car, most Casablanca households cannot afford this amenity and rely on some form of collective transportation. The most widely used are privately operated taxis. There are two types of urban taxi. "Petits taxis" (small taxis, usually Renault Dacias) can take up to three passengers. They are hailed on the curb and, within the city limits, will usually take the client to any destination requested. A small taxi can also be shared between clients headed to proximate destinations, and this is usual especially during rush hours. Also, though the fare is supposed to be calculated through a meter, taxi drivers will usually demand higher rates during rush hours and late at night. There are over 8,000 small taxis licensed in the city (Solutions 2014, 10).

"Grands taxis" (large taxis, usually diesel Mercedes 220 or 240) function differently. They take up to six passengers and are almost always shared (Le Tellier 2005). They have fixed fares and travel fixed itineraries along major thoroughfares connecting depots dispersed in neighborhoods and suburbs to those located throughout the city center. Each depot is managed by a dispatcher who insures that the taxis take their proper turn and fill in an orderly manner; a taxi will not depart until all seats are filled. Contrary to the small taxis, large taxis can operate across city limits and are also commonly used for interurban travel. They are the least expensive of all forms of urban transportation. Until recently, diesel Mercedes roadsters have been the preferred model because they have the reputation of being mechanically indestructible and can be repaired using parts from other vehicles. For decades these models of used Mercedes were imported from Europe specifically for this purpose. The desperate state of their roadworthiness has been a perennial public safety issue. In 2015, the government adopted a renewal program that aims at replacing the ancient Mercedes fleet with new seven-seat Renault Dacia-Lodgy hatchbacks, which are assembled in Tangier, Morocco. There are over 6,000 large taxis licensed in the city (Solutions 2014, 10).

Beyond transportation needs, the large taxi system also serves a social purpose. Priority in the granting of licenses to operate large taxis is given to such socially disadvantaged individuals as disabled people and widows of civil servants. These individuals then subcontract the actual operation to one or more drivers for a share of the proceeds (Le Tellier 2005, 167). This system allows a single taxi license to generate revenue for up to five families. Profit margins are tiny, however, which puts considerable pressure on drivers to complete as many runs in a day as possible, with dire consequences for road safety.

As in so many other cities around the world, the arrival of Uber into the private ride market in 2015 has upset the established taxi system. Casablanca's taxi drivers have organized strikes and demonstrations in protest. It is too soon to tell what new, hybrid, taxi-Uber system, if any, will emerge. More troubling for the registered taxis is the continued black market of car owners who illegally offer rides to strangers in return for cash (no app required). Police crackdowns on the practice have not had significant impact.

Public transit in the Casablanca agglomeration consists mostly of bus service. The service was originally publicly owned but was privatized in 2004. Called "M'dina Bus," the system currently consists of 70 bus routes (Berrada et al. 2014, 10) and serves about half a million passengers a day. While the vehicles are relatively new and mechanically reliable (which was not the case prior to the privatization), the service cannot keep up with demand. During peak hours especially the buses are packed with commuters and often cannot stop to pick up additional passengers once they have engaged their routes. Cramped rush-hour conditions are particularly problematic for women, who face frequent harassment and physical groping while onboard (World Bank 2010). Twenty-eight percent of women commute by bus, as opposed to only 18 percent of men (World Bank 2010, 5). Children and students also rely on bus service as they are eligible for preferential rates. Increasingly problematic as well, the vast new suburban neighborhoods that now extend 15 kilometers from the city center have yet to be properly serviced by the bus company, leaving their residents dependent on grand taxis. Another, tangential but no less serious problem for the bus company is that municipal buses have long been a favorite target of attack for football hooligans following matches (the fans of Casablanca's two teams, WAC and Raja, are bitter rivals and prone to attack one another in and around stadiums).

Casablanca has several commuter rail services. These serve most of the Atlantic seaboard conurbation—from Kénitra to Mohammed V International Airport, south of Casablanca. The center of the city is served by a major station, Casa-Voyageurs, and by a terminal, Casa-Port, located between the harbor and the central business district. Commuter rail service is, however, limited by the fact that it is confined to the main trunk railway of the national rail network. This trunk route is out of reach of most neighborhoods and suburbs. Since the 1970s, there have been a variety of proposals to equip the agglomeration with a more complete commuter rail system, including proposals for a subway system, an elevated monorail, and an RER (combination of rapid surface and underground system), but nothing has come of them.

The game changer for 21st-century Casablanca transportation has been the tramway. A first tramline and half of a second were inaugurated in 2012. Built and operated by a private corporation called Casa Tramway, they total 48 stations on 31 kilometers of track. Construction of the second half of the second line got under way in May 2016. The 33 new stations are scheduled for completion by the end of 2018 (Casa Transport). In addition, construction of three new lines is scheduled for completion by 2022. Should these plans materialize, Casablanca will have a comprehensive light-rail commuter service, totaling 80 kilometers of rail, covering the whole metropolitan area and integrated to the larger rail service of the Atlantic seaboard conurbation (Tantaoui 2016). At the moment, this nascent tram system suffers from under-use. The regular fare (about 70 U.S. cents per ride) is twice as expensive as regular bus fare, which makes it uncompetitive, and transfer between the two transit systems is not currently possible; commuters who need both modes must pay each fare fully and separately.

Finally, of all the modes of urban transportation, cycling is the least developed. Bicycle ownership in the city is very low (there is no data on this). There are a few designated bicycle paths, but they tend to be used by the city's mopeds rather than by cyclists. Cycling in Casablanca is in fact quite dangerous as the dominant car culture does not currently accommodate the needs of cyclists.

Eric S. Ross

See also: Pollution: Karachi, Pakistan: How Pollution Gets Out of Control; *Traffic and Transportation:* Kolkata, India: When More People Drive Their Own Cars

Further Reading
Berrada, Jaâfar, Mohamed Sebai, Fabien Leurent, and Shadi Sadeghian. 2014. *Analyser l'offre et la demande de transport dans l'agglomération du Grand Casablanca,*

Maroc (in French). Méta-observatoire de la mobilité. http://docplayer.fr/11533586-Analyser-l-offre-et-la-demande-de-transport-dans-l-agglomeration-du-grand-casabalanca-maroc.html.

Casa Transport (in French). http://casatransport.ma/pages/voir/1-societe-de-developpement-local.

City of Casablanca. "Plans stratégiques du transport urbain" (in French). http://www.casablancacity.ma/Ma-ville/Transport-et-stationnement/Plans-strategiques-du-transport-urbain.

Kingdom of Morocco, Haut Commissariat au Plan. n.d. *Recensement général de la population et de l'habitat 2014. Notes de présentation des premiers résultats. Région du Grand Casablanca* (in French). http://www.hcp.ma/reg-casablanca/Recensement-de-la-Population_a30.html.

Le Tellier, Julien. 2005. "Les grands taxis: Approche du système de transport et de mobilité au Maroc" (in French). *Annales de Géographie* 114, 642: 163–86.

Solutions: Sharing Opportunities for Low Carbon Urban Transportation. 2014. *Situation de la mobilité à Casablanca.* http://cleanairasia.org/node12666/.

Tantaoui, Younès. 2016. "Casablanca. Tramway: Les études des lignes 3, 4 et 5 confiées à un groupement franco-marocain" (in French). *Le 360*, July 8. http://fr.le360.ma/economie/casablanca-tramway-les-etudes-des-lignes-3-4-et-5-confiees-a-un-groupement-franco-marocain-78830.

World Bank. 2010. *Etude sur le genre et les transports au Maroc: Le cas de Casablanca.* http://siteresources.worldbank.org/EXTTSR/Resources/463715-1322323559362/Genre-Trsprt-Maroc-French.pdf.

Istanbul, Turkey: Building More Tunnels and Bridges Won't Make Congestion Go Away

Historically, the city of Istanbul was once dominated by the Greeks and the Romans. Under the Byzantine Empire, it served as the capital under the name of Constantinople. After the Ottoman Empire's takeover in the 15th century, the city's name was changed to Istanbul (Oxford Reference). The city's mosques and historical buildings display rich traditions and are treasures of the world's artistic heritage. Bazaars, hotels, restaurants, and nightclubs line the ancient streets. Modern highrises contrast with traditional structures, reflecting a unique scene of urban life. These intertwining streets when traveled by 3.5 million automobiles, with 30,000 new cars added each month (Istanbul in Numbers 2017), however, generate urban congestion and some of the city's biggest challenges.

TRAFFIC CONGESTION

Istanbul's geographical location is one of its unique characteristics. Straddling the Bosporus Strait that connects the Black Sea in the north and the Mediterranean Sea in the south, Istanbul is a gateway between Europe in the West and Asia in the East. Most of Turkey's international trade passes through Istanbul via the city's tunnels, bridges, and sea routes. The city's traffic congestion is notorious.

In fact, Istanbul ranks as the sixth most congested city in the world after Mexico City and Bangkok, according to the TomTom Traffic Index (TomTom Traffic Index 2017).

In addition to congested roadways, marine transportation is affected just as badly. Istanbul uses ferries more than any city in the world. In fact, the wooden paddleboats were replaced not too long ago. The Istanbul Sea Buses is the largest municipal ferry system in the world, serving as far as the Black Sea (Istanbul.com 2014). A report by the *Economist* magazine describes the situation as follows:

> Some 50,000 ships a year traverse the narrow waterway that bisects the city. A colourful mix of Polish package tourists, Indonesian pilgrims, Ghanaian textile traders, Kazakh students and honeymooning Saudis passes through its snaking airport immigration queues, and a polyglot crowd ceaselessly throngs Istiklal Street, attesting to Istanbul's growing magnetism.
>
> The city is racing ahead in other ways, too. It already has about 16m people, compared with barely 2m in 1975, and between now and 2018 it will overtake both London and Moscow as the most populous urban area in Europe. (*Economist* 2016)

The 2014–2023 Istanbul Regional Plan envisions new logistic zones, a third airport, and enlargement of existing ports. Ongoing major transportation projects, such as Marmaray and Kars-Tiblisi-Baku railroad constructions, will strengthen the region's competitiveness and increase economic growth (*Daily Sabah* 2017). On the other hand, economic expansion attracts a large residential body representing approximately 18 percent of the country's demographics. It is the largest metropolis of Turkey ahead of Ankara (the capital) at 4.75 million, Izmir at 3.04 million, and Bursa at 1.9 million (CIA World Fact Book 2016).

Due to the influx, Istanbul's squatter buildings rise in abundance, producing run-down neighborhoods. Overcrowding is a serious concern; and that problem is exacerbated by the fact that more and more middle-class families own their private vehicles. This situation is directly reflected in Istanbul's traffic pattern. Except for intercity highways, Istanbul's city streets meander in all directions following the contour of the neighborhoods. Roads tend to be narrow and hopelessly clogged by cars and pedestrians. The situation may be best illustrated by the scene of Cumhuryet Avenue in the Avcilar District, near the D100 Highway exit (https://www.youtube.com/watch?v=xKl_JseZroQ). One may find other clips on YouTube. Istanbul's traffic problems came under the limelight over a decade ago, and they were summarized by a researcher as follows:

1. Lack of sustainable, multiscale and multi-centralized urban plans.
2. Lack of high-capacity public transit.
3. Deficiency in infrastructure at intersections and parking lots.
4. Lack of effective traffic control and management system.
5. Insufficient education for drivers, passengers and pedestrians.
6. Deficiency in controlling population growth.
7. Redundant public offices resulting in poorly defined authority and responsibility (Rafet 2007; Ekenyazici Güney 2012).

EXISTING TRANSPORTATION SERVICES

Istanbul is served by a mix of public transit including metro bus, metro rails, and ferry. The city's tram system reminds one of the earliest forms of mass transit. Four tramlines were constructed in modern times; however, only two lines, T1 and T4, are in active but limited service today. The tramlines have fallen behind the metro system that incorporates the bus rapid transit and trains (Turkey Travel Planner). The passenger may purchase a universal pass and ride all public transportation. The M1 metro line, also known as the Light Metro, was opened in 1989 to satisfy the demand of the rising population. After M1, eight more metro lines were opened, and some are under construction today (UrbanRail.net). In Istanbul, the metro system has become an extension of the national rail system to provide joint service. The three other cities where national rails provide local service are Izmir, Ankara, and Adapazari (Railturkey.org 2014).

In October 2013, the first underwater Bosporus rail crossing, referred to as "Marmaray," was opened. The project includes a 13.3-kilometer Istanbul Strait crossing and the upgrade of 63 kilometers of suburban lines to create a 76.3-kilometers high-capacity line between Gebze and Halkali. It was a technological breakthrough by

Cars, trams, and people crowd the Yeni Camii mosque and Galata Bridge in Istanbul, Turkey, 2015. The city's traffic congestion is one of the worst in the world. To address the problem, the city invested heavily in expensive, high-capacity bridges and tunnels that did little to alleviate inner-city street traffic. (Madrugadaverde/Dreamstime.com)

means of an earthquake-proof immersed tunnel linked to bored tunnels from Kazlıçesme on the European side and Ayrilik Çesmesi on the Asian side. Daily traffic between continents was 1.1 million trips (Istanbul Municipality 2015). The tunnel is directly connected with the Yenikapi hub, which includes the termini for metro lines M1 and M2 (UrbanRail.net). In 2015, the Turkish government announced that the "the Three-level Big Istanbul Tunnel" will be part of the 2023 Transportation Project to further alleviate the traffic congestion. Similar to Istanbul's first sub-sea tunnel of Marmaray, the Three-level Big Istanbul Tunnel will be part of the "fast metro tunnel project" aimed at crossing the Bosporus Strait from 110 meters under the sea level and connect Europe and Asia. The tunnel will have 2×2 lines built for both metro and dual-highway Bosporus crossing. According to the announcement, "the tunnel will enable faster and cheaper transportation between the two sides of Istanbul. It will integrate nine different urban train systems with a fast metro track, which is used approximately by 6.5 million passengers on a daily basis. It will also enable easier and faster connections to ring roads; thus connecting all main arterial roads" (*Daily Sabah* 2015).

MONUMENTAL CONSTRUCTIONS, LIMITED RELIEF

Experts argue that intercity traffic represents 95 percent of the city's traffic flow, and it is the real source of Istanbul's traffic congestion. Roads are more likely congested within areas where intercity highways blend into local traffic (Albas et al. 2016). As such, while the number of cross-continent bridges and tunnels have multiplied, these developments do not seem to be of much help to solving the congestion problem. It is not surprising that many Istanbul citizens complain that politicians have squandered the transportation budget on flamboyant projects, such as highways, overpasses, and bridges, but failed to solve the real problem (Kose 2015). However, Istanbul's rankings on the TomTom World Traffic Index indicate that between 2012 and 2016 during which grand bridges and tunnels were put in use, showed some improvement: the city's ranking dropped to #6 in 2016 from #1 and #2 (#1 being the worst traffic). This could be due to more bypasses being made available around the city. However, the benefit is arguably limited and uncertain as traffic will keep increasing. The reality is, Istanbul remains one of the world's most congested cities.

In fact, more roads leading to more congestion is a common phenomenon seen in many populous cities, particularly heritage cities, for example, Beijing and Mexico City.

In the case of Beijing, with each ring road added, Beijing's traffic only gets slowed further, while its air pollution increases measurably. Beijing's strategy includes adding more public transit lines, restricting private car use, increasing parking fees, and collecting a congestion fee. However, such measures have not been significantly helpful due to the pressure of the overwhelming influx of migrant population and tourists all year round. New rounds of urban expansion have kept adding more population to the city. The census of 2010 revealed that Beijing had added 6 million residents in a 10-year period to reach 19.6 million. The census also showed that the daily peak number of passengers taking public transit alone was

15.06 million. In 2016, Beijing's population was nearly 21 million, an overwhelming pressure on the transportation system. A similar situation exists in Mexico City, where the public transit carries 14.8 million people daily, which nevertheless falls short of capacity. The poor conditions of roads and public transit fail to convince 6.8 million car users to leave their car home.

On the other hand, it seems more appealing and possibly more politically popular as well, that as city population continues to climb, the prevalent response will be to increase road budget and build more roads. And building more roads has been exactly the long-term plan of the Turkish government. In addition to the two suspension bridges on the Istanbul Strait, a third one, the Yavuz Sultan Selim Bridge, was added near the Black Sea region in August 2016. The new structure measures some 7,100 feet long, 192 feet wide, and 1,056 feet high, with four lanes of traffic in either direction as well as dual rail lines. This bridge is said to be the most prominent part of the whole project and incorporates innovative engineering to cope with some technically challenging issues. The cost of $3 billion is only a small part of the $200 billion construction initiatives pushed by President Ercep Tayyip Erdogan. Moreover, on December 20, 2016, the Eurasia Tunnel connecting the Asian and European continents under the Marmara seabed was finally opened. While these costly projects were all built in the name of relieving Istanbul's congested roads, one waits to witness the real benefit. It appears that the great strides in developing cross-strait transportation have brought in more traffic than the city could handle, and citizens' voices have not been heard (Kose 2015). To President Erdogan, however, this may be music to the ear. In hosting the opening of the Yavuz Sultan Selim Bridge he had this to say: "When man dies, he leaves behind a monument" (Moritz-Rabson 2016).

Apparently, traffic congestion in heritage cities such as Istanbul, Beijing, and Mexico City are more difficult to improve due to preservation constraints. Building more roads may mean removal of historical monuments. In the meantime, it is popularly believed that when a network is already congested, the removal of capacity can only exacerbate the situation. Here, scientific research seems to offer a different vision. A report by the European Commission titled "Reclaiming City Streets for People—Chaos or Quality of Life" published in 2004 on five congested European cities—Kajaani (Finland), Volverhamton (England), Vauxhall Cross (London, England), Nuremberg (Germany), and Strasburg (France)—shows an opposite outcome. The study shows that by reallocating traffic space through blocking strategic urban areas from cars, the congestion problem gets improved. Researchers observed that after an initial period of adjustment, some of the traffic that was in the vicinity of the scheme "disappears" due to drivers changing their travel behavior; that presumed adversary effect was less serious than believed; and, as a result, the urban environment becomes more livable in many aspects. There are many other research-based solutions and policies for city planners to draw from. Hopefully, scientific research will be able to offer more effective options than political campaigns. In the meantime, temporary solutions include "leave home early" and "buy a motorcycle" (Tapan 2017).

Jing Luo

See also: Traffic and Transportation: Beijing, China: Beijing's War on Traffic Congestion; Kolkata, India: When More People Drive Their Own Cars; Mexico City, Mexico: Improving Governance Is Key to Solving Traffic Challenges

Further Reading

Albas, Ahmet, et al. 2016. "On-Line Solution to the Bottleneck Congestion: A Case Study for Istanbul." https://www.researchgate.net/publication/242181438_on-line_solution_to_the_bottleneck_congestion_a_case_study_for_istanbul.

CIA World Fact Book, 2016. https://www.cia.gov/library/publications/the-world-factbook/geos/print_tu.html.

Daily Sabah. 2015. "Istanbul's Mega-Project: World's First Three-Level Tunnel to Be Built under the Bosporus." February 27. http://www.dailysabah.com/business/2015/02/27/istanbuls-megaproject-worlds-first-threelevel-tunnel-to-be-built-under-the-bosporus.

Daily Sabah. 2017. "First Train of Baku-Tblisi-Kars Railway to Hit Tracks Today." October 29. https://www.dailysabah.com/business/2017/10/30/first-train-of-baku-tbilisi-kars-railway-to-hit-tracks-today.

Economist. 2016. "The Lure of the City—Turkey's Urban Centers Are Modernizing at the Double." https://www.economist.com/news/special-report/21689875-turkeys-urban-centres-are-modernising-double-lure-city.

Ekenyazici Güney, Esfun. 2012. "A Study on the Effect of Transportation Systems to the Evolution of the City Image—The Case of Istanbul." *Megaron Journal* 7: 91–107. http://www.journalagent.com/megaron/pdfs/MEGARON-41713-ARTICLE-EKENYAZICI_GUNEY.pdf.

European Commission. 2004. "Reclaiming City Streets for People—Chaos or Quality of Life?" http://ec.europa.eu/environment/pubs/pdf/streets_people.pdf.

Great Istanbul.com. "Istanbul in Numbers." http://www.greatistanbul.com/numbers.html.

Hennig, Mike. 2011. "Sustainable Urban Mobility: The Example of Istanbul—A Short Survey." Federal Ministry for Economic Cooperation and Development (BMZ). http://www.sutp.org/files/contents/documents/resources/C_Case-Studies/GIZ_SUTP_CS_Sustainable-Urban-Mobility-Istanbul_EN.pdf.

Istanbul Development Agency. "2014–2023 Istanbul Regional Plan." http://www.istka.org.tr/media/24723/istanbul-regional-plan-2014-2023.pdf.

Istanbul.com. 2014. "Ferry and Seabus in Istanbul." http://en.istanbul.com/city-life/ferry-and-sea-buses-in-istanbul.html.

Istanbul Municipality. 2015. "Best Mobility Practices in Istanbul." http://19343a27nxyvlifure2nq0aw.wpengine.netdna-cdn.com/wp-content/uploads/sites/4/2015/05/9-Betul-Guney.pdf.

Kose, Pinar. 2015. "Turkey's Congestion Problem: Why New Roads Aren't the Answer." *The City Fix* (blog). http://thecityfix.com/blog/turkeys-congestion-problem-why-new-roads-arent-answer-pinar-kose.

Masters, Bruce Alan, and Gábor Ágoston. 2009. *Encyclopedia of the Ottoman Empire*. New York: Infobase Publishing.

Moritz-Rabson, Daniel. 2016. "Turkey Opens Third Bosphorus Bridge." August 27. https://www.pbs.org. http://www.pbs.org/newshour/rundown/turkey-opens-third-bosphorus-bridge.

Oxford Reference. Timeline: Ottoman Empire. http://www.oxfordreference.com/view/10.1093/acref/9780191737640.timeline.0001.

Rafet, Bozdoğan. 2007. "Solutions and Ongoing Projects to Ease Istanbul's Transportation and Traffic Problems." https://www.google.com/#q=PPT_Atilla_ALKAN_11A22.ppt.

Railturkey.org. 2014. "Public Transport by Rail in Turkish Cities." September 18. https://railturkey.org/2014/09/18/public-transport-by-rail-in-turkish-cities/.

Tapan, Mirac. 2017. "Istanbul 101: How to Beat the City's Traffic Jams." *Daily Sabah*, March 15. https://www.dailysabah.com/feature/2017/03/15/istanbul-101-how-to-beat-the-citys-traffic-jams.

TomTom Traffic Index. 2016. "Istanbul." https://www.tomtom.com/en_gb/trafficindex/city/istanbul.

Turkey Travel Planner. Istanbul Trams. http://www.turkeytravelplanner.com/go/Istanbul/Transport/IstanbulTram.html.

UrbanRail.net. "Istanbul." http://www.urbanrail.net/as/tr/istanbul/istanbul.htm.

Kolkata, India: When More People Drive Their Own Cars

Kolkata is a bustling Indian megacity standing on the banks of the Hooghly River (a distributary of River Ganga) and is home to approximately 14 million people. It is the largest city in eastern India and the third largest in India after Mumbai and Delhi both in terms of population and economic activities.

URBANIZATION AND TRAFFIC MOBILITY

Kolkata, being the commercial and educational hub of the region has always been the focus of urban migration both from neighboring Indian states and from bordering countries like Bangladesh and Nepal. It grapples with similar struggles associated with urbanization and recent upward mobility in income that are faced by many densely populated megacities especially in emerging regions like Beijing in China, Sao Paolo in Brazil, or Mexico City in Mexico, to name a few.

According to the United Nation World Urbanization Prospects (2014), a majority of the world's population, roughly 54 percent, now reside in urban areas compared to just 30 percent in the 1950s. The largest increase in urban population is expected to take place in Asia and Africa, with China, India, and Nigeria accounting for 37 percent of projected growth in urban population by 2050. Kolkata is expected to see a 1.7 percent increase in urban agglomeration between 2016 and 2030, which is lower than some other Indian cities (Mumbai, 1.9 percent; Delhi, 2.2 percent; Bengaluru, 2.5 percent) but still substantial enough to raise questions about mobility and sustainability. Kolkata, like any other large city in an emerging economy, has its struggles with overcrowding, pollution, and last but not least, traffic mobility and congestion. Traffic jams and congestion along with vehicular pollution seem to be troubling the transportation scenario in Kolkata.

TRAFFIC CONGESTION

Traffic congestion arises when existing road space struggles to keep up with increasing traffic demand. In Kolkata's major road intersections, during peak hours, the traffic corridor speed can drop to as low as 9 kilometers per hour, whereas the desired speed is around 30 kilometers per hour (Chakrabartty and Gupta 2014). One of the reasons for such low traffic mobility is because Kolkata has the lowest road space (6 percent) as compared to other large Indian megacities, such as Delhi (23 percent) and Mumbai (17 percent) (Chakrabartty and Gupta 2015).

Apart from the lack of road space, another factor that contributes to higher traffic congestion in Indian cities is the rapid growth of private vehicle ownership, and Kolkata is no exception. Economic growth and rising per capita income in the urban areas have led to greater private ownership than before. Kolkata's real GDP is projected to grow at a rate of 6.4 percent (2008–2025), making it one of the top 30 cities in terms of real GDP growth rate in the world (Hawksworth et al. 2009). Economic growth is a key factor in personal vehicle ownership. A recent report by the Brookings Institution (2015) estimates Kolkata's per capita real GDP growth at 4.7 percent, making it the second-fastest-growing city in India, surpassed only by Delhi (Parilla et al. 2015). The number of motorized vehicles in India has increased from 52.4 million in 2000 to 121.6 million in 2009, recording a growth rate of 9 percent, whereas the population growth during the same period is just 1.5 percent (Sharma et al. 2011). Even though India has a lower rate of motorization compared to other countries (22 vehicles per 1,000 population compared to 675 per 1,000 in the United States in 2009), the rate of growth of motor vehicles is faster than other countries and is a concern from the point of view of congestion, mobility, and environmental pollution.

The rate and growth of motorization are not uniformly distributed across the nation; the rural-urban divide is highly pronounced when it comes to automobile ownership. Most of these motor vehicles are concentrated in million-plus (population) cities in India. Delhi, Bengaluru, Kolkata, and Mumbai account for 14 percent of total motor vehicles in the nation, while their share in the nation's population is just 5 percent (Chakrabartty and Gupta, 2014). The rapid rate of motorization coupled with limited road space have resulted in traffic congestion and higher levels of air pollution in Kolkata. This city provides a large variety when it comes to different modes of transportation. It is a mix of modern motorized (automobiles, buses, trains, metro rail, motorcycles, auto rickshaws, electric trams) and traditional non-motorized transportation system (bicycles and cycle rickshaws). The traffic trend is Kolkata is shifting from bicycles and walking toward private motorcycles and cars, creating vehicular congestion. Lack of safety in public transport is also a reason for higher private vehicle ownership, especially among women in the city (Chakrabartty and Gupta 2014).

A recent study by Switch ON, Environment Conservation Society (2013a) showed that private cars occupy 29 percent of the road space, second only to buses and minibuses (32 percent), but they serve only a meager 6 percent of the passengers compared to buses and minibuses, which serve a massive 76 percent of the city passengers. The share of private cars in total registered vehicles is 31 percent, compared to only a 12 percent share of buses and minibuses. This is a clear picture of how public transport, especially buses, are overburdened and in dire need of investment and improvement. Most of the public and private buses operating in the city are aged and inefficient in terms of fuel use and emissions. Creating more roads is a possible solution to lower congestion, but acquiring land in a densely populated city like Kolkata is difficult, and higher road space doesn't always ease congestion. Delhi has over 21 percent road space (as a percentage of its area) and still faces traffic gridlock worse than in Kolkata. The answer lies in exploring and strengthening the already existing network of the public transportation system.

Kolkata and Mumbai have the distinction of low automobile ownership measured as automobile per 1,000 population, mostly due to a widespread network of public transportation system prevalent in these cities. In 2005, Kolkata and Mumbai reported 64 automobiles and 69 automobiles (per 1,000 population) respectively, compared to 279 in Delhi, 312 in Chennai, and 343 in Bengaluru (Reddy and Balachandra 2010). Kolkata is a leader among large Indian cities when it comes to public transportation. A study by Arthur D. Little (2014) ranked Kolkata highest among Indian cities, and 31st among world cities, when it comes to urban mobility as measured by a mobility index that takes into account share and frequency of public transport in a city, multimodality, penetration of smart cards, share of bicycles, vehicles registered per person, time taken to travel, and so on. It comes as no surprise that Kolkata, with its strong and well-developed public transportation system, ranked high in the mobility index. Switch ON (2013b) reported that Kolkata had the highest share of passengers traveling by public transport; 54 percent of the city passengers traveled by public transport in Kolkata compared to 45 percent in Mumbai and 43 percent in Delhi. Kolkata along with Mumbai had the lowest automobile share (only 8 percent of the total passengers traveled by personal cars in Kolkata and Mumbai compared to 14 percent in Delhi) amongst Indian megacities.

Unfortunately, the share of nonmotorized modes of transportation—bicycles and walking—are on the decline in the city of Kolkata, and a recent ban on bicycles by Kolkata police in 2013 to reduce congestion in major traffic intersection worsened the situation. A study published by the Centre for Science and Environment (2011) recommends that Kolkata should build on its unique strength. It should focus on its dense and well-developed network of public transportation systems comprised of buses (private and public), metro railways (both underground and aboveground), trams and nonmotorized modes of transportation (bicycles and walking). The shift should be away from private vehicle ownership and toward public mass transit systems. Kolkata's area and compact geography are conducive to walking and transportation by bicycles and other non-motorized transportations systems and use of public transportation. The report estimated that 60 percent of the total transit in the Kolkata city area is less than three to four kilometers in distance. Kolkata must realize its unique advantage and invest in a sustainable growth fueled by an energy-efficient, multimodal integrated mass transit system.

TRAFFIC AND POLLUTION

Traffic and transportation in Kolkata are also plagued by high levels of pollution and are a major contributor to poor air quality in the city and its surrounding regions. The *Times of India* (Chakraborti 2017) reported that a study by British Deputy High Commission, UKAID, and Kolkata Municipal Corporation ranked Kolkata the fifth highest among Indian cities in terms of total greenhouse gas emissions and second in terms of per capita carbon dioxide emission. The major contributor of air pollution is automobile exhaust (almost 50 percent), closely followed by pollutants from industrial processes. One major source of vehicular air pollution in the city are the diesel vehicles; 65 percent of new cars and 99 percent of commercial vehicles run on diesel in Kolkata, a disproportionately high number compared to the rest of India (Bhaduri 2013). Poor vehicle maintenance, the prevalence of aged passenger vehicles and commercial fleets, high emissions from motorcycles and cars, fuel adulteration, and ineffective traffic and pollution management further exacerbate the problem of air pollution. Prolonged exposure to emissions and automobile exhaust leads to serious respiratory diseases and higher health costs.

Kolkata is aware of the increasing threat of air pollution and alarming consequences of poor air quality. It has implemented pollution reduction programs, adopted stricter emissions standards for vehicles (Bharat Stage I to Bharat Stage IV), banned 2—stroke auto rickshaws in favor of 4—stroke engines and introduced LPG-driven vehicles, undertaken initiatives to phase out aged fuel-inefficient vehicles and replace them with green and energy-efficient buses. Pollution monitoring and reduction are a priority for the city. It is time for Kolkata to enter the second phase in pollution control and step it up.

SOLUTIONS FOR THE FUTURE

The International Association of Public Transport (UITP) identifies public transportation and mass transit as the driver of sustainable, environment-friendly growth and the future of urban mobility. Kolkata is taking actions to improve traffic mobility, lower congestion, and provide better air quality. In 2014, the Calcutta State Transport Corporation (CSTC) introduced a fleet of modern, air-conditioned buses to provide comfort and convenience to passengers in a bid to divert traffic from private cars toward shared modes of transportation. CSTC has also introduced more fuel-efficient Volvo buses, which are environment friendly and create less pollution. Further, a widespread expansion of the Kolkata Metro subway system is underway.

The Metro subway system already offers a smart card fare payment system. This can be potentially integrated with the existing network of private and public bus systems. In time, a citywide fare integration and multimodal integrated mass transit system—perhaps modeled on the Metro card in the New York Metropolitan Transportation Authority or the Oyster smart card instituted by the city of London—can be envisioned, which will allow a common smart card payment system on multiple transit modes citywide. A unified fare structure, and more importantly, a unified metropolitan transit authority, in Kolkata would go a long way in providing better transport solutions. Plans are already underway to integrate the aboveground Kolkata Circular Railway with the Kolkata Metro subway system, which will also extend a line to Netaji Subhash Chandra Bose International Airport.

Kolkata is already a pioneer in using parking policy to lower congestion. It has the highest parking rate per hour compared to other Indian megacities. This policy not only effectively discourages use of private vehicles; it also helps in generating revenue to fund investments in public transportation (Centre for Science and

Environment 2011). Kolkata has unique and innovative solutions to offer—such as the fact that Kolkata's auto-rickshaws operate like buses, running on fixed, high-density routes and always in ride-share mode. This is in contrast to auto-rickshaws operating like metered taxis in other Indian metro cities. This particular solution allows for maximum utilization of vehicles and roadways, as well as providing an affordable mode of transportation to its citizens.

For cleaner air, certain measures can immediately decrease the adverse environmental impact of passenger transport in Kolkata. They include encouraging compressed natural gas auto-rickshaws and electric auto-rickshaws, and implementing strict emission standards for the high percentage of diesel vehicles operating in the city. Kolkata has joined the C-40 Cities Climate Leadership Group to explore its options for lowering air pollution and improving its air quality. The existing tramway system should be restored to provide an environment-friendly, alternative mode of transportation and reduce reliance on petrol and diesel-powered passenger vehicles.

Making viable, livable communities in the largest megacities in the world is no mean feat. Planners and the citizens need to think boldly and work together to create a sustainable urban habitat.

Moumita Roy

See also: *Traffic and Transportation:* Mexico City, Mexico: Improving Governance Is Key to Solving Traffic Challenges; *Waste Management*: Delhi, India: Current Problems and Opportunities for the Future of the National Capital Territory

Further Reading

Audenhove, F. V., O. Korniichuk, L. Dauby, and J. Pourbaix. 2014. "The Future of Urban Mobility 2.0. Imperatives to Shape Extended Mobility Ecosystems of Tomorrow." Arthur D. Little and International Association of Public Transport (UITP). http://www.uitp.org/sites/default/files/members/140124%20Arthur%20D.%20Little%20%26%20UITP_Future%20of%20Urban%20Mobility%202%200_Full%20study.pdf.

Bhaduri, S. 2013. "Vehicular Growth and Air Quality at Major Traffic Intersection Points in Kolkata City: An Efficient Intervention Strategies." *The SIJ Transactions on Advances in Space Research & Earth Exploration (ASREE)* 1, 1 (September-October).

C 40 Cities Climate Leadership Group. 2015. "Kolkata Joins C40, Becomes Fifth Member City from India." http://www.c40.org/blog_posts/kolkata-joins-c40-becomes-fifth-member-city-from-india.

Census of India. 2011. "Urban Agglomerations/Cities Having Population 1 Million and Above. Provisional Population Totals." http://censusindia.gov.in/2011-prov-results/paper2/data_files/india2/Million_Plus_UAs_Cities_2011.pdf.

Centre for Science and Environment. 2011. "Kolkata." March 15. https://www.cseindia.org/kolkata-1748.

Chakrabartty, A., and S. Gupta. 2014. "Traffic Congestion in the Metropolitan City of Kolkata." *Journal of Infrastructure Development* 6, 1: 43–59. India Development Foundation. SAGE Publications. DOI: 10.1177/0974930614543046.

Chakrabartty, A., and S. Gupta. 2015. "Estimation of Congestion Cost in the City of Kolkata—A Case Study." *Current Urban Studies* 3: 95–104.

Chakraborti, S. 2017. "Air Pollution Level in Kolkata among Country's Highest." *Times of India*. http://timesofindia.indiatimes.com/city/kolkata/air-pollution-level-in-kolkata-among-countrys-highest/articleshow/56310086.cms.

Hawksworth, J., T. Hoehn, and A. Tiwari. 2009. "Which Are the Largest City Economies in the World and How Might This Change by 2025?" PricewaterhouseCoopers UK Economic Outlook, November. http://pwc.blogs.com/files/global-city-gdp-rankings-2008-2025.pdf.

Hemalatha, K. 2013. "Kolkata Tops Indian Cities in Public Transport Study." *Times of India*, December 18. http://timesofindia.indiatimes.com/india/Kolkata-tops-Indian-cities-in-public-transport-Study/articleshow/27553749.cms.

India Environment Portal Website. 2011. "Citizen's Report: Air Quality and Mobility in Kolkata." http://www.indiaenvironmentportal.org.in/files/file/Kolkata%20Report.pdf.

Mani, Akshay. 2014. "On the Move: The Future of Multimodal Integration." http://thecityfix.com/blog/on-the-move-future-multimodal-integration-akshay-mani.

Parilla, J., J. L. Trujillo, A. Berube, and T. Ran. 2015. "Global Metro Monitor 2014. An Uncertain Recovery." The Brookings Institution. Metropolitan Policy Program. https://www.brookings.edu/wp-content/uploads/2015/01/bmpp_gmm_final.pdf.

Reddy, B. S., and P. Balachandra. 2010. "Dynamics of Urban Mobility: A Comparative Analysis of Megacities of India." Indira Gandhi Institute of Development Research. WP-2010-023.

Sharma, R., S. Jain, and K. Singh. 2011. "Growth Rate of Motor Vehicles in India—Impact of Demographic and Economic Development." *Journal of Economic and Social Studies*. 1, 2: 137–50. http://eprints.ibu.edu.ba/1073/1/vol1-no2-pJOURNAL.OF.ECONOMIC.AND.SOCIAL.STUDIES-1-2_p137-p153.pdf.

Switch ON. 2013a. "Report—Case on Cycle NMT Ban and Kolkata Congestion Survey." http://switchon.org.in/India/congestionsurvey.pdf.

Switch ON. 2013b. "Cycle & NMT Kolkata." http://switchon.org.in/case.pdf.

United Nations, Department of Economic and Social Affairs, Population Division. 2014. "World Urbanization Prospects: The 2014 Revision, Highlights (ST/ESA/SER.A/352)." https://esa.un.org/unpd/wup/Publications/Files/WUP2014-Highlights.pdf.

United Nations, Department of Economic and Social Affairs, Population Division. 2016. "The World's Cities in 2016—Data Booklet (ST/ESA/ SER.A/392)." http://www.un.org/en/development/desa/population/publications/pdf/urbanization/the_worlds_cities_in_2016_data_booklet.pdf.

Mexico City, Mexico: Improving Governance Is Key to Solving Traffic Challenges

Mexico City is the capital of Mexico and a prominent metropolis in Latin America. The city proper has an area of 1,485 square kilometers, comparable to the size of Houston, Texas. It consists of 16 municipalities inhabited by 8.8 million residents. The Greater Mexico City is a conglomerate of dozens of municipalities, some of which belong to surrounding states, with a total population surpassing 21 million, or 18 percent of the country's population. Economically, the area generates 35 percent of Mexico's GDP (World Bank 2011).

THE CHALLENGE

Mexico City is well known for traffic congestion and air pollution. The 2017 TomTom Traffic Index ranks it no. 1 in the most congested world cities list. In the announcement, TomTom indicates:

Mexico City once again takes the top spot with drivers in the Mexican capital expecting to spend an average of 66 percent extra travel time stuck in traffic anytime of the day (7 percentage points up on last year), and up to 101 percent in the evening peak periods versus a free flow, or uncongested, situation—adding up to 227 hours of extra travel time per year. (TomTom 2017)

One of the causes, experts believe, is its road network being built on the foundation developed in the Aztec period in the 14th century. A characteristic of the pattern is the combination of the grid design in the central historical area and the irregularly oriented roads beyond the central area following shapes of the terrain. Due to such a configuration, the city's entry points can be easily jammed. In addition, the growing trend of middle-class families owning private cars, the wide swath of shanty development in the suburbs where most of the workforce reside and commute from, and an underdeveloped public transportation system all contribute to the problem.

The city's public transportation provides a wide coverage. The metro system is one of the largest in Latin America, with 12 lines and over 195 stations. The Suburban Rail extends the metro network into the suburbs, and goes as far as Tlalnepatla and Cuautitlan Izcalli. The extension project continues. The Bus Rapid Transit (BRT) and large urban buses cover a wide area in Mexico City; the lines connect central districts to the suburbs. Additionally, there are some 30,000 microbuses. These minivans, some larger than others, are privately operated; stop at a wave of the hand; and carry over 60 percent of the total passengers (Lámbarry et al. 2016). While the microbuses offer more flexible service than BRT, they are blamed for higher accident rates and vehicular pollution. Additionally, their taxi-like travel pattern (they were once called *taxi colectivo*) makes them one of the main causes of traffic congestion. There are also trolleybuses, light rail, and streetcars, not to mention services from Uber, Blablacar, and the like. One would imagine an unparalleled convenience for traveling from point A to point B, given the many options. The reality is just the opposite: these benefits cancel out in conflicts.

With 5.5 million cars on the roads, the rush hours are among the longest in the world—6:00–9:00 a.m. and 4:30–8:30 p.m. Average car speed is 11 kilometers per hour, or the speed of horse-drawn carriages of 1910 (Devpost 2016). Road rage and frustration are high, long lines of immobile cars crawl on the roads, and cops typically ignore traffic violations. One can find abundant video accounts of similar situations on YouTube. Understandably, from the perspective of commuting time, time stuck in traffic, stress, and drivers' behavior, Mexico City was also ranked "the most painful city" in an "IBM Global Commuter Pain Survey" (IBM 2011). The upshot, however, is that artists, such as jugglers and mariachi bands, find a stage in the middle of the traffic to perform their art.

Mexico City is located in a high-plateau basin 2,240 meters above sea level. Car exhaust and industrial pollutants are trapped inside, making Mexico City one of the most polluted in the world. In recent years, pollution has worsened despite the long-standing policy of *Hoy no circula* ("Don't drive today") implemented since 1989. The system allocates driving days according to plate numbers. In March 2016, the authorities issued an ozone alert prompting the closure of schools. Another one declared just two months later resulted in 40 percent of the cars ordered off the road for days (*Economist* 2016). The most recent alert, issued on May 20, 2017, belonged to the Stage 1 level, the worst. The last time Stage 1 was reached was in 1998 (Baynes 2017).

PLANNING AND POLICY SHORTFALLS

Ineffective administration is a root of the problems on its own. Housing developments expand out of control. There is virtually no enforceable zoning policy. As a result, the residents living in the shanty neighborhoods, typically low-income workers, tend to make longer journeys to work. Their travel to and from work very much depends on the public transit. Bus stations are often located far away from their dwellings. Moreover, due to the lack of complete ring roads, public transportation uses throughways with trucks and other vehicles, resulting in congestion in the city. The number of registered vehicles in the city is expected to reach 10 million, according to an estimate, as population continues to grow (World Highways 2016).

The public transport carries 14.8 million people a day, which nevertheless falls short of demand. Additionally, the conditions with these services are often rough and lack in safety standards. Pickpocketing on public transportation remains the most reported experience (Devpost 2016). Switching from one bus line to another is often time consuming. Those who have the means, particularly the middle class, avoid using public transportation and drive their own cars. As a result, 6.8 million

A traffic jam on Paseo de la Reforma, Mexico City, 2017. The city's efforts to promote its public transit system are undermined by a cultural stigma associated with public transportation. (Edmund Holt/Dreamstime.com)

people travel in private cars, which, in turn, contributes to the congestion (Godoy 2012). Relatedly, there exists a social stigma against using the public transit—public transportation is seen as incompatible with middle-class status. Most middle-class people would feel insulted to be asked to use the metro and shudder in the bumpy buses; they would rather inch along in a prolonged traffic jam (Webber 2016). Experts believe that the situation can be improved by adding new routes and developing underground subway lines. Presumably, if 10 new routes are added, the city would save 290,000 hours a day in commuting time, improve comfort of riding, and reduce emission of 11,000 tons of carbon dioxide per year. Experts also urge city authorities to develop a better fare-paying system that allows passengers to ride all public transportation with a single fare, and make bus stations more accessible (Godoy 2012).

Misallocation of funds dedicated to traffic improvement is one of the reasons why traffic conditions are never improved. It has been observed that currently three-quarters of the transport investment in urban Mexico goes into maintaining roads. There has been insufficient investment in expanding services. While investment in maintenance may improve road conditions and create jobs, it doesn't contribute immediately to the alleviation of traffic congestion and subsequent air pollution. Some Mexican urban planners advocate doubling Metro lines to 24, adding 1,000 kilometers to the BRT network, and replacing the smog-belching privately owned microbuses that account for half of passenger journeys in Mexico City. The ability to predict road conditions and assure timely operation is critical in any public transportation service. However, Mexico City is poorly prepared for a traffic technology upgrade. For example, in offering an efficient public transportation system, the city must install an electronic system to forecast traffic conditions. This information is needed to determine the best combination of Mexico City's public transit options—that is, 12 subway lines, 94 bus lines, 4 Metrobus lines, 8 trolley lines, 260 Ecobici stations (public bikes), and almost 1,400 minibus routes—to get individuals to their destinations. Thirty-two million trips are made daily, and 20 million are on public transport in Mexico City (Ochoa 2013). An information system remains elusive for public transportation in Mexico City as of this writing, and in many other Mexican cities there are no bus schedules or route maps at all.

SEEKING SOLUTIONS

The problems listed in the previous sections suggest that a number of changes can be made to improve Mexico City's traffic congestion. Experts say that, first and foremost, city authorities must improve efficiency, which implies in-depth reforms to root out corruption in the government. Sound policies must be set up to rein in the runaway housing development, so that communities can best be served by transportation facilities. City authorities may also proactively implement programs to discourage private car use, as implemented in many developed countries. Eliminating car ownership subsidies would be one such measure. During the latest global financial crisis, some municipalities introduced tax subsidies of up to 100 percent for owners of new cars. Such incentive programs are believed to only make traffic problems worse (Oxford Analytica 2016). Experts broadly recommend providing safer and more convenient public transportation service and encouraging people to use public transport instead of driving private cars. Additionally, urban planners recommend encouraging carpooling, increasing the number of parking meters, imposing a higher emission standard, and imposing a congestion charge (*Economist* 2016). In conjunction, establishing an intelligent central system for traffic forecast, flow control, signaling, and ticketing will not only contribute to the reduction of traffic jams, but also make the rides more comfortable. Arguably, when more and more residents ride the public transit, its social status will rise as well.

Jing Luo

See also: Traffic and Transportation: Beijing, China: Beijing's War on Traffic Congestion; Istanbul, Turkey: Building More Tunnels and Bridges Won't Make Congestion Go Away; Kolkata, India: When More People Drive Their Own Cars

Further Reading

Associated Press. 2016. "Smog Stays Bad; Mexico City Extends Traffic Cutback." May 4. http://www.voanews.com/content/smog-stays-heavy-mexico-city-extends-traffic-cutback/3316255.html.

Baynes, Chris. 2017. "Thousands of Cars Banned from Roads as Mexico City Chokes in Longest Pollution Alert for Two Decades." *Independent*, May 20. http://www.independent.co.uk/news/world/americas/cars-banned-mexico-city-longest-pollution-alert-smog-a7746756.html.

Business Wire. 2016. "Global Traffic Congestion at All Time High—But Shocking Differences between Continents." March 22. http://www.businesswire.com/news/home/20160321006115/en/TomTom-Traffic-Index-2016-%E2%80%93-Results-In.

Devpost. 2016. "Mexico City Mobility Challenge." https://mexicocity-mobility.devpost.com/.

Economist. 2016. "Blocking Traffic." *Economist,* May 7. http://www.economist.com/news/americas/21698258-clean-up-its-air-capital-has-spend-more-money-more-intelligently-blocking-traffic.

Global Road Safety Partnership. 2015. "Mexico City Announces Bold New Traffic Regulations." August 24. http://www.grsproadsafety.org/news/mexico-city-announces-bold-new-traffic-regulations.

Godoy, Emillo. 2012. "Sorting Out Mexico City's Chaotic Transport System." October 25. http://www.ipsnews.net/2012/10/sorting-out-mexico-citys-chaotic-transport-system/.

IBM News Release. 2011. "IBM Global Commuter Pain Survey: Traffic Congestion Down, Pain Way Up." http://www-03.ibm.com/press/us/en/pressrelease/35359.wss.

Lámbarry, Fernado, Mara Maricela Trujillo, and Cintia Guadalupe Cumbres. 2016. "Stress from an Administrative Perspective in Public Transport Drivers in Mexico City: Minibus and Metrobus." *Estudios Gerenciales* 32, 139: 112–19 (April-June). https://doi.org/10.1016/j.estger.2016.02.003.

Luhnow, David, Nicholas Casey, and Jose de Cordoba. 2011. "Just an Ordinary Day of Death in Mexico's War on Drug Traffickers." *Fox News World.* August 27. http://www.foxnews.com/world/2011/08/27/just-ordinary-day-death-in-mexicos-war-on-drug-traffickers.html.

Ochoa, Maria Catalina. 2013. "Mexico City Traffic Open Data to Avoid Traffic Jams." The World Bank, June 26. https://blogs.worldbank.org/latinamerica/mexico-city-traffic-open-data-to-avoid-traffic-jams.

Oxford Analytica Daily Brief Service. 2016. "Mexico: Weak Measures Will Not Improve Air Quality." April 28. https://dailybrief.oxan.com/Analysis/DB210794/Weak-measures-will-not-improve-Mexicos-air-quality.

Timilsina, Govinda, and Hari B. Dulal. 2010. *Urban Road Transportation Externalities: Costs and Choice of Policy Instruments.* Oxford: Oxford University Press. http://documents.worldbank.org/curated/en/751701468183286599/pdf/770100JRN0wbro0Box0377291B00PUBLIC0.pdf.

TomTom. 2017. "TomTom Traffic Index 2017: Mexico City Retains Crown of the Most Traffic Congested City in the World." http://corporate.tomtom.com/releasedetail.cfm?releaseid=1012517.

Webber, Jude. 2016. "Corruption and Car Fumes Clog Up the Capital: Mexico City Notebook." *Financial Times,* May 26. https://next.ft.com/content/55767084-1b2d-11e6-8fa5-44094f6d9c46.

World Bank. 2011. "Mexico Case Study Overview." http://siteresources.worldbank.org/INTURBANDEVELOPMENT/Resources/336387-1306291319853/CS_Mexico_City.pdf.

World Highways. 2016. "Mega City Transport in Mexico." http://www.worldhighways.com/sections/key-projects/features/mega-city-transport-in-mexico.

New York City, United States: The New York Subway

Modern cities are plagued with traffic congestion. Overpopulation and an increasing number of people driving to work overwhelm cities' roadways. In cities such as Beijing and Mexico City, there can be as many as 4 to 5 million vehicles on the city's roads. Traffic congestion not only causes loss of productivity, but more importantly, it is the main contributor of air pollution. A common solution is to promote public transportation and do everything possible to make the rides on buses and subways convenient and comfortable, so that people willingly leave their car home. In this regard, New York City's subway system is among the best in the world.

Opened in 1904 with only 28 stations in Manhattan, today the New York City subway is the preferred rapid transit system managed by the Metropolitan Transportation Authority (MTA). The New York subway is also the oldest and the largest network in the world. It has 472 stations (MTA Info-a) as of 2018, more than Shanghai Metro (337), Beijing Subway (319), Paris Metro (303), London Metro (270), and Tokyo Metro (179) (CityMetric). While nearly 85 percent of workers in the United States drive to work, four of every five rush-hour commuters to New York City's central business districts avoid traffic congestion by taking transit service. New York City's rail car riders outnumber the rest of the country's subways and commuter railroads combined (MTA Info-a). The system plays a critical role in ensuring New York's place as a world center of finance, commerce, culture, and entertainment, and offers a model of how traffic congestion in large metropolises can be reduced.

CONVENIENCE

New York City's subway system is arguably the most convenient and efficient mobility solution for a city of 8.6 million (U.S. Census Bureau 2017). Per MTA's ridership data, in 2016, the subway had a daily ridership of more than 5.6 million and an annual ridership of roughly 1.757 billion. The fleet consists of 6,400 subway cars traveled approximately 358 million miles in 2016, along 665 miles of track, 24 hours a day, seven days a week. Of the 472 total subway stations, 117 are made accessible to customers with disabilities, via elevators and ramps. NYC Transit Subway serves Brooklyn, the Bronx, Manhattan, and Queens, making 8,200 weekday trips. For added convenience, the Metrocard can be used on other kinds of transit such as MTA buses and AirTrain JFL.

The ease of riding the subway has not gone unnoticed. In 2016, a 25-year-old lawyer in New York City set the Guinness World Record of traveling to all 469 subway stations (prior to the opening of 3 new stations) in 21 hours, 28 minutes, and 14 seconds covering 660 miles of track, which beat the previous world record set by himself (Licea 2016).

ENVIRONMENTAL BENEFIT

New York City's subway saw its highest weekday ridership of about 5.67 million trips and 1.76 billion for the year in 2016, the highest since 1948, according to MTA's statistics.

In world subway ridership ranking, however, New York subway's annual total trips rank no. 7 in the top 10 of 2016, compared to (in billion units) Beijing's 3.660, Tokyo's 3.411, Shanghai's 3.401, Seoul's 2.620, Guangzhou's 2.568, Moscow's 2.384, Hong Kong's 1.716, Mexico City's 1.624, and Paris's 1.526 (MTA Info-a). A tremendous benefit of riding the subway is the reduction of air pollution. In 2010, the MTA, using a measuring system developed by the American Public Transportation Association, found that when passengers used MTA subways, buses, and commuter trains, they reduced the emission of greenhouse gases by 20 million metric tons. To help achieve this level of efficiency, the New York Power Authority (NYPA) and New York State Energy Research & Development Authority (NYSERDA) provided significant support to the MTA. On the environmental front, New York City's transportation is ahead in conscientiously achieving a sustainable urban mobility.

Table 1 Subway Ridership at a Glance

Year	Average Weekday	Average Saturday	Average Sunday	Average Weekend	Annual Total
2011	5,284,295	3,082,463	2,414,587	5,497,050	1,640,434,672
2012	5,380,184	3,172,627	2,490,736	5,663,363	1,654,582,265
2013	5,465,034	3,243,495	2,563,022	5,806,517	1,707,555,714
2014	5,597,551	3,323,110	2,662,795	5,985,905	1,751,287,621
2015	5,650,610	3,309,731	2,663,418	5,943,149	1,762,565,419
2016	5,655,755	3,202,388	2,555,814	5,758,201	1,756,814,800

Source: http://web.mta.info/nyct/facts/ridership/index.htm.

SUBURBANIZATION

The relationship between the development of transportation facilities and urban gentrification has drawn research attention. In megacities such as Beijing, Shanghai, and Mexico City, urban crowding worsens as more roads and subway lines are added. In fact, it appears reasonable to assume that subway expansion is likely to lead to growth in residential neighborhoods—more subway stations, more neighborhoods, and more traffic. This hypothesis dates back to the time when the first subway lines were opened in New York City. A commentary in a 1905 issue of the *Street Railway Journal* predicts:

> One of the most interesting features of opening new rapid transit lines for service in the densely populated districts of large cities is the effect of these additional facilities upon the volume of traffic within the tributary region. It has long been recognized that a permanent solution of the rapid transit problem in a growing city cannot be secured by the development of a single route of high-speed service. New facilities not only open up additional avenues of travel and thereby can—and often do—relieve congestion existing upon other lines; they apparently create traffic, which sooner or later grows to a volume that requires additional means of transportation to be furnished. (Hood, Nycsubway.org)

However, studies show that it may not have been by coincidence that New York City did not go this route. Data of population projection compiled by the Department of City Planning of New York City shows, the overall population changed little between 1950 and today, hovering around 8 million, with a dip to approximately 7 million between 1980 and 1990. During this period, 21 new stations were built (King 2011).

A 2011 study examined subway construction of 138 cities worldwide including in Asia, Europe and North America, and found that subways do not necessarily boost population growth. In the case of New York City, the change in station densities was found to have no measurable effect on net residential densities. However, the study does identify a correlation between commercial land use in New York City and population fluctuation in the vicinity. The study suggests that population growth is more correlated with commercial development, but the growth of the subway system per se is not significantly correlated with population growth. Hence, the effect on gentrification appears to be indirect, via its provision of mobility to commercial activities. The study further indicates that the subway's underground network does not compete with motorways, and therefore does not lead to the city's land expansion. Moreover, it suggests that the subway system seems to encourage urban decentralization, the evidence being that cities with large subway networks appear to be less centralized and more suburbanized than those without. By contrast, in megacities of developing countries, Beijing being a good example, most subway expansion happened after private cars had been popularized, and thus did not significantly reduce car use (King 2011). It is further noted that since the early 1990s, China's urban-bound migration has remained in its acceleration phase, and most migrants choose megacities as their destination. The World Bank warns that at 54 percent, China's degree of urbanization is still well below the 70 percent expected of a country with its current income level per person. The flood of migrants will continue; by 2030, Chinese cities will contain more than 1 billion people (*Economist* 2015). As such, development of public transit has the potential of contributing to urban crowding.

A similar finding was reported by a 2007 study titled "Did Highways Cause Suburbanization?" (Baum-Snow 2007). The study finds that the aggregate population of central cities in the United States declined by 17 percent despite an overall 72 percent growth in urban population between 1950 and 1990. The study attributes this change to the pro-exogenous effect of the widening distribution of highways. The study estimates that adding a highway through a central city could reduce the city's population by as much as 18 percent. On the other hand, without the interstate highways, population in central cities would have grown by 8 percent. It was observed that highways result in reduced population density and increased free urban space.

SERVING MULTIDIMENSIONS

In a sense, the functionality of the great subway system of New York is beyond the "centralizing" or "decentralizing" effects. Some argue that this is a simplification of what the concept of "city" implies. The traditional concept of city vs. suburbs reflects that of a boundary solely based on population density. In reality, however, there are different boundaries that could be drawn. In a culturally diverse city like New York City, "Just as there is a political New York, there is a health care New York, a cultural New York, a culinary New York of delicious ethnic complexity . . . Each city exists simultaneously with the others, the boundaries overlap" (Washburn 2013, 24). It is fair to say, while the New York subway facilitates suburbanization at one level, it serves residents to urbanize more conveniently at other levels.

Jing Luo

See also: Traffic and Transportation: Beijing, China: Beijing's War on Traffic Congestion; Osaka, Japan: Attracting Private Investments to Public Transportation; Stuttgart, Germany: A City with the Best Mass Transit

Further Reading

Baum-Snow, Nathaniel. 2007. "Did Highways Cause Suburbanization?" *Quarterly Journal of Economics.* May. http://qje.oxfordjournals.org/content/122/2/775.full.pdf+html.

CityMetric Staff. CityMetric.com. http://www.citymetric.com/fabric/city-doesn-t-exist-and-when-angela-merkel-made-joke-story-bielefeld-2692.

The City of New York, Department of City Planning. 2013. *New York City Population Projections by Age/Sex & Borough, 2010–2040.* The City of New York.

Economist. 2015. "The Great Sprawl of China." January 22.

Gonzales-Navarro, Marco. 2016. "Subways and Urban Growth: Evidence from Earth." May 30. http://individual.utoronto.ca/marcog/attachment/Subways.pdf.

Hood, Clifton. Nycsubway.org. "The Impact of the IRT on New York City." http://www.nycsubway.org/wiki/The_Impact_of_the_IRT_on_New_York_City_%28Hood%29.

John F. Kennedy International Airport. https://www.panynj.gov/airports/jfk-airtrain.html.

King, David. 2011. "Developing Densely—Estimating the Effect of Subway Growth on New York Land Uses." 4, 2 (Summer): 19–32. https://pdfs.semanticscholar.org/0cb6/29961b3dab87ab02d778f2a43fdf0689c182.pdf.

Licea, Melkorka. 2016. "NYC's Fastest Subway Rider Beats His Own All-Stations Speed Record." *New York Post*, July 23. http://nypost.com/2016/07/23/nycs-fastest-subway-rider-beats-his-own-all-stations-speed-record.

MTA Info-a. http://web.mta.info/nyct/facts/ridership/index.htm.

MTA Info-b. "Subways." http://web.mta.info/nyct/facts/ffsubway.htm.

NYC Tourist. "The New York City Subway." http://www.nyctourist.com/subway_page1.htm.

TomTom Traffic Index. 2016. www.tomtom.com. https://www.tomtom.com/en_us/trafficindex.

United States Census Bureau. 2017. Quickfacts: New York City, New York." https://www.census.gov/quickfacts/fact/table/newyorkcitynewyork/PST045217.

Washburn, Alexandros. 2013. *The Nature of Urban Design: A New York Perspective on Resilience.* Washington, DC: Island Press.

Osaka, Japan: Attracting Private Investments to Public Transportation

Osaka is the third-largest city in Japan, home to more than 2.5 million people. The city's population increases by another million each workday. This is due in large part to rapid postwar suburbanization. As a key part of the Osaka-Kobe-Kyoto Metropolitan Area, it is the most densely populated region of Japan with over 18 million people. As one study noted, "Within a 20 kilometer (12.4 mile) radius of Osaka's urban core live almost as many people as reside in the state of Michigan" (Hill 1996, 10; Transportation Research Board 2006, 5; Cox 2012, 1). The challenges of efficiently moving millions of commuters falls to a combination of public and private entities that operate trains, subways, trams, and buses. Itami and Kansai International—Osaka's two major airports—connect the city to the wider world.

HISTORICAL BACKGROUND: GROUND TRANSPORTATION

By the late 19th century, the national railway system formed the basis of rail transportation for Osaka—a key commercial and industrial center. By the early 20th century, several private companies began to construct interurban and commuter rail lines for Osaka residents. In 1933, the first subway opened. In the two decades after World War II, Osaka experienced rapid economic and population growth. By the 1960s, the Osaka Municipal Transportation Bureau (OMTB), in charge of the metro, tram, and bus lines, began to devote more efforts to solving the growing problem of traffic congestion. Until this decade, most Japanese did not own a car. Automobile usage comprised only 8 percent of all trips in 1965. One could not buy a car unless they had already secured a parking space. However, as the middle class expanded and simultaneously fell in love with automobiles, the city had to address the consequences of this shift by expanding the public transit system. Beginning in 1962, the central government assisted the OMTB through the Subway Construction Cost Subsidization Program, which provided 70 percent of the funding for the construction of "publicly operated metro lines." This helped finance the opening of four more subway lines by the end of the decade. Government subsidies also helped the OMTB improve stations and safety, but the metro did "not receive any operating subsidies" (Transportation Research Board 2006, 15).

RECENT DEVELOPMENTS: GROUND TRANSPORTATION

By the turn of the 21st century, Osaka was experiencing serious traffic congestion. The Millennium Cities database ranked the Osaka-Kobe-Kyoto area as having the 19th-greatest traffic density among major metropolitan areas. By 2001, for example, 39 percent of all trips within the city were by car—a huge increase over 8 percent in 1965. Yet simultaneously, the region had "the highest mass transit market share of any high-income world megacity outside Tokyo." In 2007, "57 percent of trips in the metropolitan area were by mass transit" (Cox 2012, 4). This ranked Osaka as "the second highest public transport ridership in the automotive world" (Urban Transport 2003, 1).

Regarding the mass transit mix, in the first decade of the 21st century about 2.35 million commuters used the metro and tram system every day, at least 2.94 million rode the rails, and approximately 250,000 took the bus. Seven metro lines with 112 stations provided service every two to four minutes—a frequency unheard of

Commuters board subway trains in Osaka, Japan, 2016. Osaka is known for its clean, comfortable, and efficient public transit services. (Tupungato/Dreamstime.com)

in U.S. cities. Twenty commuter rail lines, many of which connect with the subway system, stop at almost 1,000 stations. There is also a linkage with the *Shinkansen* line, which offers high-speed rail service the length of Japan (Urban Transport 2003, 1; Transportation Research Board 2006, 5–6).

In many ways Osaka's mass transit system is a success. Each day it carries millions of people swiftly, safely, in spotlessly clean vehicles, over a massive coordinated system. Yet it is facing a number of challenges in the 21st century. Like Japan as a whole, the Osaka region's birth rate is declining and its population is aging. More people are driving their cars. Ridership declined 20 percent between 2000 and 2005. Insufficient government funding is also a problem. In response, the OMTB initiated a management reform plan, upgraded signage—including English-language information—built bus shelters, added more elevators and escalators to assist the elderly and those with physical disabilities, and instituted "more convenient fare options" using a prepaid card. An unusual innovation is the No-My-Car-Day pass, which is good for unlimited rides on buses, trams, and subways during the special No-My-Car days "every Friday and the 20th of each month." This program is designed to reduce the number of people driving in the city, thereby lessening traffic congestion (Transportation Research Board 2006, 9–10). It appears, however, that the Osaka Prefectural Government's program might not be as successful as hoped. According to a 2001 *Japan Times* article, "more people drive their cars on No-My-Car Day than non-designated days, making traffic even worse" (Moriguchi 2001).

A more radical solution to some of Osaka's transit problems is the privatization of its metro system. In a 2014 *Next City* article, Stephen J. Smith asserted that the privatization of Japan's national railway system, which began in 1987, helped set the precedent for Osaka's decision to sell its municipal subway system. Smith argues that the sale of the national railways "was a roaring business success." Local political leaders also shaped this decision as Osaka Mayor Toru Hashimoto and his political compatriot Osaka Prefecture Governor Ichiro Matsu, both of the nationalist Japan Restoration Party, supported the sale as a way to stimulate the economy and reduce the size of the government. The attempt to shift control of transportation infrastructure from the public to the private sector is—according to some—a risky strategy, while others argue it is necessary to address problems associated with a declining population and a stagnant economy (Smith 2014; Sato and Urabe, 2014).

HISTORICAL BACKGROUND: AIR TRANSPORTATION

Commercial aviation began in Japan in the 1920s. Osaka's first airport for land-based aircraft opened in 1938. Typical of most airports of the time, it was located close to the Central Business District (CBD). This was advantageous for the business community, who lobbied for the airport and used the airlines. The Asia-Pacific War led to the military taking over operations. After the war the United States occupied the base until 1959 when it reverted to civilian control. Renamed Itami Airport (ITM), the facility linked Osaka to the expanding commercial aviation network as more business personnel began to take advantage of the airlines' time and cost savings. The early 1960s saw the introduction of jet aircraft, which further accelerated this trend. The advantages of jet aircraft—they could carry more passengers longer distances in a shorter time—were offset by the disadvantages as they produced much more noise than piston-engine aircraft. This led to increasing complaints from angry residents located under the flight paths to and from ITM. In response, the Ministry of Transportation instituted the first curfew in 1965, prohibiting jet aircraft from using the airport between 11:00 p.m. and 6:00 a.m. They also placed limits on the number of takeoffs and landings. Believing that the government favored business interests over citizens' well-being, in 1969 local residents filed the first "large-scale lawsuit on noise pollution" in Japan (Tsuru 2000, 107–110; Yamaguchi 2013, 15; Siddiqi 2003). Ultimately, Itami Airport could not be easily expanded to handle increased air traffic because it was hemmed in by residential development. These factors led aviation advocates and business leaders to look for a better location to build a new airport that would not be afflicted by these issues.

Senator Hoei Kato of the Osaka Prefectural Government played an important role in this process. He noted that it was clear by 1966 that a new airport was needed because of numerous restrictions at Itami. Moreover, Kato and other city boosters desired to "develop Osaka as a truly international city of the 21st century" and to do that they needed a new airport. Advocates wanted an airport that would be open twenty-four hours, would "become a hub airport for the Asia-Pacific region," and would develop into an air cargo center. This would be a key part of the economic revitalization plan for Osaka, and more broadly the Kansai region of Japan, as it would attract more post-industrial concerns such as high-tech firms, universities, research institutions, and tourists. Planning began at the local and national levels in the 1970s. To overcome local resistance, it became clear that the airport should be built offshore (Kato 1992, Aldrich 2016).

RECENT DEVELOPMENTS: AIR TRANSPORTATION

The new Kansai International Airport (KIX) opened in 1994. Constructed on an artificial island two miles into Osaka Bay, the new facility had a magnificent terminal building designed by the prestigious Italian architect Renzo Piano. Unfortunately, KIX faced a host of problems. Because it cost $14 billion to build this island airport, the debt load was enormous, making it impossible to turn a profit. Extremely high landing fees further discouraged airline use. Moreover, KIX faced increased competition from new Asian airports such as Macao in 1995, Hong Kong in 1998, and Seoul in 2001. Furthermore, it was a 25-mile trip to the CBD, the Japanese economy was declining, and the island was literally sinking into the sea and had to be stabilized. Unexpected events such as the September 11, 2001, terror attacks on the U.S. and the spread of SARS—Severe Acute Respiratory Syndrome—depressed international air travel. As a result, the original grand expectations for the new facility were not met (Sims 2001; *Japan Times* 2014; *Japan Times* 2015; Matsumoto 2005).

The fortunes of Kansai International Airport began to turn around due to several developments. The deregulation of international commercial aviation, for example, created a new market for low-cost carriers (LCC). In 2012, KIX opened Japan's first LCC-dedicated terminal. The following year, Kansai International won the "LCC Airport of the Year" award. Recently, growing economies and middle classes in nearby Asian countries such as China and South Korea, the weak yen, and additional flights by Asian LCCs led to more international tourists entering Japan via KIX (Travelbiz 2012; Yamaguchi 2013, 8; *Japan Times* 2014).

Potentially even more important to the future of KIX was the Ministry of Land, Infrastructure, Transport, and Tourism's decision to privatize all Japanese airports by 2020. The conservative Liberal Democratic Party of Prime Minister Shinzo Abe envisioned airport privatization as a means of reducing state expenditures, lowering the national debt, and attracting more private investment as a crucial part of their plan to reinvigorate the Japanese economy. The competition for the rights to operate KIX saw the number of applicants dwindle to just the Vinci-Orix group when the others were reluctant to agree to take on the $12 billion debt. Vinci-Orix signed a 44-year lease to operate both Itami—which handled only domestic flights—and Kansai. The new operating company—Kansai Airports—immediately set out to enhance the entire airport complex. For example, the growing numbers of Muslim tourists from Southeast Asia could now utilize a prayer room at KIX. In 2017, a new inexpensive "24/7" airport hotel is scheduled to open (Fujita 2015; Centre for Aviation 2016; Narioka 2015; *Asahi Shimbun* 2016; Shugo 2014).

As the *Wall Street Journal* noted, the Vinci-Orix deal represented the "the first privatization of a major airport operation in Japan" and was "part of Tokyo's efforts to tap into private-sector capital and infrastructure expertise." A number of commentators, however, had concerns about this strategy as reflected in articles in the *Japan Times*, the *Asahi Shimbun*, and Reuters. CAPA-Centre for Aviation called the decision "a private sector gamble." Supporters hope that private firms operating airports such as KIX can more quickly adapt to changing conditions and develop more revenue streams than state airport management.

Douglas Karsner

See also: *Traffic and Transportation:* Beijing, China: Beijing's War on Traffic Congestion; Istanbul, Turkey: Building More Tunnels and Bridges Won't Make Congestion Go Away; Stuttgart, Germany: A City with the Best Mass Transit

Further Reading

Aldrich, Daniel. 2016. *Site Fights: Divisive Facilities and Civil Society in Japan and the West*. Ithaca, NY: Cornell University Press.

Asahi Shimbun. 2016. "New Hotel Set for Kansai Airport as Travelers Fly 24/7" (in Japanese). *Asahi Shimbun,* August 10. http://www.asahi.com/ajw/articles/AJ2016081000041.html.

Centre for Aviation. 2016. "Osaka Kansai International Airport: A Powerful Regional Airport but Still an Investment Experiment." *CAPA-Centre for Aviation,* January 12. https://centreforaviation.com.

Cox, Wendell. 2012. "The Evolving Urban Form: Osaka-Kobe-Kyoto." *Newgeography,* March 28: 1–7. http://www.newgeography.com/content/002750-the-evolving-urban-form-osaka-kobe-kyoto.

Fujita, Junko. 2015. "Update I-Orix Only Confirmed Bidder for Kansai Airport Rights after More Drop Out." *Reuters,* May 22. https://www.reuters.com/article/kansai-bidding-idUSL3N0YD3J320150522.

Hill, Richard Child. 1996. "Detroit and Osaka: Urban Life in the USA and Japan." *Michigan Sociological Review* 10: 1–17. https://www.jstor.org/stable/40969000?seq=1#page_scan_tab_contents.

Japan Times Editorial. 2014. "Can Kansai Airport Take Off?" *Japan Times,* September 8. https://www.japantimes.co.jp/opinion/2014/09/08/editorials/can-kansai-airport-take/.

Japan Times. 2015. "Sinking under Debt, Kansai Airport Privatization Will Be Test for Abe." *The Japan Times,* March 14. https://www.japantimes.co.jp/news/2015/03/14/business/sinking-under-debt-kansai-airport-privatization-will-be-test-for-abe/#.XAbSgmhKhM0.

Kato, Hoei. 1992. "Osaka Kansai International Airport." *Trends and Issues in International Aviation,* April 30: 30–32. http://onlinepubs.trb.org/Onlinepubs/trcircular/393/393.pdf.

Kato, Shinichi. 1996. "Development of Large Cities and Progress in Railway Transportation." *Japan Railway & Transport Review,* September: 44–48. http://www.ejrcf.or.jp/jrtr/jrtr08/pdf/history.pdf.

Matsumoto, Hidenobu. 2005. "Effects of New Airports on Hub-Ness of Cities: A Case Study of Osaka." *Journal of the Eastern Asia Society for Transportation Studies* 6: 648–63. https://www.jstage.jst.go.jp/article/easts/6/0/6_0_648/_pdf/-char/en. .

Moriguchi, Kenzo. 2001. "We're Pretty Rude—and We Don't Care." *Japan Times,* May 20. https://www.japantimes.co.jp/community/2001/05/20/general/were-pretty-rude-and-we-dont-care/#.XAbofGhKhM0.

Narioka, Kosaku, and Inti Landauro. 2015. "Vinci, Orix Get Nod to Operate Two Japanese Airports." *Wall Street Journal,* November 10. https://www.wsj.com/articles/vinci-orix-get-nod-to-operate-two-japanese-airports-1447153916.

Sato, Shigeru, and Emi Urabe. 2014. "Osaka City Plans Subway Operator Initial Offering to Chase Tokyo." *Bloomberg,* April 13. https://www.bloomberg.com/news/articles/2014-04-13/osaka-city-plans-subway-operator-initial-offering-to-chase-tokyo.

Shugo, A. 2014. "The Efforts of Kansai International Airport." *Halal Media Japan*, October 15. https://www.halalmedia.jp/archives/723/efforts-kansai-international-airport/.

Siddiqi, Asif. 2003. "The Origins of Commercial Aviation in Japan." *U.S. Centennial of Flight Commission.* https://www.centennialofflight.net/essay/Commercial_Aviation/japan/Tran20.htm.

Smith, Stephen. 2014. "New Starts: Osaka Mulls Subway Sale . . ." *Next City,* April 28. https://nextcity.org/daily/entry/new-starts-osaka-mulls-subway-sale-iranian-metros-abound-madrid-metro-looks.

Transportation Research Board of the National Academies. 2006. "Innovative Techniques in the Planning and Financing of Public Transportation Projects." *Research Results Digest* 77 (May): 1–17. http://onlinepubs.trb.org/onlinepubs/tcrp/tcrp_rrd_77.pdf.

Travelbiz. 2012. "Japan's Kansai International Airport to Become Asia's Most Environment-Friendly Hub." *Travelbiz: The Leading Travel/Business News Portal for Nepal.* https://travelbiznews.com/japans-kansai-international-airport-to-become-asias-most-environment-friendly-hub/.

Tsuru, Shigeto. 2000. *The Political Economy of the Environment: The Case of Japan.* Vancouver: UBC Press.

Urban Transport Fact Book. 2003. "Osaka-Kobe-Kyoto Suburban Rail Summary." *Urban Transport Fact Book*, October.

Yamaguchi, Katsuhiro. 2013. "Evolution of Metropolitan Airports in Japan: Airport Development in Tokyo and Osaka." Discussion Paper No. 2013-3, Roundtable on Expanding Airport Capacity under Constraints in Large Urban Areas, International Transport Forum, February. https://www.itf-oecd.org/sites/default/files/docs/yamaguchtokyoosaka.pdf.

Saint Petersburg, Russia: Swamped with Traffic

The invention of the automobile was, like many inventions, both a blessing and a curse. Big-city dwellers of Saint Petersburg often point out that traffic congestion is one thing that makes them sigh about the good old days of horses clip-clopping on the streets of Russian cultural capital. Situated in the north of the Russian Federation, the city of Peter is well known for having been built on the marshlands and now, 300 years later, it is swamped with cars.

A BLANKET SOLUTION

It is hard for the government to turn a blind eye to the kind of problems people have to deal with on an everyday basis, so in the year 2014, the Saint Petersburg government issued an ordinance addressing the development of the city's transport system for the next five years. In order to deal with one general problem, it is only logical to subject it to analysis, getting several smaller and therefore manageable ones as a result.

TOO MANY HIGHS AND LOWS

Saint Petersburg has certain specific traits compared to other Western European cities. It covers a huge territory of 556 square miles and is densely populated—9,398 people per square mile, which is comparable to some European capitals, such as Warsaw and Budapest. There is, however, a significant difference in the urban development area. Whereas in Europe the townscape is more or less balanced, 90 percent of Saint Petersburg's population lives on 234 square miles, meaning that the distribution is drastically uneven, all due to some parts of the city being twice as developed as the others. In addition, despite the city's relatively low GDP per capita its economic development in the past decade led to rapid motorization, reaching 300 cars per 1,000 citizens.

More cars mean increasing demand for roads, but in spite of the high population density in developed urban areas, the road density (the ratio of the length of the total road network to the land area) there is as low as 8 miles per 1 square mile (compare to 1.55 miles per 1 square mile in general).

Built on the Neva River, Saint Petersburg developed a unique mixed road system incorporating bridges, very unlike the ring pattern of Paris or Moscow, or the rectangular pattern of New York City or Washington, D.C. Traveling from remote areas of the city to its center, people do not have many routes to choose from. Several highways (Moskovskiy proezd, proezd Marshala Zhukova, Petergoffskoe

Traffic and Transportation

expressway, etc.) connect the center and the peripheral areas, while circular highways (Sadovaya Street, Liteyniy Prospect, Vladimirskiy Prospect, etc.) allow transition between them. In the meantime, there is only one ring road in Saint Petersburg, referred to as the Ring Road. The limited choices inevitably lead to traffic congestion on most of those roads in the mornings and evenings, when coming to work or driving home.

During rush hours, which in Saint Petersburg occur from 7:30 a.m. to 10:30 a.m. and from 5:00 p.m. to 8:30 p.m. (in the remote neighborhoods, morning rush hours could be from 8:30 a.m. to 10:00 a.m.), the average speed in town does not exceed 16 miles per hour; in the most congested sections, the speed drops to 6 miles per hour. In fact, traffic congestion is widespread all over the city (Saint Petersburg Municipality 2014).

INSUFFICIENT PUBLIC TRANSPORT

Despite having been modeled after big European cities, Saint Petersburg lacks a refined and balanced transport infrastructure, the kind seen in London or Paris. Despite the impressive numbers given on the official cite of the city administration, it seems that it might just be not secure enough, not fast enough, or not efficient enough for the majority of citizens to choose public transportation over their

Cars and electric trams on an avenue in Saint Petersburg, Russia, 2017. The city's public transportation system is mediocre relative to other major European cities. Its inconvenience and expense make it an unattractive alternative to driving one's own car. (Aliaksandr Klapkou/Dreamstime.com)

personal automobile. As a result, the streets are overwhelmed with cars, and insufficient parking space only adds to the problem.

Means of public transportation available to Saint Petersburg citizens include subway (also known as "Metropolitan" or "Metro"), buses (commercial and public routes), electrical transport (streetcars and trolleybuses), railway (for commuters) and water-buses, transporting 2 billion passengers per year. Saint Petersburg Metro remains the most popular, taking on 40.6 percent of overall public transport passengers. It is also the fastest, most efficient, and most reliable means of public transportation in the city.

However, due to the low income levels of the population, the Metro is not as affordable as it is in cities of many European countries. The area covered by the public transport infrastructure is much lower than necessary for such territory and population (Saint Petersburg Municipality 2014).

CHEAPER DOESN'T MEAN BETTER

Saint Petersburg Municipality has drawn a plan for the city's development in the period of 2015–2020, taking into account the city's privileges, for example, comparing Saint Petersburg to London, Madrid, and Paris (Saint Petersburg Municipality 2014). The numbers demonstrate such correlations as free parking in the central streets of the city leading to lower speed, whereas accessibility of independent public transportation allows for faster transition during rush hour. The data suggests that free parking is not really a benefit. It is not a surprise that when lines of cars are parked free on the sides of the road in Saint Petersburg, the traffic is slowed down. In Madrid and Paris, if cars were left somewhere in the center of the city, there would be a charge as high as 1 to 3 Euros per hour. The fact that gasoline is relatively cheaper in the Russian Federation is not necessarily advantageous either. Low gasoline costs encourage people to own a personal car and spend time in it rather than in the public transit.

ROAD-UNFRIENDLY CLIMATE

Even if we put all myths of Russian weather aside, Saint Petersburg remains a northern city, situated close to the Baltic Sea. Severe climatic conditions cause faster erosion, more traffic congestion, and lower safety on roads. A humid continental climate and high average rainfall with temperatures below zero centigrade starting in November contribute to fast destruction of the asphalt pavement, which, combined with the use of cheaper materials and maintenance, is one of the main problems across the country.

Streets close due to roadwork, incessant precipitation from showers to blizzards creates dangerous situations, ice on roads results in multiple accidents. The same chart provided in the city's data shows that the number of people who died in a transportation-related accident is twice as high in Saint Petersburg as in European capitals.

SOLUTIONS

Having looked into the points the problem stems from, the Municipality of Saint Petersburg came up with a budget schedule to combat each of them separately. Overall there are five general subprograms the city started on, with the general idea of encouraging citizens to reduce their car usage in favor of public transportation and enhancing the city public transportation infrastructure in terms of accessibility and safety. Those were 1) general development of transport infrastructure, 2) main public transportation system enhancement, 3) alternative public transportation system enhancement, 4) maintenance of public roads, and 5) management and safety of transportation industry.

According to the city's 2015–2020 Plan, the aforementioned goals are to be accomplished by increasing the capacity of public transport by 6 percent to reduce overcrowding of subway cars during rush hours; introducing more modern subway cars and raising the percentage of those to 55 percent in order to boost the overall appeal, and also build more accessible subway stations to encourage people to walk to them. In an attempt to make the electric transport more convenient, the municipality made the decision to renew the fleet of trolleybuses and streetcars and modernize the public transport stops. Changing the policy on parking is also included in the plan: the municipality has decided to increase the number of parking lots, including paid ones, up to 60,000 places. In order to discourage drivers from parking on the curbs of the cities, the municipality introduced fines. These steps are aimed at alleviating traffic congestion by lowering the number of cars in the streets (Saint Petersburg Municipality 2014).

Another strategy employed by the ordinance is to offer more alternatives in terms of nonmotorized transportation. Saint Petersburg Metro, as the most effective and the most promising type of public transportation, will remain the priority with speed of 25 miles per hour (compared to 11 miles per hour of buses and streetcars or even 6 miles per hour during rush hours) and two-minute time interval between trains. The municipality has planned to put 13 new stations into service, thus connecting previously isolated areas of the city to the subway network and elongating it to 87 miles.

In search of other options, the municipality considered turning to water transport. However, water-buses were seen by the citizens solely as tourists' and visitors' means of transport, and with their limitations of routes (4) and times (June–October), by the year 2016 only the major route remained operational.

Such alternatives as bicycles gained attention as well. Overall, being eco-friendly, economical, and not prone to get stuck in traffic jams, bicycles tend to be quite popular with young people living in cities. And yet, with the shortage of bikeways and virtually no bicycle parking facilities, this choice has been dismissed by many. In order to change this situation, the ordinance budgeted quintupling bikeway mileage and raising the number of bicycle parking facilities up to 120 parking lots.

Finally, not to forget about pedestrians, the municipality also included on the list of budgeted activities the reconstruction and maintenance of pedestrian areas and traffic-free zones. Judging by the fact that according to the ordinance statistical data, more than 60 percent of road accident victims are pedestrians, this kind of enhancement is very much called for.

Two of the five subprograms listed in the ordinance concern the poor condition of roads far from the central part of the city and highway structures—that is, bridges (416) and tunnels (36) made necessary due to waterways and railways. At the moment of the issuance of the ordinance about one-fifth of all the structures required attention. The municipality allocated a substantial part of the overall budget to the cause.

THE BENEFITS TO REAP

As matters stand now, according to the yearly report of the Committee of Transportation and Transportation Infrastructure Development published in December 2015, the implementation of the transportation plan has been more or less successful. In particular, this pertains to the maintenance and reconstruction of public roads and alternative public transportation system enhancement. In addition, the municipality seemed quite successful in creating and maintaining new parking lots and public transportation pavilions for the bus and streetcar stops.

In terms of alternative transportation development, several promotional campaigns on cycling have been launched, including introducing bicycle rental stations for the spring, summer, and autumn months. The number of stations tripled in the year 2015, with the number of rides growing eight times (Saint Petersburg Municipality 2015).

Russian Federation Transport Strategy 2030

Reports indicate that major cities in Russia are experiencing worsening traffic congestion, particularly in large low-income cities. According to a report by the World Bank, primary contributors to the deteriorating conditions include lack of a coherent legal basis, challenges in financing urban transport systems, weak physical and operational integration of public transport services, and automobile-related policies and investments. To improve urban transportation and enhance mobility, the Russian government has set up pilot programs in leading cities as part of the Russian Federation Transport Strategy 2030 initiative, one of which is the open data program in Saint Petersburg. The project aims to reduce congestion and pollution by developing a comprehensive parking management plan for the city's historic center, and improving traffic management and passenger information systems. The World Bank encourages open transport data programs worldwide; it believes that integrated information of passengers, traffic conditions, and public transport services can be an effective solution. In the case of Saint Petersburg, experts believe, a policy of open transport data will provide an effective traffic solution, and will also be consistent with the city's existing policies, as well as with the Federal Government's Open Government policies and programs. Furthermore, the World Bank has made its own recommendations as well for the city regarding improving passenger information, setting legal and technical policies, establishing standards for data sharing, promoting best practice in data handling, and improving transparency at both the city and government levels. Experts believe delivering timely information on the flow of urban traffic, providing instant access to information on traffic congestion, the availability and cost of parking spaces, and current public transit routes will effectively address Saint Petersburg's challenges in managing its canal and bridge systems.

As to the issue of overall modernization, Saint Petersburg Metro and electric transport now accept credit cards and feature traffic data display boards at every station. Data obtained through the monitoring of passenger traffic help the transportation authority to adjust the routes of public transport to the needs of the citizens. The report actually mentions that according to 2004–2015 surveys analysis, a significant number of citizens now opt for using public transport over driving. However, no specific data is given.

Anastasia Kovalyuk

See also: Traffic and Transportation: Beijing, China: Beijing's War on Traffic Congestion; Istanbul, Turkey: Building More Tunnels and Bridges Won't Make Congestion Go Away; Mexico City, Mexico: Improving Governance Is Key to Solving Traffic Challenges

Further Reading
Administration of Saint Petersburg Official site on Transport infrastructure (in Russian). http://transport.orgp.spb.ru/Portal/transport/main?lang=en.
Saint Petersburg Municipality. 2014. "Governmental Ordinance of Saint Petersburg Municipality on Saint Petersburg Transportation System Development for 2015–2020 Years" (in Russian). July 30. http://spbstrategy2030.ru/wp-content/uploads/2014/07/Развитие-транспортной-системы.pdf.
Saint Petersburg Municipality. 2015. "Annual Report for the Year 2015 on the Implementation of the Saint Petersburg Transportation System Development Plan for 2015–2020 Years" (in Russian). December. http://gov.spb.ru/static/writable/ckeditor/uploads/2016/05/06/05%20%D0%A2%D1%80%D0%B0%D0%BD%D1%81%D0%BF%D0%BE%D1%80%D1%82%20%20%D0%BE%D1%82%D1%87%D0%B5%D1%82%202015%20(%D0%B8%D1%82%D0%BE%D0%B3).docx.
The World Bank Group. 2014. "Opportunities and Strategies for Mainstreaming Open Data in Transport Projects in Saint Petersburg." *World Bank.* December. http://documents.worldbank.org/curated/en/947031468295545087/pdf/936810WP0Box3800Petersburg00PUBLIC0.pdf.

Stuttgart, Germany: A City with the Best Mass Transit

Not to be confused with a city of the same name in Arkansas, Stuttgart is the largest metropolis and the capital of Baden-Wuerttemberg, a state in Germany. Traffic and transportation have special importance in Stuttgart given that German automaker Karl Benz invented the automobile there. Today Stuttgart is home to Mercedes-Benz and Porsche, expensive brands of automobiles. Prominent in industry, agriculture, science, and technology, Stuttgart has a long tradition of innovation. Its scientists and engineers boast many patents to their name. The city takes pride in its system of mass transit. Yet many residents still rely on the automobile, and traffic jams and congested roadways are too frequently a fact of life in Stuttgart. The automobile and its reliance on fossil fuels have many detractors, and the city must take steps to improve the daily commute.

THE PROBLEM

Stuttgart, and Germany at large, deserves credit for its mass transit systems, and Germans own fewer automobiles per person than do Americans. Yet a reliance on the automobile is part of life in the city. Statistics on the number of cars are hard to uncover, but it seems clear that these cars cause traffic jams, congestion, and frustration on the roads. Compiling statistics on traffic patterns worldwide, global positioning satellite (GPS) company TomTom concluded in 2015 that Stuttgart is Germany's worst city for traffic congestion (Lukyen 2015). According to the company, a 30-minute commute to work finds the average driver stuck in traffic 22 minutes daily. Over the duration of an average year such a commuter will spend 84 hours motionless in a traffic jam. This predicament must cause duress. The German Automobile Association, alert to the problem, has dubbed Stuttgart the "the traffic jam capital of Germany" (Lukyen 2015).

The association faults the city for the problem, charging that Stuttgart authorities have done too little to maintain roads, bicycle lanes, and its mass transit system. Regrettably, the situation is not improving. In a trend notable worldwide, traffic congestion has worsened in Stuttgart in recent years. In this context, Baden-Wuerttemberg, the German state that contains Stuttgart, has witnessed a rise in traffic congestion of a magnitude comparable with events in its capital.

In the context of traffic travails elsewhere, Stuttgart's problems rank the second worst in Europe. In 2015, INRIX, a company that tracks and analyzes traffic patterns worldwide, issued its annual Traffic Scorecard, revealing that year that Stuttgart's traffic congestion worsened by 14 percent (Burfeind 2016). No other European city matched this magnitude of increase. The *Local*, an online news outlet, in 2013 compared Stuttgart's traffic problems to the woes that assail drivers in Los Angeles, California, Paris, France, Sydney, Australia, and Rome ("Stuttgart Faces Worst Traffic Jams" 2013). Stuttgart's drivers spend 33 percent more time in traffic, according to the *Local*, than those who travel roads free from congestion.

MASS TRANSIT

Already a strength, mass transit is a potential solution to the problem of traffic congestion in Stuttgart. The city's public transportation options include a train, a subway, and a street railway system. Electricity powers these options and requires an expense on the part of the city and its residents. The train, subway, and street railway operate daily between 5 a.m. and 1 a.m., according to Stuttgart Information, a website run by the Public Transportation Association ("Train and Bus"). Moreover, buses roam the city on weekend nights to take passengers to their destinations. Buses offer an important service because they operate when the train, subway, and street railway are closed. Gasoline and diesel power the buses. Diesel is particularly important in Stuttgart and other regions of Europe. As elsewhere, residents and tourists must pay for these services to defray the cost of fuel and maintenance. Ticket prices vary by route and duration. The shortest routes, irrespective of form of public transit, offer fares as low as 1.2 Euros, according to TripAdvisor.com. This price covers only one-way trips. As in many other cities, it is possible to purchase a ticket that entitles a person to ride the public transportation system all day. Rates for groups of people are also available. Simplicity is an aim of this system, so it is possible to buy only a single ticket that will allow that person to change lines multiple times during a day rather than requiring him or her to buy multiple tickets. Depending on the route and time, students and tourists may qualify for discounts.

The diversity of the public transit system means that tickets vary in duration. The cheapest are valid for only two hours during the day, whereas the tickets with the longest tenure may remain valid an entire year. The longer the duration of the ticket, the greater tends to be the discount on the price. As many as five people may share a single ticket and qualify for a group rate. The Verkehrs-und Tarifverbund Stuttgart (VVS) has created a system of vending machines that sell these tickets. Larger VVS stations, of course, sell tickets. In addition, a person may purchase a ticket from the driver of a bus or streetcar. To encourage tourists to use public transportation, hotels and inns sell tickets good for three days, a suitable duration for a conference goer or a person on a brief visit to the city. These tickets, known as StuttCards, allow a rider unlimited use of whatever means or combination of public transit he or she chooses during these three days. Attendees at special events like music concerts may purchase a Kombi Ticket, valid from three hours before the event until late into the night to allow the purchaser time to exit the city by bus. Purchasers buy Kombi Tickets through the VVS. The event planner sends the ticket through the mail to these buyers. The best value is available to college students, who may ride the train, subway, streetcar, or bus free any weekday until 6 p.m. and all weekend or holidays. A student identification suffices in lieu of a ticket. This option is known as the StudiTicket.

The public transit system is extensive enough to connect Stuttgart with its suburbs. The city's autoworkers congregate in the suburbs. Stuttgart's rolling terrain, with several hills and valleys, has influenced the layout of public transit lines. Despite critics, Stuttgart maintains roads and rail lines so that its system of public transportation is among the most modern and efficient in Europe. This system is a collaboration between city government and the private sector, both of which contribute money to the system's upkeep. The principal government agency in charge of the public transit system is the VVS. Public and private subsidies allow people to use public transportation at a fraction of what it would otherwise cost. In partnership with the VVS, the Stuttgart Stadtbahn manages the fleet of buses.

Public transportation is essential because Stuttgart has its population dispersed throughout the city rather than concentrated in dense enclaves. For this reason, the train, subway, streetcars, and buses cover a large swath of territory. As a rule, the streetcars and buses receive the heaviest use. The train receives lighter use, though with termini downtown and in Stuttgart's shopping district, it offers public transportation for residents and tourists intent on shopping. Residents and tourists know the train as the Standseilbahn, and it is popular among visitors. Whatever the form of public transportation, users need wait only a few minutes for the next train, subway, streetcar, or bus. Termini and the VVS website post the times of arrival and departure, and the forms of public transportation adhere to these times. The result is a dependable, regular system of travel.

An important part of this system is the Stuttgart metro, known to residents as the Stadtbahn, an impressive network of light railways that augments the route of streetcars and buses. The system is extensive with 77 stations and routes totaling 195 kilometers as shown in "Metro of Stuttgart." Operational since 1966, the Stadtbahn features aboveground lines and about 30 kilometers of underground lines near downtown. These lines are near some 2.6 million residents of Stuttgart, offering ready access to this form of public transit. This system uses a letter and number to code for the route. For example, U1, U2, and U14 take passengers along the main valley in Stuttgart. U5, U6, U7, and U15 run north and south through the city, whereas U4 and U9 cross through Stuttgart east and west. U3 and U13 are peripheral lines that do not take commuters directly through the city but rather funnel them to destinations outside Stuttgart.

These lines vary in duration. For example, U1 extends a little more than 17 kilometers. Along this route are 31 stations. A passenger may travel the entire length in 40 minutes. A longer route, U2, extends 36.1 kilometers. Along the route a traveler encounters 28 stations. A traveler may complete the entire route in 38 minutes. U3 is comparatively short at just under 8 kilometers. The route has 11 stations and may be completed in its entirety in 15 minutes. Even shorter, U4 has just 3.5 kilometers of track. The route has 21 stations and requires 34 minutes to complete. The longest route appears to be U14, which stretches nearly 21 kilometers. It has 32 stations and requires 45 minutes to complete. There are many other routes, and all need not be tabulated to gain a sense of the scale of light rail in Stuttgart and the many options available to residents and tourists. These routes are particularly impressive when one considers that they represent just the train. Many other avenues exist for the streetcars, the subway, and the buses, giving people a multiplicity of choices. The reader should keep in mind that a single ticket gives passengers access to all these routes, not merely to the extensive routes of the light rail. It is not surprising that Stuttgart's residents take pride in their mass transit.

A desirable if easy to overlook feature of Stuttgart's light rail is its capacity to carry bicycles along with passengers. This extra feature complements the city's residents who use their bicycles as a mode of transportation. By combining the bicycle and train, people can cover long distances with relative ease and minimum expense. Bicycle paths comb the city to encourage cyclists to travel distances safely. Drivers appear willing to share the road with cyclists. In some cases, the cyclist must buy a ticket for his or her bicycle to use the train. An advantage of the bicycle is its suitability for the commute from suburb to city.

CARPOOLING

There are other ways to ameliorate the problem of traffic congestion in Stuttgart. One popular option is carpooling. Stuttgart sponsors Pendlernetz Stuttgart, a website where people advertise the desire for and the availability of carpooling. For example, a person might announce the intention of attending a soccer match (Europeans refer to soccer as football) in Stuttgart and ask whether any reader might wish to carpool to the game. This service is valuable because some 50,000 people attend Stuttgart soccer matches. Traffic for such events tends to clog roads because soccer is such a popular sport for the city's residents. By carpooling, however, spectators can lessen this congestion by sharing a ride with another fan or group of

> ### Baden-Wuerttemberg
>
> In southwestern Germany, Baden-Wuerttemberg borders Switzerland to the south and France to the west, with the Rhine River forming the border between Baden-Wuerttemberg and France. Nearly 14,000 square miles (35,750 square kilometers), Baden-Wuerttemberg is Germany's third-largest state. Its population approaches 11 million, roughly 600,000 of whom live in its capital, Stuttgart. German tribes colonized what is today Baden-Wuerttemberg in prehistory. Relations were uneasy with the Romans, who invaded in the early second century CE. Rome's decline in late antiquity led to Baden-Wuerttemberg's absorption into the Holy Roman Empire in the Middle Ages. The Reformation of the 16th century, important throughout much of Germany, left Baden-Wuerttemberg largely Catholic. In 1871, Baden-Wuerttemberg became part of the German nation. The state formed from formerly independent Baden, Hohenzollern, Wuerttemberg, and sections of Swabia. After World War II, Baden-Wuerttemberg became part of West Germany, but was again reunited with the rest of Germany in 1990. Despite having few natural resources compared to other regions in Germany, Baden-Wuerttemberg has a robust economy and low unemployment. Technology firms including software companies and factories, among them high-end automakers Daimler AG, Porsche, and Robert Bosch GmbH, provide jobs and competitive wages. Baden-Wuerttemberg's countryside produces food and lumber.

fans. Anyone may use the Pendlernetz Stuttgart website free, so advertisements for rides incur no fee. The Stuttgart Mobility Centre operates this website for the benefit of all residents and travelers to Stuttgart.

Carpooling, of course, has potential beyond easing the traffic congestion to and from sporting events. Stuttgart's residents might carpool to and from work or pair with one another for shopping excursions. If implemented in a large way, carpooling has the potential to halve the number of automobiles on the road. Carpooling can extend beyond the bounds of Stuttgart to mobilize people traveling to the city from a neighboring area and so broaden the appeal of this alternative transportation.

Christopher Cumo

See also: Energy and Sustainability: Frankfurt, Germany: Protecting the City from Climate Changes; *Traffic and Transportation:* Zurich, Switzerland: Improving Traffic and Transportation through All Possible Venues

Further Reading

"Bicycle-Train Commuting around Stuttgart." 2011. Toytown Germany, March 30. https://www.toytowngermany.com/forum/topic/210596-bicycle-train-commuting-around-stuttgart/.

Burfeind, Mark. 2016. "Stuttgart Sees the Highest Rise in Traffic Congestion in Europe, Overtakes Cologne as Germany's Most Congested City." INRIX, March 16. http://www.inrix.com/press-releases/scorecard-de-english.

Lukyen, Jorg. 2015. "Stuttgart Worst City for Traffic Jams." *The Local*, March 31. https://www.thelocal.de/20150331/stuttgart-worst-city-for-traffic-jams.

"Metro of Stuttgart." http://www.mapa-metro.com/en/germany/Stuttgart/Stuttgart-stadtbahn-map.htm.

"Stuttgart Faces Worst Traffic Jams in Germany." 2013. *The Local*, April 5. http://www.thelocal.de/20130405/48951.

"Stuttgart: Public Transportation." https://www.tripadvisor.com/travel-g187291-s303/stuttgart:germany:public.transportation.html.

"Train and Bus: Public Transportation." http://www.stgt.com/stuttgart/trans_city_transport_eng.htm.

Zurich, Switzerland: Improving Traffic and Transportation through All Possible Venues

Situated in northern and central Switzerland, Zurich touches the northern shore of Lake Zurich. The city is the largest in Switzerland and the capital of the canton (province) of the same name. Zurich's origins go back more than 6,000 years. Historically it has not been heavily populated, a circumstance that remains true today. Zurich is, however, a financial center whose economic activity brings people to the city. The aggregation of people in Zurich has congested the city's roads. Conscious of this problem, Zurich encourages residents and those who commute to the city for work to favor public transportation over the automobile. City authorities boast of a modern, efficient mass transit, which includes trains, streetcars, and buses. Beyond these modes of transportation, the city is working to make roads safe for bicyclists and to create paths for them. Zurich authorities hope to encourage more people to commute to work by bicycle. Such alternatives have the potential to alleviate the city's traffic congestion and thereby improve transportation.

THE PROBLEM

According to a 2011 report, Zurich ranked as the world's sixteenth-worst city for traffic congestion (Allen 2011). Traffic jams force the city's drivers to spend too much time idle on the roads, causing duress and aggravation. The main roads are along Zurich's business district, and more than one-fourth of them are clogged with traffic. Other reports, including commentary in the *New York Times*, fault the city for these ills, noting that traffic lights are timed to favor Zurich's streetcars rather than the automobile. Moreover, pedestrian crossings, which were once underground to avoid conflict with traffic, are now aboveground, pitting pedestrian against automobile. Global positioning satellite (GPS) company TomTom has calculated that more than 27 percent of Zurich's roads are so heavily traveled that drivers must inch ahead at speeds 70 percent slower than the velocity of drivers who travel at night when roads are more lightly used (Allen 2011).

Zurich's authorities are holding their own against these criticisms. A member of Zurich's civil engineering department, Pio Marzolini, affirms that the city is different from many others worldwide. In many cities, traffic takes pride of place over pedestrians, but in Zurich authorities strive to treat pedestrians and automobiles equally (Allen 2011). Traffic jams may be an unfortunate byproduct of a system that seeks to reward people for walking, cycling, or taking a streetcar rather than clogging the road with automobiles. Pedestrians and streetcar riders, like drivers, are equally indignant when they face delays, prodding Zurich authorities to craft policies that respect their rights as much as those of car drivers.

The Zurich chapter of the Touring Club of Switzerland, an organization that represents motorcars and their drivers, believes that the city is doing too little to placate the automobile drivers. The chapter faults Zurich authorities for having few policies that benefit the automobile. Part of the problem, according to the chapter, may be that Zurich has too few roads, especially roads that could take cars out of the city to reduce congestion within it. The chapter cites the Uetliberg Tunnel, opened in 2009, as a good first step because it can funnel traffic south of the city, thereby relieving congestion. The chapter hopes for more projects along these lines and cites the notoriously congested Gubrist Tunnel as an example of a road that needs enlargement. Because of the traffic congestion, the chapter estimates that Zurich loses $118 million per year in tardiness for work and in delays in the delivery of goods within the city (Allen 2011).

OVERVIEW OF PUBLIC TRANSIT AND THE VERKEHRSBETRIEBE ZURICH

Public transportation has long been popular in Zurich and may be an antidote to traffic congestion. Not only residents, but tourists and other visitors to the city use public transportation in robust numbers. Perhaps as many as half the trips within the city are taken on public transportation. Options for travel by public modes are numerous, including train, bus, streetcar, electric bus, boat, and cable-powered car. Some of these modes are integrated into a single operating system. The wait for

Zurich Main Station is the largest railroad hub in Switzerland, and the center of Zurich's popular public transportation system. As many as 3,000 trains and 500,000 travelers pass through the station each day. (Bumbleedee/Dreamstime.com)

the next streetcar, bus, or other mode of transit is seldom longer than a few minutes. As in some other cities, Zurich strives to simplify the purchase and use of tickets. Rather than buy several tickets to use when a passenger switches from one mode of transit to another, a single ticket allows that person to use any and all modes of transit during a day. In other words, there is no additional fee for switching from, say, a streetcar to a bus.

The center of activity may be the Zurich Main Station, the largest railroad hub in Switzerland and one of the busiest in Europe. Service is available not merely within the city but between Zurich and neighboring countries, including Italy, Germany, France, and Austria. Onlookers may gain a sense of the magnitude of traffic to and from the station by observing the nearly 3,000 trains that enter and depart from it on an average day. As many as 500,000 people may use the trains daily at Zurich Main Station.

Zurich, Switzerland, delegates decisions about the mass transit system to a publicly owned company, the Verkehrsbetriebe Zurich (VBZ). More than a century old, the VBZ controls Zurich's trains, streetcars, buses, trolleybuses, and a funicular. In Zurich, as in the rest of Europe, the streetcars are commonly known as trams. A trolleybus is a bus that runs on a track and is powered by electricity. Because the tracks cannot be electrified for fear of electrocuting people who step on them, power must be supplied by a copper wire running above the bus. A funicular is a type of train that can climb steep grades because a cable pulls it.

The VBZ has grown with the city. Operating the first buses in 1927, the VBZ grew by 1939 to operate a system of trolleybuses in addition to the diesel-powered buses of its earlier venture. The tempo of growth slowed during World War II even though Switzerland was not a combatant. After the war, the VBZ became part of a larger public transit system, allying with the Zurich Transport Network in 1990.

STREETCARS

Zurich has a network of streetcars or trams that penetrate every neighborhood within the city. Many residents depend on the trams to the extent that they do not need to own an automobile. This convenience accounts for the fact that per capita car ownership in Zurich is lower than is the case for many American cities.

Electricity powers these trams, but this source of energy was not always used. The first streetcars in Zurich were latched to horses. Horses did not supply power and speed equivalent to electricity, and they caused the noxious problem of polluting city streets with dung that city workers had to remove from the pavement. These first horse trams operated in Zurich as early as the 1880s, but electricity quickly supplanted the horse during the next decade.

In fact, Zurich's first electric tram patrolled the streets in 1888, only six years after the introduction of the horse tram. At first the tram was a private venture, with several companies vying for passengers within the city. Most of these companies ceased operation within a few decades or were subsumed into the VBZ when Zurich authorities took charge of the trams. As companies faded from view, the trams underwent other changes, including the consolidation of lines. Recent decades, however, have witnessed an expansion of service as the streetcars compete with the trolleybuses for riders.

TROLLEYBUSES

The operation of trolleybuses does not differ in principle from that of the trams. Both require electricity as their source of power. The advantage of the trolleybus is its capacity to carry very large numbers of people. This feature benefitted the city because the maintenance of a small number of large trolleybuses did not cause the magnitude of traffic congestion that was common with a proliferation of trams or, even worse, automobiles.

In its early days, the VBZ maintained a fleet of just six trolleybuses to serve all the residents of Zurich. Growth was rapid, so that by 1957, the VBZ counted 57 trolleybuses under its auspices. By 2012, the number had grown to 114. Most of these trolleybuses are articulated, meaning that they have joints between cars that pivot. By pivoting, these vehicles can travel rapidly along curves. The automaker Mercedes-Benz, however, is experimenting in Zurich with trolleybuses that do not have these joints that pivot.

THE S-BAHN

Zurich's S-Bahn, a dense network of tracks, is another mode of transportation. The tracks and trains that run atop them extend throughout Zurich. The most extensive of these lines connect Zurich to cities in Germany. Akin to the practice at airlines, the S-Bahn offers luxury accommodations for first-class travelers, an option unusual among modes of public transit.

The first of these rail lines began operating in 1968, providing service near Lake Zurich. This first line served commuters, most of them affluent from the industrial boom that followed the end of World War II, from the north shore of the lake who wished for regular service into the city. The area near the north shore of Lake Zurich had once been a center of viticulture, but postwar industrialization had transformed it into an area of successful entrepreneurs and industrialists. As population grew, passengers became more numerous, straining this rail line so that service slowed and overcrowding became a source of irritation.

Responding to a demand for improvements, Zurich authorities began planning an expansion of the rail system about 1970. Sleek models of trains followed. Locals dubbed them "Mirages" after the fighter jets of the same name. These trains were fast and had features that reduced travel time further. For example, doors opened and closed automatically to streamline service. These trains accelerated rapidly and had state-of-the-art brakes to decelerate when necessary.

Zurich authorities developed several plans of new lines in the 1970s, but financing was not always easy to secure. As part of the public transit system, these new trains depended on taxpayer funding, but the residents of Zurich were not at first eager to vote for such spending, perceiving the trains as a system that disproportionately benefited the wealthy of northern Lake Zurich who should not need

> ### Lake Zurich
>
> Sharing the name of the city to its northwest, Lake Zurich owes its origins to the Glarus Alps, central Switzerland's portion of the Alps. The water collected there as rain in warm weather and snow and ice in cold weather flows down the mountains through the Linthal River, which has its source near Linthal, a village in the Swiss canton of Glarus. Until the early 19th century, the Linthal River emptied into Lake Zurich, providing it with the water that sustains it. But in 1811, Swiss engineers diverted the river into Lake Walen, a large body of water in both the cantons of Glarus and St. Gallen. Deprived of water, Lake Zurich would over time have shrunk and possibly disappeared from evaporation, but engineers dug the Linthal Canal in 1816 to carry water from Lake Walen to Lake Zurich. By a circuitous route, therefore, the Linthal River continues to replenish Lake Zurich. Picturesque scenery makes the lake and its environs ideal for tourists, especially during summers. Sailing, swimming, kayaking, paddle boating, wake boarding, wake surfing, and canoeing are popular. The beach hosts sunbathers and volleyball enthusiasts.

taxpayer subsidies. Despite these misgivings, voters approved funding for an expansion of these rail lines in 1981.

The opening of these new lines in 1990 coincided with other developments. The most prominent may have been the city's integration of the public transit system such that a single ticket entitled the buyer to travel on any one or several of the modes of public transit. A train ticket was thus more than a train ticket, being redeemable for travel on a streetcar, trolleybus, bus, or other mode of transportation. In 2002, Zurich began operating these trains at night in addition to during the day. The tempo of operation varies by line, with some trains operating every 20 minutes whereas others operate on the hour. Zurich aims to improve service so that no passenger will need to wait more than 15 minutes for a train by 2030.

BICYCLE

Zurich authorities are committed to making the city safe and inviting for bicycle commuters. The city aims to encourage all residents, particularly the young and those in robust health, to bicycle to work or for errands. To this end the city is planning bicycle routes that separate cyclists from traffic and so do not expose them to the danger of accidents. For example, an underground tunnel below the airport will take cyclists away from traffic. The city will also need shelters for the storage of bicycles to protect them from inclement weather and thieves. These developments are in the planning stages, and cycling enthusiasts complain that progress has been too slow. For example, the underground tunnel, originally to have opened in 2016, has been postponed until 2019. Until improvements are made, bicyclists must venture onto the crowded roads of Zurich.

Christopher Cumo

See also: Energy and Sustainability: Copenhagen, Denmark: Striving to Be Carbon-Neutral by 2025; *Traffic and Transportation:* Stuttgart, Germany: A City with the Best Mass Transit

Further Reading

Allen, Matthew. 2011. "Zurich's Streets among Europe's Most Congested." July 7. http://www.swissinfo.ch/eng/zurich-streets-among-Europe-s-most-congested/30634398.

"Underway with Public Transport in Zurich." http://www.zuerich.com/en/visit/public-transport.

"Zurich: Public Transportation." https://www.tripadvisor.com/travel-g188113-s303/zurich:switzerland:public.transportation.html.

Violence, Corruption, and Organized Crime

OVERVIEW

The 21st century sees urbanization progressing at an accelerated pace. According to a 2018 report by the World Bank, today over 50 percent of the world's population reside in urban areas and 80 percent of the world's economy is produced in cities. Cities have become the places where job creation, education, and innovation take place. However, the urban environment is also the most vulnerable to violence, corruption, and crime. The World Bank's 2011 *World Development Report* shows that urban violence is a particularly significant barrier to sustainable development. Articles in this section of our book analyze some of the major sources of violence, corruption, and crime, including criminal and organized conflicts, drug trade, corrupt governance, wars, and disturbances caused by climate change.

Struggle to Restitch the Society

In maintaining peace and order in the city, the government's responsibility is the most important factor. Experience shows that where the governance fails, violence, corruption, and crime thrive. However, building an efficient and corruption-free government can be an extremely complex and slow process.

Baghdad is the capital city of Iraq and the second-largest Islamic city in the world. In the past three decades, the city experienced the 1980–1988 Iran-Iraq War, the 1991 Persian Gulf War, and the 2003 U.S.-led invasion. The latter ended with the removal of Saddam Hussein and his Baathist government. The liberation, however, failed to bring the intended peace, safety, and prosperity to the city. Instead, as Karsner shows, revenge killings were rampant after the U.S.-led invasion, and 3 million people are currently living in slums. Security walls built to protect neighborhoods have been found to segregate communities and make people's lives more difficult. Corrupt guards use checkpoints to extort money, and corrupt government officials are behind economic crimes that lead to hate, insurgency, and sectarian conflicts. In addition, the prolonged decline of oil prices has made the sufferings even worse. In his article, Karsner reviews a series of historical events, both domestic and external, to identify factors that have delayed the process for rebuilding a valid government.

Syria, a close neighbor of Iraq, has also been plagued with instability. Once the western end of the Silk Road where global traders met, Aleppo is Syria's largest city. Within just five years, from 2012 to 2017, the civil war reduced the city to rubble. Some scholars compare the destruction of Aleppo to the German siege of Stalingrad in World War II. Since then, Aleppo has become a battleground of religious factions and a haven of extremist groups, one of which is ISIS. Syria's civil war has driven millions of refugees around the world. While most scholars attribute the causes of the war to an ethnic and political divide, Johansen explores a more encompassing root cause. He contends that climate changes are likely to have played a critical role in the events. The warmer temperature in the region had led to frequent droughts in recent years, and eventually driven millions of farmers into large cities such as Aleppo, Homs, and Damascus. He argues that when a sudden influx drains the city's resources and makes people with divided ideologies crowd into densely populated quarters, conflicts are more likely to happen. Johansen urges governments to be prepared for more conflicts of this kind, as climate changes appear to be continuing and with increasing severity.

Kabul, the capital city of Afghanistan, has been through wars and chaos for decades. Major wars include the Soviet invasion of 1979–1989, the Civil War of 1992–1996, and the U.S.-led invasion in 2001. Instead of coming out a stronger government capable of maintaining order and reviving the economy, Kabul hit the bottom. It was ranked 166 out of 168 countries on the 2015 Transparency International's Corruption Perception Index. It has been named a "failed city," a "city of chaos" in several reports. At the top level, corrupt officials have embezzled billions of dollars in aid funds. High-level corruption is believed to pose more threat to the national security than terrorist groups today. The law enforcement forces, such as the army and the police force, are among the most corrupt of the government branches. Lack of law enforcement has turned Kabul into a haven of international organized crime. Terror attacks have become deadlier and more frequent over time. At the grassroots level, bribery is commonplace. This situation is certainly not what the U.S.-led international coalition had sufficiently anticipated and prepared for. However, by some accounts, crime, violence and, corruption are worse after the 2001 U.S.-led occupation, as Karsner indicates. Some critics argue that the invasion was based on a "frighteningly simplistic view of Afghanistan," and the consequences benefited insurgent groups and undermined American goals of building a stable government to serve its people. Through a careful review of historical events, Karsner provides an insightful assessment of what has led to the current situation.

Handling Challenges of Domestic and International Migrations

The 21st century has been challenged by tremendous pressure from international migration right from the beginning. Large cities all over the world have become destinations of choice. Most cities are unprepared to handle cultural differences;

nor do they have the capacity to forcefully contain terrorists who infiltrate migrant populations. Adaptation will likely be a steep curve.

Beijing is the capital city and one of the four provincial-level cities of China. It is also a tourist city receiving 8 million visitors per year. Duncan examines the safety and security conditions of Beijing and finds that the city has to deal with some common challenges seen in the West. While organized crime is not prevalent in Beijing, thanks to the city's close monitoring of criminal groups, petty crimes such as robbery and street violence have been on the rise since the late 1970s. Duncan offers two reasons: 1) the sudden arrival of migrant population overwhelms the city's resources; and 2) the economic reform has weakened the closely knit neighborhoods, rendering the traditional neighborhood watch obsolete. Additionally, economic gaps and gender imbalance are arguably among the most important generators of crime as well. He indicates that Beijing is nevertheless a safer city than most, due to the city's intensive police surveillance and harsh anticrime measures. A noticeable law enforcement practice, Duncan indicates, is that Beijing readily employs severe punishment including the death penalty and life imprisonment for economic crimes. Multiple top-ranking officials have been given such penalties. Despite the harsh crackdowns, however, China's ranking in perceived corruption is low.

Brussels, the capital of Belgium, is a world-recognized secure city. Unlike Beijing, Brussels is a more open and liberal society. However, as Duncan points out, Brussels faces many challenges recently. As waves of refugees arrive in Europe in recent years and more migrant camps are set up in and around Brussels, crimes such as robbery, rape, sexual assault, and forced prostitution are on the rise. These crimes often make immigrants their victims of choice. Gangs formed by migrants from Africa are among the major perpetrators of street violence. The prevalence of street crimes appears to be higher in Brussels compared to other world cities. Duncan observes that, unlike in Beijing where criminal groups are mostly subdued, organized crime is active in Brussels, particularly in the city's red-light districts. The trade of sex workers exploits girls and women from poor nations such as Albania. Another high-profile crime of recent years is terror attacks, one of which happened in 2016 in an airport and a metro station, resulting in 32 people killed. The terrorists in that event were found to be connected with the 2015 attack in Paris. These attacks also triggered a backlash in the form of threats against Muslim neighborhoods. As such, Belgian security must monitor several nationalist groups in and around Brussels. As a result, heavily armed personnel are seen stationed on the premises of many public transportation facilities.

Sicily is a highly urbanized region of Italy with a population of approximately 5 million. Like many cities and regions in Europe, Sicily has experienced an influx of migrants especially from Africa in recent years. As Lesneskie's analysis of the well-known crime group Cosa Nostra shows, recent social changes have produced opportunities for organized crime to rise. A characteristic of the Italian mafia is that it performs certain social services to cloak criminal activities. In the case of Cosa Nostra, the gang operates drug trades and prostitution rings by themselves and through migrant gangs. Extortion of money is a main operation often targeting migrants, as Lesneskie observes. On the other hand, members of Cosa Nostra help the government by providing social work, such as settling disputes and helping with disaster relief. The assistance is known for higher efficiency compared with the government's aid. However, the group expects a "tax" or *pizzo* from the beneficiaries. While the Sicilian public and local governments seek every way to combat Cosa Nostra, success is not easily achieved, due to the criminal groups' wide connections and the complex social functions they perform.

Maintaining Equality and Justice Is Key to Stability

Inequality is a hotbed that breeds violence, crime, and corruption. The experiences of Seoul and Mexico City demonstrate that progress in democracy involves overcoming certain established traditional values.

The progression of democracy in South Korea represents an unrelenting struggle and serves as a model for neighboring countries. In this regard, the people of Seoul have always stood in the forefront. The rise of the middle class has been a process of breaking the tradition of authoritarianism and the *chaebols* (large family-run conglomerates dominating the economy) who take advantage of it. The political elites representing a network of interests typically use their resources to sway public opinion in their favor. Their political maneuvering has a broad range of objectives, from accumulating personal wealth, staying in power by rigging elections, living an extravagant life, to getting their children enrolled in prestigious universities. However, the primary goal of the elite class is to suppress the middle class who demand their fair share. Historically, the struggle for democratic rights has been dealt with by bloody crackdowns by the government, resulting in loss of lives. However, using democratic means, the Korean public has succeeded in deposing the dictators one after another. From 2016 to 2017, Seoul saw tens of thousands of demonstrators taking to the streets to demand impeachment of President Park Geun-hye on the grounds of corruption and influence peddling. Eventually, in 2017, Park became the first democratically elected president to be removed from office. Through a succinct review of democratic struggles in South Korea, Long contends that the ouster of President Park represents the culmination of a social transformation showing that the South Korean civilian-led democracy is maturing.

When Spaniards colonized Mexico, they intended to build a society like Spain's, with the nobles enjoying privileges at the expense of the rest of the society. Donahue argues that the outcomes of a pyramid regime, such as the corruption and injustice seen today in Mexico, are traceable to the conquistadors. Likewise, historical tensions within the Spanish kingdom find their parallel in the regimes of Mexico today, and even the solutions bear a resemblance. Although modern democracy is different from the feudal tradition, rule of law is not immune to corruption. Corrupt candidates with money and power may rig elections in their favor. As Donahue points out, when opportunities are unequally distributed, violence and crime rise. One way the impoverished classes in Mexico react to the government's corruption is through open protests that may involve violence. Donahue examines a number of examples of unfair government policies in recent decades and the resulting social instability. He argues that to curb corruption, crime, and violence in the society, the Mexican government must constantly reform itself and maintain a policy of transparency.

Cultivating Social Capital Contributes to Crime Prevention

Interpersonal trust and mutual expectations are what bond communities together; they constitute the "social capital." Successful urban management tends to protect its social capital by bridging divides, building networks of reciprocity, and extending opportunities to criminals to help them rehabilitate. Strengthening social equity through effective law enforcement is critical to the cultivation of social capital.

Tokyo, the capital of Japan, has a population of more than 9 million. Its safety record is one of the world's best. Tokyo has been ranked the "safest city in the world" by multiple indices, a recent one being its inclusion in "The Safe Cities Index 2015" by the *Economist* magazine. According to the index, the per-100,000 murder rate in Tokyo was .4 compared to New York City's 5.6. Tokyo's tips include "informal social control," "absence of internal social conflicts," and "strong sense of group identity." An important factor, not surprisingly, is the constant presence of neighborhood policing in the form of *koban* (police box). However, what may be most critical to Tokyo's low violence level, according to Karsner, is the fact that very few people own guns. The procedure for buying a gun in Japan can be so complicated that it would discourage most potential buyers. However, violence and corruption do exist. The sarin nerve gas attack that killed 13 and injured 6,000, the Yakuza gang, and political corruption are evidence. One type of criminal offense widely found to disturb people's daily life is *chikan*—men sexually groping women in public transits. Tokyo's residents demonstrate ingenuity and courage in fighting the perpetrators.

Chicago, with a population of 2.7 million, is an economically dynamic and the third most populous city in the United States. It attracts tens of thousands of tourists each year. The city's fame, however, is tarnished by a notoriously high crime rate. In 2016 alone, 4,000 shootings were reported. In some neighborhoods, there have been cases of minor disputes settled by gun-related violence. Lesneskie contends that one of the factors spurring the violence is the modeling effect, that is, gang members worshipping violence as a way of life. Additionally, when larger gangs break up into smaller ones, which happens more frequently when economic conditions deteriorate, members of smaller groups are likely to follow their own rules; in which case they tend to become more violent. In countering violence, Chicago stresses prevention. The city employs a comprehensive approach integrating deterrence and education. Two programs dubbed Strategic Subject List and Operation Cease-Fire are aimed at changing the violence culture.

Further Reading

The World Bank. 2011. World Development Report 2011: Conflict, Security, and Development. https://openknowledge.worldbank.org/handle/10986/4389.

The World Bank. 2018. "Urban Development—Overview." http://www.worldbank.org/en/topic/urbandevelopment/overview.

Aleppo, Syria: Drought, Global Warming, and Civil War

By 2017, much of Aleppo, Syria's largest city (which had been home to 2.3 million people in 2005), lay in ruins, having been bombed by the United States, Russia, and Syrian air forces. A large proportion of the city had been abandoned, several hundred thousand of its people dispersed as refugees around the world. Ancient Aleppo had been one of the longest continually inhabited cities in the world (since about the third millennium BCE, or 5,000 years); as the western terminus of the Silk Road it drew a wide variety of peoples from China and points between. It had been a Middle Eastern trading center for centuries. A customer could buy raw silk from Iran and dyes from India in Aleppo's *souqs* (markets). It was Syria's industrial and financial center as well. How did the once-great, prosperous city of Aleppo meet this fate? And why? The answer may be surprising to anyone who isn't a student of climate science.

HISTORICAL CONTEXT

For centuries, Aleppo was the third-largest city in the Ottoman Empire, after Cairo and Constantinople (now Istanbul, Turkey). It also was a major world transport center until the Suez Canal opened in 1869. It appears in historical records much earlier than Damascus, which is now Syria's capital and best-known urban area. The city is referenced in William Shakespeare's *Macbeth* (1606). Aleppo has long been majority Muslim (more than 80 percent, the vast majority Sunni), but also has been home to large numbers of Christians and Jews.

Aleppo also was long considered a major center of Arabic traditional and classical music. The city hosted several annual music festivals and shows and festivals in its citadel amphitheater, including the Silk Road Festival, the Syrian Song Festival, and the Khan al-Harir Festival. It also was a center of education, with the University of Aleppo and several other higher-education institutions, as well as several large museums.

Just as a severe drought set in around 2011, triggering circumstances that led to one of the most devastating civil wars in recent world history, France's International Academy of Gastronomy awarded Aleppo a culinary prize for its outstanding restaurants. Within a few years, the people of Aleppo were eating grass. The city's once-famous pubs and boutique hotels, some of which had occupied ancient oriental mansions built by affluent Silk Road traders, were bombed-out shells.

After 2012, Aleppo and the rest of Syria became a collision point between a complex mixture of regional ideologies, including the Assad regime versus rebels within Syria, Sunni and Shia factions of Islam, as well as an international rivalry between the United States and Russia, and extremists affiliated with the Islamic State (ISIS),

The British Broadcasting Corporation described the many players in this complex war:

> On the government side, state forces are being supported by Russian air strikes and Shia militias, including fighters from Iran, Iraq, Afghanistan, Lebanon and Pakistan. The predominantly Sunni Muslim opposition is made of several rebel groups,

many of whom have received financial aid from key opponents of President Assad, including the United States, Saudi Arabia and Turkey. Hard-line Sunni Islamist groups are involved too, most notably ISIS, as well as Jabhat Fateh al-Sham, which earlier this year changed its name from the Nusra Front and announced it was cutting ties with al-Qaeda. (What's Happening? 2016)

Within five years (2012–2017), Aleppo had become the worst-devastated city in the Syrian civil war. By March 2013, according to the Syrian Foreign Ministry, more than 1,000 factories in Aleppo had been plundered. The prolonged siege of Aleppo and the devastation of civilian populations caused some historians to recall the German siege of Stalingrad during World War II. By 2017, an estimated 33,500 buildings had been damaged or destroyed in one of the longest sieges in the history of warfare. At least 31,000 people had died.

THE CLIMATIC CONTEXT

Prior to the breakout of armed conflicts, Aleppo had become a focal point for refugees, many of them former farmers, whose wheat crops, as well as olive, fig, fruit, and pistachio groves, had died. They were fleeing rising temperatures and the worst drought in memory, which has been associated by scientists with a broader, prolonged drought in the region (beginning in 2007) that has roots in global warming.

The drought intensified after 2007. According to Elizabeth Kolbert, writing in the *New Yorker* (2015, 23), "The country [in 2008] experienced its driest winter on record. Wheat production failed, many small farmers lost their herds, and prices of basic commodities more than doubled." Within months, as the drought intensified, hundreds of thousands of people abandoned their homes and farms in the countryside and moved to Damascus, Aleppo, Homs, and other cities, crowding them into urban areas already strained by the arrival of more than a million refugees from the ongoing war in Iraq. By 2017, more than 4.5 million Syrian refugees had moved to Turkey, Lebanon, and Jordan, as well as several European countries. By 2016, NASA had issued a report using tree rings to determine that the drought in this region from 1998 to 2012 was the worst in at least 900 years (NASA 2016).

Researchers from the University of California Santa Barbara and Columbia University described civil unrest linked to the collapse of farming in Syria and the migration of 1.5 million farmers to cities, with related poverty that provoked civil unrest beginning in 2007. Because of the civil war, weather records after that time are scarce. Droughts have become more frequent and intense in Syria; three of the country's longest droughts have occurred during the last 30 years, as temperatures have risen and winter precipitation has declined.

"There are various things going on, but you're talking about 1.5 million people migrating from the rural north to the cities," said climate scientist Richard Seager, a coauthor of the study in the Proceedings of the National Academy of Sciences. "It was a contributing factor to the social unraveling that occurred that eventually led to the civil war" (Borenstein 2015). The study's lead author, Colin Kelley, said that climatic change combined with oppression by the Assad regime, immigration of at least 1 million refugees from Iraq, and political instability across the region had caused the civil war. However, said Seager, this is the "single clearest case" ever presented by scientists of climate change playing a part in a conflict because "you can really draw a blow-by-blow account with the numbers" (Borenstein 2015).

THE MOST SEVERE DROUGHT ON RECORD

Kelley and colleagues summarized the situation in the Proceedings of the National Academy of Sciences (2015):

> Before the Syrian uprising that began in 2011, the greater Fertile Crescent experienced the most severe drought in the instrumental record. For Syria, a country marked by poor governance and unsustainable agricultural and environmental policies, the drought had a catalytic effect, contributing to political unrest. We show that the recent decrease in Syrian precipitation is a combination of natural variability and a long-term drying trend, and the unusual severity of the observed drought is here shown to be highly unlikely without this trend. Precipitation changes in Syria are linked to rising mean sea-level pressure in the Eastern Mediterranean, which also shows a long-term trend. There has been also a long-term warming trend in the Eastern Mediterranean, adding to the drawdown of soil moisture. No natural cause is apparent for these trends, whereas the observed drying and warming are consistent with model studies of the response to increases in greenhouse gases. Furthermore, model studies show an increasingly drier and hotter future mean climate for the Eastern Mediterranean. Analyses of observations and model simulations indicate that a drought of the severity and duration of the recent Syrian drought, which is implicated in the current conflict, has become more than twice as likely as a consequence of human interference in the climate system.

CLIMATE CHANGE A TRIGGER FOR CONFLICT

The Syrian civil war has become a vivid illustration of a country in which climate-related crises have been fundamental to violent conflict. A paper in the Proceedings of the National Association of Sciences traced conflict and climate generally to societies with existing social and political conflicts that fracture along ethnic lines. The authors of this paper assigned climate change a role as a triggering mechanism:

> This overall state of affairs is likely to be exacerbated by anthropogenic climate change and in particular climate-related natural disasters. Ethnic divides might serve as predetermined conflict lines in case of rapidly emerging societal tensions arising from disruptive events like natural disasters. Here, we hypothesize that climate-related disaster occurrence enhances armed-conflict outbreak risk in ethnically fractionalized countries. (Schleussner et al. 2016)

"This debate comes up time and again—is climate change really something like a trigger for violent conflict?" said Hans Joachim Schellnhuber, director of the Potsdam Institute for Climate Impact Research (Harvey 2016). Schellnhuber and colleagues applied climatic criteria to a list of armed conflicts bretween 1980 and 2010, analyzing each disaster, which "found a significant link between climate disasters and the outbreak of violent conflict specifically in countries with high degrees of

A neighborhood in Aleppo destroyed during the Syrian civil war, 2013. The war in Syria may have resulted from political and social instability caused by the effects of climate change—like severe drought. (Richard Harvey/Dreamstime.com)

ethnic fractionalization . . . about 23 percent of armed conflicts in highly ethnically divided nations coincided with climate-related disasters." "We cannot explain the full complexity of the emergence of violent conflict, but here we have found something really robust, a factor that really matters," Schellnhuber said (Harvey 2016).

Syria is one dramatic example where millions of people in a single nation have become refugees because of war with origins in environmental crisis. During the 21st century, the phrase "environmental refugee" has become more familiar around the world. Lowland residents who could be forced out of their homes by a three-foot rise in sea levels during the present century include 26 million people in Bangladesh, 70 to 100 million in China, 20 million in India, and 12 million in the Nile Delta of Egypt (Gelbspan 1997, 162). In Egypt, a one-meter sea-level rise could cost 15 percent of the country's gross national product, including much of its agricultural base (Edgerton 1991, 72–73). A 14-inch rise in sea levels could flood 40 percent of the mudflats that ring Puget Sound in Seattle, obliterating a significant habitat for shellfish and waterfowl (Gough 1999, 48). These locations are only a few of a great many examples, because the earth's junctures of seas and rivers have been important crossroads for human trade (as well as fertile farming areas) throughout human history. Many river deltas are densely populated and very vulnerable to even a small amount of sea-level rise.

The World Bank released a report in 2013 listing the 10 cities in the world that may incur the highest bills for damage from sea-level rise. They are: Miami, New York City, New Orleans, Tampa, Boston, all in the United States; as well as

> **Weather vs. Climate**
>
> With regard to global warming, climate is the plot, but weather is the story. While weather varies, there is an underlying trend in temperature, and it is rising. It will continue to rise as long as carbon dioxide's level in the atmosphere increases. As of 2018, that level was close to 410 parts per million, compared to a range of 180 to 280 ppm before the fossil-fuel age began about 1850. Weather is inherently variable, and responds to patterns other than rising carbon-dioxide levels that provoke warming in global temperatures long-term. Conditions vary from place to place on various dates, sometimes causing confusion.
>
> One example of many: in 2018, air currents over the Arctic guided storms through the Bering Sea from south to north repeatedly, often drawing abnormally mild air from tropics and mid-latitudes into the region on a jet stream that then plunged southward into the central and eastern United States, bringing record cold, ice, and snow. The U.S. Northeast suffered back-to-back blizzards while rain fell near the North Pole.

Guangzhou, China; Mumbai, India; Nagoya, Japan; Shenzhen, China; and Osaka, Japan. The bank surveyed prospective damage in 136 large coastal cities and concluded that damage could rise to $1 trillion a year. Directed by World Bank economist Stephane Hallegatte, with the Organization for Economic Cooperation and Development (OECD), the study warns that "Coastal cities face a high risk from increasingly costly flooding as sea levels rise amid climate change. Their current defenses will not be enough as the water level rises" (10 Coastal Cities 2013). Many of these cities are at risk not only because of rising seas, but also subsiding land.

Bruce E. Johansen

See also: Violence, Corruption, and Organized Crime: Baghdad, Iraq: Restitching a Torn Society Isn't Easy; Kabul, Afghanistan: What Went Wrong?; *Waste Management:* Baghdad, Iraq: Hauling Garbage in Hell on Earth

Further Reading

Borenstein, Seth. 2015. "Syria's Civil War Linked Partly to Drought, Global Warming." PhilStar Global, March 4. https://www.philstar.com/world/2015/03/04/1429923/syrias-civil-war-linked-partly-drought-global-warming.

Edgerton, Lynn T. 1991. *The Rising Tide—Global Warming and World Sea Levels.* Natural Resources Defense Council.

Gelbspan, Ross. 1997. *The Heat Is On: The High Stakes Battle over Earth's Threatened Climate.* Reading, MA: Addison-Wesley.

Gough, Robert. 1999. "Stress on Stress: Global Warming and Aquatic Resource Depletion." *Native Americas* 16: 46–48.

Harvey, Chelsea. 2016. "How Climate Disasters Can Drive Violent Conflict around the World." *Washington Post*, July 25. https://www.washingtonpost.com/news/energy-environment/wp/2016/07/25/how-climate-disasters-can-drive-violent-conflict-around-the-world/.

Kelley, Colin, Shahrzad Mohtadi, Mark A. Cane, Richard Seager, and Yochanan Kushnir. 2015. "Climate Change in the Fertile Crescent and Implications of the Recent Syrian Drought." *Proceedings of the National Academy of Sciences* 112:8 (March). http://www.pnas.org/content/112/11/3241.

Kolbert, Elizabeth. 2015. "Unsafe Climates." *New Yorker* [Talk of the Town], December 7, 23–24.
NASA: Recent Mideast Drought Worst in 900 Years." 2016. *Omaha World-Herald*, March 4, 7-A.
Schleussner, Carl-Friedrich, Jonathan F. Donges, Reik V. Donner, and Hans Joachim Schellnhuber. 2016. "Armed-Conflict Risks Enhanced by Climate-Related Disasters in Ethnically Fractionalized Countries." *Proceedings of the National Association of Sciences* 113 (July 25): 30. http://www.pnas.org/content/early/2016/07/20/1601611113.
"10 Coastal Cities at Greatest Flood Risk as Sea Levels Rise." 2013. Environment News Service, September 3. http://ens-newswire.com/2013/09/03/10-coastal-cities-at-greatest-flood-risk-as-sea-levels-rise/.
"What's Happening in Aleppo?" 2016. British Broadcasting Corporation (BBC) News, December 23. http://www.bbc.com/news/world-middle-east-38132163.

Baghdad, Iraq: Restitching a Torn Society Isn't Easy

In recent decades, the people of Baghdad have endured the repressive rule of Saddam Hussein's Baathist regime, the consequences of the Iran-Iraq War of 1980–1988, the devastation of the 1991 Persian Gulf War followed by years of severe sanctions, and the profound impact of the 2003 U.S.-led invasion and subsequent occupation, which led to an insurgency and sectarian civil war. Increased violence, corruption, and organized crime have plagued the capital city since 2003. Yet Baghdad—it should be recalled—is one of the oldest cities in the world, the second-largest Islamic city, and formerly a cosmopolitan city comprised of people of diverse religious beliefs and ethnicities that in the period of the 1950s to the early 1980s had attracted renowned urban planners and architects such as Frank Lloyd Wright and Walter Gropius to chart an even greater future (Schulz and Banna 2015).

BACKGROUND TO THE CURRENT URBAN CRISIS

In a 1968 coup, the Baath Party seized power. Eleven years later, Saddam Hussein took control of the government. Though the Baathist government did not tolerate corruption by low-level civil servants, top members of the ruling party connected to Hussein used state funds to "indulge in whatever earthly pleasures they desired." Most of this revenue came from the oil industry that the government had nationalized in the 1970s—at the same time that oil prices skyrocketed as a result of the 1973 and 1979 oil embargoes (Al-Ali 2014).

In 1980, Hussein made the fateful decision to invade Iran, leading to eight years of brutal warfare. After this conflict ended, the huge war debt coupled with the decline in oil prices led to reduced wages and rising unemployment. It also led Hussein to make another fateful decision to invade Kuwait. In response, the United States led a coalition of nations to push Iraqi forces out of Kuwait. The 1991 Persian Gulf War began with a massive aerial attack on Iraq. Coalition forces repeatedly bombed Baghdad, destroying most of its infrastructure and killing many civilians. The city was devastated. Severe sanctions that followed the end of the war destroyed the economy, increased poverty, undermined social stability, and significantly reduced funding to repair Baghdad's severely damaged infrastructure (Al-Ali 2014).

THE 2003 U.S.-LED INVASION AND AFTERMATH

According to Zaid Al-Ali, a lawyer who worked for the United Nations Assistance Mission for Iraq, the March 2003 U.S.-led invasion transformed Iraq "into the world's most recent incarnation of the Wild West, in which corruption and incompetence reigned supreme." While this assessment might seem harsh, many other experts have drawn similar conclusions (Al-Ali 2014).

In her master's thesis for Columbia University's Graduate School of Architecture, Planning & Preservation, Sarah Almukhtar argued that the 2003 invasion was a "crucial turning point in the history of Iraq" because "this war was a particularly urban war" where the "front lines were in the city streets" of Baghdad. The war directly affected the daily life of Baghdadis, upending work and school routines, forcing many to migrate, and leading to many casualties (Almukhtar 2014).

Most analysts agree that the formation of the Coalition Provisional Authority (CPA) under the leadership of L. Paul Bremer in April 2003 was another turning point. The CPA was given executive, legislative, and judicial authority. Shortly after his arrival in Iraq, Bremer issued CPA Order No. 1, which purged senior members of the Baath party "from public employment." Iraqi emigres working for the State Department's Future of Iraq Project made the original proposal. It was modeled on the de-Nazification program in Germany after World War II. The plan gained broad interagency support within the U.S. government. The goal was to remove Iraqis from the government who would oppose U.S. policies. Bremer also issued CPA Order No. 2, which "disband(ed) the Iraqi army." U.S. military officials argued that since the Iraqi army had "already self-demobilized," the order essentially confirmed the existing situation. Moreover, U.S. officials believed this order would serve an "important symbolic purpose" as it would prove to the Iraqis that the United States would not allow "Saddam's instruments of repression" to return (Dobbins et al. 2009).

A RAND Corporation study characterized these decisions as "the most controversial" of Bremer's tenure. The RAND study also noted that Lt. General Jay Garner, who headed the Office of Reconstruction and Humanitarian Assistance—the predecessor agency to the CPA—recommended that Bremer not issue the rulings, but his advice was ignored. It should be noted, however, that at the time no other senior U.S. official publicly opposed disbanding the army (RAND 2009).

Others, however, were more critical than RAND. Professor of Public Policy James Pfiffner argued that Bremer's two decisions laid the groundwork for the insurgency by "alienating hundreds of thousands of Iraqis who could not support themselves or their families; undermining the normal infrastructure necessary for social and economic activity; ensuring that there was not sufficient security to carry on normal life; and by creating insurgents who were angry at the U.S., many of whom had weapons and were trained to use them" (Pfiffner 2010).

Military historian John Keegan stated, "in retrospect the disbandment of the army was a serious mistake" (Norton-Taylor 2004). Moreover, since the CPA handled the distribution of billions of dollars to rebuild Iraqi society, the lack of accountability regarding the allocation of funds led to increasing opportunities for corruption. Al-Ali added an important contextual point that "after more than thirteen years of international sanctions, billions of dollars were suddenly flowing into the country unimpeded, most of it in cash." The consequences for the reconstruction of Baghdad were profound. "Schools that were supposedly rebuilt were left in ruins; projects that were supposed to create employment were in fact staffed by ghost employees, with the salaries being pocketed by a handful of individuals" (Al-Ali 2014).

One of the few positive aspects of Saddam Hussein's repressive regime was that Baghdad's streets were relatively safe. In sharp contrast, after the U.S. invasion there was a substantial upsurge in violence. The CPA during its 14-month existence was unable to provide security for the people of Baghdad. Starting in May 2003, "there was a wave of murders and revenge killings, especially of Baathists." During May, almost 300 "bodies showed up at the Baghdad morgue, all of which met violent deaths." Nationwide, 547 Iraqi civilians died that month, averaging almost 18 per day. These numbers pale in comparison to civilian death totals in the 2004 to 2006 period (e.g., July 2005 saw 3,266 civilian deaths, or 105 per day), as a sectarian civil war between Sunnis and Shia devastated Baghdad and ripped apart the country. Journalist Paul Wing, who has published extensively on Iraq, concluded that "the U.S. invasion led to the undoing of society. The occupying forces were not ready to secure the country, and the ensuing chaos opened the door to foreign terrorists, insurgents, and militias to fill the void" (Perito 2006; Wing 2013).

"CITY OF WALLS"

Attempting to contain the violence and gain control of the city, the U.S. military began to build walls throughout Baghdad. According to Major John Spencer with the Modern War Institute at the U.S. Military Academy in West Point, "the growing numbers of IEDs" (improvised explosive devices) placed alongside major roads led to the installation of the first walls. Soon it became clear that the best way to achieve the "strategic goals of providing security, protecting populations, establishing stability, and eliminating terrorist threats" was to construct walls throughout the city. Spencer, who served in Iraq during the war, characterized concrete as the U.S. military's "most effective weapon" in urban warfare (Spencer 2016). These walls included "12–20 foot high concrete" blast walls and "shorter 'Jersey' barriers" similar to those "used as highway dividers in the U.S." Many walls cordoned off Sunni neighborhoods (Almukhtar 2014). Sarah Almaki observed that the Western media usually portrayed the walls as "security walls," while most Iraqis considered them "occupation walls." In her 2015 study of Baghdad, she calculated that 144 miles of blast walls surrounded sections of Bagdad. In comparison, the Berlin Wall was only 96 miles. Almaki provocatively asserts that "this military urbanism scheme was modeled after the West Bank wall." Moreover, she argues

An Iraqi woman passes by the site of a car bomb explosion in Baghdad's Hurriyah neighborhood, 2016. Behind her is a cement wall constructed by the U.S. military to mitigate the effects of IEDs (Improvised Explosive Devices). (Sabah Arar/AFP/Getty Images)

that "like the Palestinians, Iraqis complained of being treated like caged animals" (Almaki 2015).

Urban life was profoundly affected. Baghdad had been a city where approximately 75 percent of its neighborhoods were comprised of different ethnic and religious groups—Sunni, Shia, and Christian. Walling Baghdad led to increasingly segregated neighborhoods. Almaki contends that politics influenced many decisions on where to erect walls because the Shia-majority Iraqi government wanted to "marginalize" the Sunni minority. Many Baghdadis were disconnected from their former neighbors and their places of work, education, health care, and worship. This led to an increase in displaced persons and heightened economic inequalities. Moreover, checkpoints set up throughout the city greatly lengthened the time it took to travel from one section to another. Time-consuming traffic jams and security procedures caused urban residents many headaches and hurt business activity. Schulz and Banna note that "residents complain about arbitrary decisions made at checkpoints by security guards and their reputation for taking bribes." In an even more extreme example, some "gated communities" began to require that one had to have a biometric scan before they could enter the neighborhood (Almaki 2015; Schulz and Banna 2015). One University of Baghdad professor depicted the impact of walls and checkpoints on daily life by noting that "it took me three hours to reach home compared to the 15 minutes before 2003" (Almukhtar 2014). Perhaps the logical conclusion in the walling of Baghdad was observed in a 2016 *USA Today* article that noted that the Iraqi Interior Ministry had begun work on a "wall and trench around Baghdad" to help "secure the city from terror attacks" by ISIS (Michaels 2016).

ORGANIZED CRIME

One of the unintended consequences of the UN sanctions imposed on Iraq after the 1991 Persian Gulf War was that Saddam Hussein utilized criminal networks to evade restrictions in order to maintain power. For example, oil was smuggled through various countries such as Turkey and Syria, which brought in desperately needed funds. Criminal gangs thus helped the regime stay in power, and the regime helped the gangs profit. After the U.S. invasion, the state collapsed, political instability increased, and limits on Iraqi criminal organizations disappeared. An environment favorable to criminal activity was further enhanced by Hussein's decision to release tens of thousands of criminals from jail shortly before the invasion, followed by insufficient U.S. troop presence to establish security in the immediate postinvasion period (Wing 2010).

Professor of International Security Phil Williams argues in a 2009 study that "the rise of organized crime in Iraq was a strategic surprise for (US) decision makers and military planners." Furthermore, he contends that the passive reaction "in the face of widespread looting was a major mistake, creating a climate of citizen insecurity and criminal impunity." Organized criminal networks participated in oil smuggling, kidnapping, drug trafficking, and various other illegal activities. Corrupt government officials in Baghdad as well as growing violence facilitated the rapid rise of organized crime post-2003. These developments in turn help fuel the insurgency and sectarian conflict (Williams 2009).

CONCLUSION

In a 2012 Transparency International study, Iraq ranked "169 out of 174" in the "global corruption perceptions index" (Al-Ali 2014). In a 2017 report on crime and safety in Baghdad, the Overseas Security Advisory Council characterized Baghdad as a "critical threat" to Americans, urging government and business personnel to follow "strict security guidelines." Anti-American sentiment and political violence coming from terrorist groups such as the Sunni-affiliated ISIS and Shia-related Kata'ib Hizballah made life in Baghdad subject to sudden death (OSAC 2017).

Despite these extensive problems, municipal officials continue to develop plans to enhance urban life. Recently the $35 million Mansour Mall opened in Baghdad. The city promoted this project because, among other factors, it helped "create an image of beautification and development." Critics, however, argued that this type of development did "not really address the structural problems on the ground which affect Baghdadi residents daily." Urban planning expert Sarah Almukhtar, for example, contends that the best method to enhance urban life is to utilize "active community-based initiatives" that would benefit the majority of the city's residents, not just the elites. Based on three case studies conducted in Baghdad, she insists that incorporating the perspectives of young, college-educated adults would help revitalize the city (Almukhtar 2014). Architectural specialist Sarah Almaki developed a proposal to construct an urban bridge alongside the walls "to restitch the fragmented city through pedestrian movement." This elevated walkway would "relink the severed city of Baghdad through the act of leisurely walking"—a "civil right" that she claims U.S. authorities took away when they began to wall the city more than a decade ago (Almaki 2015).

Could Almukhtar and Almaki's proposals significantly improve conditions in Baghdad? Could they help address the persistent problems of violence, corruption, and organized crime in the capital? It seems they would improve certain aspects of urban life. However, serious challenges would still exist. In May 2016, for example, thousands of Iraqi protesters stormed the Green Zone and rampaged through the Parliament building. Inspired by the Shiite cleric Moqtada al-Sadr, they demanded an end to government corruption and mismanagement. For many Baghdadis, the Green Zone has for years been seen as "a safe haven for corrupt politicians" living a luxurious life "separated from the grim daily realities faced by most ordinary Iraqis." In 2016, economic conditions worsened as the price of oil declined, the costs of fighting the Islamic State increased, and the government payroll swelled "from 2 million to 7 million people" (Peterson 2016). Moreover, Baghdad's growing slums now hold almost 3 million people scrambling to survive, and the numbers appear to be increasing. This, according to executive editor of the *Al-Mada* newspaper Adnan Hussein, is a recipe "for terrorism and organized crime" (Hussein 2017).

Douglas Karsner

See also: *Violence, Corruption, and Organized Crime:* Aleppo, Syria: Drought, Global Warming, and Civil War; Kabul, Afghanistan: What Went Wrong?; *Waste Management:* Baghdad, Iraq: Hauling Garbage in Hell on Earth

Further Reading

Al-Ali, Zaid. 2014. *The Struggle for Iraq's Future: How Corruption, Incompetence and Sectarianism Have Undermined Democracy.* New Haven, CT: Yale University Press.

Almaki, Sarah. 2015. "The Urban Bridge: Walking Baghdad." Master's thesis, Carleton University, Ottawa, Ontario. https://curve.carleton.ca/system/files/etd/3a9bf829-0f7c-41c1-b6cf-74bd35939aa4/etd_pdf/70511f54e48ff5f51d3c1438cfef7fc0/almaki-theurbanbridgewalkingbaghdad.pdf.

Almukhtar, Sarah. 2014. "The Effects of Urban Conflict and the Role of Community-Based Initiatives in Baghdad." Master's thesis, Columbia University, May 9. https://academiccommons.columbia.edu/doi/10.7916/D8ZP447X.

Dobbins, James, Seth Jones, Benjamin Runkle, Siddharth Mohandas. 2009. "Occupying Iraq: A History of the Coalition Provisional Authority." *RAND National Security Research Division.* https://www.rand.org/pubs/monographs/MG847.html.

Hussein, Adnan. 2017. "Baghdad and Its Growing Slum Problem." AlArabiya.net via Middle East Newsstream, June 24. https://english.alarabiya.net/en/views/news/middle-east/2017/06/24/Baghdad-and-its-growing-slums-.html

Michaels, Jim. 2016. "Iraq to Build Wall and Trench around Baghdad." *USA Today*, February 3. https://www.usatoday.com/story/news/world/2016/02/03/iraq-wall-trench-baghdad-isil/79767764/.

Norton-Taylor, Richard. 2004. "Violence Blamed on US Decision to Disband Iraq Army." *Guardian*, April 7. https://www.theguardian.com/world/2004/apr/07/iraq.usa2.

OSAC. Overseas Security Advisory Council. 2017. "Iraq 2017 Crime & Safety Report: Baghdad." Overseas Security Advisory Council, Bureau of Diplomatic Security, US Department of State, March 1. https://www.osac.gov/pages/ContentReportDetails.aspx?cid=21351.

Perito, Robert. 2006. "Policing Iraq: Protecting Iraqis from Criminal Violence." Peace Briefing, The United States Institute of Peace, June 29. http://www.usip.org/publications/2006/06/policing-iraq-protecting-iraqis-criminal-violence.

Peterson, Scott. 2016. "Storming Iraq's Green Zone: Wake-Up Call for Political Reform?" *Christian Science Monitor* via Middle East Newsstream, May 2. https://www.csmonitor.com/World/Middle-East/2016/0502/Storming-Iraq-s-Green-Zone-Wake-up-call-for-political-reform.

Pfiffner, James. 2010. "US Blunders in Iraq: De-Baathification and Disbanding the Army." *Intelligence and National Security* 25, 1 (February): 76–85. http://www.pfiffner.gmu.edu/files/pdfs/Articles/CPA%20Orders,%20Iraq%20PDF.pdf.

Schulz, Sebastian, and Niran Banna. 2015. "Planning in Baghdad: How Years of Conflict Have Shaped the Design of the City." *Global Urbanist*, January 22. http://www.globalurbanist.com/2015/01/22/planning-in-baghdad.

Spencer, John. 2016. "The Most Effective Weapon on the Modern Battlefield Is Concrete." *Modern War Institute*, November 14. https://mwi.usma.edu/effective-weapon-modern-battlefield-concrete/.

Williams, Phil. 2009. "Criminals, Militias, and Insurgents: Organized Crime in Iraq." *Strategic Studies Institute*, June. https://ssi.armywarcollege.edu/pdffiles/PUB930.pdf.

Wing, Joel. 2013. "A History of Violence in Iraq through Iraq Body Count's Archive." *Musings on Iraq*, February 11. http://musingsoniraq.blogspot.com/2013/02/a-history-of-violence-in-iraq-through.html.

Beijing, China: Tight Surveillance and Harsh Punishment

Despite international recognition as one of the safest cities in the world, Beijing still encounters problems with violence, organized crime, and corruption. For violent crime, offenders target visitors from other nations, typically after-hours and in the city's nightlife districts. The most common violent crime is robbery with a financial motive, but assaults occur as well and predominantly involve excessive alcohol consumption. Organized crime, though present, is not as prevalent in Beijing as in other capital cities. The centralization of China's strong government leadership in the city certainly limits the power of organized crime. Regarding corruption, Communist Party General Secretary Xi Jinping has prioritized ending this practice, and several notable cases involving government officials in Beijing have resulted in public trials, convictions, and punishments.

Being one of four municipalities in China, government in Beijing is primarily administered at the national rather than the provincial level. Nonetheless, the city has locally elected and appointed officials, and is divided into four urban and six suburban districts. In addition, eight rural counties surround the city's urban area. Primarily, the Public Security Bureau handles law enforcement and judicial functions, with each government district having police jurisdictions and substations, as well. The majority of crime statistics in Beijing and other provinces in China are limited to estimates based on government arrest tabulations. Specifically, only a small portion of crimes result in arrest, and substantial numbers are never reported to authorities for a variety of reasons (e.g., fear of police, victim involvement in criminal activity, fear of offender retaliation, etc.). As such, estimates of crime in Beijing, similar to that of other cities around the world, only provide a partial image of the overall crime and violence problem.

For visitors to Beijing, the U.S. State Department designated the jurisdiction as a low-threat location in terms of property and violent crime victimization likelihood. The State Department cautions that the most common type of violence affecting nonresidents is assault, which frequently occurs in bars or clubs in the jurisdiction's popular nightlife districts. Contributors to the violence typically include alcohol consumption and cultural miscommunication. Overall, Beijing's favorable international reputation for infrequent crime and violence aided in the city's successful bid and then hosting of the 2008 Summer Olympic Games.

In 2015, the *Economist*'s Safe Cities Index ranked Beijing no. 37 overall in terms of favorability in the context of crime, population health, and environmental issues. Compared to other cities in China, Beijing finished behind Shanghai, Shenzhen, and Tianjin. In the same study, Beijing finished no. 48 in the world for personal safety, a category comprised of the security of citizens from theft and violence, the level of police engagement, and resident perceptions about safety. Similar to challenges faced by nations globally, violent crime due to mental illness occurs infrequently. In publicized stories from 2013, a disgruntled man detonated a homemade bomb at the Beijing Airport injuring himself, while two days later a 50-year-old man attacked residents at a shopping mall, killing one and injuring three others, including a 2-year-old.

Despite Beijing's comparatively low frequency of violence, crime rates in the city and the nation have increased steadily since the 1970s. Paralleling the vast economic growth of the past three decades for China, criminologists attribute more violence and property crime to the weakening of informal social controls, among other issues. Specifically, once close-knit neighborhoods are now interspersed with floaters or transient workers who relocate for economic reasons. This lack of familiarity among residents reduces informal social controls over behaviors. When violence does occur, the incidents garner substantial public attention. For instance, in the summer of 2013, the murder of a sleeping two-year-old in Beijing after a traffic dispute involving the child's mother and another party generated spirited negative reactions from citizens against the perpetrator. Support for executing the child's killer was widespread, with some even advocating torture as acceptable for retribution.

In addition to loosening social controls, economists and sociologists have explored the potential contributions of two other factors to the republic's increasing crime rate. First, a significant income disparity exists for residents of this capital city. In 2013, Beijing ranked no. 38 in terms of gross domestic product (GDP), with the vast majority of residents earning lower-middle annual income between $10,000 and $30,000. With perceived insurmountable obstacles to success, frustrated community members may turn to crime to achieve goals. This is not limited to property crime rates, but is also applicable to violence, where monetary gain is a motivator through traditional offenses like armed robbery and carjacking.

A second aspect alleged to indirectly influence violent crime in China is the nation's one-child policy. Instituted in 1979 to limit family sizes, only to be revoked in 2015 to allow two children per couple, the government's aim was to control population growth and improve the quality of births. The result has been a surplus of boys, as approximately 113 boys are now born in the country for every 100 girls. The prospect of millions of boys with limited prospects of marriage in a country that socially values that path can create stress on individuals. Further, marriage has been shown to globally contribute to lower individual involvement in crime, thus this social policy can motivate violent and petty crime offenders in cities like Beijing.

Between 2005 and 2014, more than 40,000 robberies and thefts were reported in Beijing. The city has a large student population, and seasonal upticks in the general crime rate are common. Specifically, more crime occurs in the summer and parts of the winter when students are not in school and have increased mobility and social interactions. Interestingly, robbery and theft rates decreased significantly during the summer of 2008, when the city hosted the Olympic Games—likely a reflection of the increased law enforcement presence to support this international event. Further, an additional type of violent crime described as increasing in Beijing is that of workplace violence.

Even without the Olympics, Beijing is a popular travel destination, and hosts almost 8 million tourists during China's National Day holidays in October. For violent and petty crime prevention, police in Beijing recently expanded government surveillance within the city to 100 percent coverage. Law enforcement officials reportedly employ over 46,000 video cameras and more than 4,000 police officers to monitor every street corner in the city.

In general, organized crime is more active outside the urban area of Beijing. This is reflective of the heavy law enforcement presence and restrictive government controls centered in China's capital city. Nationally, the government's strategy is to disperse organized crime into smaller sects. Large crime syndicates are rare, and organized efforts in illegality are more frequently comprised of smaller groups numbering from 50 to 200 members. For instance, in 2006, authorities in Beijing successfully prosecuted 34 members of an organized crime ring that had committed a series of local aggravated assaults and briberies. Beijing media characterized this prosecution as the first of its kind, since the founding of the People's Republic of China in 1949.

Chinese criminal organizations have used human trafficking and organ harvesting as illicit sources of revenues. The vast majority of those enterprises exist in areas other than Beijing, again as the capital city houses such a large police presence. Regarding human trafficking, China acts as a source, conduit, and destination for illicit workers. Some victims, especially those under age, are lured to the country by false promises of employment and then forced into prostitution at the nation's coal mines or in urban areas like Beijing. China does not fully comply with collaborative international efforts against human trafficking, but has made significant improvements in the investigation and prosecution of such crimes. For instance, in 2014, the Republic arrested 194 individuals for human trafficking offenses.

Although begging is illegal in the city, it is commonplace on Beijing's public transportation as employees rarely prioritize prohibiting such activities. Interestingly, those panhandling on Beijing's subways are said to be controlled by organized crime. If an individual does not have permission to solicit money at a location, senior members of the criminal community will use threats and violence to ensure compliance.

Street gangs represent a form of organized crime that has generated fear among Beijing residents and visitors. Visible media exposure coupled with violence have led to the perception that these groups are becoming more active. Typically, non-Chinese victims are targeted with robberies and/or aggravated assaults in and around the city's bars and clubs. In recent published reports describing the assaults, multiple perpetrators armed with bats attack the victims without provocation, and then flee the scene using vehicles. Police theorize that some of these violent crimes are racially motivated—certainly not an issue limited to China.

As discussed previously, organized crime activities in Beijing are limited, but the participation of juveniles in gangs continues to be troubling. In general, criminologists attribute youth crime problems in the republic to weakened informal social controls, and economic disparities that tend to ostracize community members at an early age. In 2008, two juvenile street gangs, the Hall of Princes and the Black Clothes Gang, received national media attention for brutal assaults and other violence. The Hall of Princes was reportedly established by a 20-something local to help defend marginalized high school students from bullying. Primarily comprised of students from Beijing's vocational schools, both gangs quickly morphed into rivals that focused on organized efforts at extortion and violence.

With the added media exposure of the street violence, police and school officials became more involved in proactively addressing juvenile gang problems in the city, but the issue remains problematic for both residents and visitors. A recent high-profile arrest by police in Beijing netted 15 suspected gang members ranging in age from 13 to 17. The youth, all attending school, were suspected of multiple armed robberies in the city's entertainment district. The juveniles chose to confront each robbery victim in isolated areas (e.g., a parking lot or alley after dark), threaten victims with knives and clubs, and present an overwhelming number of assailants to guarantee compliance.

Characterized as prevalent in all levels of business and government, eliminating official corruption in China remains challenging. The frequency and extent of corruption is difficult to assess, as authorities are protective of such information that could damage the city and country's image. In 2012, to combat such illegal and unethical practices, Communist Party General Secretary Xi Jinping announced an anticorruption campaign that emphasized arrests of violators, as well as a widespread informational campaign to laud individual integrity. With corruption consistently ranked as a despised social problem, the Chinese people have responded favorably to these government initiatives.

The increased enforcement netted several high-profile government officials for corruption-related offenses. Former director of the Beijing Municipal Bureau of State Security Liang Ke and former government security chief Zhou Yongkang were both taken into custody in 2014 and accused of official corruption. Once considered the republic's godfather of security, Zhou's case generated national attention. The former leader was a member of the party's top decision-making body, the Politburo Standing Committee, and chaired the committee that oversees China's law enforcement and courts. The arrest led to a bribery conviction in 2016.

Interestingly, Fu Zhenghua, formerly Beijing's police chief and leader of the investigation against Zhou, has been promoted several times since the case. Recently, top party officials named Fu to probe insider trading and other corruption alleged to be occurring in the financial markets based in Beijing. Despite similar recent crackdowns, Transparency International ranked China no. 76 out of 170 nations in their annual Corruption Perceptions Index 2016.

Coupled with visible and well-funded anticorruption efforts, the Chinese government uses harsh punishments as well to deter official misconduct. For instance, in 2010, a former director at the Beijing City Public Security Bureau was sentenced to death for accepting bribes that had allowed Internet companies to obtain unvetted sales permits within China. Corruption sentences involving capital punishment are nonexistent in Westernized nations, but are common in China. In sum, reducing corruption has been a recent priority for the nation's leaders headquartered in Beijing, and the government continues to use high-profile efforts in conjunction with severe punishments to deter illegal and unethical practices.

Scott Duncan

See also: Energy and Sustainability: Beijing, China: Battling Water Shortage; *Traffic and Transportation:* Beijing, China: Beijing's War on Traffic Congestion

Further Reading

Cheong, Tsun Se, and Yanrui Wu. 2015. "Crime Rates and Inequality: A Study of Crime in Contemporary China." *Journal of the Asia Pacific Economy* 20, 2: 202–23.

The Economist Intelligence Unit & NEC. 2015. "The Safe Cities Index 2015: Assessing Urban Security in the Digital Age." http://safecities.cope.economist.com/wp-content/uploads/sites/5/2015/06/Safe_cities_index_2015_EIU_report-1.pdf.

Hu, Xiaofeng, Peng Chen, Hong Huang, Ting Sun, and Dan Li. 2017. "Contrasting Impacts of Heat Stress on Violent and Nonviolent Robbery in Beijing, China." *Natural Hazards* 87: 961–72. https://www.researchgate.net/publication/315344800_Contrasting_impacts_of_heat_stress_on_violent_and_nonviolent_robbery_in_Beijing_China

Ignatius, David. 2016. "China's Intelligence Shake-up Mirrors Its Political Tumult." *Washington Post*, March 31. https://www.washingtonpost.com/opinions/chinas-intelligence-shake-up-mirrors-its-political-tumult/2016/03/31/bb62d77c-f78b-11e5-9804-537defcc3cf6_story.html.

United States Department of State, Bureau of Diplomatic Security: Overseas Security Advisory Council (OSAC). 2017. "China 2017 Crime & Safety Report: Beijing." https://www.osac.gov/pages/ContentReportDetails.aspx?cid=21824.

Brussels, Belgium: Facing Safety Challenges in the 21st Century

The historic capital of Brussels is a popular tourist destination, and a desirable place to live and work. In terms of serious crime, this urban area is generally considered safe, but still experiences problems with violence, organized criminal groups, and corruption. As with most cities, violent crime is more frequent in areas of either high unemployment or those that attract tourists and the wealthy (i.e., individuals at risk for robberies). In addition, several high-profile terrorist attacks have put Belgian officials and citizens on alert, cognizant of the potential for future violence. In the past decade, organized crime in the form of criminal gangs has garnered more media attention through high-profile acts of violence including murder, robbery, and rape. Also contributing to the violence through increases in sexual assaults, organized groups involved in human trafficking operate within the city. Finally, public criticism from recent incidents of corruption has embarrassed local officials and resulted in reform efforts.

Brussels is considered a secure city with low levels of violent crime. In terms of personal and public safety, the 2015 Safe Cities Index ranked it a favorable 22nd of the world's major urban areas. Moreover, the city recently experienced its lowest crime totals on record. Most incidents are petty property offenses, but violent crimes like assault and robbery do occur. For instance, city police recorded 17,797 assaults in 2016. Strong-arm robberies, including purse snatchings, periodically occur at the city's primary train terminals of Noordstation, Gare Central, and Gare du Midi, the latter being the city's primary international hub.

In recent crime statistics, Brussels averaged about three murders per 100,000 residents. For perspective, Brussels would be considered safer than Caracas (122 murders per 100,000) and New York City (5.6), but rated higher than London (1.6) and Toronto (1.5). Surprisingly, aggravated assaults involving knife attacks have recently increased, but overall violent crime in the city is significantly lower than in the majority of other world capitals.

Sadly yet similar to other cities, authorities in Brussels face challenges from the violent crimes of rape and sexual assault. Though Belgium's reported rate of 29.5 incidents of rape per 100,000 community members is considered high in comparison to other countries, this statistic should be considered within context. Specifically, Belgium and other progressive nations encourage victims to report sexual assaults, and as a result, these supportive police practices produce more documentation and accurate crime counts. As a result, comparing Belgium rape totals to countries with less supportive reporting practices can lead to mischaracterizations about the crime's frequency.

Some investigations involving sexual assaults in the capital city have attracted international attention. Recently, Brussels police examined a string of 23 sexual attacks over several years. Specifically, offenders posed as taxi drivers and targeted intoxicated women who were walking alone at night or in the early morning hours. After accepting car rides from the offenders, the victims were transported to the park area of Ter Kamerenbos in the city and sexually assaulted. In response, police launched a public information campaign to build community awareness about the incidents, and to educate residents regarding how to identify licensed taxi drivers.

As in other European capitals, the increase in migrant camps in and around Brussels represents gatherings of populations vulnerable to violent crimes. Interviews of more than a hundred refugees from Africa and Eastern Europe coordinated by researchers from Ghent University elicited reports of robbery, rape, sexual assaults, and forced prostitution. Since these victims often lacked the formal documents required for work and government services, they were subsequently targeted while in the city, with little recourse to resist or report the crimes. As such, perpetrators, including individuals, gangs, and other groups involved in organized crime, view these victims as targets for violence. The two primary languages in the country are Dutch and French, which many of those relocating do not speak, further isolating migrants and increasing the likelihood of victimization

Sadly, Brussels has also struggled with violence in the form of terrorism. In May 2014, a terrorist attack involving gunfire and targeting the Jewish Museum of Belgium resulted in the deaths of four people. The shooter was later identified as a French national with a long history of violence and connections to established terrorist groups. After confessing, the offender remains imprisoned in Belgium, awaiting extradition to France to face additional criminal charges.

Following the tragedy of the November 2015 Paris attack, Belgian authorities raised the country's terror alert rating to Level 3, indicative of probable terrorism. At the same time, officials increased the warning system specifically for the Brussels Capitol Region to Level 4 or "imminent attack." This was only the second time since World War II that the nation's leaders had implemented a Level 4 alert.

Violence occurred again in 2016 as terrorists detonated three bombs in the city: two at the airport and another at a busy metro station. The coordinated attack killed 32 victims, 3 perpetrators, and injured more than 300. The bombings occurred shortly after authorities had raided several locations of a terrorist cell that had connections to the 2015 Paris attack. In another incident in 2017, a soldier shot and killed a perpetrator who was attempting to detonate a nail bomb at Brussels

Mounted police patrol the streets of Brussels, Belgium, after terrorist bombs struck the city, 2016. (Pictura/Dreamstime.com)

Central Station. With such threats against residents and visitors, police in Belgium employ heavily armed personnel and high-visibility tactics to deter violence in areas of public transportation.

After the 2016 terrorist attack in Brussels, residents of predominantly Muslim neighborhoods in the city, like Molenbeek, received a backlash of violent threats. At a memorial site in the city for terrorism victims, Belgian riot police used water cannons to quell violent outbursts from anti-immigration advocates. Belgian security services, concerned about the risk of future violence against immigrant populations, continue to monitor several nationalist groups in and around Brussels.

Finally, Belgium operates an open borders policy that can complicate investigations of violent offenders operating in Brussels, as well as other parts of the country. Similar to other European countries, this policy promotes tourism and economic pursuits, but unfortunately, also permits accessible escape avenues for perpetrators of violence. As such, an offender fleeing the scene of a crime can access Brussels's convenient and efficient transportation systems to exit the country and elude authorities.

Beyond the danger of terrorism from violent groups, the capital city faces threats from other structured criminal entities. Organized crime is heavily active in Brussels's sex-worker trade. For decades, criminals have exploited and forced girls and women from nations like Albania to work in the city's red-light districts. For instance, Place de l'Yser is a short walk from the center of the city, and offers a range of adult entertainment to attract customers from the thousands of tourists and locals frequenting the area. Organized crime like the Albania Mafia use deception, threats, or even complicity from the victims' families to traffic workers into Brussels, and then launder profits via real estate purchases.

To combat human trafficking, the nation frequently cooperates with other countries. Overall, Belgium has a favorable international reputation for proactive measures against this type of crime. In 2016, Belgium received a top Tier 1 ranking by the U.S. Department of State for full compliance with the Trafficking Victims Protection Act's minimum standards. Despite this, prosecuting these cases can be difficult, as authorities in Belgium must collaborate with underfunded, understaffed, and sometimes corrupt officials from each victim's nation of origin.

Brussels's efficient airport and rail systems function as a primary transportation hub for travel within the country and to neighboring nations. As such, Belgium attracts organized crime from around the world, including from Italy and the Far East. In response, the nation's customs officials regularly investigate and seize illegal narcotics and contraband at these transportation centers. Further, migrants, the homeless, and undocumented workers frequent the city's railway stations, thereby attracting perpetrators from organized gangs and human traffickers.

Organized crime in the form of street gangs presents challenges for authorities in Brussels as well. African gangs in the city's urban districts have also increased in power over the past few decades. In 2012, authorities estimated that approximately 13 gangs comprised of migrants from Africa's Great Lakes Region had from 30 to 50 members per organization. Although gangs were involved in numerous violent acts, it was the high visibility of street assaults that garnered national attention. These gang fights and targeted assaults received publicity from traditional news sources, as well as gained visibility via social media. In 2013, officials lamented a government report indicating that the number of new street gangs in Brussels had nearly doubled from that of previous years. This increase was in contrast to decreases in total organized crime membership for the country.

The 2016 release in Belgium of the movie *Black*, which features a romance between rival gang members, further increased the notoriety of gangs in Brussels. Though fictional, the film's story depicts two real rival street gangs in the city: a Moroccan group called the 1080-ers, which is in reference to the postal code for Molenbeek, and the Black Bronx from another neighborhood of the capital. Molenbeek is one of Belgium's most impoverished areas with a jobless rate of around 30 percent, and one in four of the neighborhood's estimated 95,000 inhabitants lack a Belgian passport. These factors serve to ostracize Molenbeek residents, and increase tensions with citizens from other parts of the city and country.

The film's release coincided with the aftermath of the 2016 Brussels terrorist attack, and some concerned theater owners refused to show the movie fearing additional violence. At the film's premiere, Brussels police had to disperse a crowd of rock-throwing juveniles, as residents feared additional outbursts. In response, government officials increased security around theaters and required patrons to be at least 16 years of age for admittance.

Official corruption in Belgium and Brussels has been problematic for authorities, and a source of contention with residents in maintaining viable levels of trust in government. A 2014 report released by the global accountability agency Transparency International revealed that Belgium had performed better than other European Union states, but still needs improvement. The report stated that government efforts toward transparency exceed neighboring German standards, but were weak in practice.

For instance, about 6,000 professional lobbyists complied with national standards and registered in Brussels in 2014. In contrast to those official tallies, researchers estimated that twice the number of lobbyists actually existed. Unfortunately, authorities had implemented few checks and balances to monitor lobbyist authorizations, and enforcement practices were lax. To bolster public trust in government officials, it was suggested that the lobbyist registration program be revamped to include more layers of accountability.

After the 2016 Brussels terrorist attack, critics leveled allegations that government nepotism, corruption, and unethical behaviors acted as facilitators to the violence. In 2017, the multinational organization Group of States Against Corruption condemned Belgium's failure to comprehensively adopt 15 reforms to better prevent deputies, judges, and prosecutors from financial entanglements that can lead to corruption. Despite criticism, the nation's law enforcement, judiciary, and public administration officials typically rank favorably in terms of independence and reliability versus other major cities around the world.

Certainly, recent high-profile scandals involving officials in Brussels have done little to bolster public confidence. In 2017, Yvan Mayeur resigned as the mayor of Brussels after an internal audit revealed that he had been paid thousands of Euros for work allegedly not performed. Specifically, the former mayor had received compensation for board meetings regarding the city's homeless that he had not attended or participated in. Similarly and a few months prior to Mayeur's impropriety, several of the city's politicians were accused of accepting money from an energy distribution company, evidently to help maintain economic influences in the region.

In sum, recent incidents of official corruption in Brussels have damaged public trust in government authorities. With the threat of terrorism faced by residents of the nation especially for those in the capital city, corruption reduction efforts will continue to be an emphasis into the future. Accordingly, the actions of government officials will remain closely scrutinized.

Scott Duncan

See also: Energy and Sustainability: Beijing, China: Battling Water Shortage; *Traffic and Transportation:* Beijing, China: Beijing's War on Traffic Congestion; *Violence, Corruption, and Organized Crime:* Chicago, United States: Stop the Crimes before They Spread

Further Reading

Cendrowicz, Leo. 2017. "Is Belgium Fighting Hard Enough against Corruption?" *Brussels Times*, April 19. http://www.brusselstimes.com/opinion/8047/is-belgium-fighting-hard-enough-against-corruption.

The Economist Intelligence Unit & NEC. 2015. "The Safe Cities Index 2015: Assessing Urban Security in the Digital Age." http://safecities.cope.economist.com/wp-content/uploads/sites/5/2015/06/Safe_cities_index_2015_EIU_report-1.pdf.

Keygnaert, Ines, Nicole Vettenburg, and Marleen Temmerman. 2012. "Hidden Violence Is Silent Rape: Sexual and Gender-based Violence in Refugees, Asylum Seekers and Undocumented Migrants in Belgium and the Netherlands." *Culture, Health, & Sexuality* 14, 5: 505–20.

United States Department of State, Bureau of Diplomatic Security: Overseas Security Advisory Council (OSAC). 2017. "Belgium 2017 Crime & Safety Report: Brussels." https://www.osac.gov/pages/ContentReportDetails.aspx?cid=21158.

Van Hellemont, Elke. 2012. "Gangland Online: Performing in the Real Imaginary World of Gangstas and Ghettos in Brussels." *European Journal of Crime, Criminal Law, and Criminal Justice* 20, 2: 165–80.

Chicago, United States: Stop the Crimes before They Spread

Some neighborhoods in Chicago have become synonymous with violence. Violence is defined as behaviors that intend to hurt or kill another human being. In 2016, from January through November in Chicago, there were over 4,000 shootings with the intent to harm another human (Gorner 2016a). Violence in this city has been surging since 2012, and much of it has been attributed to gang members and individuals who have adopted violence as a cultural norm. Culturally normalized violence is essentially when violence has become legitimized. Determining what exactly spurred this increase in violence is difficult, but in part, it is believed to be due to the fracturing of once highly organized street gangs (Heinzmann 2016). The gangs are now smaller and more autonomous, with little regulation of behavior. Further, with this increased autonomy of street gangs, violence has become a normative behavior in some neighborhoods, and petty or minor disputes are now settled by gun-related violence. Methods to reduce violence have naturally been undertaken by law enforcement and the community. Programs such as Operation CeaseFire and the use of computer algorithms to predict individuals who are likely to commit violent acts are some of the ways that Chicago is attempting to prevent and reduce violence.

CHICAGO GANGS

Historically, Chicago is known for organized street gangs like the Black Disciples, Latin Kings, and Vice Lords. In many instances, these gangs were highly organized hierarchical groups, and the focus was to make profits from the drug trade (Venkatesh 2007). Essentially, there was a clearly defined division of labor for the drug trade with leaders and line workers. Control over the gangs was centered amongst small number of older gang members, and the younger gang members were primarily involved in street-level drug dealing and violence. Although the organized gangs did commit high rates of violence, there was at least some regulation and oversight of members' behaviors. However, by the early 2000s, the leaders of many of the organized street gangs were prosecuted and imprisoned, resulting in the fracturing of the gangs into smaller leaderless gang sects (Heinzmann 2016). These gang sects are now based on personal relationships rather than a rigidly defined hierarchy of membership. Thus, it appears that regulation of members' behavior is reduced, and members are freer to engage in behavior of their choosing.

Further, gang turfs were once based in and around much of Chicago's low-income public housing projects, such as the Robert Taylor Homes. Much of the city's public housing was dismantled beginning in the early 2000s. Prior to the dismantling of public housing, members from a particular gang generally lived in the same building or area. Thus, even if the leaders were incarcerated, the infrastructure of residing in the same building helped to maintain continuity and to establish new leadership for the gang. However, the dismantling of the housing projects relocated families across the city. With this relocation, there was also a redistribution and eradication of gang territories. What were once stabilized gang and drug turfs are now volatile due to rival gang members residing in the same neighborhood. With the destabilization and restructuring occurring almost concurrently with the gang leaders being imprisoned, gang members and other individuals are freer to engage in behaviors that previously were regulated by the structure of the highly organized street gangs. Gang members are now able to engage in violence to promote self-interest. As more individuals engage in violence, it becomes a normative or subcultural behavior in some neighborhoods of Chicago.

CHICAGO VIOLENCE

Violence, in particular lethal violence, reached the highest numbers during the early to mid-1990s, with more than 900 homicides a year in Chicago (Gorner 2016a). The number of homicides occurring in 2016 is over 700 incidents. Although, the current number of homicides is less than during the 1990s, this amount of lethal violence has not occurred at this level in about 20 years. As previously mentioned, this surge in violent behavior in recent years can be attributed to the subculture or the normative nature of violence. In many cities across the United States, including Chicago, a relatively small number of neighborhoods and individuals produce the majority of violent incidents. For example, one Chicago neighborhood, Garfield Park, experienced a homicide rate of 55 per 100,000 residents in 2012 (Papachristos and Kirk 2015). The homicide rate for this neighborhood was more than 10 times higher than the national homicide rate; meanwhile, other Chicago neighborhoods experienced a zero-homicide rate (Papachristos and Kirk 2015). Further, the total population of Chicago is around 2.7 million residents, but only about 1,400 residents are responsible for the bulk of the violence (Davey 2016). Specifically, according to Papachristos et al. (2015), less than 6 percent of Chicago's population was responsible for about 70 percent of all nonfatal shootings occurring in the city. These violent incidents committed by these individuals can take two forms: expressive and instrumental. Expressive forms of violence are violent reactions to an insult or slight, while instrumental forms of violence are when violence is used to accomplish a goal. With many of Chicago's gang and violent individuals, expressive forms of violence seem to be the most prevalent type. This expressive type of violence is often believed to be socially contagious, meaning it is retaliatory in nature. Many scholars indicate that gang- and drug-related violence is a sequence of retaliatory acts that leads to the creation of violence being socially normative in the community (Papachristos 2009). In the case where violence becomes normative, a violent act is looked upon as being similar to gift giving. For example, during the holiday seasons, if a gift is received and none is returned, often there is a feeling of shame or embarrassment. In order to reduce such feelings, a gift is then given in return. Similarly with violence, when you or an associate is targeted by a rival, then in order to save face or maintain status in the community, you must retaliate against that individual or group. Thus, over time, this sequence of violence becomes a common theme or norm in the community. Recognizing this, Chicago is developing and using strategies to target individuals who are responsible for these acts and attempt to change community norms of violence in neighborhoods.

STRATEGIC SUBJECT LIST

Assessing and predicting the risk of engaging in violence is a hot topic in criminology. Essentially, characteristics of an individual are statistically computed to predict the likelihood that the person will engage in violence. The Chicago Police Department, in 2013, began utilizing the Strategic Subject List to target individuals who are prone to commit violent acts (Davey 2016). This is a repeat-offender-focused policing strategy that uses a computer algorithm that assigns a score to a person based on his or her past behaviors. Some of these past behaviors include arrests, convictions, whether the individual has been shot, activities of associates, and arrests for weapon offenses. The computer algorithm assigns a score from 1 to 500, based on the aforementioned characteristics (Gorner 2016b). The higher the score, the greater the predicted risk that the individual has of engaging in violence or being a victim of violence. Individuals with high scores based off the algorithm are placed on the Strategic Subject List and are visited by police officers, social workers, and community leaders at their homes. These visitations are part scare tactic and part education about potential opportunities. The police officers warn the at-risk individual about the legal consequences if he or she engages in violence, the social workers and community leaders offer opportunities to leave gangs, to enroll in drug treatment if warranted, to find stable housing, and help with job skills training.

The Strategic Subject List is not without criticisms and concerns, especially in the realm of profiling individuals and legal rights (Davey 2016). However, the underlying premise of this policing tactic is based on past criminological research and theory. Typically, research has indicated that a small number of offenders commit the majority of crimes. With this past research in mind, the Strategic Subject List focuses on a small number of offenders who exhibit the highest scores based on the computer algorithm. Further, this strategy is based on deterrence theory. There are two types of deterrence, general and focused. General deterrence, through severity, swiftness, and certainty of punishments, attempts to prevent the general population from engaging in certain criminal behaviors. Meanwhile, focused deterrence, is when efforts to reduce crime and violence are targeted toward groups or individuals who are involved in a specific behavior. The Strategic Subject List and the subsequent contact from law enforcement and social services takes the form of focused deterrence. By identifying the at-risk individuals, they will be deterred to commit crime through the police warnings that they are under close scrutiny and if they do not stop offending, arrest and prosecution are highly likely.

OPERATION CEASEFIRE

Starting in 2000, Chicago introduced the Operation CeaseFire program, which is a street violence reduction initiative (Ransford et al. 2016). Operation CeaseFire is based on the premise that violence is learned behavior and employs a three-step process to prevent it. This program takes on the model utilized in public health to stop epidemic disease outbreaks. The heart of the program is to attempt to stop violence before it becomes contagious and spreads. The first goal of the program is to detect and interrupt potentially violent conflicts. To detect such conflicts, outreach workers identify and talk to key people in the community about the disputes, recent arrests, and prison releases. Through this interaction, the outreach workers use mediation techniques to interrupt or dissolve the potential conflict. Second, the program is designed to identify and help those individuals who are at high risk of engaging in violence. The outreach workers discuss the cost of using violence and facilitate seeking the needed services such as job training and drug treatment. The third aspect of this model is to change the community norms by reversing the subculture or normative violence in the neighborhood. Along with the outreach workers, community residents, local business owners, and religious leaders send the message that violence should not be normal behavior and that it needs to be stopped. National evaluations of Operation CeaseFire indicate that it has had a significant reducing effect on violence in U.S. cities that employ it. In Chicago, from 2000 to 2007, there was a reduction in shootings from 73 percent to

41 percent in neighborhoods that utilized the program (Ransford et al. 2016). However, it appears recently that Operation CeaseFire has only been partially or sporadically implemented due to funding issues. The reduced levels of funding coincided with a spike in violence starting in 2015. Thus, the reduced implementation of the program many have had at least a small impact on the spikes in violence during 2016 (Ransford et al. 2016).

CONCLUSION

Methods that are currently being utilized by Chicago to reduce violence include the Strategic Subject List and Operation CeaseFire. Both of these programs have similarities in providing employment and/or rehabilitation opportunities as outlets to violence. Yet there are differences: the Strategic Subject List has more of a deterrence focus in warning the individuals on the list that they are being watched, while Operation CeaseFire is partly designed to change the norms of the community. Violence is influenced by a variety of factors, and in Chicago it appears that a subculture of violence is present in some neighborhoods and is instilled in the fabric of daily life for some individuals. Violence will never be totally eradicated, but employing multiple strategies, like Chicago is doing, will prove to be more fruitful than simply using one type of program or method. By employing the Strategic Subject List, a focused deterrent effect will take place when the police identify those at risk for engaging in violence. However, this focused deterrent effect is not likely to occur unless the subcultural violence norms of the community are changed. Changing community norms to prevent socially contagious violence and the utilization of novel policing practices may prove productive for Chicago in reducing the overall levels of violence occurring in the city.

Eric G. Lesneskie

See also: Violence, Corruption, and Organized Crime: Beijing, China: Tight Surveillance and Harsh Punishment; Sicily, Italy: Fighting Organized Crime in the New Era

Further Reading

Davey, Monica. 2016. "Chicago Police Try to Predict Who May Shoot or Be Shot." *New York Times,* May 23. http://www.nytimes.com/2016/05/24/us/armed-with-data-chicago-police-try-to-predict-who-may-shoot-or-be-shot.html.

Gorner, Jeremy. 2016a. "Chicago Tops 700 Homicides with a Month to Go in Violent 2016." *Chicago Tribune,* December 2. http://www.chicagotribune.com/news/local/breaking/ct-chicago-violence-700-homicides-met-20161201-story.html.

Gorner, Jeremy. 2016b. "With Violence Up, Chicago Police Focus on a List of Likeliest to Kill, Be Killed." *Chicago Tribune,* July 22. http://www.chicagotribune.com/news/ct-chicago-police-violence-strategy-met-20160722-story.html.

Heinzmann, David. 2016. "Leaderless Chicago Street Gangs Vex Police Efforts to Quell Violence." *Chicago Tribune,* July 29. http://www.chicagotribune.com/news/local/breaking/ct-chicago-violence-gangs-20160728-story.html.

Papachristos, Andrew. 2009. "Murder by Structure. Dominance Relations and the Social Structure of Gang Homicide." *American Journal of Sociology* 115: 74–128.

Papachristos, Andrew, and David Kirk. 2015. "Changing the Street Dynamic: Evaluating Chicago's Group Violence Reduction Strategy." *Criminology & Public Policy* 14: 525–58.

Papachristos, Andrew, Christopher Wildeman, and Elizabeth Roberto. 2015. "Tragic but Not Random: The Social Contagion of Nonfatal Gunshot Injuries." *Social Science & Medicine* 125: 139–50.

Ransford, Charles, Tina Johnson, Brent Decker, Mark Payne, and Gary Slutkin. 2016. "The Relationship between the Cure Violence Model and Citywide Increases and Decreases in Killings in Chicago (2000–2016)." September. http://cureviolence.org/post/why-is-chicago-violence-skyrocketing.

Venkatesh, Sudhir. 2007. *Gang Leader for a Day: A Rogue Sociologist Takes to the Streets*. New York: Penguin Books.

Kabul, Afghanistan: What Went Wrong?

In recent decades, residents of Kabul have endured the effects of several successive conflicts. Starting with the 1979–1989 Soviet invasion of Afghanistan, Kabul has had to contend with the civil war of 1992 to 1996, the rule of the Taliban, and the consequences of the U.S.-led invasion beginning in 2001. These events produced much violence, fostered corruption, and created the conditions for a substantial expansion of organized crime. This has led some analysts to label Kabul a "failed city" or "city of chaos" (Esser 2004). Thus, in 2017, Kabul confronts severe challenges that would test the mettle of any urban government to resolve. This situation is further complicated by the many tribal and ethnic groups that comprise Afghan society, the influence of warlords who have become part of the political elite, and huge infusions of outside financial aid intended to rebuild Afghan society but distributed with little or no oversight.

An indicator of the enormity of the problem can be found in the March 2017 report of the U.S. Department of State's Overseas Security Advisory Council (OSAC). In this assessment, OSAC asserts that "criminal activity is widespread" in Kabul. Crime is connected to "international terrorist organizations," and "transnational organized crime (related to the drug trade) remains a serious problem." Violent street crime is common, as are politically motivated attacks on foreigners. Improvised explosive devices make urban travel a dangerous activity. Local law enforcement is ineffective (OSAC 2017). This study admittedly reflects an official U.S. perspective concerned with protecting American nationals. However, when combined with other recent reports by different organizations discussed below, one can conclude that these analyses provide a fairly accurate summary of numerous serious problems still affecting the capital city.

SOVIET INTERVENTION

The Soviet invasion and occupation of Afghanistan from 1979 to 1989 had a major impact on Kabul. Initial efforts aimed to strengthen the urban economy along the lines of the Soviet development model. Authorities promoted industry and urban construction, including housing complexes, government offices, and schools (Esser 2004). Jonathan Steele, a British journalist who visited Kabul many times during the Soviet occupation, noted that there were no "car bombs and suicide attacks . . . during the Soviet period." According to Associate Professor of Islamic History

Brian Glyn Williams, this type of tactic was "alien . . . to Afghan martial culture" until 2004 when the success of Iraqi suicide bombers began to "spillover" into Afghanistan (Steele 2011; Williams 2007).

Though major violence did not afflict Kabul at this time, fighting did intensify in the countryside. As Soviet military tactics led to many civilian casualties, millions of Afghans fled the rural areas to the cities—including Kabul (Metcalfe and Haysom 2012). The huge increase in displaced persons overwhelmed the city's infrastructure (Esser 2004). This in turn contributed to greater urban conflict among different tribal and ethnic groups, due in part to the mixing of these various groups in once homogenous neighborhoods (Payind 2013; Ittig 2010).

AFGHAN CIVIL WAR AND RULE

After the Soviet Union withdrew its military forces, several *mujahideen* (jihadist) factions occupied Kabul. Their struggle for control led to civil war from 1992 to 1996. The intense fighting caused severe damage to the capital's buildings and infrastructure and led to more than 100,000 residents fleeing the stricken city. The Taliban faction eventually won the internal struggle. Many Afghans initially perceived this as a positive development. They resented the warlords' violent rule and widespread corruption. The Taliban promised to eliminate graft and increase security. This they did, but their anti-urban philosophy coupled with their ultraconservative religious views crippled the former cosmopolitan city, neglected urban development projects, eliminated numerous social services, purged women from city jobs, and persecuted ethnic and religious minorities. By the end of the 20th century, Kabul was an extremely oppressive place to live (Metcalfe and Haysom 2012; Esser 2004; Esser 2013; Goodman and Sutton 2015; Forsberg and Sullivan 2016).

U.S.-LED INVASION AND OCCUPATION

On October 7, 2001, the United States invaded Afghanistan in response to Al-Qaeda—then based in Afghanistan—attacks on the U.S. on September 11. For the second time in less than a decade, war devastated the city. This time the U.S.-led coalition did the damage. Though quickly defeating the Taliban, U.S. policies produced many negative consequences for Kabul and Afghanistan more generally.

VIOLENCE

After the United States established a degree of control in the capital, many Afghans perceived Kabul to be safer than the countryside. As a result, millions moved to the city. The presence of international peacekeeping forces probably helped make the capital a relatively safer environment. Yet violence still plagued urban life. The 2012 Metcalfe and Haysom study argues that violence connected to land and resource disputes, drug smuggling, arms trafficking, as well as attacks on women and children represent significant problems. They also point out that the

The scene following a suicide bombing in Kabul, Afghanistan, on June 1, 2017. At least 90 people were killed and over 400 were wounded in the explosion. Such incidents support the criticism that Kabul's government cannot protect its citizens from violence. (Haroon Sabawoon/Anadolu Agency/Getty Images)

central government has been unable to enforce the law and effectively protect its citizens (Metcalfe and Haysom 2012). A 2014 study by Assistant Professor Daniel Esser of the American University's School of International Service noted there were 85 insurgent attacks in Kabul between 2002 and 2012, of which 57 were suicide attacks. While these spectacular acts of violence attracted much international media attention, there was little coverage of the large increase in violent crime directed against Afghan women and children. When compared with the extensive global media focus on "crimes against women" during the Taliban period, Esser wondered if this did not reflect "a highly selective depiction of violence" that benefited the occupiers at the expense of Kabul's residents (Esser 2014). Overall, some experts calculated that at least 40,000 Afghan civilians lost their lives between 2001 and 2012. Exact statistics for Kabul were unknown (Payind 2013).

CORRUPTION

According to a 2015 Center for American Progress study, "corruption reemerged as a potent force in Afghan life following the U.S.-led international coalition's overthrow of the Taliban in 2001." Moreover, corruption "has pervaded virtually every aspect of government operations and the daily existence of its citizens." Paying a bribe to various officials became commonplace. The worst offenders were the political elite who siphoned off "billions of foreign aid dollars." Corruption existed before the invasion. Years of conflict hindered the establishment of strong government oversight. The United States, however, made the situation far worse by aligning with crooked warlords to help defeat the Taliban, by utilizing corrupt Afghan contractors to transport supplies, and by pumping billions of dollars in military and economic assistance into Afghanistan—some $73 billion between 2002 and 2012—without properly monitoring the funds. Polling indicated that corruption and insecurity were the two issues that most concerned Afghans (Goodman and Sutton 2015).

Jamil Danish writing for the *Guardian* in 2016 noted that "Afghanistan was ranked 166 out of 168 countries on Transparency International's corruption perception 2015 index." Danish, previously an advisor for the Afghan government, concluded that "government has often become a self-serving means of enriching the political class." The spirit of greed rather than public service seems to motivate most elite. Corruption reigns from small infrastructure projects to the largest bank in the nation—the Kabul Bank—which lost $850 million to fraud. Even more important, Danish contends that the pervasive influence of corruption coupled with the lack of accountability—few are punished—undermine the people's support of the government. This, in turn, helps the insurgents garner support because citizens feel betrayed by the Western-backed central government (Danish 2016).

In a 2015 article in *The Diplomat*, Najibullah Gulabzoi, who previously worked on projects with the Counter Narcotics Police of Afghanistan, asserted that "the direct involvement of hundreds of senior and mid-level government officials in the drug trade pose a far greater threat to national security and economic prosperity of Afghans than the Taliban insurgency does." Thus, almost all efforts by the central government in Kabul are compromised from the start (Gulabzoi 2015). Laine Gutcher argues that Hamid Karzai, the Afghan president from 2004 to 2014, was "reluctant to go after corrupt warlords and officials close to him because, having become president without a power base, he has had to cut deals with them to shore up his position." Under pressure from coalition forces and international lenders, Karzai finally did establish the High Office of Oversight and Anti Corruption in 2008. However, he did not encourage serious efforts to eradicate corruption, sometimes blaming Westerners for causing the pervasive problem (Gutcher 2011).

Corruption has enveloped the government officials charged with insuring law and order. The judiciary, the Afghan National Army, and the Afghan National Police are considered amongst the most corrupt forces in Afghan society (Goodman and Sutton 2015). According to a 2012 report, "the police in Kabul are reportedly implicated in a range of illegal activities, from corruption to drug smuggling and arms trafficking." Residents of Kabul complain that police officers regularly expect bribes, and that they favor the rich over the poor in disputes (Metcalfe and Haysom, 2012).

ORGANIZED CRIME

Organized crime has flourished under these conditions. In their 2016 study, Forsberg and Sullivan argue that criminal patronage networks (CPNs) "undermined US . . . attempts to stabilize Afghanistan after 2001." Combined with widespread corruption, "organized crime has helped foment instability and insurgent violence."

The narcotics trade forms the basis of the CPNs' power. Since so many in the government—from mid-level to senior officials—are directly linked with this illicit trade, and large amounts of funds continue to pour in from abroad, it has been very difficult to reduce the power of organized crime (Forsberg and Sullivan 2016)

CONCLUSION

Many of the problems confronting Kabul today stem from decades of conflict and the resulting social fragmentation, magnified by the U.S. invasion and occupation. On October 7, 2011—exactly one decade after U.S. intervention—U.S. General Stanley McChrystal observed that "the United States began the war with a frighteningly simplistic view of Afghanistan. . . . We did not know enough and we still don't know enough." In their 2013 study, Alam Payind, Director of the Middle East Studies Center at the Ohio State University, argued that the U.S.-led coalition committed "a series of self-inflicted wounds" that angered Afghanis, benefitted insurgent groups, and undermined the American goals of establishing a viable Afghan government that had the support of the people (Payind 2013). Designed for 1 million people, by 2012 Kabul housed more than 4 million—equal to 50 percent of Afghanistan's urban population. Approximately 70 percent of the population lived in "unplanned settlements without access to basic services" (World Bank 2014).

Yet there are signs of progress. Some urban infrastructure has been rebuilt, and technology is connecting city residents to the outside world. New construction led to Kabul's first shopping mall and five-star hotel opening in 2005. Coca-Cola started production at a new plant in 2006. That same year, President Karzai, foreign experts, and investors began planning for "New Kabul City" north of the old city to provide desperately needed housing for residents as well as additional job opportunities. These developments, however, did not benefit everyone. According to Daniel Esser, "Kabul's recent transformation from a destroyed shell of a city to a bustling urban center . . . only enriches a few while failing to provide sustainable livelihoods for the many" (Payind 2013; Esser 2013; Telegraph 2011).

ADDENDUM

As this writer was completing this essay, a huge truck bomb exploded in Kabul, killing more than 80 people and injuring about 500. A May 31, 2017, *New York Times* article characterized the explosion as "one of the deadliest strikes in the long Afghan war and a reminder of how the capital itself has become a lethal battlefield." The authors further pointed out that this terrible incident was just one of an increasing number of attacks that have occurred since 2014 as the security situation has deteriorated. In an observation reflecting the fatalism of many, the authors concluded that for residents of the capital city life had "become of game of chance." In Kabul that unfortunate day, a number of people "just were not lucky" (Mashal et al. 2017).

Douglas Karsner

See also: Violence, Corruption, and Organized Crime: Aleppo, Syria: Drought, Global Warming, and Civil War; Baghdad, Iraq: Restitching a Torn Society Isn't Easy; *Waste Management:* Baghdad, Iraq: Hauling Garbage in Hell on Earth

Further Reading

Danish, Jamil. 2016. "Afghanistan's Corruption Epidemic Is Wasting Billions in Aid." *Guardian.* November 3. https://www.theguardian.com/global-development-professionals-network/2016/nov/03/afghanistans-corruption-epidemic-is-wasting-billions-in-aid.

Esser, Daniel. 2004. "The City as Arena, Hub and Prey—Patterns of Violence in Kabul and Karachi." *Environment & Urbanization* 16, 2 (October). https://journals.sagepub.com/doi/abs/10.1177/095624780401600219.

Esser, Daniel. 2013. "The Political Economy of Post-Invasion Kabul, Afghanistan: Urban Restructuring beyond the North-South Divide." *Urban Studies* (November). https://journals.sagepub.com/doi/abs/10.1177/0042098013487773.

Esser, Daniel. 2014. "Security Scales: Spectacular and Endemic Violence in Post-Invasion Kabul, Afghanistan." *Environment & Urbanization* 26, 2 (October). https://journals.sagepub.com/doi/abs/10.1177/0956247814544098.

Forsberg, Carl, and Tim Sullivan. 2016. "Criminal Patronage Networks and the Struggle to Rebuild the Afghan State." In Michelle Hughes and Michael Miklaucic, eds. *Impunity: Countering Illicit Power in War and Transition.* https://cco.ndu.edu/News/Article/780086/chapter-1-criminal-patronage-networks-and-the-struggle-to-rebuild-the-afghan-st/.

Goodman, Mary Beth, and Trevor Sutton. 2015. "Tackling Corruption in Afghanistan: It's Now or Never." *Center for American Progress*, March 17. https://www.americanprogress.org/issues/security/reports/2015/03/17/108613/tackling-corruption-in-afghanistan-its-now-or-never/.

Gulabzoi, Najibullah. 2015. "The Narco-State of Afghanistan." *The Diplomat,* February 12. https://thediplomat.com/2015/02/the-narco-state-of-afghanistan/.

Gutcher, Lianne. 2011. "Afghanistan's Anti-Corruption Efforts Thwarted at Every Turn." *Guardian,* July 19. https://www.theguardian.com/world/2011/jul/19/afghanistan-anti-corruption-efforts-thwarted.

Ittig, Annette. 2010. "Urban Development in Kabul: An Overview of Challenges and Strategies." Institute of Afghan Studies. http://www.institute-for-afghan-studies.org/Contribution/Projects/Dr-Ittig/UrbanDev.htm.

Mashal, Mujib, and Fahim Abed, and Jawad Sukhanyar. 2017. "Deadly Bombing in Kabul Is One of the Afghan War's Worst Strikes." *New York Times*, May 31. https://www.nytimes.com/2017/05/31/world/asia/kabul-explosion-afghanistan.html.

Metcalfe, Victoria, and Simone Haysom, with Ellen Martin. 2012. "Sanctuary in the City? Urban Displacement and Vulnerability in Kabul." HPG Working Paper, Humanitarian Policy Group, Overseas Development Institute, June. https://www.odi.org/sites/odi.org.uk/files/odi-assets/publications-opinion-files/7722.pdf.

OSAC. Overseas Security Advisory Council. 2017. "Afghanistan 2017 Crime & Safety Report." Overseas Security Advisory Council, Bureau of Diplomatic Security, U.S. Department of State, March 6. https://www.osac.gov/Pages/ContentReportDetails.aspx?cid=21383.

Payind, Alam. 2013. "Inside Afghanistan 23 Years after the Soviet Withdrawal." *Journal of Asian and African Studies* April 15. https://journals.sagepub.com/doi/abs/10.1177/0021909613478394?journalCode=jasa.

Steele, Jonathan. 2011. "Car Bombs and Suicide Bombers Were Unknown in Soviet-era Kabul." *Guardian*, September 27. https://www.theguardian.com/world/2011/sep/27/no-car-bombs-soviet-kabul.

Telegraph. 2011. "Afghanistan: 'New Kabul' to Be Built North of War-Torn Capital." *Telegraph*. April 1. https://www.telegraph.co.uk/news/worldnews/asia/afghanistan/8420577/Afghanistan-New-Kabul-to-be-built-north-of-war-torn-capital.html.

Williams, Brian Glyn. 2007. "Suicide Bombings in Afghanistan." *Islamic Affairs Analyst*, September. http://brianglynwilliams.com/IAA%20suicide.pdf.

World Bank. 2014. "Afghanistan Reconstruction Trust Fund, Project Appraisal Document on a Proposed Grant in the Amount of US$110 Million Equivalent, to the Islamic Republic of Afghanistan for a Kabul Municipal Development Program." *World Bank Report No. 80177-AF*, March 25. http://documents.worldbank.org/curated/en/885711468187133218/pdf/801770PAD00P12000PUBLIC00KMDP000PAD.pdf.

Mexico City, Mexico: Crime, Corruption, and Violence Have Deep Roots

When the Spaniards who colonized the portion of the Americas to which they laid claim set about the business of setting the foundation of the new society that was to be forged, they did so not by imagining what might be but rather by imitating what had already been. Their model was the triangularly shaped social structure of their motherland, which, for centuries up to that point, had been primarily feudal in nature. The foundation of the new, ethnically and racially diverse society was to slant more favorably in the direction of the Spaniard of noble lineage, transplanted directly from Spain to the Americas, and to slope downward from there, based primarily on social class and race.

In retrospect, certain outcomes of the Spanish colonization of the Americas, and the subsequent establishment of new nations from those colonies, were to be anticipated from the beginning. Among these outcomes could be counted: corruption, which typically arises when those who benefit from an imbalance in power coerce that power in order to maintain the favored status of the privileged segment of the society. Also included in this list would be a reaction against the implicit injustices of the social system that the less privileged segments of the society were forced to endure. In cases of consistent institutional corruption, the reaction against the status quo also becomes institutionalized (or organized). The presence and persistence of social dysfunction results in another anticipated outcome of a society inherently flawed in its structure: violence. Because where one finds injustice, corruption, and crime, one inevitably finds violence. If crime and violence were neither immediate nor constant within the newly established Spanish jurisdiction, they would become so eventually. Given the fact that current-day Mexico and most of its Latin American neighbors were colonies of a classist, racist, medieval system of government for a longer period of time (from around 1492 until the wars of independence in the early 19th century) than they have yet to be nations (from around 1820 until the present day), it is not difficult to understand that the process of cutting itself free from the medieval roots that served for so long as its lifeline has been an arduous, painful and ongoing task.

Relevant to the study of the period during which the present-day nations of Spanish America waged war in order to gain their independence from Spain is the fact that, for similar reasons, throughout the 19th and into the 20th century, political tendencies in Spain paralleled those of Latin America. At the same time the newly forming nations were shuffling off the grasp of Spanish rule, Spain was undergoing its own period of internal debate regarding socially progressive forms of governance. The *Cortes de Cádiz*, a gathering of political delegates in Cádiz, Spain, convened in 1810, consisted of Spanish political figures who wished to address the future governance of their country. At the time of the *Cortes*, Spain was under the control of Napoléon Bonaparte via his brother, Joseph Bonaparte, who acted as king of Spain from 1808 until 1813. That is, Spain, the country that had established its unsustainable political system in the Americas, was dealing with the same lack of sustainability with regard to its own governance. Progressive, liberal forces within Spain had begun to counter traditional, conservative authoritarian systems of government headed by monarchs and royal families. The short-lived Spanish Constitution of 1812 favoring a constitutional monarchy, model of the Mexican Constitution of 1824, was born of the *Cortes*. Had the ideas that arose out of the progressive *Cortes de Cádiz* taken root and held firm, Spain would have been an early example of a country to have successfully embraced a representative system of government. Unfortunately, the century-long, back-and-forth struggles between progressive and conservative forces in Spain ultimately ended up, following the horrific Spanish Civil War (1936–1939), in the hands of an authoritarian dictatorship headed by Francisco Franco (1892–1975), who ruled Spain from 1939 until his death in 1975.

If Spain and its former colonies were undergoing similar challenges regarding their form of government, Mexico was quicker to boil over into civil war than Spain was. The Mexican Revolution (*La Revolución Mexicana*) took place between the years of 1910 and 1920, having the acknowledged ending date of 1917 (the year in which the resultant Constitution of 1917 (*Constitución Política de los Estados Unidos Mexicanos*) was promulgated, even though the fighting continued on and off for another few years before it can be said that the revolutionary process had come to an end.

The Mexican Revolution of 1910 came about after a series of progressive 19th-century constitutions (*Constitución Federal de los Estados Unidos Mexicanos de 1824*, *Constitución Política de la República Mexicana* [1857]) had not been able to withstand the tendency—widespread in Latin America—toward authoritarian rule despite the deliberated and popular will for representational government. Following each of the previous constitutions (1824, 1857), Mexico had fallen into the trap of extended presidencies and dictatorships. Agustín de Iturbide (1783–1824) was proclaimed emperor following the political deliberations resulting from the successfully fought battle against Spain for independence. It was a short-lived position, as Republican aspirations outweighed the impetus to return to a state resembling a monarchy. The curious career of one of the very heroes of Mexican independence from Spain who had championed progressive models of governance, Antonio López de Santa Anna, reflects the give and take between opposite forces during this time. Santa Anna was six times president, the last time proclaiming himself dictator, *Su Alteza Serenísima*, "His Most Serene Highness" (1853–1855).

The following exchange between Santa Anna and Joel Roberts Poinsett (U.S. Minister to Mexico 1822–1823) during Santa Anna's visit to the United States following Mexico's defeat in the Texas Revolution (1835–36), is telling of the status of progressive politics in Mexico at the time:

> While Santa Anna was in confinement at the Phelps plantation, he was visited by a gentleman who bore him a message from Mr. Poinsett at his home in South Carolina. When Poinsett was minister to Mexico in 1824, he was a great apostle of republican ideas, and had a happy acquaintance with the young leader who had just overthrown the empire, and was the avowed champion of popular government.
> "Say to General Santa Anna that when I remember how ardent an advocate he was of liberty ten years ago, I have no sympathy for him now, that he has gotten what he deserves."
> To this very unkind message, *El Presidente* made this deliberate reply:
> "Say to Mr. Poinsett that it is very true that I threw up my cap for liberty with great ardor, and perfect sincerity, but very soon found the folly of it. A hundred years to come my people will not be fit for liberty. They do not know what it is, unenlightened as they are, and under the influence of a Catholic clergy, a despotism is the proper government for them, but there is no reason why it should not be a wise and virtuous one." ("Santa Anna's Captivity")

The lack of effectiveness of certain articles of the Constitution of 1824, made apparent by the dictatorship of Santa Anna, led to the 1857 Constitution. Before long, the effectiveness of this Constitution was also being challenged. Porfirio Díaz was elected in 1876 and ruled until his ouster in 1911, with a single lapse of four years during which he had an ally occupy the presidency while the Constitution was modified to allow presidents to serve for consecutive terms. The move to end his continued political viability is perhaps the element most responsible for the outbreak of the Mexican Revolution in 1910.

The revolution was, in essence, a complex outgrowth of widespread displeasure with the results of a century of failed politics following the wars that earned the Spanish colonies their independence. Discontent toward the strong-handed machinations of the 30-year reign of Porfirio Díaz (known as the *Profiriato*) extended from all sides. The displeasure of the wealthy trickled down to the middle class, while the protests of the impoverished lower classes and indigenous rose from below. During the decade-long revolution, the concerns of different sectors involved in the fight morphed and allegiances changed. In the end, it would be difficult to say that any of the factions achieved precisely what it was fighting for. In essence, the end of the conflict resulted in the promulgation of the new Constitution of 1917, along with a transfer of power, but the chaotic and changing nature of the conflict and its participants resulted in little change to the social structure that originally led to the chief complaints of the combatants.

The newly formed *Partido Revolucionario Institucional* (Institutional Revolutionary Party, or *PRI*) was the political entity that came out of the conflict in power. While the presidents of the party changed according to the dictates of the new Constitution (presidents are limited to a single term of six years), the corruption that led to the affinity of Mexican politicians to remain in power did not. "Between 1929 to 1982, the PRI won every presidential election by margins of over 70 percent—which were obtained usually by massive electoral fraud. The party also held an overwhelming majority in the Chamber of Deputies, every seat in the Senate, and every state governorship. . . . During its long reign, the PRI learned not only how to buy votes but also how to corrupt the army, exploit the media, buy off criminals and absorb the opposition. . . . Loyalty, discipline, discretion and silence—already deeply rooted in society—became essential to the political system's survival" (Weiner 2013).

At the outset of this essay, it was suggested that governing a large, complex citizenry with a clear tendency to favor one segment of that citizenry is prone to lead to a number of undesirable outcomes (corruption, crime, violence). Two horrific episodes serve as witness to the fact that in Mexico, the maintenance of power and its ensuing corruption still loom large.

In 1968, Mexico City was preparing to host the Summer Olympics (Games of the XIX Olympiad). As was the case in other parts of the hemisphere, social unrest in Mexico was on the rise, particularly in the form of student protests that served as repeated public challenges to the government's lack of response to their concerns. On October 2, 1968, 10 days prior to the start of the Summer Olympics, a student demonstration took place in the *Plaza de las Tres Culturas* (Plaza of Three Cultures), commonly referred to by the name of the *Tlatelolco* archeological site contained within the plaza. Protests had been on the rise, and the approaching date of the opening of the Olympics was a matter of significant import to the government. As the Tlatelolco protest began to ramp up, different branches of the government's armed forces disrupted it, setting off a violent slaughter of students and innocent bystanders. The Mexican government has only recently begun to acknowledge its role in the massacre, and to aid in gathering the evidence that is required to clarify exactly how events unfolded. The facts point toward an intentional, violent confrontation aimed at putting an end to that day's events and to any future student protests in light of the pending start to the Olympic Games. While the government acknowledges that there were upward of 30 students and bystanders killed in the massacre, unofficial reports indicate that the number was much higher. What was clear from the event was that the government was neither able nor willing to listen to the protests of the citizens it was supposedly representing.

Flash-forward to 2014, and incidents similar to those surrounding the Tlatelolco massacre—public student demonstrations of dissatisfaction toward an inattentive, authoritarian government—lead eerily to unidentified armed forces reacting to a protest in an apparently organized fashion, wounding and killing participants and innocent bystanders on-site, and, even more horrifyingly, removing over 40 students from a bus and "disappearing" them. The whereabouts of the disappeared students is still unknown, and the alleged perpetrators of the crime—associated with government agencies—have gone largely unpunished.

While these events do not speak directly to the issues of organized crime and violence in Mexico City, they speak very clearly to the nature of governance in Mexico, which up to the present day gives ample rise to protest from within but offers no solution to protest other than violence.

With regard to organized crime in Mexico, the Mexican government's involvement in combating the organized crime associated with the lucrative business of

Relatives and comrades of the 43 students of the teacher training school in Ayotzinapa who went missing in September 2014 hold a demonstration to mark 43 months since their disappearance, Mexico City, April 26, 2018. (Yuri Cortez/AFP/Getty Images)

trafficking heroin, cocaine, marijuana, gold, and humans into the United States comes largely under the auspices of the United States. The practice began with the Nixon administration in the 1970s and continued fervently under the Reagan and Bush administrations. The corruption resulting from the relationship was so extreme that it led at one point to the United States utilizing drug trafficking networks in Mexico and Central America to provide arms illegally to the *Contra* rebels fighting against the Sandinista government in Nicaragua.

A noteworthy surge toward controlling narcotrafficking occurred in 2006 with the administration of Felipe Calderón (2016–2012). According to InsightCrime.org, "Calderón sent some 6,000 troops to his home state of Michoacán to control violence generated by warring drug gangs. A few months earlier gunmen had dumped five severed heads on a disco dance floor. By the end of Calderón's administration there were 75 military bases around the country dedicated to public security, and that number has more than doubled under Peña Nieto's watch; there are now 162 military bases around the country" (Bonello 2017). Ahmed and Schmitt (2016) suggest that "the unique relationship between the military and the government [in Mexico] dates back more than 70 years, to the period after the country emerged from civil war. To maintain stability, historians say, the governing Institutional Revolutionary Party reached a pact with the armed forces: In exchange for near total autonomy, the military would not interfere in politics." The objective consensus regarding curtailing crime related to narcotrafficking is stated clearly by Deibert:

"From Richard Nixon's famous first speech announcing the war on drugs in 1971 until 2012, the United States has spent more than $1 trillion fighting it, a war to which plainly there can be no end.... The drug policies of the major drug-consuming countries can and must change. The arguments against decriminalization and a non-military approach to the problem of drug addiction have now been thoroughly exposed for what they are, cynical lies put forth by politicians panhandling for votes through fear and government agencies and private industries seeking funding. They all know the fallacy of their argument" (234–235).

Meanwhile, a recent uptick in crime in Mexico City, which has largely avoided the widespread violence associated with narcotrafficking, has been reported. Bonello writes that in 2015, "violent homicides rose by 21% to 566 in the first eight months of the year compared with the same period in 2014, according to figures from the local attorney general's office. That's high for Mexico City, where the number of homicides had been dropping, although still nowhere near as high as in other parts of the country. The capital district's homicide rate ranks seventh among Mexico's 32 regions" (Bonello 2015). It is likely that this rise is due mostly to the government's violent targeting of large, organized cartels. Once thwarted by intense targeting by the Mexican military, some of the larger cartels have splintered into smaller groups in new areas, such as Mexico City, while they reorganize.

While Mexico City does not represent a good snapshot of organized crime in Mexico, it nonetheless provides excellent insight into the matters of urban crime and violence. While some might find it convenient to write off the violence in Mexico City as cartel-related, one excellent study suggests that to do so is a mistake. Vilalta and Muggah (2016) provide outstanding evidence that crime rates in Mexico City can be attributed to the same principal causes of crime and violence that are found in other large urban areas that are not infected with narcotrafficking. In starting from the premise that "crime arises when legitimate opportunities are unequally distributed and certain segments of society have no way to attain basic social and economic goals" (3), the authors conclude, with regard to the Mexico City Metropolitan Area, that "in line with what is predicted by both theories [social disorganization theory and institutional anomie theory], crime rates correlate . . . positively with migration, bars/restaurants, female headed households and income inequality" (22). Finally, the central thesis of their study corroborates the central notions put forth in the present essay regarding the social stressors associated with Mexico today: "The most common response to crime tends to involve increasing police deployments, raising penalties on would-be offenders, and increased incarceration. Yet the insights raised from testing these two theories suggest that targeted prevention is central to reduce crime in the Mexico City Metropolitan Area. At the moment, social crime prevention policies are virtually non-existent. Notwithstanding a growing discourse around violence prevention, it continues to be confined to wishful thinking rather than pragmatic interventions. While the government and law enforcement agencies in Mexico cannot be held responsible for restoring family structures, they could, however, redouble investments in social protections and targeted subsidies for working families, single-headed female households, and unsupervised youth—not least due to their crime prevention impacts" (17). As a footnote, it should not be overlooked that the Mexican people are jealous of their hard-won democracy even if some of those in power subscribe to the motto *"el que no tranza, no avanza"* ("He who does not cheat does not advance"). A recent grassroots movement referred to as *"3de3"* ("3 of 3") is encouraging politicians to negotiate anticorruption legislation that requires elected officials to provide legal documents related to their income and business interests. In a country in which high-ranking members of the government, including the president, state governors, and other prominent members of government have been ensnared in embarrassing corruption scandals in recent years, and in which corruption has been proven to be claiming an increasingly significant percentage of the country's GADP each year, times *may* be changing for politicians in Mexico.

Christopher J. Donahue

See also: Traffic and Transportation: Mexico City, Mexico: Improving Governance Is Key to Solving Traffic Challenges

Further Reading

Ahmed, Azam, and Eric Schmitt. 2016. "Mexican Military Runs Up Body Count in Drug War." May 26. https://www.nytimes.com/2016/05/27/world/americas/mexican-militarys-high-kill-rate-raises-human-rights-fears.html.

Angel, Arturo. 2016a. "Mapping Mexico's Current Organized Crime Landscape" (in Spanish). *InSight Crime: Investigation and Analysis of Organized Crime.* July 15. http://www.insightcrime.org/news-analysis/mapping-mexico-current-organized-crime-landscape.

Angel, Arturo. 2016b. "Radiografía del narco: cárteles del Pacífico y Jalisco, dominan; Templarios y Zetas se repliegan." *Animal político.* https://www.animalpolitico.com/2016/07/asi-se-reparten-carteles-de-la-droga-en-mexico/.

Archibald, Randal. "Rights Groups Contend Mexican Military Has Heavy Hand in Drug Cases." *New York Times,* August 2. http://www.nytimes.com/2011/08/03/world/americas/03mexico.html.

Bonello, Deborah. 2015. "In Mexico City, a Body Hanging from a Bridge Portends a Shift in Violence." *Los Angeles Times,* October 21. http://www.latimes.com/world/mexico-americas/la-fg-mexico-city-violence-20151022-story.html.

Bonello, Deborah. 2017. "GameChangers 2016: After Decade-long Drug War, Mexico Needs New Ideas." January. http://www.insightcrime.org/news-analysis/gamechangers-2016-after-decade-long-drug-war-mexico-needs-new-ideas.

DEA Intelligence Report. 2016. "National Heroin Threat Assessment Summary-Updated." June 16. https://www.dea.gov/sites/default/files/divisions/hq/2016/hq062716_attach.pdf.

Deibert, Michael. 2014. *In the Shadow of Saint Death: The Gulf Cartel and the Price of America's Drug War in Mexico.* Guilford, CT: Lyons Press.

"Mexico 2016 Crime and Safety Report: Mexico City." 2016. *Overseas Security Advisory Council.* March 3. https://www.osac.gov/pages/ContentReportDetails.aspx?cid=19202.

Montes, Juan. 2015. "Rise in Violent Crime Shakes Mexico City." *Wall Street Journal,* September 27. https://www.wsj.com/articles/rise-in-violent-crime-shakes-mexico-city-1443398548.

Pestano, Andrew V. 2016. "Mexican President Peña Nieto Apologizes for $7 Million Corruption Scandal." *United Press International,* July 19. http://www.upi.com/Top_News/World-News/2016/07/19/Mexican-President-Pea-Nieto-Apologizes-for-7-million-corruption-scandal/8601468932469.

"Santa Anna's Captivity." http://www.tamu.edu/faculty/ccbn/dewitt/santaanna4.htm.

Semple, Kurt. 2016a. "Grass-Roots Anticorruption Drive Puts Heat on Mexican Lawmakers." *New York Times,* May 28. https://www.nytimes.com/2016/05/29/world/americas/grass-roots-anticorruption-drive-puts-heat-on-mexican-lawmakers.html.

Semple, Kurt. 2016b. "Missing Mexican Students Suffered a Night of 'Terror,' Investigators Say." April 24. https://www.nytimes.com/2016/04/25/world/americas/missing-mexican-students-suffered-a-night-of-terror-investigators-say.html.

Vilalta, C., and R. Muggah. 2016. "What Explains Criminal Violence in Mexico City? A Test of Two Theories of Crime." *Stability: International Journal of Security and Development* 5, 1: 1–22. http://dx.doi.org/10.5334/sta.433.

Viñas, Silvia. 2015. "The History of Organized Crime in Mexico, Told through Data." *Columbia Journalism Review* (December 11). http://www.cjr.org/analysis/the_history_of_organized_crime_in_mexico_told_through_data.php.

Weiner, Lawrence. 2013. "How Mexico Became So Corrupt: From Sicily to Tijuana, How Monopolies and Governments Perpetuate One Another." *Atlantic,* June 25. http://www.theatlantic.com/international/archive/2013/06/how-mexico-became-so-corrupt/277219.

Wood, Duncan. 2016. "Fighting Corruption in Mexico: Taking It to the People." *Foreign Affairs: Council of Foreign Relations.* June 22. https://www.foreignaffairs.com/articles/mexico/2016-06-22/fighting-corruption-mexico.

Seoul, South Korea: The Continuing Public Fight for Democracy

With a long history of political struggle against overbearing autocrats, the Korean people have become quite adept at confronting dictatorships in many forms. So we should not be surprised that the South Korean public took to the streets of Seoul from the fall of 2016 through the spring of 2017; this time to protest the charges of corruption and influence peddling by South Korean President Park Geun-hye. She became the first democratically elected president to be removed from government through impeachment. Moreover, the circumstances that led South Koreans to march in the streets seem very 21st century in nature: the bizarre relationship between President Park and her longtime confidant Choi Soon-sil, the daughter of a religious cult leader, and the "reality-TV" spat between Choi and a friend over taking care of a puppy that led to the initial accusations of fraud and collusion (*BBC News* 2016). Finally, this impeachment also hints at another political rupture opening in South Korea's "identity politics." This time scholars argue that a new generational rift is developing that we can add to the regionalism, the differing ideas about reunification, class identity, and most importantly the struggle between democracy and autocracy that has characterized much of South Korea's birth and maturation to a democratic government and a civil society.

THE PUBLIC STRUGGLE AGAINST AUTHORITARIAN RULE, 1945–1988

In his study of the confrontations between the South Korean state and its civil society, political scientist Jang Jip Choi argues that multiple political conflicts have characterized state-society relations during this period of autocratic leadership.

From the liberation of the Korean peninsula from Japanese rule in 1945 through the April 19 Student Uprising in 1960, Choi asserts that the public fight for a democratic government to challenge the authoritarian rule of the U.S. military government from 1945 to 1948, and then the dictatorial leadership of Syngman Rhee from 1948 to 1960, ended in favor of the state. The Korean War (1950–1953) was the decisive factor here, Choi suggests, because anticommunism justified the state's excessive use of force to control the people and the land. Moreover, the U.S. government provided ample funding so that Syngman Rhee could provide bribes to form a coalition made up of the wealthy landed elites and those former Korean collaborators from the Japanese colonial bureaucracy to run the newly created Republic of Korea (Choi 1993, 21–22). Rhee overplayed his hand in 1960 when he attempted to extend his tenure in office by rigging the election. This time, university students demonstrated in the streets of Seoul, as the press revealed Rhee's dirty tactics in the newspapers. Rhee departed for Honolulu and retirement, leaving an opening for political change. The idealistic students used this space to advocate reunification with the North Korean people, which, in turn, prompted an immediate anticommunist response when General Park Chung-hee led the May 16 military coup in 1961 (Choi 1993, 24–26).

With no political mandate beyond preventing the spread of Communism on the peninsula, Park Chung-hee deflected the public's aspirations for democratic rule by emphasizing the industrial capitalist development of the South Korean economy. Where Rhee had used corruption to keep himself in power, contributing little to national economic development (GlobalSecurity.org), Park jailed the businessmen and fined them. He forced them to work with his military government from 1961 to his death in 1979 to build companies and to pursue economic development for the country (Clifford 1998, 39–40). To do this he created a closed loop of political rule among the military, bureaucrats, and the financial leaders of the *chaebŏl* (large business corporations like Hyundai, Samsung, Daewoo, and LG) that spurred the "miracle on the Han river" in the 1970s and 1980s. As the economy grew, the Park government was able to quiet the demands for political democracy, but instead, rising incomes spurred the desire for economic justice, particularly for those who saw the least financial gains from this growth, the factory workers, who began to push for a more equal distribution of the wealth.

Despite the call to share the wealth, the South Korean middle class, on the whole, chose to support the Park administration's economic and political policies, which limited the involvement of the urban middle class, who watched the clashes between dissident groups and the government, instead of participating in them (Choi 1993, 32–35). Thus, it was not a social movement that brought an end to the autocratic rule of Park Chung-hee, but the head of the Korean CIA, Kim Chae-kyu, who gunned down President Park while they were dining on October 26, 1979. Kim had opposed Park's continued use of violence to suppress worker demonstrations in the Masan-Pusan area (Seth 2016, 207). What followed then, was a bloody military coup where General Chun Doo-hwan in 1980 asserted his control over the army first, and then took the reins of government until 1988.

Chun continued the economic and political policies of his predecessor, but unlike the Park regime, which issued emergency decrees to rule, the Chun government often resorted to military force to control the population (Choi 1993, 36). In the spring of 1980, university students—soon reinforced by the citizens of Kwangju, a large provincial city in the southwestern part of the Korean peninsula—protested the arrest of opposition political leader Kim Dae-jung, a native son of the region. Chun responded by sending in paratroopers to secure the city. Instead, the Kwangju residents came together, armed themselves, and drove out the troopers. Chun then ordered a division of army troops to recapture the city, killing many civilians in the process. As historian Michael Seth notes, "Kwangju became a symbol of civilian resistance to military rule and helped to radicalize the student and dissident movement and alienate much of the middle-class population from the government" (Seth 2016, 209). On the one hand, the student movement—a group largely influenced by a mix of anti-imperialist nationalism, a neo-Marxist understanding of unequal economic development in South Korea, with an emphasis on the common people and Korean folk traditions—who spearheaded the political dissent in the south, reflected the increased education levels of South Korean society in general (Seth 2016, 222–224, 210–211). On the other hand, the urban middle class that represented the growing prosperity in the south, but who had been skittish about joining the students and workers out on the streets, finally participated in the 1987 summer protests against the Chun regime's brutal crackdowns on workers, students, and protestors, clogging the public spaces in Seoul (Choi 1993, 36–40).

In many ways, the Chun regime became the victim of the Park government's successful education and economic modernization programs of the 1970s. Eventually, the dissident movement and the urban middle class came together, forcing the government to revise the constitution and allow direct presidential elections in 1988. With the transition to a political democratic system, Choi in his article published in 1993 wrote that South Korean society was already witnessing the decoupling of the middle class's political and economic interests from those guiding the leading groups of the dissident movement. Yet, in unleashing the power of popular democratic forces within South Korea civil society, Choi anticipated first a continuing readjustment of the power relationship between the State and society; and second, that the balance of power within civil society itself would depend on "how effectively the populist democratic forces can mobilize and organize their strength vis-à-vis the ruling power bloc . . . , and whether they can outmaneuver and neutralize the power of the state" (Choi 1993, 50). Accordingly, the ouster of Park Geun-hye in 2017 would seem to represent the culmination of this transformation of civil society in favor of the middle class and the generation who fought with the dissident movement in the 1970s and 1980s.

HISTORICAL AND SOCIAL ROOTS OF CORRUPTION IN KOREAN POLITICS

Yet, while the fight for democratization turned a corner with the June Democracy Movement in 1987, the struggle against political and economic corruption remains. Historian Kyung Moon Hwang argues that the traditional Confucian emphasis on hierarchy and reciprocity established cultural and social expectations of repaying a show of kindness and obedience with certain favors. Combined with the customary Korean social hierarchy based on birth, Hwang asserts that for many government officials, holding political office became a means of validating one's social status in Korean society, not a chance to serve the people. Native dictatorships from 1948 to 1987 simply modernized the means of evading accountability, controlling the populace, and masking the economic and political relationships among the government, bureaucracy, and the chaebol, Hwang explains (Hwang 2016).

Sociologists Markus Pohlmann and Jaok Kwon-Hein contend that several other factors enable this corruption today for the privileged elite. Above all is the "clan structure" of the chaebol, whose members share similar educations from the elite universities in Seoul, and whose networks of interests are situated in Seoul where "the social circles of the economic and power elites are constantly and inevitably overlapping," Pohlmann and Kwon-Hein observe (Pohlmann and Kwon-Hein 2017). Thus, even with this transition to a democratic political system, corruption has followed every administration. Both Chun Doo-hwan and fellow general Roh Tae-woo, who ruled from 1988 to 1993 as the first democratically elected president, were tried and sentenced to prison on corruption charges. The family members of Presidents Kim Young-sam (1993–1998), Kim Dae-jung (1998–2003), Roh Moo-hyun (2003–2008), and Lee Myung-bak (2008–2013) also have been imprisoned on corruption charges. Hence, in spite of the shift to a democracy, Pohlmann and Kwon-Hein stress that what is new with the Park Geun-hye scandal is the widespread public support for legal steps to put an end to the corruption that maintains the privileged elites' place in Korean society (Pohlmann and Kwon-Hein 2017).

CIVIL SOCIETY COMING INTO ITS OWN? THE PARK GEUN-HYE SCANDAL

On March 10, 2017, eight justices of the South Korean constitutional court confirmed a parliamentary motion on December 9, 2016, to impeach President Park Geun-hye for several violations of the constitution and remove her from the office of president. Polls showed that over three-quarters of the South Korean population agreed with the decision, but a number of conservative protest groups vowed to resist the decision. The *Economist* reported that "over 21,000 riot police were today [March 10th] deployed in central Seoul," and that the police parked buses in the streets to keep apart the anti-Park and pro-Park demonstrators (*Economist*). Political scientist John Nilsson-Wright argues that these police barricades highlight an emerging divide in civil society (Nilsson-Wright 2017).

In his analysis of South Korea's "identity politics," Nilsson-Wright highlights the age gap between Park's supporters and the opposition. Park's supporters, who are in their sixties and seventies, view the impeachment proceedings against her as an attack on the narrative of economic success that her father Park Chung-hee is credited for directing during his rule. For those in the pro-Park camp, then, Nilsson-Wright notes that they view impeachment as a "politically motivated witch-hunt, based on rumor and unsubstantiated allegations" (Nilsson-Wright 2017). Those in the anti-Park camp, however, see the impeachment as a victory for the

Anti-government activists march toward the presidential Blue House after the announcement of the Constitutional Court's decision to uphold the impeachment of South Korea's president Park Geun-Hye in Seoul on March 10, 2017. Park became the first democratically elected president to be removed from office through impeachment. (Jung Yeon-Je/AFP/Getty Images)

historical fight against political corruption and authoritarian rule in South Korea, an alternative narrative that emphasizes the unending struggle to democratize the South Korean political system.

Park's opponents are made up of younger and middle-aged voters who, in addition to interpreting this as a win for democracy, also celebrate the impeachment decision as an indictment of the privileged elite in South Korean society. One of the main accusations upheld by the court was that Park had pressured several chaebol leaders to contribute around $70 million to foundations run by her friend and confidant Choi Soon-sil. As a result, the vice-chairman and heir apparent of the Samsung chaebol, Lee Jae-yong, has been arraigned on a number of charges related to this scandal, including the purchase of a $900,000 horse for Choi's daughter, who was part of the South Korean Olympic equestrian team (Fifield 2017). Another sore point for the anti-Park camp is that Park used her influence to grant Choi's daughter, Chung Yoo-ra, admission to Ewha Woman's University, one of South Korea's prestigious universities (*Associated Press* 2017). Such a show of favoritism strikes at the heart of the South Korean education system that is based on merit, allowing ordinary citizens to rise up in Korean society. Finally, her critics also accuse Park of misusing her authority to intimidate her political rivals in academic circles and to blacklist artists, writers, and members of the liberal media (Nilsson-Wright 2017). Thus, the public struggle against corruption, nepotism, favoritism,

> ### Chaebol
>
> South Korea is the fifth-biggest exporter in the world today. Its electronic products are used by almost every household. The South Korean economy has some noticeable characteristics, one of which is the chaebol, or family-owned conglomerates. There are 45 chaebols according to Korea's Fair Trade Commission. The top 10 own approximately a third of South Korea's business assets. According to Bloomberg News, the biggest five—Samsung, SK, Hyundai, LG, and Lotte—own 54 percent of the Korean stock index, and of which the top chaebol, Samsung, owns 30 percent. The chaebols have played an important role in the miraculous rise of South Korea's economy since the 1960s. However, these privately owned conglomerates are also known for sidetracking South Korea's democratic system and using bribery to get ahead. In 2017, Jay Y. Lee, the de facto head of Samsung, was sentenced to five years for bribery involving paying tens of millions of dollars to a close friend of ex-president Park Geun-hye to secure his leadership transition in the Samsung empire. Ex-president Park, as a result and in conjunction with coercion and abuse of state power, was deposed and sentenced to 24 years in prison. Another chaebol, Lotte retail group's 95-year-old founder, was sentenced to four years in jail for embezzlement. The company's chairman was sentenced to 30 months in prison in a trial of corruption related to ex-president Park. Massive protests in recent years have revealed people's growing discontent. Many believe that the model of family-owned conglomerates is no longer compatible with the 21st-century Korean society and that it is time for a systematic revamp of the chaebol conglomerates.

and the autocratic tendencies of the political and economic elite in South Korea is far from over, and it is certainly one of the challenges that the newly elected South Korean president Moon Jae-in will face in his leadership of the country. Yet, as former U.S. ambassador to South Korea Kathleen Stephens emphasizes, President Moon and the three-quarters of the population who supported the impeachment of Park Geun-hye from office must feel encouraged that a political and judicial solution ended Park's reign (Altshuller 2017, 61). This is more evidence that South Korea's flourishing civil society can assert its will over the State when necessary, and that the South Korean civilian-led democracy is maturing.

Jeff E. Long

See also: Pollution: Seoul, South Korea: When Every Citizen Takes It to Heart; *Violence, Corruption, and Organized Crime:* Tokyo, Japan: Violence, Corruption, and Organized Crime

Further Reading

Altshuller, Maria. 2017. "Scandal in South Korea: An Interview with Former US Ambassador Kathleen Stephens." *Harvard International Review*, May 2. http://hir.harvard.edu/article/?a=14523.

Associated Press. 2017. "How Protests at a South Korean University Led to the Downfall of President Park Geun-hye." *Associated Press*, March 14. http://www.cbc.ca/news/world/south-korea-downfall-of-president-park-geun-hye-1.4023811.

BBC News. 2016. "Park Geun-hye Impeached: Did a Puppy Bring Down South Korea's President." *BBC News*, December 9. https://www.bbc.com/news/world-asia-38259068.

Choi, Jang Jip. 1993. "Political Cleavages in South Korea." In Hagen Koo, ed. *State and Society in Contemporary Korea*. Ithaca, NY: Cornell University Press, 13–50.

Clifford, Mark. 1998. *Troubled Tiger: Businessmen, Bureaucrats, and Generals in South Korea*. Rev. ed. Armonk, NY: M. E. Sharpe.

Economist. 2017. "Leadership in South Korea: South Korea's President Is Permanently Stripped of Her Powers." *Economist*, March 10. https://www.economist.com/asia/2017/03/10/south-koreas-president-is-permanently-stripped-of-her-powers.

Fifield, Anna. 2017. "South Korean President Removed from Office over Corruption Scandal." *Washington Post, Asia & Pacific*, March 10. https://www.washingtonpost.com/world/asia_pacific/south-korean-president-impeached-from-office-over-corruption-scandal/2017/03/09/23666a46-0488-11e7-a391-651727e77fc0_story.html.

GlobalSecurity.org. "Korean Corruption." https://www.globalsecurity.org/military/world/rok/corruption.htm.

Hwang, Kyung Moon. 2016. "Historical Origins of Korea's Political Corruption." *Korea Times*, February 3. http://www.koreatimes.co.kr/www/news/nation/2016/06/633_197187.html.

Koo, Hagen, ed. 1993. *State and Society in Contemporary Korea*. Ithaca, NY: Cornell University Press.

Nilsson-Wright, John. 2017. "Park Geun-hye: How Identity Politics Fuelled South Korean Scandal." *BBC News*, March 10. https://www.bbc.com/news/world-asia-39228815.

Pohlmann, Markus, and Jaok Kwon-Hein. 2017. "Corruption in Korea—A Never Ending Story?" *Max-Weber-Institut für Soziologie*, May 4. https://www.soz.uni-heidelberg.de/?p=4846.

Seth, Michael J. 2016. "South Korea: Creating a Democratic Society, 1953–1997." In *A Concise History of Modern Korea*. Vol. 2, *From the Late Nineteenth Century to the Present*. 2nd ed. Lanham, MD: Rowman & Littlefield, 201–34.

Sicily, Italy: Fighting Organized Crime in the New Era

Change occurring in a society, whether social or technological changes, has historically produced new opportunities for crimes to occur. Crimes does not happen in a vacuum; it is influenced by a variety of different forces and one such force is rapid social change. Sicilian cities are experiencing such a change that has produced new opportunities for organized crime and criminal network exploitation. Like many other regions in Europe, Sicily is experiencing an influx of migrants, particularly from North African countries in social unrest. This mass migration of individuals has altered the daily functioning of destination cities and has provided opportunities for organized crime groups, such as the Sicilian Cosa Nostra, to predatorily profit off the hardships of others. Often working in tandem with migrant criminals, members of Cosa Nostra have expanded their criminal activities to migrant smuggling and manipulating the drug distribution and prostitution in Sicilian cities (Tondo 2016).

HISTORY OF COSA NOSTRA

In Italy, organized crime is divided into four main groups: Cosa Nostra, Camorra, 'Ndragheta, and Scara Corona Unita. These groups generally operate in separate regions across Italy, with Cosa Nostra predominately operating in Sicily. Cosa Nostra, interpreted as "our thing," comprises almost a hundred different criminal families with an estimated 3,500 members (Paoli 2004). By the most basic definition, an organized criminal group is a network of individuals that make money predominately through illegal and criminal activities. Cosa Nostra groups control an estimated 91 percent of all organized criminal activities in Sicily, but their sphere of involvement in crime extends worldwide (Calderoni 2014). The majority of profits, about 68 percent, come from criminal activities occurring directly in Sicily, with the other 32 percent coming from other parts of Italy and other countries (Calderoni 2014). It is estimated that Cosa Nostra groups earn at least an estimated $1.4 billion each year from their involvement in criminal activities (Calderoni 2014). Organized criminal groups, such as Cosa Nostra, establish continuity by providing goods and services that are in demand. Such goods and services can include illicit drugs, selling stolen newly produced technology, and prostitution. These are in demand due to their illegality or short supply. Organized criminal groups also use violence or threat of violence to make money and protect themselves from arrest or prosecution through corruption or bribery of key individuals.

Established in preindustrialized towns in Sicily during the 1860s, Cosa Nostra is often viewed are the archetypal form of organized crime (Paoli 2004). The early forms of Cosa Nostra were not predatory in nature. These were groups established to provide law and order when the local governments failed or were inadequate. The early forms of Cosa Nostra would settle disputes and provide services and protection to citizens of a town. This is very similar to the role that a local government provides, but in this case, the private groups would act in the governmental role. In exchange for the services provided, citizens would pay a pizzo to the local Cosa Nostra group. Historically and even currently, Cosa Nostra groups are based on their strong collective identity with shared customs and practices (Paoli 2004). A key component of this shared collective identity is the oath of *omertà*. *Omertà* is a code of silence and loyalty to Cosa Nostra, which prohibits the speaking or disclosing of criminal activity to individuals outside of the criminal group, especially law enforcement. This strong adherence to the code of silence helps to insulate the criminal group from prosecution. Further, Cosa Nostra follows a code of honor that limits their direct involvement in certain activities. There is much secrecy and many unknowns about these groups, but membership is limited, and one must be Sicilian or have Cosa Nostra family bonds.

Organized criminal groups, through bribery and corruption, often have ties and involvement in legitimate businesses and local governments. These connections allow for the criminal group to operate unfettered. Organized criminal groups such as Cosa Nostra often specialize in certain stable criminal ventures such as extortion or drug sales. But they also exploit opportunities for economic gain. The profitably of criminal opportunity motivates organized criminal groups to branch out and become involved in these ventures. Essentially, these groups rationally calculate the costs and benefits of committing a criminal act by planning and engaging in bribery to reduce the opportunities of getting apprehended. One such example of this opportunistic involvement in criminal activities is the exploitation of migrants from countries in turmoil to destination cities in Sicily and other European countries. The pure opportunity to make large sums of money off of the hardships of the migrants has enabled and motivated Cosa Nostra groups to take advantage of the situation.

CRIMINAL OPPORTUNITY: MIGRANTS

Fleeing war or poverty for the hope of a better life, over 105,000 migrants arrived in Italy between January and August 2016 alone (London 2016). Due to this social change occurring in Sicily, Cosa Nostra organized crime groups are making millions of dollars by exploiting these refugees and migrants from North Africa. Cosa Nostra groups have relationships with North African smugglers and have arranged transportation, food, and shelter for the migrants, in exchange for exorbitant sums of money (Tondo 2016). In order for the process to play out smoothly and as planned, often public officials at ports and the countries of origin and destination must be bribed to allow the passage of migrants. Cosa Nostra groups have the connections and ability to bribe these corrupt officials. Further, even after migrants make initial payment for transportation to destination counties, there are opportunities to make money with the threat or use of violence to extort the migrants. One such example was the kidnaping of six children from a migrant camp in Sicily (Tondo 2016). The children were kidnapped to send the message to the migrants who fail to pay for services provided by Cosa Nostra groups. Essentially, if payment is not received, then harm will come to them or their families.

Many of the migrants remain illegally present in Sicily and this opens up more opportunities for exploitation by organized crime groups. Cosa Nostra groups are making profits by utilizing the migrants for drug trafficking and prostitution once the migrants are located in Sicily (Reguly 2016). Cosa Nostra groups, due to their strong code of honor, often does not become directly involved with certain criminal ventures. However, this does not stop the groups from collecting a pizzo from those that do engage in the prohibited activities. For example, in addition to non-criminal migrants, a small number of criminal gangs from North African countries have also migrated to cities in Sicily. These migrant gangs or criminal groups, mostly Nigerian, have established ties to Cosa Nostra groups and now distribute drugs and run prostitution rings on a daily basis. In exchange for the drugs and permission to operate, the Nigerian gangs pay a large percentage of the profits back to Cosa Nostra groups. In essence, there is a pizzo that is paid by the Nigerian gangs to be able to operate their criminal ventures in the area. By working with the migrant gangs, the Cosa Nostra groups are insulated and protected from the day-to-day criminal behaviors, which reduces the odds of getting arrested.

COMBATING COSA NOSTRA

Any criminal act causes harm in some way, whether in the form of physical, economic, psychological, or societal harms (Maltz 1990). However, when criminal groups are involved, there is greater capacity for harm to take multiple forms, compared to when a single individual is committing a criminal act (Finckenauer 2007). Thus, combating organized criminal groups, such as Cosa Nostra, is a vital and difficult undertaking. Often these groups have infiltrated governments through bribery and corruption, which allows for the group to operate with relative immunity. However, efforts are being made to combat these groups and to stop their activities. Traditional law enforcement strategies are being used such as criminal intelligence, electronic surveillance, wiretaps, and informants. Further, Italy employs a witness protection program that enables individuals to inform on members of organized crime. These programs have been shown to be productive because many individuals are fearful of testifying and speaking out against these groups. Thus, by providing protection, witnesses are more willing to testify, and this increases the likelihood of legally prosecuting organized criminals.

Cosa Nostra groups, with their participation in human smuggling, are involved with transnational organized crime. Combating this kind of crime is difficult due to the different laws present in each nation. Yet law enforcement efforts are being made through the use of wiretaps to identify the individuals who are controlling and organizing the smuggling. By using wiretaps in this way, efforts can be made to arrest and prosecute. Prosecuting the upper-echelon individuals will help to dismantle the criminal network. Further, efforts are being made to target the migrant gang members who run prostitution rings and distribute drugs. In November 2016, Sicilian police arrested 20 members of a Nigerian gang in a series of raids (Offord 2016). Law enforcement was tipped off by an informer that gave the names of the 20 high-level Nigerian gang members.

Grassroots movements have also been established to fight Cosa Nostra and other organized criminal groups. Essentially, these movements attempt to reverse the culture of organized crime that is ingrained in the fabric of everyday life in many Sicilian cities. Libera is an anti–organized-crime campaign that encompasses over 1,200 groups, schools, and individuals committed to promoting a culture of lawfulness and opposition to organized crime. This group educates the public on how to fight corruption and about the negatives associated with organized crime. By educating the public, the culture of corruption and organized crime can be reversed, and eventually the strength of organized crime groups like Cosa Nostra will be weakened. For instance, hundreds of businesspeople in Sicilian cities refuse to pay a pizzo to the local Cosa Nostra group. By refusing to pay, this indicates that the culture of organized crime is slowly starting to change.

A purpose of most organized crime groups is to make money quickly and easily through illicit behavior. Often, some of the profits are used to expand and branch out to different criminal ventures. To address this key purpose of organized crime, asset seizures are often utilized by law enforcement to combat and cripple criminal organizations. Having their assets seized hinders organized criminal groups by the loss of properties, which are often used to further generate income and for money-laundering purposes. Italy has been using this method to combat organized crime since 1996, when a law was passed that allows the Italian government to seize possessions of convicted organized crime figures. For instance, from 2011 through 2014, Italian police seized 1,474 properties in Rome (ANSA 2014). Worth over $800 million, these properties included companies, restaurants, and apartment buildings (ANSA 2014). Cosa Nostra members, along with members of other Italian organized crime groups, buy properties and businesses as investments and as opportunities to launder money. Furthermore, once seized, the government can turn these assets over to community organizations. Many agricultural groups have turned previously owned Cosa Nostra villas into community centers and organic farms. Confiscating possessions and property and converting them into pro-social and beneficial uses also helps to reverse the culture of organized crime.

Social change produces new opportunities for criminal behavior. Organized crime is pervasive in many Sicilian cities; and with the influx of migrants to Sicily, there is opportunity for Cosa Nostra groups to make large sums of money. The harm that is caused to society from Cosa Nostra's involvement in criminal behavior is substantial. Thus, traditional law enforcement tools, such as wiretaps, surveillance, and informants, are being used to arrest and prosecute members of Cosa Nostra groups. Additionally, efforts are being made to reverse the culture of citizens being subservient to Cosa Nostra groups by unifying and educating the public on the harms caused by organized crime.

Eric G. Lesneskie

See also: Pollution: Rome, Italy: Reducing Spatial Segregation Contributes to Pollution Control; *Violence, Corruption, and Organized Crime:* Chicago, United States: Stop the Crimes before They Spread; *Waste Management*: Naples, Italy: Coping with a Rubbish Crisis

Further Reading

ANSA. 2014. "51 Million Euros in Mafia Assets Seized: Alfano Says Police Working to Infiltrate Organized Crime." ANSA General News, March 25. http://www.ansa.it/english/news/general_news/2014/03/25/51-million-euros-in-mafia-assets-seized_d8f2853d-f6e3-441c-ab0d-8f27017d9c8c.html.

Calderoni, Francesco. 2014. "Mystical Numbers and the Proceeds of Organized Crime: Estimating Mafia Proceeds in Italy." *Global Crime* 15: 138–63.

Finckenauer, James. 2007. *Mafia and Organized Crime: A Beginner's Guide.* Oxford: Oneworld.

London, Breitbart. 2016. "Migrants Mass in Libya in Deadly 'Race against Time.'" Reuters, August 31. http://www.breitbart.com/london/2016/08/31/migrants-mass-libya-deadly-race-time-cross-mediterranean.

Maltz, Michael. 1990. *Measuring the Effectiveness of Organized Crime Control Efforts.* Chicago: Office of International Criminal Justice.

Offord, Jen. 2016. "Italian Police Arrest Members of Notorious Black Axe Mafia Gang." *International Business Times*, November 19. http://www.ibtimes.co.uk/italian-police-arrest-members-notorious-black-axe-mafia-gang-1592454.

Paoli, Letizia. 2004. "Italian Organized Crime: Mafia Associations and Criminal Enterprises." *Global Crime* 6: 19–31.

Reguly, Eric. 2016. "Sicily after Dark: Where the Refugee Crisis Meets the Mafia." *Globe and Mail*, June 10. http://www.theglobeandmail.com/news/world/sicily-after-dark-where-the-refugee-crisis-meets-themafia/article30390326.

Tondo, Lorenzo. 2016. "How the Mafia Make Millions out of the Plight of Migrants." *Time*, January 18. http://time.com/4134503/mafia-millions-migrants.

Tokyo, Japan: Violence, Corruption, and Organized Crime

In 2015, the *Economist* rated Tokyo as the "safest city in the world." In "The Safe Cities Index 2015," they analyzed several safety categories for the largest cities around the globe: personal, infrastructure, digital, and health ("Tokyo Name Safest" 2015). That Tokyo came out on top is not surprising for anyone who has been there in recent years. Stories abound regarding how little violent crime exists in Tokyo, especially when compared to major cities within the United States. Visitors relate tales of seeing expensive golf clubs lying exposed—and undisturbed—in the back seat of cars. They hear of individuals who accidentally left their wallets on trains having them returned with all the cash and credit cards intact. While Tokyo deserves its reputation, residents and visitors do have to contend with some forms of violence. Moreover, various types of corruption seem to be endemic to Japan's capital city. Finally, organized crime is an element of Tokyo life, though the shape it takes has changed over the years.

VIOLENCE

That Tokyo has been an incredibly safe city for a long time is borne out by data. In 1987, for example, people committed 133 murders and 412 robberies. In sharp contrast, New Yorkers experienced 1,627 murders and 78,890 robberies. In 2009, data indicate that Tokyo's homicide rate was 0.4 per 100,000 people, compared to New York's 5.6 per 100,000. A 2016 U.S. State Department report on crime and safety in Tokyo noted that "violent crime is rare." Why Tokyo's crime rate is so low is a matter of debate. Urban geographer Roman Cybriwsky notes that many scholars argue that the social characteristics of the Japanese people are crucial factors—they cite, for example, "informal social control" by various institutions, an "absence of internal social conflicts," and a "strong sense of group identity." Other factors noted include little drug use and less inequality compared to the United States (Cybriwsky 1998, 46–47; *Guardian* 2012; U.S. Department of State 2016; Engel 2014).

Cybriwsky also cites several other reasons. One key factor is the *koban*—or neighborhood police box. In the mid-1990s, Tokyo had more than 1,200 kobans, most staffed 24 hours a day. In addition, officers also walk the local communities, thereby coming to know the residents and business owners. This allows them to more easily spot crimes as well as serve as a deterrent. This type of ground level community-based policing is in sharp contrast to most American cities, where officers patrol in police cars. Recently, as more foreign tourists visit Japan and in preparation for the 2020 Olympics, the National Police Agency has begun placing officers with foreign-language ability in kobans located in tourist and shopping areas where many foreigners visit. Since September 2016, English-speaking police officers have been stationed in the Kabukicho and Shibuya sections of Tokyo. The Kabukicho koban also has a Chinese-speaking officer. Moreover, police boxes are also being equipped with tablet devices that can translate 20 languages (Cybriwsky 1998, 47; *Japan News* 2016; "English Language Services" 2016; Gordenker 2015).

Another key factor is that very few people own guns. The origins of gun control in Japan go back to the 16th century. After World War II, the Diet (Japanese legislature) passed increasingly strict gun control legislation. This helps to explain why only 10 gun homicides occurred in Japan in 2008. The same year, gun homicides in the United States killed more than 12,000 people. In fact, fewer Japanese were shot to death during all of 2008 than the number of Americans killed in one mass shooting incident that same year at an Aurora, Colorado, movie theater. In Tokyo—and throughout Japan—to purchase a gun one has to file an application, pass a series of tests, and store the gun and bullets in separate locked safes. As a result, "there were 236,979 guns registered with (Japanese) authorities in 2013, in a country of 127 million people. Compare that with almost one privately owned gun for each of the more than 300 million people in the United States." As one commentator noted, "American law is designed to enshrine access to guns, while Japan starts with the premise of forbidding it." Thus, it is not unusual to see even elementary school children walking the streets and taking the subways by themselves. Parents and children feel quite safe (Fisher 2012; Fifield 2015; Law Library of Congress 2015; Leonard 2016).

Crime does exist. One crime that is very common on the crowded Tokyo train and subway lines is men sexually groping young women. Known as *chikan* in Japanese, this is a long-standing problem. Starting in 2000, some metro lines introduced women-only cars to try to address the issue. Yet a 2009 poll indicated that about two-thirds of young women had been groped. A National Police Agency (NPA) survey the following year found that 90 percent of women who were sexually harassed did not report the crime to the police. In fact, 53 percent of the victims endured the groping at the time. They acted this way because they were too embarrassed to complain and did not want to bring undue attention to themselves or disturb others around them—values most Japanese hold. Authorities have responded by placing undercover police officers on the lines with the greatest number of incidents. One senior high school student, tired of being groped and distressed that the police and even fellow passengers were not doing much about the situation, started an anti-groping campaign in 2016. First she placed a card on her school bag stating that if a chikan touched her she would cause a public commotion. This was successful, so she then had anti-groping badges designed with the message "I won't tolerate (groping) in silence" and sells them to young women (Tanaka and Kawai 2016; McCurry 2009). This type of assertive action signals a change among some Japanese young people.

Violent crime, though rare, also exists. Probably the most shocking example was the March 20, 1995, sarin nerve gas attack by members of the Aum Shinrikyo cult on commuters riding three Tokyo subway lines. The gas attack killed 13 people and injured more than 6,000. According to *Los Angeles Times* staff writer Teresa Watanabe, the attack "deeply shook this tranquil nation" (Watanabe 1995). *LATimes* correspondent Sam Jameson expanded on Watanabe's point, asserting, "the subway attack shook to the roots Japan's longstanding confidence in its public safety" (Jameson 1995). Why this horrific attack occurred is debated. Journalist Murray Sale argued "Aum joined basic Buddhism to an apocalyptic vision . . . that current society must be destroyed before universal enlightenment can be achieved." Furthermore, he asserted that the cult's guru, Shoko Asahara, "had political visions; a lust for worldly power" (Sayle 2001). At the memorial service marking the 21st anniversary of the event in 2016, Prime Minister Shinzo Abe stated, "the public should never forget that the sarin gas attack took place. [The government] will take all measures to prevent another terrorist attack from happening" (Shiori 2016).

CORRUPTION

Various forms of corruption have plagued Tokyo—and Japan—over the decades. In a July 28, 2016, editorial, the *Asahi Shimbun* argued that "one thing remains unchanged in Japanese politics. It is the power of money that keeps breeding graft and corruption" (*Asahi Shimbun* 2016). They trace this current problem back 40 years to the 1976 Lockheed bribery scandal under Prime Minister Kakuei Tanaka. *Asahi* pointed out recent examples of this trend when Economic Revitalization Minister Akira Amari and Tokyo Governor Yōichi Masuzoe both resigned over corruption charges. The *Diplomat* and the *Japan Times* also covered these scandals. The former noted that Amari stepped down due to allegedly receiving "illegal donations from a construction company" (Pollmann 2016). The latter pointed out that Masuzoe quit "after being accused of using millions of yen in political funds for private purposes" (Kikuchi and Murai 2016). Moreover, the *Japan Times* noted how Tokyoites were tired of the negative impact of political corruption on their city, observing that the previous Tokyo governor, Naoki Inose, also resigned. Amari was a member of the Liberal Democratic Party (LDP), and both Inose and Masuzoe received support from the LDP. Some observers contend that the LDP's long-running hold on power—they have dominated Japanese politics since the 1950s—is one key reason why political corruption is endemic. In its editorial, *Asahi* did note that reforms have been passed in recent years, including the Political Fund Control Law designed "to remove special-interest money from politics." They also urged further reforms. The new Tokyo Governor Yuriko Koike, the first woman elected to this key position in the world's most populated city, clearly sensed the importance of this issue when she quickly began to investigate a scandal linked with the new site for the Tsukiji fish market and overspending connected with the upcoming 2020 Tokyo Olympics (Osumi 2016).

Corruption is not limited to politicians. Some experts think that bureaucratic corruption is as widespread as political corruption. Various scandals have occurred in the Foreign Ministry, Ministry of Finance, National Policy Agency, among other bureaucracies, all headquartered in Tokyo. Sociologist David Johnson argues that "police corruption is a double problem" leading to police abuses and preventing the "police from properly enforcing criminal laws against other bureaucratic wrongdoers" (Johnson 2001). Some experts argue that corruption is actually declining compared to the past, while others assert that it is getting worse.

ORGANIZED CRIME

The issue of corruption is quite complicated because it is frequently linked with organized crime. In Japan, organized crime groups are known as the *yakuza* or *boryokudan* (violence groups). The yakuza's origins date back to the 17th century. They started out as gamblers. After 1945, they increased their power by expanding into the postwar black market, prostitution, smuggling drugs, and protection rackets. Moreover, the yakuza have long been involved in the construction business (Rankin 2012). During the buildup for the 1964 Tokyo Olympics, for example, the yakuza "brought in the laborers, supplied temporary lodging, ran the food concessions, the after-hours gambling dens and brothels, and . . . provided 'protection'" (Whiting 2014). For many years they also aligned themselves with ultranationalist right-wing groups in opposition to leftists and unions. Investigative journalist Jake Adelstein states they were a crucial power base of the Liberal Democratic Party (LDP), as "gang bosses funded and supported LDP candidates and elected officers, and were rewarded with public works projects, political favors, and an agreement that no serious crackdown . . . would take place" (Adelstein 2010, 64). Moreover, the yakuza depicted themselves as "ultra-Japanese," protecting "Japanese traditions, untainted by Westernization" (Reilly 2014). These activities gave them significant political influence.

In the 1980s, the yakuza increasingly shifted into white-collar crime—in particular, financial crime—including manipulation of the stock market and corporate fraud. This serious development threatened the financial sector of the economy and Japanese businesses. It is the key reason for the 1991 Anti-Boryokudan Law and subsequent revisions, as well as related laws such as the 2000 Organized Crime Punishment Law and the 2007 Transfer of Criminal Proceeds Prevention Law. According to lawyer Edward Reilly, the public has taken an increasingly negative view of the yakuza as a result of these developments. Perhaps taking advantage of this changed atmosphere, Tokyo Governor Shintaro Ishihara instituted a series of "crackdowns on illegal sex businesses and gambling dens in the Shinjuku and Roppongi districts of Tokyo, cutting off the yakuza's *shinogi*, or revenue streams" (Adelstein 2010, 68). In recent years, the yakuza have tried to improve their image. For example, they quickly sent aid to the victims of the 1995 Great Hanshin earthquake and the 2011 Great Tohoku earthquake and tsunami. Some commentators asserted the yakuza responded quicker than the national government (Reilly, 2014; Rankin 2012). Whether the government offensive against the yakuza will be able to keep organized crime from regaining a more prominent role in Japanese society remains to be seen.

Douglas Karsner

See also: Violence, Corruption, and Organized Crime: Beijing, China: Tight Surveillance and Harsh Punishment; Seoul, South Korea: The Continuing Public Fight for Democracy

Further Reading

Adelstein, Jake. 2010. "The Last Yakuza." *World Policy Journal* 27, 2 (Summer): 67–71. https://www.jstor.org/stable/27870341?seq=1#page_scan_tab_contents.

Asahi Shimbun. 2016. "Editorial: Corrupt Politics Linger 4 Decades after Lockheed Bribery Scandal." *Asahi Shimbun*, July 28.

Cybriwsky, Roman. 1998. *Tokyo: The Shogun's City at the Twenty-First Century*. London: John Wiley & Sons.

Engel, Pamela. 2014. "How Japan's Murder Rate Got to Be So Incredibly Low." *Business Insider*, April 11. https://www.businessinsider.com/why-japans-murder-rate-is-so-low-2014-4.

"English Language Services Available at Two Police Koban in Tokyo." 2016. *Japan Today*, October 1. https://japantoday.com/category/national/english-language-services-available-at-two-police-koban-in-tokyo.

Fifield, Anna. 2015. "In Japan, Even the Gun Enthusiasts Welcome Restrictions on Firearms." *Washington Post*, June 29. https://www.washingtonpost.com/world/in-japan

-even-the-gun-enthusiasts-are-in-favor-of-gun-control/2015/06/27/283cfaea-19a6
-11e5-bed8-1093ee58dad0_story.html.

Fisher, Max. 2012. "A Land without Guns: How Japan Has Virtually Eliminated Shooting Deaths." *Atlantic*, July 23. https://www.theatlantic.com/international/archive/2012/07/a-land-without-guns-how-japan-has-virtually-eliminated-shooting-deaths/260189/.

Gordenker, Alice. 2015. "Police Who Stand with Big Sticks." *Japan Times*, March 20. https://www.japantimes.co.jp/news/2015/03/20/reference/police-who-stand-with-big-sticks/#.XAnWi2hKhPY.

Jameson, Sam. 1995. "Japan Cult Leader, Aides Indicted in Fatal Gas Attack." *Los Angeles Times*, June 7. http://articles.latimes.com/1995-06-07/news/mn-10536_1_gas-attack.

Johnson, David. 2001. "Bureaucratic Corruption in Japan." *Japan Policy Research Institute: JPRI Working Paper* No. 76, April. http://www.jpri.org/publications/workingpapers/wp76.html.

Kikuchi, Daisuke, and Shusuke Murai. 2016. "Tokyo Voters Seek Out Corruption-Free Governor." *Japan Times*, July 14. Kikuchi, Daisuke, and Shusuke Murai. 2016. "Tokyo Voters Seek Out Corruption-Free Governor.".

"Koban Police Boxes Going Multilingual Ahead of 2020 Games." 2016. *Japan News* by *Yomiuri Shimbun*, November 12. http://jp-gate.com/u/news/ryu64lbnhoz82s.

Law Library of Congress. 2015. "Firearms-Control Legislation and Policy: Japan." loc.gov/law/help/firearms-control/japan.php.

Leonard, Abigail. 2016. "For Some Expats, US Gun Violence Makes Japan Feel Like a Haven." *Stars and Stripes*, July 19. https://www.washingtonpost.com/world/asia_pacific/for-some-expats-us-gun-violence-makes-japan-feel-like-a-haven/2016/07/18/0edca7d4-4840-11e6-8dac-0c6e4accc5b1_story.html.

McCurry, Justin. 2009. "Japanese Police Launch Crackdown on Commuter Gropers." *Guardian*, September 17. https://www.theguardian.com/world/2009/sep/17/japan-tokyo-police-commuter-gropers.

Osumi, Magdalena. 2016. "New Tokyo Gov. Koike Names Toyosu Scandal, Olympic Overspend as Policy Priorities." *Japan Times*, September 28. https://www.japantimes.co.jp/news/2016/09/28/national/politics-diplomacy/new-tokyo-gov-koike-names-toyosu-scandal-olympic-overspend-policy-priorities/#.XAnYV2hKhPY.

Pollmann, Mina. 2016. "Japan's 'TPP Chief' Resigns over Corruption Scandal." *Diplomat*, January 29. https://thediplomat.com/2016/01/japans-tpp-chief-resigns-over-corruption-scandal/.

Rankin, Andrew. 2012. "21st-Century Yakuza: Recent Trends in Organized Crime in Japan, Part 1." *Asian Pacific Journal/Japan Focus* 10, 2 (February). https://apjjf.org/2012/10/7/Andrew-Rankin/3688/article.html.

Reilly, Edward. 2014. "Criminalizing Yakuza Membership: A Comparative Study of the Anti-Boryokudan Law." *Washington University Global Studies Law Review* 13, 4 (Winter). https://openscholarship.wustl.edu/law_globalstudies/vol13/iss4/9/.

Sayle, Murray. 2001. "Haruki Murakami and the Tokyo Gas Attack." *Japan Policy Research Institute: JPRI Critique* VIII, no. 1 (January). http://www.jpri.org/publications/critiques/critique_VIII_1.html.

Shioiri, Aya. 2016. "Memorial Events Held to Mark Sarin Gas Attack Anniversary." *Asahi Shimbun*, March 21.

Tanaka, Yoko, and Mamie Kawai. 2016. "Long-Suffering Schoolgirl Leads Project to Stop Gropers on Trains." *Asahi Shimbun*, March 18.

"Tokyo Named Safest City in World; Osaka No. 3." 2015. *Rocket News*, February 5. https://japantoday.com/category/features/lifestyle/tokyo-named-safest-city-in-world-osaka-no-3.

United States Department of State, Bureau of Diplomatic Security. 2016. "Japan 2016 Crime & Safety Report: Tokyo." www.osac.gov/pages/ContentReportDetails.aspx?cid=19134

Watanabe, Teresa. 1995. "Japanese Guru Arrested in Fatal Subway Attack: Crime: Shoko Asahara Found during Raid on Cult's Mt. Fuji Compound. Warrant Is First to Link Sect to Poisoning." *Los Angeles Times*, May 16. http://articles.latimes.com/1995-05-16/news/mn-2520_1_shoko-asahara.

"Where Are World's Deadliest Major Cities?" 2012. *Guardian*, November 30. https://www.theguardian.com/news/datablog/2012/nov/30/new-york-crime-free-day-deadliest-cities-worldwide.

Whiting, Robert. 2014. "Negative Impact of 1964 Olympics Profound." *Japan Times*, October 24. https://www.japantimes.co.jp/sports/2014/10/24/olympics/negative-impact-1964-olympics-profound/.

Waste Management

OVERVIEW

Waste management receives the urban world's increasing focus, as more than half of the world population lives in cities today, and urban dwellers will account for nearly 70 percent of the world's population by 2050, according to an estimate of 2014 by the Department of Economic and Social Affairs of the United Nations. Proper treatment of municipal solid waste (MSW), the major form of urban waste, is critical to sustainable urban development. The UN-recommended course of action is to implement the Waste Management Hierarchy that stresses prevention, reuse, recycling, recovery, and disposal, with emphasis on prevention. New technologies are allowing cities to turn the traditional waste treatment into waste-to-energy conversion. However, properly managing MSW requires financial resources, government leadership, and citizens' participation. These are not readily available to all cities in the world. Articles included in this section demonstrate challenges and success stories of cities under different economic and social conditions.

Waste Management along the Economic Fault Line

Cities that are war-torn or suffering from widespread poverty face the worst challenge. Typically, they lack efficient government and funding to provide public services in general. Corruption and insecurity further complicate the situation. These cities face constant threats from waste-borne diseases.

An extreme case is the city of Baghdad. The Iraqi capital has 9 million residents; the city generates 11,000 tons of waste daily. Disposal infrastructure is virtually nonexistent, and there is no effective restraint on random dumping. International funding for garbage disposal is largely embezzled by corrupt officials. Additionally, there is danger for waste management workers—bombs hidden under the refuse have been responsible for the deaths of many waste management employees. It is literally "hell on earth" to handle waste in Baghdad, as Johansen describes it. The poorest districts simply do not have disposal services at all. Residents pile up the garbage along the streets, which ends up infesting waters and spreading diseases around. Locals remember Saddam fondly, because under his tyrannical reign at least garbage got picked up. Johansen suggests that the key to providing services in the war-torn city is to strengthen the local governance. However, the unsuccessful efforts so far prove that just throwing more money at the Baghdad municipality is unlikely to make it better.

In a city of extreme poverty, waste management is not considered a priority. Port-au-Prince, the capital of Haiti and home to over 2.5 million people, is one of the poorest urban areas in the Caribbean. In Port-au-Prince, the widespread MSW pollution problem is further complicated by social instability, poor governance, shortage of funding, and irresponsible disposal practices, as Haney observes. In 2015, only 62 percent of the population had access to an improved water source, and 24 percent had access to improved sanitation facilities. Outbreaks of cholera have happened and remain a real threat. Because most residents, regardless of social status, use the gullies to remove waste, flooded gullies spread waste in the community in rainy seasons and damage the ecology in rivers. The greatest barrier to effective treatment, however, is the city's inefficient management, as Haney points out. The management fails to collect data on MSW generation and disposal. It leaves a main disposal site of hundreds of acres near the capital city open to unmanaged dumping. The overall failure in infrastructure and governance appears to have rendered Port-au-Prince incapable of providing MSW management to its citizens. To reverse the situation, Haney recommends that the municipal government make improvement in a number of areas, including quantifying waste discharge and adopting proper technologies. Moreover, the municipality must assume its leadership and encourage citizens, collectors, and educators to work together.

Experience shows that by involving citizens' participation, cities can improve waste management despite unfavorable conditions. Dakar, the capital city of Senegal in West Africa, has a population of approximately 3 million. Because the city is located in a peninsula, there is no room for expansion. As a result, high population density, scarcity of space, shrinking agricultural land, shortage of water supply, along with other issues, constitute an unhealthy urban environment. One major challenge is to separate the city's wastewater from its food chain, since the local agriculture that supplies produce to the city uses the city's discharge to irrigate farms. Prior to 2008, irrigation water was mixed with wastewater and sludge from the city's cesspits, causing outbreaks of typhoid. Today, farms purchase treated wastewater for use as fertilizer. However, over 90 percent of the wastewater discharged into the ocean is untreated. Another challenge is to provide a better MSW treatment. Households in Dakar habitually discard or burn garbage where service is unavailable. When gullies clog in rainy seasons, they send waste to the streets. To make up for the shortfall in service, Dakar youths form cleaning crews known as "Set-Setal" to unclog the drainage lines. While most waste treatment problems are unresolved with these operations, Ross indicates that it is often the small-scale private actors in Dakar who step up to save the city.

Cairo, the capital city of Egypt, is one of the largest Islamic cities in the world, and the most populous city in Africa. Greater Cairo has a population of 20 million. The population density could top 50,180 per square mile in some regions, higher than anywhere else in Africa. As a result, properly managed urban waste is a historical challenge. Inefficiency in treating the city's 15,000-ton MSW generated daily has led to pollution to the environment and tainted the tourist industry. Under these circumstances, a unique workforce (as well as an ethnic group), the Zabaleen, has been recognized for their hard work in providing disposal service. The Zabaleen work in family-based units, utilizing donkey carts as a means of transportation and pigs to reduce organic materials. Their hard work contributes to the removal of as much as 40 percent of the urban waste. Meanwhile, their cultural tradition of Coptic Christianity contributes to Cairo's cultural diversity.

Cities of emerging economies, such as China, India, and Pakistan, face tremendous challenges in handling urban waste. New Delhi is the National Capital Territory of India, with a population of 18 million. The city generates 11,558 tons of MSW per day. Kumar indicates that large population, increased economic activities, lack of regulations, and law enforcement are some of the factors that make waste management difficult. The city's waste collection is notoriously inefficient, Kumar observes. Only 70 to 80 percent of MSW is collected by services; the remainder is found discarded illegally. The city's poor air quality is partially blamable on the widespread illegal burning of waste that releases toxic smoke into the atmosphere. Additionally, landfills that receive most of the MSW are known to have leakage problems. In some cases, the leachate has caused outbreaks of dengue and chikungunya, two deadly mosquito-borne diseases. The New Delhi municipality strives to improve waste management by adding new landfills and giving private waste pickers proper recognition.

Practice of Developed Cities—Putting Prevention First

Compared to economically strained cities, the cities in economically well-off countries enjoy more means to handle their MSW. They have better access to technologies, broad participation from citizens mindful of environmental protection, and an efficient management to streamline treatment efforts. The successful cities tend to be those where citizens avidly implement the waste management hierarchy.

In North America, San Francisco, United States, and Calgary, Canada, are two model cities in waste management. San Francisco is a large city with a population of over 860,000. Located at the tip of a narrow peninsula, surrounded by water, the city has limited spaces available for waste disposal. Yet San Francisco has become a leader in waste management, and is well-positioned to achieve its goal of zero-waste by 2020. A 2013 report indicates that the city had already achieved 80 percent of that goal. In a 2016 report, the *New York Times* labeled the city "the Silicon Valley of recycling." In addition to successfully diverting MSW from landfills, Giraldo remarks, the key to San Francisco's success is to be able to reduce waste at the household level. For example, the city encourages residents to acquire a number of simple habits, such as bringing their own bags when going shopping, purchasing products that can be recycled or made of recycled materials, buying local products that don't require transportation, and reusing bags and packaging materials. In a larger framework, these practices are part of the waste management hierarchy promoted by the United Nations—"prevention, reuse, recycle, recovery, and disposal." San Francisco's success story serves as a good working model for what citizens can do to keep their city clean.

Open dumping leads to environmental degradation by causing contamination of the groundwater and nearby soil. However, open dumping has been how people discard waste for a long time, as Moghadam indicates. The current standard practice in North America and Western Europe is to maximally divert MSW from landfill. The widely adopted practice, the "integrated waste management," promotes the three "R's"—reduce, reuse, and recycle. Recovering energy from waste is sometimes called the fourth "R." Landfill, as a traditional method of disposal, is carefully managed today to avoid contamination. Canada invests heavily in managing MSW. Federal, provincial, and local governments have their own share of responsibility within the jurisdiction of each level. In the province of Alberta and its largest city Calgary, the waste management project is known as the Too Good to Waste strategy. As Moghadam explains, Calgary has established a detailed set of procedures to facilitate the "3 Rs." The city distributes color-coded bins, for example, to help households sort waste materials, and uses specific collecting methods to recycle e-waste. Calgary's waste management practice is a good example of how the goal of prevention can be achieved.

Among the European cities, Oslo and Naples are two examples of different management styles. Oslo, the capital city of Norway, has a population of 5.26 million. Keeping the city green and sustainable is arguably taken more seriously by citizens of Oslo than anywhere else in Europe. In June 2017, Oslo received the European Green Capital Award for 2019 honoring its sustainable development and high environmental standards. There are a number of things that the city does successfully, according to Schmidt. Encouraging citizens to recycle, reuse, and repair has been a success. Oslo has been a leader in establishing used clothing collection centers. The city is responsible for transporting tons of used clothes and unused food from distributors to charity organizations. Another example is collecting and sorting waste materials into proper recycling bins as a popular passion. The city sponsors waste collection contests. Optical sorting technology is used to separate food and plastic waste. Because 53 percent of food waste is produced by the household, Oslo stresses preventing waste at the kitchen table. The media provides tips for proper planning in consumption. Meanwhile, kitchen waste from households is used to generate bioenergy. These efforts have made Oslo a model of sustainable urban life.

Naples, with 1 million residents, is the third-largest city in Italy, trailing Rome and Milan. The traditional disposal uses incineration and landfills. However, Naples no longer has access to these solutions, as landfills have run out of space, and air pollution is already severe, as Cumo indicates. The problems of waste-covered streets peaked in the early 2000s, and put strong pressure on politicians who ran for offices. Italian politicians were smart and quick to quell the pressure: the mayors of Naples paid foreign companies to haul away the city's garbage and get it burned outside Italy. Cumo remarks that by having the trash burned elsewhere, Naples only shifted the problem, but did not reduce pollution. With respect to MSW control, Cumo argues that frugality rather than prodigality must become the new order of the day in Naples.

Among Asian cities, Singapore City and Kobe, Japan, are two cities that stand out with excellent performance. Together, these cities showcase a great dedication to waste management, as well as their craftsmanship in implementing treatment plans in every detail.

Singapore City has 5.6 million people in an urban space the size of Chicago. The limited space does not allow the luxury of building ample dumpsites; neither does the tropical climate preserve strewn waste for an extended period, if citizens were to choose to discard garbage at random. Singapore is ranked as one of the cleanest cities in Asia and the world. The very high environmental awareness seems to have been fostered by the island's natural constraints. Arguably, the environment-friendly mentality has driven the citizens to be extremely mindful with waste disposal. A top challenge for Singapore's densely populated urban environment is it has to handle a large amount of food waste on a daily basis. To solve the problem, Singapore strives to achieve waste reduction in households, schools, restaurants, and hotels. On the other hand, the city uses anaerobic digestion and incineration to harvest energy from food waste. The process reduces landfill to the minimum. However, what is exemplary are the city's efforts in making reduce, reuse, and recycle part of the residents' habit.

Kobe, Japan, has the reputation of being the cleanest city in the world. In many ways, Kobe is similar to Singapore: both are portal cities and have little space available for building landfills. One difference in Kobe's favor is that its population is only one-fifth that of Singapore, which makes waste management easier. For example, food waste is not Kobe's most acute challenge. However, the city has to deal with industrial waste discharged by steel and power plants. Another difference is in management styles. Unlike Singapore, Kobe implements a "pay as you trash" system, letting citizens be responsible for their own waste. In practice, every citizen must watch out for the waste materials put out on the curb, with price tags in mind. For visitors, the detailed price list may be mind-boggling. Many believe, however, that if "pay as you trash" works for Kobe, it may be applicable in other cities too.

Further Reading
The Department of Economic and Social Affairs of the United Nations. 2014. *World Urbanization Prospects.* https://www.compassion.com/multimedia/world-urbanization-prospects.pdf.
United Nations Environment Programme. 2013. "Municipal Solid Waste: Is It Garbage or Gold?" https://na.unep.net/geas/getUNEPPageWithArticleIDScript.php?article_id=105.

Baghdad, Iraq: Hauling Garbage in Hell on Earth

In a country at war, with constant factional violence (including terrorist bombings nearly daily), as summer temperatures now rise regularly to 120 degrees Fahrenheit or higher, disposing of ordinary, everyday garbage can be quite a problem. Baghdad's teeming streets and reeking landfills make Dante's visions look downright pleasant. Garbage hauling in Baghdad is literally hell on Earth. "In the absence of modern and efficient waste handling and disposal infrastructure most of the wastes are disposed in unregulated landfills across Iraq, with little or no concern for both human health and environment," one consultant's report said. Across Iraq, "Spontaneous fires, groundwater contamination, surface-water pollution and large-scale greenhouse-gas emissions have been the hallmarks of Iraqi landfills" (Alnajjar 2015).

"Waste management" in Baghdad, by 2017 a rapidly expanding metropolis of about 9 million people, usually means hauling part of the city's 11,000 tons of daily garbage and trash to a huge and growing landfill. With poverty increasing, there is never any shortage of rag pickers. Trash collecting itself is high-risk work in a place where, wrote Michael Luo in the *New York Times* (2006), "a bomb could be lurking beneath any heap of refuse, and where insurgents are willing to kill to prevent them from being discovered, [and] an occupation that pays only a few dollars a day has become one of the deadliest." A large majority of the 500 Baghdad municipal workers killed in a typical year are trash collectors. "When we are working, we are working nervously," said garbage collector Sabah Atia, age 29, in 2006. "We are carrying our souls in our hands" (Luo 2006).

In Baghdad, much of the garbage does not reach the dump; it is strewn across vacant lots and streets, stinking in the heat, drawing feral dogs, vermin, and swarms of flies, as well as an informal recycling economy maintained by many ragged people with no other source of income. Observers can rank the degree of affluence in a

A woman walks past a pile of garbage in the Sadr City area of Baghdad, Iraq, 2008. Baghdad's deplorable waste management situation is due in part to a virtually nonexistent waste disposal infrastructure, and a highly corrupt municipal government. (Robert Nickelsberg/Getty Images)

neighborhood by the depth of garbage along its streets. Like most city services (such as power, water, and sewers), garbage collection is notable for its absence in the poorest, most violent parts of the city. In some areas, garbage is so deep that bombs can be hidden beneath it. The number of trash-compacting trucks dropped to 380 from 1,280 after Saddam Hussein's regime fell (Luo 2006). New York City, with 8 million people, roughly the population of Baghdad, has 5,700 waste-removal vehicles.

Ola Sami, who lives in a third-floor apartment in an area strewn with garbage, said that disease worried her. "Forget about how badly it smells," she said. "My son got infected because of the piles" (Luo 2006). Even in Masbah, a wealthy central Baghdad neighborhood that years ago hosted several foreign embassies, garbage lines the streets. Saddam may have been a tyrant, many residents complain, but under his rule most of the garbage was picked up.

In a few areas, however, the situation has improved. One is Sadr City, a large Shiite slum. Local militias commanded by Moqtada al-Sadr have guaranteed the safety of trash haulers, who haul garbage into trucks with shovels. Even so, with one truck (with a driver and a shoveler) serving about 25,000 residents, the garbage often piles up more quickly than it can be removed. The city government estimated in 2016 that roughly half of Baghdad's 11,000 tons of daily garbage ends up on the streets or in vacant lots (Sadr City, which is Shiite, was neglected under Saddam Hussein's Sunni-dominated regime).

The other half of the garbage ends up in the landfill, where one report dated August 24, 2016, described the situation: "Despite its huge untapped oil and gas reserves and steadily rising oil output and revenue, 23 percent of the population [of Iraq] live below the poverty line," according to the Ministry of Planning.

Poverty was rising in 2016 to unprecedented levels in Baghdad, as, according to a report by the Institute for War & Peace Reporting, "Decades of conflicts and economic sanctions, paralysis of the Iraqi economy, the sharp decline in oil prices, runaway spending on the war against the Islamic State (ISIS), in addition to the absence of strategic planning and rampant financial and administrative corruption, have left the Iraqi treasury nearly empty" (Omar 2016). The city's population was swelling with refugees from areas to the north that had been seized by the Islamic State (ISIS). Some of these people ended up culling the landfills for anything they could sell. By 2015, the number of squatters in Baghdad had risen to about 2.5 million people.

"Terrorism has caused thousands of victims, including orphans, widows, impaired people and mass displacement that left scores in deep poverty, forcing many to resort to begging to make a living," said social researcher Wathek Sadek (Omar 2016). According to Deputy Director of Baghdad provincial council Atwan al-Atwani, "The local government has no data on the numbers of beggars and street children although this phenomenon has increased in an unusual and alarming way lately." He warned that rampant poverty increased the numbers of those dropping out of school, delinquency rates and prostitution among young girls (Omar 2016).

Qasim Dawood, a member of the Health and Environment Committee of the Iraqi Parliament, said, "Baghdad is not like other places, and the issues are complex. The municipality is not doing its job properly, but at the same time we lack laws that prohibit the public from littering and polluting. This is why we are unable to provide a healthy environment." According to Dawood, all manner of trash is clogging the alleys and bazaars of Baghdad, including household waste, construction debris, nondegradable plastics, and rotting organic waste (Baghdad's Trash 2010).

"In some areas," according to Dawood, "trash heaps have blocked off entire roads and residents throughout the city complain of foul odors, insects and rodents. Local media has reported a rise in packs of scavenging dogs, putting their number in Baghdad at over one million. Unchecked garbage is destroying the quality of life in Baghdad. Dumps are everywhere and sometimes near water pipes and rivers. This creates all kinds of bad fungi that lead to food poisoning and diarrhea, and can bring on diseases such as typhoid and cholera" (Baghdad's Trash 2010).

The stench of rotting garbage can reach intolerable levels in summer. Baghdad's temperatures, always hot in June, July, and August, and often well into September, have risen steadily in recent years because of global warming. Official high temperatures of 120 to 125 degrees Fahrenheit are taken in the shade. The Baghdad landfill has no shade. The routine readings in Baghdad are hotter than California's Death Valley, making it, in summer, the most miserable urban area on Earth.

The United States spent several million dollars on waste collection before its troops withdrew, to little effect. Much of the money may have been embezzled. Municipal authorities also required the use of plastic bags (to limit the spread of infections from festering garbage) and passed them out, but most people ignored them. The heat retained in the bags merely sped up decay of the garbage, especially in the heat. The city then tried distributing large yellow bins, but many of them were stolen and sold as scrap.

Talk was cheaper than garbage service: "Having garbage everywhere in the city is just uncivilised. It affects people's health as well as the environment. We need to educate people about how cleanliness is good for our health, but no group or agency is doing this, even local NGOs [nongovernmental organizations] because we lack money and support," said Salama Dhaeia Naeif, the head of the Love and Peace Messengers organization in Baghdad (Baghdad's Trash 2010). As Naeif spoke, the garbage piles continued to grow. Consulting firms were hired and reports compiled describing plans to build new waste-processing facilities not only in Baghdad, but across Iraq. The reality of poverty and war intruded, and very few plants were built.

Residents blamed the city and officials blamed the residents: "The Baghdad municipality makes great efforts to clean the city, but these efforts are mostly wasted by the citizens who throw trash everywhere, anytime. For example, a man puts trash outside his house in an open box four or five times each day. So when a cat or dog passes by, the garbage is scattered everywhere. Now, take into account the millions of citizens in Baghdad and you can imagine what the city is like. . . . Citizens throw trash everywhere," said Sabah Sami, head of the Baghdad municipality's media department (Baghdad's Trash 2010).

The large numbers of squatters who stay alive by picking through the landfill tell stories. In Baghdad, such informal recycling may sustain several thousand

> **Baghdad's Garbage Breeds Diseases**
>
> In addition to hiding bombs, Baghdad's garbage is also an incubator of disease, a situation complicated by the city's long, hot summers. With temperatures now rising to 120 degrees Fahrenheit on some summer days, according to an account in the *New York Times*, "The danger to trash collectors is at the root of one of the most visible symptoms of collapse in Baghdad. Garbage is ubiquitous, especially in dangerous neighborhoods, blanketing street medians, alleys and vacant lots in stinking, fly-infested quilts" (Luo 2006).
>
> The lack of enough functioning sanitation trucks allows garbage to fester in the heat, even in affluent neighborhoods, such as Arasat, where trash heaps sometimes have reached waist high. "If we try to sit in the garden, we cannot because of flies and mosquitoes," said Muhammad Amin, 45, who lives next to one of the larger heaps of trash on his block. "We cannot even sit in the garden to enjoy the weather" (Luo 2006). The flies and mosquitos that flourish on the trash heaps are primary disease vectors—and affluent areas that produce more waste food and other garbage have at least as many problems as poorer neighborhoods where waste is scarce. Trash and garbage also pile up alongside streets that are too narrow for modern garbage haulers, adding to the potential for infection.

people. "There are no jobs, so what else can I do but this. A lot of families depend on this business," said Haider Muhsin, 36, as he stood by the machine compacting plastic bottles (Kami 2011).

Garbage collection was one of the tasks listed in an International Labor Organization report on dangerous jobs for children; minors engaged in this activity often risked violence and serious injury (Baghdad Rubbish 2016). By 2016, The *Arab Weekly* said that "In addition to large numbers of beggars, shantytowns and complexes taken over by squatters are visible across Baghdad" (Poverty in Iraq 2016).

Abbas Mohammed, a 12-year-old living in Sadr City, spends his school holidays picking through garbage in the summer heat before selling his daily haul to a middleman. He sells each kilogram (2.2 pounds) of plastic bottles or soda cans for 250 Iraqi dinars (around 20 U.S. cents), earning between 2,000 and 4,000 dinars ($1.50–$3) a day.

Used plastic bottles and empty aluminum cans have been keeping Mohammed's family alive, Reuters reported. "Mohammed works the refuse dump near [his] home in the Iraqi capital's impoverished district of Sadr City, where men, women and children swarm over the stinking piles of garbage" (Kami 2011). Mohammed and others start in the mornings. "We collect Pepsi cans, plastic bottles and then we sell them. I have been working in this place since I was three years old" (Kami 2011). His mother and one of his brothers work with him in and around Sadr City. "The three of them bring in around $250 to $400 a month, meager earnings to support a large family" (Kami 2011).

Mohammed is as diligent at school as he is on the landfill. With an education, he wants to escape life in Baghdad's hell on Earth and become a teacher.

Bruce E. Johansen

See also: Green Spaces: Moscow, Russia: Planting 1 Million Trees; *Pollution:* Krakow, Poland: Old Furniture, New Fuel Source

Further Reading

Alnajjar, Ashraf Yahya. 2015. "Waste Management in Iraq." BioEnergy Consult. October 1. https://www.bioenergyconsult.com/waste-iraq/.

"Baghdad Rubbish Dump." 2016. AVAX News, August 24. http://avax.news/fact/Baghdad_Rubbish_Dump.html.

"Baghdad's Trash Piles Up." 2010. Institute for War & Peace Reporting. July 2. https://iwpr.net/global-voices/baghdads-trash-piles.

Kami, Aseel. 2011. "For Baghdad's Poor, City Garbage Brings in the Bread." Reuters, June 22. http://www.reuters.com/article/us-iraq-poverty-idUSTRE75L4XI20110622.

Luo, Michael. 2006. "Even Picking Up Trash Is a High Risk in Baghdad." *New York Times*, October 13. http://www.nytimes.com/2006/10/13/world/middleeast/13trash.html.

Omar, Oumayma. 2016. "Baghdad's Trash Piles." Institute for War & Peace Reporting, March 4. https://iwpr.net/global-voices/baghdads-trash-piles.

"Poverty in Iraq Dramatically Rises." 2016. *Arab Weekly*, March 4. http://www.thearabweekly.com/Opinion/4112/Poverty-in-Iraq-dramatically-rises.

Cairo, Egypt: The Zabaleen

Located on the East bank of the Nile River, the capital city of Egypt Cairo has been an Islamic cultural center for about 1,000 years. Greater Cairo has an area of 175 square miles, and is the largest city in Egypt and in Africa as well. The climate divides into two seasons—summer and winter. Summer months lasting from June to August have an average temperature of 70 to 90 degrees Fahrenheit, while winter months' temperature ranges from 47 to 67 degrees Fahrenheit. After the 1970s, Cairo went through significant gentrification. As a result, some of the city's main challenges today are high population density due to influx, severe traffic congestion, and acute pollution (AlSayyad et al. 2019). The city proper, or Cairo Governorate, has an area of about 83 square miles, and a population density of 50,180 per square mile. In terms of demographic composition, residents of Cairo are 12 million, while metropolitan Cairo's population is as high as approximately 20 million. While the population is predominantly Muslim, it includes several larger ethnic groups, one of which is Egyptian Christians, who observe the Coptic Orthodox faith (AlSayyad et al. 2019; World Population Review 2019). In the past two decades, the influx of job seekers rose rapidly. The situation reflects a general trend affecting cities in developing countries—populations from poorer regions tend to move directly, bypassing small and medium cities, to megacities where there are more employment opportunities. When crowded neighborhoods are poorly managed, they become hotbeds of crisis. The most urgent problem faced by Cairo is to improve the city's waste management—removing municipal solid waste (MSW) from the streets and the pungent odor from the air. One visitor had this to say:

> It's hard to keep your mind off it for very long when you first arrive. The trash is everywhere, all over the streets, the sidewalks, the steps, in the grass of the parks, and on the ground surrounding the occasional empty unused trash can. Any vacant spaces are almost immediately converted into impromptu garbage dumps. It would seem on first glance, to a new visitor, there is no system whatsoever for disposing of waste in Cairo. (Yacoub 2015)

COMPARISON IS CRUCIAL FOR IN-DEPTH UNDERSTANDING

Comparing different practices may be helpful here. In the U.S., laws and regulations are set up at federal and local levels to manage MSW. In general, managing solid waste includes a number of procedures, starting from identifying waste to collection, separation, and storage. Typically, solid waste is reduced locally before being transported to appropriate sites for disposal to ensure that waste materials are treated, through thermal or bioprocesses, to the level that they do not pose a threat to the environment. The most popular treatment methods in households are reuse and recycling, both help to maximally reduce landfill. Landfill is considered the most undesirable strategy, due to the fact that the buried materials may exist for a long time while leaking toxicity into the environment. When it is necessary to landfill, the burial pit must be well sealed so that leakage of gas or toxic liquid is prevented from contaminating air and aquifer. Recuperating energy from MSW is considered an optimal strategy. Thermal treatment, for example, transforms waste materials through incineration to generate energy to produce electricity or for heating purposes. This process may generate air-polluting gasses if not properly managed. Biotreatment includes composting or anaerobic digestion. In the United States, composting is widely used to treat yard waste.

Given the impact on public health, waste management is often a public service in the West funded by tax money. Governments typically contribute most of the resources and management. In the U.S., the Environmental Protection Agency (EPA) closely monitors treatment of MSW and publishes data on a regular basis. In 2014, for example, the U.S. generated about 258 million tons of MSW; over 89 million tons of MSW were recycled and composted, equivalent to a 34.6 percent recycling rate. In addition, over 33 million tons of MSW were combusted with energy recovery, and 136 million tons were landfilled. About 90 percent of corrugated boxes were recycled, and 61 percent of yard trimmings were composted. Organic materials such as paper and paperboard (26 percent); yard trimmings and food (28 percent); and leather, rubber, and textile (9 percent) were the largest component of MWS. Recycling and composting reduced greenhouse gas (GHG) emission. In 2014, 89 million tons of MSW recycled and composted provided an annual reduction of over 181 million tons of carbon dioxide equivalent of emissions, comparable to the annual emissions from over 38 million passenger cars (EPA 2017).

CAIRO UNDER SIEGE

In Egypt, the legal environment for waste management is weak: the two backbone legislations, the Law of 1967 for Public Cleaning and the Law of 1994 for the Protection of the Environment, lack specificity. As a result, statistics are unreliable due to the fact that standards are unclear, and there is no consistent and efficient plan for managing MSW. When regulations are unenforceable, trash generated by households, industries, and commercial activities is found littered in public areas, and the pungent odor of decomposing garbage fills the city's air. According to the Egyptian government's report, more than 80 percent of the generated MSW in Egypt is simply dumped, as the overall recovery rate is less than 11.5 percent

Shenuda, a Coptic Christian and Zabaleen, collects garbage in Cairo, Egypt, 2011. (Marco Bulgarelli/Gamma-Rapho via Getty Images)

(Tchobanoglous and Kreith 2002). Conditions like this are exacerbated in high-density neighborhoods in Cairo.

The Cairo governorate has been working hard toward a better solution, including envisaging sound national planning, strengthening the legal framework, finding better ways to involve private companies, setting up procedures of cost recovery to let polluters pay fines that will be used to fund MSW projects, training and capacity building, providing incentives to parties that create services and infrastructure, and so on (Ibrahim and Mohamed, 2016). In 2012, Cairo became the first city to set up observatories to follow the trail of garbage disposal, starting from a households' doorstep, to the removal from the premises by collecting companies, and on to the final steps of reduction, recycling, and reuse. In 2013, the Ministry of Environment launched a national campaign to improve solid waste management by reinforcing transportation and collection. A focus of the action was to coordinate efforts of the public and private sectors (Al-Akkad 2017).

However, progress has been slow, due to the rapid increase of population and shortage of processing centers. Cairo produces more than 15,000 tons of solid waste every day, putting great pressure on the city's infrastructure. Waste collection is handled partly by the public companies, such as Cairo Cleanliness and Beautification Authority (CCBA), and by individual garbage collectors who use various means of transportation and methods, from trucks to donkey carts. Yet the result is unsatisfactory—only 60 percent of the solid waste is removed and processed somehow; the remainder is littered on the streets or discarded in illegal dumpsites, such as canals and the Nile River (Al-Akkad 2017).

THE ZABALEEN—"DIAMOND IN THE ROUGH"

Since 2002, Cairo has employed international waste management companies, such as Alexandria and Giza, to provide services. However, by 2009, it became clear that these modern firms had lower efficiency compared to the traditional Zabaleen collectors who have made a living out of garbage removal for generations since the 1940s. Today, members of Zabaleen communities are estimated to be between 30,000 and 70,000 and are emerging as Cairo's main cleaning force (Guirre 2015).

The word "Zabaleen" means "garbage collectors" in the Arabic language. The majority of the Zabaleens are Coptic Christians who emigrated from southern Egypt fleeing from religious intolerance. The Coptic Orthodox Church is the main Christian Church in Egypt and has between 6 and 11 million members ("Coptic Orthodox Church" 2009). Copts believe in the Holy Spirit that inspired men to write down the words in the Holy Bible. Marriage is held within the faith (BBC 2009). The life of Zabaleen communities is told in a 2009 film, *Garbage Dreams*, for example, produced by Iskander Films and broadcast by PBS and other networks.

The operation of Zabaleen collectors is labor intensive. They use donkey carts and pickup trucks to collect garbage door to door, and transport the materials to their own residence. Muqattam is one of the neighborhoods that processes MSW, and is known as "the garbage city." After the men return home with the collected garbage, sorting work falls on the women and children, who spend 10–12 hours daily to separate the garbage into various categories prior to resale or landfill. The dirty and backbreaking work brings a daily income of below US$1. Not surprisingly, Zabaleen neighborhoods generally have poor hygienic conditions and a low level of education (Aguirre 2015). The Zabaleen are hardworking people who remove 40 percent of Cairo's solid waste, of which 80 percent is recycled, which is considered high efficiency by world standards (MacBride 2017). Despite reports that they often skip poor neighborhoods to serve the affluent ones (Zafar 2016), the Zabaleen are lauded as "Egypt's diamond in the rough" in the garbage collection business (Aguirre 2015).

In addition to their reputation for hard work, the Zabaleen are also known to be successful entrepreneurs. They have been able to establish dozens of recycling companies and put a significant number of people to work. Having been neglected for decades, they finally received recognition from the current post-Mubarak government. The Cairo municipality praised the Zabaleen for having established 44 waste disposal companies employing a labor force of 1,000 families. In addition, the municipality decided to arm the Zabaleen with uniforms and vehicles, and grant them urban contracts. The new minister of the environment, Leila Iskandar, is reported to have said:

> Over the years the Zabaleen have created an efficient ecosystem that is both viable and profitable, with a recycling capacity of almost 100 percent. It provides work for women and young people who are the first to suffer from Egypt's unemployment. We need to use this local organization. (Aguirre 2015)

The administration's change of attitude, however, was not without a twist: since 2009, the city has been under pressure to hire more labor to remove increasing amount of MSW. Part of the urgency was caused by the slaughtering of 300,000 pigs in 2009 in an effort to prevent the H1N1 Influenza, also known as swine flu.

The cull had created a sudden shortage of labor in garbage sorting, the first step of the sorting work being to let pigs scavenge the organic waste. The disappearance of pigs in the work process resulted in a shortage of storage space for unsorted materials. Moreover, the post-swine flu recovery of the pig population was slow due to government restrictions. As such, the collectors had to reduce their garbage collection. The situation, in turn, resulted in garbage piling up on Cairo's streets (Slackman 2009). Additionally, the cull removed one of the two income sources of the Zabaleen family—selling pork to Cairo's meat markets, which resulted in further financial hardship (Fraser 2009). On the other hand, while the cull of pigs did not seem to have caused a wide interruption of the meat supply, as the majority Muslim residents abstain from consuming pork, those whose diet included pork were denied it for years (Kingsley 2014).

ENVIRONMENTAL IMPROVEMENT COMES FROM COLLABORATION

It is obvious that cleaning up Cairo's streets and neighborhoods is a complex task. So, what could be in the list of Cairo's action plan? The aforementioned practices in the United States may provide some ideas. Experts' top recommendation is to minimize solid waste at the source. This requires arming citizens with scientific knowledge and ethical standards. It also requires greater participation of the local communities. On the government's end, policies should be established to require waste management features as part of initial infrastructure building. Future urban plans should include building landfill sites with modern features. Additionally, the government needs to be more proactive in supporting private-sector partnerships (Ibrahim and Mohamed 2016). The experience of most megacities shows that mobilizing all groups of the society to take action in creating and protecting a healthy living environment is essential. For Cairo, the fundamental challenge lies in whether the city will be able to make its society more open and tolerant.

Jing Luo

See also: Waste Management: Dakar, Senegal: Peri-Urban/Urban Agriculture and Urban Waste Management; Port-au-Prince, Haiti: Challenges of Waste Management under Poor Governance

Further Reading

Aguirre, Itziar. 2015. "Cairo's 'Zabaleen' Garbage Collectors: Egypt's Diamond in the Rough." *Global Risk Insights*, June 12. http://globalriskinsights.com/2015/06/cairos-zabaleen-garbage-collectors-egypts-diamond-in-the-rough/.

Al-Akkad, Farah. 2017. "Focus: Egypt's Garbage Problem." *Al-Ahram Weekly.* http://weekly.ahram.org.eg/News/14892.aspx.

AlSayyad, Nezar, and Janet L. Abu-Lughod. 2019. "Cairo—National Capital, Egypt." *Encyclopaedia Britannica.* https://www.britannica.com/place/Cairo.

Cairo Population. n.d. http://worldpopulationreview.com/world-cities/cairo-population/.

"Coptic Orthodox Church." 2009. BBC. http://www.bbc.co.uk/religion/religions/christianity/subdivisions/coptic_1.shtml.

Fraser, Christian. 2009. "Struggling after Egypt's Pig Cull." *BBC News*, Cairo, August 6. http://news.bbc.co.uk/2/hi/middle_east/8185844.stm.

Kingsley, Patrick. 2014. "Morsi's Overthrow Helps Egypt's Pork Famers Get Their Sizzle Back." *Guardian*, March 28. https://www.theguardian.com/world/2014/mar/28/morsi-overthrow-egypt-pork-farmers-sales-growth-pigs.

MacBride, Elizabeth. 2017. "In Cairo's Garbage City, These Entrepreneurs Could Be the World's Best Recyclers." *Forbes*, January 28. https://www.forbes.com/sites/elizabethmacbride/2017/01/08/in-cairos-garbage-city-the-lure-of-profits-is-strong-so-are-the-mothers/#6c243cd11c39.

Mohamed Ibrahim Mohamed Ibrahim, and Nanis Abd El Monem Mohamed. 2016. "Towards Sustainable Management of Solid Waste in Egypt." *Procedia Environmental Sciences*, 34: 336–47. http://ac.els-cdn.com/S1878029616300524/1-s2.0-S1878029616300524-main.pdf?_tid=ace67c80-2318-11e7-a2b7-00000aacb361&acdnat=1492397634_80ca7bdf9d6f4d4dc907e8f1c5b9eaec.

The Regional Solid Waste Exchange of Information and Expertise Network in Mashreq and Maghreb Countries—SWEEPNET. 2012. *Country Report on Solid Waste Management. Cairo, Egypt*. http://nswmp.net/wp-content/uploads/2015/05/2012_Country-Report_SWM-EGYPT_SWEEP-Net.pdf.

Slackman, Michael. 2009. "Belatedly, Egypt Spots Flaws in Wiping Out Pigs." *New York Times*, September 19. http://www.nytimes.com/2009/09/20/world/africa/20cairo.html.

Tchobanoglous, G., and F. Kreith. 2002. *Handbook of Solid Waste Management*. 2nd ed. New York: McGraw-Hill.

United States Environmental Protection Agency (EPA). 2017. "Advancing Sustainable Materials Management: Facts and Figures." https://www.epa.gov/smm/advancing-sustainable-materials-management-facts-and-figures.

World Population Review. 2019. "Cairo Population 2019." http://worldpopulationreview.com/world-cities/cairo-population/.

Yacoub, Ahmed. 2015. "Documenting Cairo's First Impressions." https://www.youtube.com/watch?v=aZ8maE2WOpo.

Zafar, Salman. 2016. "Garbage Woes in Cairo." *EcoMENA*, March 2. http://www.ecomena.org/tag/waste-management-in-cairo/.

Calgary, Canada: Waste Management Is a National Effort and Calgary's Priority

INTRODUCTION

Despite being an eyesore, open dumping of waste was a common way of life up to recent times. The discovery of links between open dumps and environmental degradation, especially the contamination of ground- and surface water and their negative health consequences, have brought enormous public pressure on how waste is managed (Hettiaratchi 2007). In response to these concerns, many local governments have adopted waste management approaches such as sanitary landfills to reduce environmental degradation and human health risks.

The objective of a waste management is not to achieve zero contamination or health risks, which would be extremely expensive if not impossible, but rather to reduce risks to an acceptable level (Hettiaratchi 2007; Davidson 2011). While open dumping is still practiced in many parts of the world, the past decades have witnessed a gradual shift toward a new and more proactive integrated waste management approach (especially in North America and Western Europe) to divert waste from land disposal. Studies suggest, the central principle of an integrated waste management approach is to extract the maximum benefits from waste and generate the minimum amount of disposal. An integrated waste management system aspires to prevent or reduce the generation of waste in the first place, promote reuse and recycling, recover as much of energy as possible, and finally manage the disposal of the remaining waste in a sanitary way.

The main emphasis of an integrated waste management system is to mitigate the consequences of 1) increasing volume of waste, and 2) decreasing available landfill space through a concept known as the three "R's"—"reduce, reuse, and recycle." Waste reduction is usually achieved through redesign of products to reduce the creation of waste in the first place or changing consumers' pattern of consumption and waste generation. Furthermore, waste can be reduced when a product is reused more than once. Recycling refers to the possibility that waste can be taken apart into new valuable materials. Finally, recovering of energy, sometimes referred to as the fourth "R," is a treatment that aims to recover energy in the form of electricity, heat, or steam from a waste source. In addition to being financially beneficial to consumers, these concepts can minimize the use of natural resources to produce new products, and reduce the generation and costs of waste disposal.

Nonetheless, the last component of an integrated waste management system is the disposal of waste to a sanitary landfill. The most common landfills in North America are dry-tomb landfills where waste is kept dry by banning liquid, and keeping moisture out by covering waste daily. These landfills use a bottom liner and a final cover to prevent ground and surface-water contamination. A dry-tomb landfill is not a silver bullet and cannot address all the issues related to waste disposal. For example, it 1) has a very low biodegradation, which requires long-term monitoring for any possible environmental contamination; 2) does nothing to address the generation of gases such as methane and volatile organic compounds; and 3) requires a new landfill space every few years.

In recent years, newer generations of sanitary landfills such as bioreactor and biocell have been developed to address some of the aforementioned shortcomings. In a bioreactor landfill, rather than avoiding liquid, leachate (water that leaches out of waste) is collected, supplemented with water, and reintroduced to the landfill to stimulate the growth of micro-organisms responsible for decomposition of waste. This process can accelerate the decomposition of biodegradable waste, which in turn will reduce the mass of biodegradable components, creating more space for dumping; and will substantially reduce the time needed for monitoring a landfill.

A biocell or "sustainable bio-cell" is a newer variation of bioreactor landfills that has all the aforementioned benefits of a traditional bioreactor landfill, and in addition aims to address the problems associated with the continuous need of finding new space for landfills. The process uses a hybrid of anaerobic (air is not introduced into the landfill) and aerobic (air is pumped into the landfill) methods, where in the anaerobic phase the production of methane is maximized and in the aerobic phase compost is produced and extracted to open up space (Hettiaratchi 2007; Hettiaratchi, et al. 2010; Davidson 2011). While with the current technologies these processes are not cost-effective yet, if the volume and rate of methane generation are high enough, methane can be economically converted to energy.

WASTE MANAGEMENT IN CANADA

Municipal solid waste in Canada is regulated by the provinces and territories, and is either directly managed by municipal authorities or contracted to a waste management industry. The federal government is only in charge of waste management on federal lands or where the international and interprovincial movements of hazardous waste materials are of concern (Giroux Environmental Consulting 2014).

Table 1 represents current local governments' expenditures on waste management by activities. Overall, local government across Canada spent CAN$2.9 billion on waste management for which they only received CAN$2.3 billion in operating revenues in 2010. The largest portion of the expenditures were collection and transportation of municipal waste (more than 42 percent of current expenditures), followed by the operation of disposal facilities (almost 18 percent of current expenditures). Residential waste accounted for slightly more than one-third of the total waste disposed (Giroux Environmental Consulting 2014).

It is reported that Canadians on average spent CAN$ 58.18 per capita on waste management in 2010. Nova Scotia with CAN$82.39 and Saskatchewan with CAN$33.3 per capita have the highest and lowest per capita expenditures on waste management, respectively.

The residential and nonresidential waste disposed in Canada amounted to 25 million tonnes in 2010. While the most populous provinces (Ontario and Quebec) are also the ones with the highest volumes of waste disposal, in per capita basis Alberta

Table 1 Current Local Governments' Expenditures on Waste Management (Thousand CAN$)

Activities	2008	2010
Collection and transportation	1,105,294	1,236,696
Tipping fees	368,260	424,773
Operation of disposal facilities	465,221	516,991
Operation of transfer stations	168,638	145,960
Operation of recycling facilities	113,643	157,248
Operation of organics processing facilities	71,045	74,525
Contributions to landfills post closure and maintenance fund	58,401	93,171
Other current expenditures	265,139	270,564
Total	2,615,641	2,919,928

Source: Statistics Canada, 2013.

with 1,052 kilograms of waste disposal per person ranked no. 1 in 2010 (compared to 729 kilograms of waste disposal per person for Canada).

The amount of waste diverted to recycling or organic processing facilities in Canada was 8.1 million tonnes, or 236 kilograms per person, in 2010. On average, 32.4 percent of total waste disposed was diverted to recycling or organic processing facilities in 2010. Among all provinces and territories, Nova Scotia with 72.3 percent diversion rate ranked first (281 of 389 kg per capita waste disposed was diverted to recycling or organic processing facilities in Nova Scotia), and Saskatchewan with 15.2 percent diversion rate ranked last (137 of 897 kg per capita waste disposed was diverted to recycling or organic processing facilities in Saskatchewan).

WASTE MANAGEMENT IN ALBERTA, CANADA

In 2007, the government of Alberta approved a provincial roadmap for waste reduction and management (Too Good to Waste Strategy). While the primary objective of the strategy is to develop innovative waste management programs to reduce overall waste disposal, it also intends to complement a set of broader strategies in Alberta. For instance, it plans to complement Alberta's climate change, rural development, alternative energy, and water sustainability through increasing the volume of recycled waste materials and reducing the disposal of organic residuals at municipal landfills (Alberta Environment Information Centre 2007).

The current annual expenditures on waste management for the local governments in Alberta have increased by the average rate of 10.4 percent per year from CAN$129.8 million in 2000 to CAN$385.4 million in 2010, respectively. The increase in the expenditures was much faster than the annual inflation rate of 2.4 percent during the same period in Alberta. In addition, the increase in the expenditures is not uniform across the years. The biggest increase was after the approval of the Too Good to Waste Strategy, where the annual expenditures increased by an average rate of 15.14 percent per year from 2008 to 2010.

During the same period, the annual waste disposal per person in Alberta increased by 1.29 percent per year. This was despite the downward trend after the approval of the Too Good to Waste strategy, where the annual waste disposal per person actually decreased by 3.1 percent per year from 2008 to 2010. Initially, the Too Good to Waste strategy set a goal of reducing landfill waste to 500 kilograms per capita by 2010; however, the target was deemed to be unattainable, and as a result, the government of Alberta has opted for an annual basis target instead.

The annual waste diversion per capita in Alberta has increased by the annual rate of 2.91 percent from 2000 to 2010. Contrary to what one may expect, after the adaptation of the Too Good to Waste Strategy, the annual waste diversion has actually decreased by the annual rate of 1.84 percent from 2008 to 2010. The additional CAN$132.9 million in the local governments' current annual expenditures from 2008 to 2010 had only prevented 103 kg of waste generation per capita or 230 million tonnes for the entire province of Alberta, but had a negative impact on waste diversion—that is, in 2010, waste diversion per capita was 11 kg lower than the levels in 2008 or 15.4 tonnes lower for the entire province of Alberta.

As can be seen in Table 2, Alberta is ranked last in per capita expenditure to divert 1 percent waste generated. On average, Albertans spend CAN$3.45 to divert 1 percent of waste generated compared to CAN$1.8 for Canada and CAN$1.14 and CAN$1.15 for the most cost-effective provinces of Nova Scotia and British Columbia.

WASTE MANAGEMENT IN CALGARY

Calgary, with a population of more than 1.2 million, is the largest city in Alberta and the third-largest municipality in Canada (Statistics Canada 2017). Calgary's metropolitan area is home to more than one-third of the population in Alberta. Municipal waste contains a large percentage of organic materials. In Calgary, 65 percent of the garbage for a typical single-family home is compostable (The City of Calgary 2017). Out of the remaining 35 percent, 15 percent is recyclable and the remainder will end up in the landfills. The city has three sanitary landfill sites (Spyhill, Shepard, and East Calgary) where residents can take residential waste, chemicals, and recyclable items.

Calgary started its first pilot residential recycling with blue-box and drop-off depots that collected newspapers, glass, and metal cans in 1991. During the 1990s, the city offered its first Christmas tree drop-off, accessible landfill site for small vehicles, tire recycling project, and backyard composter sale. The city reported that the Christmas tree recycling program not only helps to save money, but recycling trees into mulch (material applied to the surface of soil for conservation of soil moisture) also keeps trees out of the landfill (The City of Calgary 2017).

Table 2 Percentage Waste Diverted, Per Capita Local Governments' Current Annual Expenditures (CAN$) for Selected Provinces in 2010

	Percentage of Waste Diverted	Per Capita Expenditure	Per Capita Expenditure to Divert 1 Percent Waste
Canada	32.40	$ 58.18	$1.80
Nova Scotia	72.29	$ 82.39	$1.14
British Columbia	54.81	$ 62.80	$1.15
Quebec	40.31	$ 56.21	$1.39
Ontario	29.73	$ 57.41	$1.93
New Brunswick	28.93	$ 57.70	$1.99
Saskatchewan	18.76	$ 33.30	$2.19
Manitoba	18.20	$ 43.00	$2.29
Alberta	15.22	$ 62.74	$3.45

Source: Statistics Canada, 2013.

Under the tire recycling project, the province charges a CAN$4 environmental fee for new tires to pay for the cost of recycling, but residents can dispose of their tires free of charge. This is to free landfill space, save natural resources, and conserve energy.

With the widespread use of electronic devices, Calgary introduced its first electronics recycling program in 2003. Several locations in Calgary are designated for electronics recycling where residents can drop off their electronic devices such as televisions, laptops and desktop computers, printers, scanners, fax machines, and monitors free of charge. In 2004, Calgary opened its compost facility and a curbside collection of residential recyclable, yard, and food waste. The city introduced its landfill gas recovery to generate electricity in 2006. The blue-cart recycling, black-cart collection, and green-cart composting pilots were introduced in 2009, 2010, and 2012, respectively. The purpose of blue-cart is to help with recycling paper; cardboard; plastic bottles, jugs, and bags; food containers, cans, and foils; and bottles (The City of Calgary 2017). The green-cart is used to collect all the food and yard waste in one bin to turn into nutrient-rich compost; and the black-cart is used to collect the things that are at the end of their useful life and cannot be recycled or composted. In 2017, Calgary opened its new composting facility with the goal of diverting 70 percent of waste in the city by 2025.

Arian Moghadam

See also: Energy and Sustainability: Toronto, Canada: A City with a Passion for Energy Conservation; *Green Spaces:* Halifax, Canada: Near-Urban Wilderness Protection; *Waste Management:* Oslo, Norway: Prevention and Reduction, What Makes Oslo Clean

Further Reading

Alberta Environment Information Centre. 2007. *Too Good to Waste: Making Conservation a Priority.* Edmonton: Alberta Environment Information Centre.

The City of Calgary. http://www.calgary.ca/SitePages/cocis/default.aspx.

The Conference Board of Canada. 2013. *International Ranking—Municipal Waste Generation.* http://www.conferenceboard.ca/hcp/details/environment/municipal-waste-generation.aspx.

Davidson, G. 2011. *Waste Management Practices: Literature Review.* Halifax, Nova Scotia, Canada: Dalhousie University, Office of Sustainability.

Giroux Environmental Consulting. 2014. *State of Waste Management in Canada.* Kanata, Ontario, Canada: Giroux Environmental Consulting.

Hettiaratchi, J. P. A. 2007. *New Trends in Waste Management: North American Perspective.* Chennai, India, 9–14.

Hettiaratchi, J. P. A. C. Hunte, and S. Kumar. 2010. *Full Scale Operation of a Unique Landfill Bioreactor: The Calgary Biocell.* Shanghai, China, RILEM Publications SARL, 340–48.

New Energy Corporation. 2017. *Waste Hierarchy.* http://www.newenergycorp.com.au/what-we-do/waste-hierarchy/.

Statistics Canada. 2013. *Waste Management Industry Survey: Business and Government Sectors 2010.* Ottawa: Minister of Industry.

Statistics Canada. 2017. *Population and Dwelling Count Highlight Tables, 2016 Census.* http://www12.statcan.gc.ca/census-recensement/2016/dp-pd/hlt-fst/pd-pl/Table.cfm?Lang=Eng&T=302&SR=1&S=86&O=A&RPP=9999.

Dakar, Senegal: Peri-Urban/Urban Agriculture and Urban Waste Management

Dakar, the capital city of Senegal in West Africa, presents a diversity of conditions related to urban and peri-urban agricultural activities, as well as the management of both solid and liquid waste. These two sectors of urban life intersect in a variety of ways, and they have major impacts on employment, revenue generation, politics, the economy, culture, health, and the environment. Garbage, and the practices and discourses surrounding it, has had a lasting impact even on Dakar's art scene. While the government plays a role in how both agriculture and waste management have developed in an urban context, small-scale private actors remain the driving force. In many respects Dakar exemplifies how these urban phenomena are managed across the global South generally, and across Africa specifically.

Dakar is located on the Cape Verde Peninsula, on the Atlantic coast at the westernmost tip of the African continent. The agglomeration, which consist of the city proper (1,146,000), as well as the populous suburbs of Pikine (1,171,000), Guediawaye (330,000), and Rufisque (491,000), had over 3 million inhabitants according to the 2013 census (Republic of Senegal 2015). This represented just over 23 percent of Senegal's total population and about half of its urban population. Dakar is thus exemplary of the type of macrocephalous primate city that characterizes the urban network of many African countries. In the case of Dakar, the high concentration of the national population in the capital and biggest city is compounded by the constraints of the city's site and location at the extremity of a peninsula. Among the urban planning problems this causes are scarcity of land for urban expansion, disappearance of agricultural land, difficulty of water supply, and traffic congestion.

While greater Dakar is densely populated (averaging about 4,000 inhabitants per square kilometer), various forms of agriculture are practiced within or contiguous to the urbanized area. Over 4,000 hectares of land in the Dakar region are currently under cultivation. Agricultural production sustains 18,000 direct jobs in the region, with a further 10,000 spin-off jobs in food processing, distribution, etc. (Sy et al. 2014, 16). Furthermore, upwards of 200,000 inhabitants of the city supplement their incomes with agricultural activities of one type or another (Sy et al. 2014, 15).

The most important form of agriculture in the metropolitan region, and the earliest one to develop, is market gardening and horticulture in coastal depressions called Niayes. Niaye interdunal depressions are found all along Senegal's Atlantic coast from Dakar north all the way to the city of Saint Louis, at the mouth of the Senegal River. The water table in these depressions remains high all year round, and the clay-rich soils contrast with the sandy soils that predominate in most of the rest of Senegal's arable land. The Niayes of Dakar produce 60 percent of the vegetables (namely tomatoes, onions, cabbage, potatoes, peppers, and eggplant) consumed in the city (Sy et al. 2014, 13). Farms are generally very small, less than a hectare in size (Tounkara 2015, 243).

Niaye agriculture not only contributes substantially to feeding the metropolis; it also consumes a substantial proportion of its organic wastes. Most irrigation water in the Niayes comes from shallow watering holes. This used to be complimented by wastewater and sludge from the city's cesspits. This wastewater was mixed with groundwater in the watering holes before use. The high proportion of nitrates in domestic sewerage enhances the importance of this agricultural input. Nonetheless, there are major health risks associated with this agricultural practice. In 2004, approximately 400 case of typhoid fever were linked to vegetables contaminated by human waste (Tounkara 2015, 169), and in 2008 the practice was banned (Tounkara 2015, 24).

Another agricultural input for Niaye market gardens is urban compost, mostly from kitchen waste. Organic kitchen waste is collected by hand from fresh produce markets and various kinds of garbage dumps around the city by small operators, usually a man and a mule cart. The waste is then sold to the farmers in the Niayes who compost it on-site (Tounkara 2015, 111). Various manures produced in the city (horse, mule and donkey manure, chicken droppings, waste from fish processing) are also collected and distributed in this way. Large amounts of such organic wastes are produced in Dakar every day. Draught animals remain an important component of urban transportation, and most animal protein consumed in the city comes from local fish and poultry production. Moreover, many city dwellers raise chickens (fed with stale bread) and a sheep or two (fed with vegetable scraps from the kitchen) in their courtyards. Animal droppings from this microscale production are also fed into neighborhood agriculture.

Beyond the Niaye depressions, which are intensely cultivated year-round, small-scale urban gardening characterizes all of Dakar's working-class neighborhoods and suburbs. Small informal market gardens occupy vacant lots and open stretches

A local resident tends the micro-garden at Derklé Social Center in Dakar, Senegal, 2016. The government of Dakar promotes micro-gardens as a means for poor families to supplement food intake and generate revenue. (Seyllou/AFP/Getty Images)

along thoroughfares. Most are farmed by women, who supply the labor, manufacture the soil (from compost), and provide the irrigation water (by bucket). While the legality of this land use and occupancy is often doubtful, the produce from these little plots supplies the dinner tables of those who farm them, and some even finds its way into the neighborhood vegetable market through curbside vending, generating revenue for the small-scale producers.

In the early 2000s, a new form of gardening, called micro-gardening, was introduced to Dakar. Micro-gardening is a very intensive form of urban agriculture (Tounkara 2015). It is conducted in raised crates, or in watertight tubs for the hydroponic variety, which occupy rooftops, balconies, terraces, carparks, and courtyards in even the densest urban fabrics. Micro-gardening requires the creation of special types of soils and/or liquid solutions that make use of readily available composted organic wastes (kitchen scraps). The composting (in specialized buckets) also requires very little space. Even the physical support of crates and tubs can be built of reused or recycled materials. As an urban practice, micro-gardening originated in Latin America. It was introduced to Senegal through a development program run by the Food and Agriculture Organization and the University of Milan. It requires a certain amount of training, initially provided by these international partners, as well as access to a number of specialized inputs that need to be purchased on the market. The purpose of promoting micro-gardening in Dakar was twofold: to supplement food intake for poor families and to generate revenue for poor women (most micro-gardeners are women). A variety of vegetables (lettuce, watercress, celery, tomatoes, peppers) as well as kitchen herbs and medicinal plants are cultivated in this way (Sposito 2010).

Dakar's various forms of urban and peri-urban agriculture not only play an important role in feeding the city; they also help transform much of the waste it produces. Lack of publicly funded and managed infrastructure hamper efficient waste management. Only 40 percent of an estimated 180,000 m^3 of wastewater produced in the agglomeration on a daily basis are collected through the sewer system (Sposito 2010, 121). The remainder uses various types of septic systems. Of waste collected through the sewers, only 4 percent is treated before it is emptied into the ocean. Farms near the treatment plants (at Cambérène, next to the Niayes in particular) are able to purchase the treated waste for use as fertilizer. Other farmers simply puncture the sewer mains to access the waste.

The Dakar agglomeration produces approximately 2,000 metric tons of solid refuse per day. About 1,200 tons of this is collected, mostly from well-off neighborhoods, and dumped in the city's largest landfill site at Mbeubeuss, on the city's northeastern outskirt (Diawara 2010, 88). From 1971 to 2012, a succession of different private corporations, some of them transnational firms, held the municipal garbage collection contract (Badiane 2006). The chronic mismanagement of Dakar's garbage, and the exploitation of garbage collectors by these companies, fed into a major political struggle between Senegal's Liberal president, Abdoulaye Wade, and the city's Socialist mayor Khalifa Sall. The struggle was resolved after the 2012 presidential election when Dakar's garbage collection was returned to public municipal control and jointly managed with the union of garbage collectors (Fredericks 2013).

Due to deficiencies of infrastructure, not all household waste is effectively collected by the municipal workers. It can be disposed of in a variety of ways. Small informal and completely illegal dump sites can be found in all the poorer neighborhoods and shantytowns. Some garbage is simply burnt in empty lots. Garbage is also dumped, illegally, into Dakar's numerous open-air drainage ditches (clogging them and contributing to flooding during the rainy season) as well as into the ocean from the city's cliffs and beaches.

The lack of centrally managed garbage collection across the agglomeration provides opportunities for myriad small-scale garbage collectors. These often consist of a single individual or two who operate an animal-traction cart (donkey, mule, or horse). Each operator has a more or less precise geographical circuit. As there is no garbage sorting at the source, in households the small-scale private-sector collectors ensure much of the sorting as they go. Organic waste, as discussed above, can be sold on to urban and peri-urban farmers. Various nonorganic waste also finds a market. Cloth, clothing, and fabric (jute sacks from imported cereals) can be recycled by upholsterers or, if still usable, will re-enter the market as used clothing. Various kinds of metal are also reused or recycled (old pots smelted into new kitchen utensils). Cardboard, glass, plastics . . . virtually every type of rubbish can find a buyer. Thus, Dakar's garbage is a resource not only for its small-scale independent garbage collectors but for a host of petty trades: upholsterers, cobblers, tailors, even toy-makers, adept at reuse and recycling. These trades are mostly cottage industries operating out of homes or small market stalls, and they form the mainstay of the so-called "informal" economy.

Dakar's main landfill, at Mbeubeuss about 30 kilometers from the center of the city, is also part of the reuse-recycle economy. Occupying a dry lake bed, Mbeubeuss dump opened in 1968. It is currently home to an estimated 300–500 recyclers and their dependents, including children, who reside on-site in a number of "villages" (Diawara 2010, 122). Here, the same kinds of post-sorting reuse and recycling go on, albeit far more intensely. Organic solid waste is composted on-site before being sold on. However, the Mbeubeuss compost is not considered by local Niaye farmers to be of good quality as it is contaminated by heavy metals (lead, zinc, mercury), among other things (Diawara 2010, 118). Many of the resident recyclers specialize in specific materials (plastics, ferrous or non-ferrous metal, fabrics, paper and cardboard, glass). While much of the material is sold-on as raw material to businesses elsewhere, many of the landfill residents recycle material on-site (e.g., metal working). Living conditions for those who work the Mbeubeuss dump are very unhealthy. ENDA-Tiers-Monde, an international NGO, operates a health clinic there (Diawara 2010, 123). Traumas range from cuts and burns (from the burning garbage) to more serious infections and intoxications caused by the presence of hazardous materials (heavy metals) and of discarded electronics in particular.

Dakar's garbage problems have impacted the city's social, cultural, and artistic life. In 1989, torrential rains caused severe flooding in Dakar's low-lying poor neighborhoods. Exasperated when they saw that the municipal authorities were unable to handle the mess, local youth groups and sports teams spontaneously took on the

> **Dak'art**
>
> Dak'art is Dakar's art biennial that showcases the works of contemporary visual artists from across Africa and the African diaspora. The international event lasts a month and has been held every two years since 1990. Exhibit sites are spread throughout the city's central neighborhoods and include both "in" and "off" sites. "In" sites are in official buildings, such as the former Court House, the National Art Gallery, and City Hall, and host exhibits that have been officially sponsored by Dak'art's main patron, Senegal's Ministry of Culture. By contrast, "off" sites, more numerous and visible than the former, are organized by artists' collectives, individuals, business, and associations in a great variety of urban locations, including art galleries, nightclubs, hair salons, gas stations, and various and sundry outdoor public spaces. The "off" exhibitions tend to be edgier than the official "in" ones. They offer great latitude for artists to address critical social, economic, and political issues. While Dak'art has put Dakar on the world art map, integrating it into the global art world economy, its increasingly popular and sophisticated "off" exhibits have greatly boosted the city's creative economy, legitimizing its "arts sector" and situating artists as legitimate actors in urban life.

task themselves, initiating what became known as Set-Setal (meaning "clean and clean up"). They unclogged the blocked storm sewers, swept up the rubbish, and carted it away. Dakar's young people also turned garbage into public art. In order to shame the authorities, they erected expressive installations assembled from metal and plastic junk on street corners and roundabouts. Lampposts and electricity poles, too, were festooned with colorful garbage. The cleanup was accompanied by the painting of street murals conveying clear social and political messages about civic life and public affairs. Streets and intersections were even given new evocative names by neighborhood residents (Hechte and Simone 1994).

The Set-Setal movement was a success not only in that local people managed to clean up their neighborhoods on their own, but because it shamed the municipal authorities into taking action after years of negligence. Soon afterwards, NGO-backed community-based waste management programs, heavily reliant on the free labor of neighborhood women, were implemented in various working-class districts (Fredericks 2015). Local popular direct action involving garbage continues to be a feature of civic life in the city. Set-Setal has morphed into "Tilim-Tilimeul" ("deliberate dirtying"), where installations of garbage are artfully piled up in the middle of intersections and in prominent public spaces as a means for residents to communicate their frustration over poor waste management.

Dakar's innovative art scene, too, has taken garbage on board. Many Senegalese artists integrate used, found, or discarded objects into their paintings, sculptures, and installations (Kart 2009). Objects include those of everyday life—a commentary on global throw-away consumer culture—as well as such rare and exotic items as plastic trash from Brazil that washes up on Dakar's beaches. Known as "récupe" (an abbreviation of "récupération" in French), reuse of found objects and flotsam is now a distinguishing feature of Dakar's art scene, and of the Dak'art biennial (Grabski 2017).

Eric S. Ross

See also: Housing and Infrastructure: Touba, Senegal: A Spiritual Solution to Affordable Housing

Further Reading

Badiane, Boubacar. 2006. "Diagnostic organisationnel des sociétés de gestion des déchets solides urbains de Dakar: Cas de la SOADIP, SIAS et AMA Sénégal." Master's thesis, Dakar: Institut Supérieur de Management des Entreprise et des Organisations.

Diawara, Amadou Bélal. 2010. "Les déchets solides à Dakar: Environnement, société et gestion urbaine." PhD dissertation, Bordeaux: Université Michel de Montaigne.

Fredericks, Rosalind. 2013. "Disorderly Dakar: The Cultural Politics of Household Waste in Senegal's Capital City." *Journal of Modern African Studies* 51, 3: 435–58.

Fredericks, Rosalind. 2015. "Dirty Work in the City: Garbage and the Crisis of Social Reproduction in Dakar." In Katie Meehan and Kendra Strauss, eds. *Precarious Worlds: Contested Geographies of Social Reproduction.* Atlanta: University of Georgia Press, 139–55.

Grabski, Joanna. 2017. *Art World City: The Creative Economy of Artists and Urban Life in Dakar.* Bloomington: Indiana University Press.

Hechte, David, and Maliqalim Simone. 1994. *Invisible Governance: The Art of African Micropolitics.* New York: Autonomedia.

Kart, Susan. 2009. "The Phenomenon of Récupération at the Dak'art Biennale." *African Arts* 42, 3: 8–9.

Republic of Senegal, Ministère de l'économie, des finances et du plan. 2015. Direction des statistiques démographiques et sociales, Division du recensement et des statistiques démographiques. *Rapport Projection de la Population du Sénégal 2013–2063.* Dakar.

Ross, Eric S. 2008. *Culture and Customs of Senegal.* Westport, CT: Greenwood.

Sposito, Tommaso. 2010. "Agriculture urbaine et périurbaine pour la sécurité alimentaire en Afrique de l'Ouest: Le cas des micro-jardins dans la municipalité de Dakar." PhD dissertation, Toulouse: Université Toulouse le Mirail II.

Sy, Moussa, Mamadou Khouma, Marie Sophie Gueth Ndong, Ndèye Yacine Badiane, Youga Niang, Mohamed Oumar Diagne, Mouhamadou Lamine Dial, Idy Niang, and Ousseynou Diop. 2014. *Renforcer la résilience des systèmes agricoles urbains: Évaluer l'agriculture urbaine et périurbaine à Dakar, Sénégal.* Edited by J. Padgham and J. Jabbour. Nairobi: United Nations Environment Program.

Tounkara, Sidy. 2015. "La valorisation des déchets organiques dans l'agriculture 'périurbaine' à Dakar (Sénégal): Analyse d'une multifonctionnalité stratégique." PhD dissertation, Milan: Università degli Studi di Milano.

Delhi, India: Current Problems and Opportunities for the Future of the National Capital Territory

Safely collecting and managing municipal solid waste (MSW) is a key challenge for the rapidly growing and urbanizing cities in the developing world. Cities in India, China, and Pakistan are producing waste at unprecedented levels, primarily because of rapid population growth, an increase in economic activity, and the adoption of Western-style consumerism by the city residents. Insufficient collection and improper disposal of MSW have exposed these cities to significant health and environmental risks. A good waste management system requires an integrated approach that includes waste generation, segregation, transfer, sorting, treatment, recovery, and disposal of solid waste to ensure the highest standards of public health and environmental protection. The idea of what constitutes MSW varies within and between countries. UN-Habitat provides a working definition for MSW: "Wastes generated by households, and wastes of a similar nature generated by commercial and industrial premises, by institutions such as schools, hospitals, care homes and prisons, and from public spaces such as streets, markets, slaughter houses, public toilets, bus stops, parks and gardens" (2010, 6).

MUNICIPAL SOLID WASTE MANAGEMENT IN DELHI

Delhi, or the National Capital Territory of India (NCT), is the largest city in India, and the fifth most populous city in the world with a population of roughly 18 million. Population growth, mass rural-urban migration, rapid urbanization, and a change in the people's lifestyles have contributed to a significant increase in the amount of municipal solid waste that is generated in Delhi. The NCT generates about 11,558 tons of MSW per day, up by more than 50 percent from 2007.

Municipal solid waste management (MSWM) in Delhi is the primary responsibility of three urban local bodies (ULBs): The Municipal Corporation of Delhi (MCD), New Delhi Municipal Corporation (NDMC), and Delhi Cantonment Board (DCB). These municipal bodies are often supported informally by other stakeholder groups such as waste pickers, waste dealers, and recyclers. MSWM in Delhi is governed by a set of act and rules, including the Municipal Solid Waste (Management and Handling) Rules (2000), and the Delhi Plastic Bag and Non-Biodegradable Garbage Act (2000), each of which provide a set of procedures for managing MSW and for the treatment of specific types of MSW.

MSWM is considered to be one of the most neglected areas of the municipal system in Delhi, with poor collection and disposal of MSW. The system also ignores segregation and the treatment and recovery of MSW, all of which are considered integral to a good waste management system. The government's policies for MSWM are piecemeal and often poorly implemented. Already considered one of the world's most polluted cities, the improper treatment and disposal of MSW is contributing to worsening Delhi's air quality.

According to Talyan and colleagues (2008), only 70–80 percent of the municipal waste generated in Delhi is collected for disposal and treatment. The MSW Rules 2000 require that the three municipal bodies provide a door-to-door collection of solid waste. However, the requirement has not been entirely implemented because of a lack of resources. In areas where the door-to-door collection is not available, owners and occupants of residential houses and industrial establishments deposit their solid waste in municipality-provided waste receptacles. Several of these receptacles are open, and their placement does not follow any standards. In addition, there is an unequal distribution of the waste receptacles within and between different zones of the city. Improper monitoring makes the collection of solid waste from these receptacles highly inefficient. According to Kumar (2013), there is also a lack of litter bins in the city. The consequence is large amounts of unattended waste on streets or in small dumps.

Only 9 percent of all the MSW collected is treated. The lack of waste segregation reduces the efficiency of waste treatment, and precludes the monetary and environmental benefits from recycling. Composting is the primary treatment method used in Delhi. There are three composting plants in Delhi, but they operate below intended capacity, primarily because of the high operating and maintenance costs. The high costs make compost less competitive in the market, where commercial fertilizers are available for a much lower cost. In addition, because of a lack of waste segregation in Delhi, the MSW sent to composting plants contains plastic and glass, which degrades its quality. The other popular method for treating MSW is waste incineration. Delhi only has one plant for the incineration of MSW. The plant was set up in 1989, but was shut down soon after. The waste produced in Delhi has a very low calorific value, and is therefore considered unfit for burning.

Ninety-one percent of all collected MSW is disposed in landfills. The municipal authorities in Delhi use three landfill sites on the outskirts of the city. These are located at Bhalswa, Okhla, and Ghazipur. The landfills are poorly maintained, and waste is often dumped in an uncontrolled way. The requirement that MSW be covered with construction and demolition waste to prevent odor and rodent infestation is not complied with. In addition, these landfills were created without any base liner, and have no provision for the collection, treatment, or disposal of leachate. Leachate is the liquid that collects at the bottom of the landfill, and contains various harmful chemical constituents that contaminate groundwater. Various studies have confirmed that the groundwater of residential areas near landfills is significantly contaminated by leachate percolation (Talyan et al. 2008; Mor et al., 2006; Kumar and Alappat 2003). A report published in the *Daily Mail* (Adak 2014) claimed that the ground soil of the three landfill sites harbored organic pollutants exceeding the permissible limits by 158 times. In addition to groundwater contamination, the landfills provide a breeding ground for mosquitoes, in a city that recently witnessed a large-scale outbreak of dengue and chikungunya, both serious illnesses caused by viruses transmitted by mosquitoes.

Landfill sites in Delhi also emit methane and other gases like toluene and methylene chloride, which are trapped under the layers of garbage. The spontaneous combustion of Methane burns landfill, including plastic which sends nauseating white smoke in to the city. According to a recent report published in the *Hindustan Times* (Joshi and Sharma 2016), the landfill sites of Ghazipur and Bhalswa were emitting several toxic gases, including copious amounts of methane into Delhi's air.

The Clean Air Act in the United States prohibits the burning of unsegregated MSW, citing the adverse impact on the environment and local residents. Though illegal in India, it is a common practice for waste disposal at the landfills in Delhi. Observers have found that burning MSW at landfills is contributing to worsening Delhi's air quality. It has also increased the presence of chlorides in the air, which is responsible for weak immune systems and several respiratory ailments for those living around the landfills. According to reports, the Bhalswa landfill was on fire for more than a week in April 2016, which produced large amounts of carbon monoxide and other toxic gases. Rajiv Aggarwal, the director for a think tank, Toxic Link, in an interview in Asian Age (Grover 2016) argued that the landfills in Delhi are susceptible to large fires, which would be dangerous for pollution levels in the city, and also to the well-being of residents in the neighborhood. He also believes that the authorities are not doing enough to check the illegal disposal of waste, or monitoring the conditions at these landfills.

The Delhi Pollution Control Board has argued that all three landfill sites are way past their shelf lives, and should not be used as dumping grounds anymore. The Bhalswa landfill, for example, reached its capacity in 2006, but still receives 2,700 tons of garbage per day.

MUNICIPAL SOLID WASTE MANAGEMENT IN BEIJING, CHINA

Beijing, with a comparable population of roughly 22 million generated 6.35 million tons of MSW according to a 2010 statistic. Li and colleagues (2009), show that MSW generation has increased rapidly in Beijing in the last three decades. A large population, together with an increase in the purchasing power of the urban dwellers, has contributed to higher levels of MSW. The changing composition of the MSW also reflects a change in the lifestyle of the urban population. Paper and plastic waste are a significant component of Beijing's MSW. Food waste accounts for more than 60 percent of the total MSW. As in Delhi, landfill is the most prominent form of waste disposal in Beijing. About 90 percent of the MSW generated in Beijing is landfilled. There are 15 landfill sites in Beijing, but their designed capacity has been unable to cope with the actual quantity of waste generation. Zhao and colleagues (2011) believe that the current system for MSW management has created significant adverse environmental impacts, primarily through methane emissions from landfills.

In addition to landfills, Beijing also uses two waste-to-energy (WTE) incinerators, which can recover energy from discarded MSW and produce electricity and/or steam for heating. Beijing also uses two waste-composting plants. Wang and Chunmei (2012) suggest that there is now increasing government support, and several financial incentives, for the development of WTE technology in China. According to Zhao and colleagues (2011), incinerators may not have the desired environmental impact because of the low calorific value of mixed waste, and the fact that these incinerators would require significant amounts of auxiliary fuels to support combustion of wet waste.

Beijing has, however, made significant progress in separating waste at the source, an issue that Delhi is still struggling with. Waste separation allows for the proper disposal and recycling of waste. According to a recent report (Cohen et al. 2015), Beijing had achieved a 50 percent separation rate, primarily by actively involving the citizens and recognizing the important role of waste pickers who manually pick up and recycle waste.

LESSONS FOR THE FUTURE

In the master plan (2005–2021) for Delhi, it was noted that the three landfill sites have been saturated and have outlived their normal life. The Ministry of

Environment and Forest for the Government of India (GOI), in its rules for Solid Waste Management and Handling published in 2000, asked that new landfill sites be engineered in each direction of the city to ensure efficient SWM. The Supreme Court of India has also directed the Municipal Corporation of Delhi to acquire land for engineered landfills in low-lying areas and line them appropriately to prevent gases and leachate from contaminating the groundwater. According to Gupta and Arora (2016), not much has been achieved in terms of setting up new landfill sites.

Even though waste disposal leaves a lot to be desired, the MCD has taken some concrete steps to improve the collection of MSW in Delhi. Collection and segregation have been privatized in several parts of the city. Like in Beijing, there is also a call for active participation and cooperation by the Resident Welfare Associations (RWAs) to encourage door-to-door collection and the segregation of MSW. The very important role performed by waste pickers is also receiving greater recognition in Delhi. Efforts are being made to utilize the services of this informal sector to improve MSWM in Delhi. There is still a need for better implementation of the existing policies and to develop the infrastructure for recycling MSW.

Nakul Kumar

See also: Employment and Jobs: Mumbai, India: Exploring Employment Solutions in Temporary Jobs; *Pollution:* New Delhi, India: Success of Pollution Control Depends on Effective Collaboration

Further Reading

Adak, Baishali. 2014. "Delhi at Risk as Landfill Sites Leak Cancer-Causing Chemicals into Water Supply." *Daily Mail India,* December 7. https://www.dailymail.co.uk/indiahome/indianews/article-2864658/Delhi-risk-landfill-sites-leak-cancer-causing-chemicals-water-supply.html.

Adak, Baishali. 2016. "Delhi's Flaming Hell." *Daily Mail India*, April 18. http://www.dailymail.co.uk/indiahome/article-3546535/Delhi-s-flaming-hell-40-acre-landfill-site-Bhalswa-fire-WEEK-thanks-42C-temperatures-leaving-locals-choking-putrid-black-smoke.html.

Cheng, Hefa, and Y. Hu. 2010. "Municipal Solid Waste (MSW) as a Renewable Source of Energy: Current and Future Practices in China." *Bioresource Technology* 101, 11: 3816–24.

Cohen, Steven, Hayley Martinez, and Alix Schroder. 2015. "Waste Management Practices in New York City, Hong Kong and Beijing." http://www.columbia.edu/~sc32/documents/ALEP%20Waste%20Managent%20FINAL.pdf.

Ghose, Debobrat. 2016. "Waste Management Is Imperative in Delhi as the National Capital Inches Closer to Another Deonar." *First Post*, January 28. http://www.firstpost.com/india/waste-management-is-imperative-in-delhi-as-the-national-capital-inches-closer-to-another-deonar-2697564.html.

Grover, Nishtha. 2016. "Norms Being Flouted in 'Simmering' Landfill Sites." *Asian Age*, May 20. http://www.asianage.com/delhi/norms-being-flouted-simmering-landfill-sites-962.

Gupta, Bhavik, and S. K. Arora. 2016. "Municipal Solid Waste Management in Delhi—the Capital of India." *International Journal of Innovative Research in Science, Engineering and Technology* 5, 4: 5130–38.

Joshi, Mallica, and Mohit Sharma. 2016. "Landfills or Pollution Bombs? Delhi's Garbage Dumps Spewing Toxic Gases." *Hindustan Times*, May 5. http://www.hindustantimes

.com/delhi/landfill-sites-or-pollution-bombs-garbage-dumps-spewing-toxic-gases/story-2abfwizFWqY5NzsFzbuFdN.html.
Kumar, Ashwani. 2013. "Existing Situation of Municipal Solid Waste Management in NCT of Delhi, India." *International Journal of Social Sciences* 1, 1: 6–17.
Kumar, D. and B. J. Alappat. 2003. "A Technique to Quantify Landfill Leachate Pollution." Proceedings of the 9th International Landfill Symposium, Cagliari, 6–10 October 2003, Paper No. 400.
Lahiri, Ishadrita. "Residents Choke on Smoke as Delhi's Landfills Burns Unchecked." *New Delhi Television*, October 16. http://www.ndtv.com/delhi-news/residents-choke-on-smoke-as-delhis-landfills-burn-unchecked-1474721.
Li, Zhen-shan, Yang Lei, Qu Xiao-Yan, and Sui Yu-mei. 2009. "Municipal Solid Waste Management in Beijing City." September 2009. *Waste Management* 29, 9: 2596–99. https://doi.org/10.1016/j.wasman.2009.03.018.
Magnier, Mark. 2012. "For Many in India, Landfill Is a Livelihood and Home." *Los Angeles Times*, April 22. http://articles.latimes.com/2012/apr/22/world/la-fg-india-trash-mountain-20120422.
Mor, Suman, Khaiwal Ravindra, R. P. Dahiya, and A. Chandra. 2006. "Leachate Characterization and Assessment of Goundwater Pollution Near Municipal Solid Waste Landfill Site." *Environmental Monitoring and Assessment* 118, 1–3: 435–56. https://doi.org/10.1007/s10661-006-1505-7.
Talyan, V., R. P. Dahiya, and T. R. Sreekrishnan. 2008. "State of Municipal Solid Waste Management in Delhi, the Capital of India." *Waste Management* 28, 7: 1276–87.
United Nations Human Settlements Programme (UN-HABITAT). 2010. *Solid Waste Management in the World's Cities*. London: Earthscan.
Wang, Hao, and W. Chunmei. 2012. "Municipal Solid Waste Management in Beijing: Characteristics and Challenges." *International Solid Waste Association* 31, 1: 67–72.
Zhao, Yan, T. H. Christensen, W. Lu, H. Wu, and H. Wang. 2011. "Environmental Impact Assessment of Solid Waste Management in Beijing City, China." *Waste Management* 31, 4: 793–99.

Kobe, Japan: The Cleanest City in the World

Kobe is a port city of Japan and one of the first port cities of the country that was opened in the mid-19th century for trade with the West. The total area of the city is 557 square kilometers, slightly smaller than the city of Chicago, with a population of about 1.5 million (Kobe City 2018). It is located at the eastern end of the Inland Sea, on Osaka Bay, about 20 miles to the west of Osaka. Together with Osaka and Kyoto, the three cities constitute the second-largest urban and industrial agglomeration in Japan. In 1995, a devastating earthquake struck Kobe and killed more than 5,000 people (Encyclopaedia Britannica 2018). The city has since recovered from the natural disaster, and thanks to the city's excellent waste management, Kobe has been ranked one of the cleanest cities in Japan and in the world by a number of agencies year after year.

OVERVIEW OF JAPAN'S WASTE MANAGEMENT

As an island country of 377,915 square kilometers, Japan has limited construction space. Building additional waste dump sites has always been a challenge. As such, environmental preservation is constantly on people's minds. In the Japanese language, the word *mottainai* ("wasteful") is often used to remind people to save and appreciate. Author Chiba Hiroshi explains *mottainai* as follows:

> We often hear in Japan the expression "mottainai," which loosely means "wasteful" but in its full sense conveys a feeling of awe and appreciation for the gifts of nature or the sincere conduct of other people. There is a trait among Japanese to try to use something for its entire effective life or continue to use it by repairing it. In this caring culture, people will endeavor to find new homes for possessions they no longer need. The "mottainai" principle extends to the dinner table, where many consider it rude to leave even a single grain of rice in the bowl. The concern is that this traditional trait may be lost. (Hitroshi 2002)

One story Hiroshi tells in his writing is about a "toy hospital" in Tokyo, founded in 1977, where volunteer "doctors" come in every Sunday afternoon to repair toys thrown away due to slight damage, a tradition that continues today. Hiroshi's concern about erosion of the *mottainai* spirit in modern Japanese society, however, is not without reason.

Since the beginning of the 20th century, as Japan rose to become one of the richest nations in Asia, and as consumerism encroached on the Japanese lifestyle, the traditional respect for the environment has been weakening, and waste and pollution have been on the rise. Pollutants have also become more diverse, harder to remove, and riskier to public health.

During the "rapid economic growth period" of the 1960s and 1970s, mass production, particularly of plastics-based products, became a major source of pollutants. Improper incineration of disposed plastics generated acidic gases and soot, polluting the air and water. Urbanization advanced at a faster pace, and lack of laws to restrict companies from illegal dumping worsened environmental deterioration. Sludge, synthetic resin waste, and waste oil were dumped untreated. Two pollution-induced diseases in the 1960s, Niigata Minamata disease or methyl-mercury poisoning, and Yokkaichi asthma or neural and respiratory diseases caused by sulfur oxide, devastated many parts of Japan. In 1970, the Japanese government enacted the Waste Management and Public Cleaning Act. This law categorized waste materials into two categories—municipal waste and industrial waste, and assigned responsibility of waste treatment to the city and source industries, respectively. During this period, the government also enacted regulations on water and air pollution control and landfill management. Meanwhile, the government called on the Japanese people to join the "War against Waste."

From the 1980s to the 1990s, the Japanese economy grew rapidly, reaching an unsustainable stage known as the "bubble economy period." Packaging materials, such as water bottles, became major challenges for treatment at this time. An increase in consumption generated more waste, while landfill and incineration capacities failed to catch up with demand. In 1995, the Law for the Promotion of Sorted Collections and Recycling Containers and Packaging was issued and was enacted two years later. Dioxins, by-product of the incineration process and in some cases toxic, were found in the atmosphere and in foods. Social protests against building more landfills further exacerbated the situation. As a result, illegal dumping was rampant. Teshima Island landfill, for example, received 620,000 square meters of industrial waste containing chromium, mercury, and cadmium.

Eventually, the Japanese government had to pay for the costly cleanup (Ministry of the Environment 2014).

Due to the slowdown of the Japanese economy in the 1990s, the government invested in waste management programs as part of the efforts to rejuvenate the economy. The period of the 1990s to the 2000s is known as the "era of establishment of a sound material-cycle society" (Ministry of the Environment 2014). In the early 2000s, the government enacted several laws and regulations aiming at enforcing accountability, which included the Law for the Promotion of Recyclable Resources, the Container and Packaging Recycling Law, the Electric Appliance Recycling Law, the Food Recycling Law, and the Basic Act for Establishing a Sound Material-Cycle Society (Basic Recycling Act). In practice, the society works together to implement the three "R's" or "reduce, reuse, and recycle." At the household level, families carefully sort materials into color-coded bags, avoid food waste, and bring their own bags for grocery shopping. At the industrial level, according to the Basic Recycling Act, the government requires industries to set targets for productivity, recycling rate, and waste disposal amount. A fourth "R" that has recently been added refers to "recovery," or harvesting green energy from the waste treatment process. Nevertheless, the shortage of landfill sites remains a pressing issue, despite the fact that more efficient management could somewhat extend the residual time (time for a landfill to fill up).

KOBE'S WASTE MANAGEMENT

Kobe has six sewage treatment plants servicing 98.7 percent of the population (Kobe City n.d.). Its modern sewage project dates back to the early 1950s when the city designed separated sewage processing systems. Its sewer line runs 4,700 kilometers; the average volume of treated wastewater is now 550,000 cubic meters per day. The "separate sewage system" is more advanced than the "combined system" in that it separates rainwater from municipal wastewaters that typically include black water from toilets and grey water from households, such as bathwater. As such, the separate system is more efficient than the combined system, since it allows surface rainwater runoff to be reused for gardening and agricultural purposes with simple treatment, whereas industrial waters must be given more extensive treatment. The maintenance, however, is costlier.

Sludge treatment has become a renewable energy source in Kobe. Since 2008, the city has deployed a biogas project for automobile fuel consumption, general urban use, and co-power-generation. Since 1990, Kobe has invested in wastewater recycling. Kobe Steel Group and Shinko Kobe Power are two leading industries in recycling industrial water for reuse. Currently, Kobe recycles 60,000 cubic meters of water per day (Kobe City n.d.).

RUBBISH DISPOSAL BY HOUSEHOLDS

Kobe's renowned cleanliness is the result of extensively detailed rules and schedules for household disposal. The principle behind the rules and regulations is "pay-as-you-trash." Residents are required to purchase bags with appropriate color-coding,

Bags of carefully sorted recyclable materials ready for pickup in Kobe, Japan, 2016. (Tharakorn Saengsuratham/Dreamstime.com)

weight, and size limits for different kinds of materials. Garbage is collected by trucks from "Clean Stations." Disposers can also bring bagged waste to Clean Stations. Kobe's "Rules of Sorting and Putting Out Garbage and Recyclables" is held as a model across Japan. An overview of these rules, which some find tedious, may be helpful for understanding why Kobe enjoys the reputation of being the cleanest city.

Visitors would readily agree that the garbage collection schedule is more frequent than many countries in the West. Moreover, the classification of waste materials can be mind-boggling. Common household garbage is collected twice a week, once for cans, bottles and PET bottles, and once for plastic containers and trays. Households are encouraged to return recyclable bottles, such as beer bottles, to vendors. Cans and bottles must be emptied and washed and put in designated bags; PET bottles must be crushed. Food containers, wraps, and shampoo/lotion bottles must be cleaned before being put into designated bags. If not cleanable, these items must be placed in bags marked "burnable garbage." Burnable garbage includes kitchen waste. One must remember to drain bones and shells before bagging them. Paper, leather, fabrics, shoes, plastic items, wooden items, and diapers are also burnable materials. Oil-soaked items must be placed into their own designated bags. Items made of whole bamboo must be broken open (to avoid explosion in the incinerator). The disposal guidance advises households to recycle newspapers, cardboards, and cotton clothes, with a reminder printed on the guidance flyer—"Isn't it wasteful to dispose of recyclables as burnable garbage?"

To dispose of large items, Kobe has special rules to encourage people to maximally recycle them. In many cases, one must make phone calls to prearrange. For example, to dispose of oversize garbage, such as anything larger than what a 45-liter bag can hold (the bag must be fastened on top), or weighs more than five kilograms, such as furniture, used bicycles, and microwaves, one must call the Oversize Garbage Reception Center to arrange pickup. Oversize garbage tickets must be purchased and attached to the items. Unregistered items are not picked up.

Certain items are collected twice per month. These include nonburnable items, such as glass, ceramics, and small metal or electrical appliances. Knives and sharp-edged items must be placed in designated bags and mark with "danger" on the bags. Fluorescent light tubes must be treated the same way. Gas cartridges and spray cans must be emptied and punctured in well-ventilated areas. These items must be separated from the nonburnable garbage and put out on the designated collection day.

Clean Stations do not collect large items such as air conditioners, televisions, and washing machines. Putting these items out may result in a fine. Likewise, personal computers must not be put out with regular garbage. To dispose of these items, one must contact relevant agencies to arrange a pickup or self-delivery. Also worth noting, dead animals are picked up at a charge of 4,000 yen ($35). However, if the owner delivers the dead animal's body to a designated center, the cost is half that amount.

In general, when in doubt, one should inquire. The disposal guidance instructions come with a detailed list of phone numbers to call. In most cases, post offices and banks handle fee payments. The consequence of not following these rules may be a maximum fine of 100,000 yen ($883) by the city of Kobe.

FUTURE OF KOBE

Kobe City's goal is to achieve five town planning objectives: 1) ensuring that people can stroll with a smile; 2) ensuring that people can move around comfortably; 3) enhancing the city's attractiveness to draw many more people; 4) advertising the unique atmosphere of Kobe, a city with the sea and mountains; and 5) providing support and protection, promoting growth and disseminating information. The city's exemplary performance in waste management has enabled it to achieve these objectives year after year.

Jing Luo

See also: Waste Management: Calgary, Canada: Waste Management Is a National Effort and Calgary's Priority; Singapore City, Singapore: Managing Food Waste

Further Reading

AJ Website. 2017. "Guidance on Garbage Collection in Kobe." https://www.alljapanrelocation.com/news/garbage-collection-kobe/.

Encyclopaedia Britannica. 2018. "Kobe." https://www.britannica.com/place/Kobe.

Hitroshi, Chiba. 2002. "Restyling Japan: Revival of the 'Mottainai' Spirit." https://web.archive.org/web/20040405084940/http://www.lookjapan.com/LBcoverstory/02NovCS.htm.

Japan Info Website. "A Guide to Garbage Disposal in Japan." http://jpninfo.com/9826.

Kobe City. n.d. "Rules for Sorting and Putting Out Garbage and Recyclables." http://www.city.kobe.lg.jp/life/recycle/waketon/img/english.pdf.

Kobe City. 2018. "Pocket Statistics: Outline of Kobe: Population" (in Japanese). http://www.city.kobe.lg.jp/information/data/statistics/toukei/sougoudata/pocket.html.

Kobe City Environmental Bureau. n.d. "Business Waste Disposal Rules." http://www.city.kobe.lg.jp/business/regulation/environment/enterprise/jigyokeirulebook_en.pdf.

Ministry of the Environment, Japan. n.d. "Solid Waste Management and Recycling Technology of Japan." https://www.env.go.jp/en/recycle/smcs/attach/swmrt.pdf.

Ministry of the Environment, Japan. 2014. "History and Current State of Waste Management in Japan." http://www.env.go.jp/en/recycle/smcs/attach/hcswm.pdf.

Stauffer, Beat, and Dorothee Spuhler. "Separate Sewers." http://archive.sswm.info/category/implementation-tools/wastewater-collection/hardware/sewers/separate-sewers.

Naples, Italy: Coping with a Rubbish Crisis

The collection and disposal of waste are a basic function of any town, city, and nation. In the United States, Americans tend to refer to this solid waste as garbage or trash. In Europe, the term is rubbish or refuse, but the character of these wastes is unchanged. By solid waste this entry means discarded paper and paper products including cardboard, food scraps, the solid waste like metals from industrial processes, and any other solid debris. Organic wastes such as human excrement are generally considered a separate type of solid waste often termed as sewage. Because the collection and disposal of solid wastes are basic to any program to maintain minimal levels of sanitation, these activities generally have a high priority among civic authorities. In the 21st century, Naples, an ancient city south of Rome and sometimes considered the gateway to southern Italy, has had numerous problems with the collection and disposals of these wastes. These problems have endangered the health of people, other animals, the soil, the air, and various other components of the environment. As such, Naples has been the site of controversy and sometimes aggressive action to combat the deleterious effects of garbage.

WASTE MANAGEMENT AS A PROBLEM OF DENSE POPULATIONS

It is axiomatic that the more people who reside in an area, the more garbage they produce. Naples is a classic example of this dour trend. As of 2012, Naples, at just under 1 million residents, was the third most populous city in Italy, trailing only Rome and Milan to the north. Naples is easily southern Italy's most populous city. Anyone who has visited Naples knows how congested and overcrowded it is. In such a situation the aggregate of people inevitably generates trash in large amounts. But mere population dynamics are not the only problem. Industries contribute to these solid wastes, exacerbating the problem of their collection and disposal. The collection of solid wastes is in principle a simple matter involving the use of large trucks to collect and transport garbage to one or more central locations. Of course, the destination of these locations need not be central. Naples and several other cities have had a long history of transporting garbage to the periphery of the city so that it will not be an eyesore. The disposal of trash has traditionally taken two forms in Naples as in several other cities: disposal in landfills and incineration. By a landfill, we mean nothing more than an area that serves for the dumping and sometimes burial of trash. The idea is that once the trash is in the soil, microbes will decompose the paper and food scraps. Of course, other items of garbage are not so easily gotten rid of. Styrofoam and other forms of plastics, by which we mean petroleum-based products, are resistant to decay and can remain in landfills, perhaps for millennia. Some metal containers like those made of iron will rust over time and so degrade, but other metal containers like those made of aluminum will persist in a landfill much longer. Those items not taken to a landfill may be burned. Incineration will reduce paper products and other carbon-based garbage to ashes, the black ashes being carbon in pure form. Incineration thus reduces the volume of trash and at first appears to be an attractive solution. Some cities burn certain types of garbage to generate electricity. This is true of some cities in Hawaii and Brazil where the residues of sugarcane stalks (*bagasse*) are burned to generate electricity. Naples, however, has no such program. As a long-term solution, incineration is not viable because of the pollution it causes. Trash that is burned in the open can cause pollution that contaminates soils and air. These precious resources have already been degraded in Naples and other densely populated cities and should not be subject to still more pollution.

THE ROOT OF THE WASTE MANAGEMENT CRISIS

The waste management crisis in Naples, a problem of the 21st century, had its roots in the 1990s. We have noted the ill effects of population pressure combined with prodigal industries that produce too much waste. This dual problem emerged in the 1990s, when the first signs arose that Naples's landfills were overfilled with trash. Several factors compounded this problem. According to authorities, elements of the mafia-controlled trash collection and disposal in landfills in Naples. These people were not receptive to government oversight and the timely management of the problem of overflowing landfills before crisis could be averted. Perhaps an even more important problem was the role of industries in producing wastes to be deposited in landfills. The industries of Naples would have been a problem by themselves, but the government in Naples compounded what was becoming a crisis by inviting industries in parts of northern Italy to pay to dump their garbage in Naples's landfills. The sheer volume of this trash was too large for the city's landfills to cope with. Even had the mafia been responsive to the impending crisis, the volume of trash imported into Naples's landfills signaled an inability to plan rationally for the collection and disposal of garbage. The Pianura landfill in Naples was the first to suffer from an overflow of trash, with other sites following later in the decade.

Naples's trash collectors worked long hours to collect and dispose of trash in landfills. That they coped with the problem for more than a decade is to their credit, but on December 21, 2007, matters had reached a crisis. Overworked Naples trash collectors refused to collect and dispose of any additional garbage. In effect, they launched a strike to protest arduous working conditions and durations. With no one

Garbage piles up along a street in Naples after overworked city trash collectors refused to collect or dispose of any additional garbage, 2007. (Carlo Hermann/AFP/Getty Images)

to pick up garbage, the result was disastrous as trash piled up in streets, creating a public health crisis. With trash in the streets, rodents, insects, and other vermin multiplied. These animals carried diseases, creating unsanitary conditions that must have been unimaginable in modernity. Naples was failing in one aspect of its basic social contract with its citizens, the collection and disposal of trash. Such conditions were unacceptable, and Naples resorted to illegal measures in desperation in an attempt to combat this public health crisis. The Camorra, a part of the mafia in Naples and the surrounding area of Campania, collected trash from various sources, combining industrial waste including chemicals with residential paper, plastic, and food scraps. They dumped this mix along roads, burning it in place in violation of a city ordinance. The toxic fumes from these burnings endangered the health of the city's residents. In Naples, then, the issue of waste management combined with the larger issue of pollution.

Understandably, residents were unhappy. In response to protests, the city closed one landfill on the last day of 2007, but this did little to improve conditions because it did not get to the core of the problem of the lack of trash collection and the illegal burning of garbage. In 2008, news reports implicated the Camorra in these illegal burnings and stoked additional protests. The media turned on the government for its failure to act. Anger at political inactivity caused two gubernatorial administrations to collapse in quick succession in spring 2008. One Naples governor,

Romano Prodi, had taken dramatic action, dispatching the army to take bulldozers to the streets to push trash out of the way. He appointed a former police chief to be the new commissioner of waste, but none of these actions satisfied voters, who turned Prodi out of office that May. By one estimate, that month some 200,000 metric tons of trash remained to litter Naples's streets.

May elections elevated millionaire Silvio Berlusconi to prime minister. Aware of conditions in Naples, his first action as prime minister was to convene his cabinet in the city. Berlusconi appointed the former chief of the Civil Protection Department, Guido Bertolaso, to be the new waste commissioner. Acting quickly, Bertolaso opened a new landfill and built a new trash incinerator in June and July 2008 in the city. He used public funds to pay Hamburg, Germany, to incinerate some 700 metric tons of Naples's trash per day. Bertolaso was determined to make Naples a trash exporter not an importer as it had been. Funding the construction of still more incinerators, the waste commissioner declared the crisis at an end by the close of July, but some trash remained on the streets until that September.

In March 2009, Bertolaso translated his success into a promotion that took him to Rome. Yet Naples was not in pristine condition. Landfills were still overfilled, and the new incinerators only increased the problem of pollution. Moreover. all of southern Italy seemed to suffer from the problem of overfilled landfills, especially in the countryside. Bertolaso's movement north to Rome may be interpreted as an abandonment of the problems with sanitation in Naples and other parts of southern Italy. By September 2009, journalists were once more reporting of an impending crisis in Naples and elsewhere in the south. This news began to percolate up the ladder of media coverage, and by 2010 a prominent American magazine, *Newsweek*, was focusing on conditions in Naples. That September, Terzigno, a city about 20 kilometers east of Naples, experienced riots so severe that they destabilized conditions in Naples. Garbage collection again ceased, and trash appeared once more in the streets of Naples. Residents again protested a return to near chaotic conditions, calling for Prime Minister Berlusconi to resign on charges that he had failed to avert

---

Campania

Visualizing Italy as a boot, the lower portion of the shin is the region known since antiquity as Campania. Its principal city is Naples, though readers should not overlook Salerno, one of southern Italy's chief ports. In southwestern Italy, Campania borders the Mediterranean Sea to the west. The province began as home to three indigenous Italian peoples, all of whom spoke now-extinct Oscan. In the eighth century BCE, Greeks colonized Campania, the principal city being Cumae, whose ruins document an impressive civilization. During the fourth century BCE the Romans incorporated Campania into the republic. Campania suffered during the Second Punic War (218–201 BCE) when Cumae switched loyalties from Rome to Carthage, leading Rome to slaughter its inhabitants upon recapture. Yet the region was too valuable to ignore because it produced food for Rome, whose population neared 1 million by the end of the first century BCE. During the Middle Ages, Naples and Sicily competed to control Campania. In modernity, European powers like Spain and France fought for it. Only Italian unification in 1871 brought stability. Like much of southern Italy, Campania remains largely rural, with fruits, vegetables, and flowers being leading crops.

this crisis and that he was involved with the mafia. At this junction, Berlusconi erred by announcing the building of a large landfill in Vesuvius National Park, named after Mount Vesuvius, an active volcano in southern Italy. But the national park was to be pristine, an oasis free from filth, trash, and pollution. Berlusconi's call for the building of a landfill in the park would be tantamount to President Donald Trump announcing the building of a garbage dump in Yellowstone National Park in the United States. With this news, the riots, initially confined to Terzigno, now spread to Naples. Disorder only compounded the problem of trash in the streets, and the residents of Naples demanded change. They elected a new mayor of Naples, Luigi de Magistris, a judge who had built his reputation on handing down harsh prison terms to convicted members of the mafia. With a no-nonsense reputation, Magistris went to work. When he turned to the problem of garbage in June 2011, Naples's streets overflowed with roughly 2,500 metric tons of trash. By November, the streets were clean again. Eager to act aggressively, Magistris floated the old ideas of building more landfills and incinerators, but he changed course when residents balked at these suggestions. Magistris even proposed that some trash, paper products and plastic especially, be recycled, but here again the people of Naples had no appetite for this action. In the end, Magistris took the easy solution of paying The Netherlands to take Naples's overflow of trash. In January 2012, according to a contract between the government of Naples and the private company AVR, the Dutch firm agreed to take one shipload of trash from Naples per week. AVR burned this trash in Rotterdam. An interesting point is that Naples, and Europe at large, did not solve the problem of too much trash in the landfills so much as it shifted the burden to other parts of Europe. The trash burned in Rotterdam or Hamburg rather than in Naples still caused pollution, just in a different region of Europe. Naples has yet to solve the overarching problem that its densely populated environs generate too much trash for a city of its size. Residents and businesses are both to blame, and until they can reduce their production of trash, the collection and disposal of garbage will continue to haunt Naples, the rest of Italy, and the rest of the European Union. Frugality rather than prodigality must become the new order of the day.

Christopher Cumo

See also: Violence, Corruption, and Organized Crime: Sicily, Italy: Fighting Organized Crime in the New Era

Further Reading

Brebbia, C. A., J. F. Martin-Duque, and L. C. Wadhwa, eds. 2002. *The Sustainable City II: Urban Regeneration and Sustainability.* Southampton, UK, and Boston: WIT Press.

Mendez-Vilas, Antonio, ed. 2006. *Modern Multidisciplinary Applied Microbiology: Exploiting Microbes and Their Interactions.* Weinheim, Germanys: Wiley-VCH.

Oslo, Norway: Prevention and Reduction, What Makes Oslo Clean

Norway's capital, Oslo, has ambitious goals when it comes to sustainability. In June 2017, the city won the European Green Capital Award for 2019, which honors sustainable urban development and high environmental standards. Oslo's proactive approach using technology and innovation is also mirrored in its waste management strategy. By 2025, the city aims to reuse and recycle 100 percent of its waste.

WASTE TRENDS IN NORWAY AND OSLO

Norway has a population of 5.26 million (2017), about the size of the state of Minnesota, which has a population of 5.52 million. About 13 percent of Norwegians (658,390) live in its capital and largest city Oslo (Statistics Norway 2016, 1). Oslo is a compact city surrounded by the Oslo Fjord and the Marka forest, a nationally protected recreational area. Oslo's population has a high standard of living, so consumption levels are high (Stenmarck et al. 2016). Over time, as consumption increases, so does waste generation. Figure 1 shows the amount of waste produced in Norway from 1995 to 2014 for selected sectors. A total of 11.9 million tonnes of waste was produced in 2014. The amount of waste generated has increased in most categories except manufacturing, which is still the biggest waste category. Household waste has been steadily increasing over the years and only started leveling off in 2012 (Statistics Norway 2014).

How does Norway fare in comparison to other European countries? The European Environment Agency (EEA) keeps track of municipal waste management in 32 EEA countries. In terms of municipal waste generated per person in 2014, Norway ranked 23 out of the 32 countries with 423 kg of municipal waste per capita. In comparison, Denmark generated 758 kg, Germany 618 kg, and Poland 272 kg of municipal waste per person (European Environment Agency 2016). Even though it is difficult to compare these numbers across countries because of different data collection methods, wealthier countries usually generate more waste per person. The European Commission proposed new targets for recycling of municipal waste in 2015. By 2025, 60 percent of municipal waste should be recycled and by 2030, 65 percent. Norway ranks 10, with 42 percent of municipal waste recycled. In comparison, Germany recycled 64 percent, Poland 30 percent, and Slovakia 10 percent in 2014 (European Environment Agency 2016). Norway appears to be well on track to reach the proposed recycling targets. However, when it comes to household waste, continuous effort is required.

Table 1 shows average household waste trends in Norway. Total household waste has increased by 9 percent from 2010 to 2016 with rather marginal changes from year to year. On average, Norwegians generated 433 kg of waste per inhabitant in 2016. Even as waste created has increased, less waste was recycled (decreased by 1 percent from 2010 to 2016) (Statistics Norway 2017).

In what follows, an overview of Oslo's waste management system will be provided; and given that household waste has been steadily increasing over the past decade, household waste will be examined closer with a special emphasis on food waste.

Table 1 Household Waste Trends in Norway[1]

	Total (1,000 tonnes)			Percent	
	2010	2015	2016	2010–2016	2015–2016
Municipal Waste	2088	2289	2277	9	−1
Sent to material recovery.[2]	880	867	868	−1	0
	Per Capita (kg)			Percent	
Municipal Waste	424	439	433	2	−1
Sent to material recovery.	179	166	165	−8	−1

[1] The figures have been adjusted to correct for interference of industrial waste in household waste.
[2] Sent to material recovery includes composting and fermentation.
Source: Statistics Norway. 2017.

TOWARD A SOLUTION

The city of Oslo works continuously to encourage its citizens to reuse and prevent the creation of excessive waste in the first place. In Oslo's 2016–2025 waste management strategy, the city states that it aims to reuse and recycle 100 percent of its waste. In June 2017, it won the 2019 European Green Capital Award, which is awarded by the EU commissioner for Environment, Maritime Affairs and Fisheries. The award addresses 12 environment indicators, which include waste management, air quality, biodiversity, noise, and others (EU Commission, 2016b-1).

Oslo provides many opportunities for its citizens to re-use, recycle, and repair. Throughout the city, over 350 curbside points for clothes collection are available. The donated clothes, over 3,700 tonnes in 2015, are then given to two nonprofit organizations. All recycling stations in Oslo have reuse facilities. Overall, not-for-profit organizations collected over 900 tons of items that could be re-used. In addition, in the Alna District of Oslo, a reuse community center has been established leading to 3,200 kg of items re-used by more than 2,700 visitors of the center in 2016. Oslo also provides subsidies for the use of cloth diapers (EU Commission 2016b, 1). Oslo established its Food Bank in 2013. Beside its main social function, one of the goals of the food bank is to reduce food waste by redistributing large consignments from producers and wholesalers to charities. In its first year of operation, 607 tons of food was redistributed. The food bank's work covers a wide area of Eastern Norway, and in its first year over 3,500 meals were served daily (Stensgård and Hannssen 2015).

WASTE COLLECTION AND TREATMENT

Oslo's waste management system is cycle based. Household waste is separated at the source: food waste and plastic packaging are placed in green and blue plastic, respectively (EU Commission 2016b, 1). The colored bags to separate food from plastic waste are available free of charge at Oslo's supermarkets. Electrical waste, glass, and metal packaging are recycled through extended producers responsibility systems (EPR). EPR essentially means that producers are responsible for taking back used goods and recycling them (EU Commission 2014).

The waste is managed through two optical sorting plants for separating food and plastic waste; two incinerator plants to handle residual waste, with a capacity of 310,000 and 100,000 tons each; a biogas plant, with capacity for 50,000 tons of food waste; hazardous waste facility; composting plant, handling garden waste and recycling stations (three large and eight small with more planned) (EU Commission 2016b, 1). In the sorting plants, the colored bags are detected through industrial vision technology and separated for treatment. Any other colored bags will go straight into incineration. Since the collection of food waste in green bags has started, food waste volume has decreased by 5 percent. Food waste is reused by turning it into biogas for buses and waste trucks in Oslo and liquid fertilizer for farmers. Other European cities are inspired by Oslo's waste separation system. For example, Stockholm, Sweden, will implement optical separation of waste starting in 2018 (Holmertz 2015).

Different campaigns, such as door-to-door, media, and celebrity campaigns, were introduced by the city to encourage and promote the use of source separation and better waste management. An analysis conducted in 2016 showed that 44 percent of food waste, 77 percent of cardboard/paper, 27 percent of plastic, and 62 of glass and metal were separated. At least 90 percent of households in Oslo are less than 300 meters away from a recycling station (EU Commission 2016b, 1).

Despite having these initiatives in place and receiving the European Green Capital Award, Oslo still has some issues when it comes to waste management. For example, in early 2017, numerous newspapers reported that the city was struggling with garbage collection. Historically, household waste collection has been done through public procurement. At the end of 2016, a new company won a competition to collect waste in Oslo. After many issues with garbage collection, the company went bankrupt and the municipality took over again in February 2017. However, complaints were still ongoing (Pourramedani 2016; Anon 2017).

SPECIAL FOCUS: FOOD WASTE

Food waste has become a pressing issue for developed countries (Millock 2014). As a result, reducing food waste has gained considerable traction in the last decade in academic research and the popular press. The bulk of studies focus on estimating the amount and impact of food waste, which is hard to do given the lack of reliable data. However, more research is being conducted on what can be done to reduce food waste. Food waste has great environmental impacts and contributes to food insecurity, as wasting food increases demand, which in turn increases the cost of food for everyone. At the household level, wasting less food simply pays off because less money will be spent on the grocery budget.

At the EU-28 level (Norway is not part of the EU-28), it has been estimated that a total of 88 million tonnes of food waste is generated annually (reference year 2012). However, these numbers include edible and inedible parts, and there is great uncertainty around these values. Households are estimated to contribute the most

(47 million +/– 4 million tonnes), followed by the processing sector (17 million tonnes +/– 13 million tonnes). Together these sectors account for over 72 percent of the EU-28's food waste (see Figure 2). The overall cost of food waste in the EU-28 is estimated to be around €143 billion (USD$170 billion) (Stenmarck et al. 2016; Fusions EU 2016b, 1). Recognizing the importance of food waste as a societal issue, a number of countries have implemented or are planning to implement food waste policies and interventions.

According to Stensgård and Hannssen (2016), about 13 percent of total consumption in Norwegian households ends up as food waste, meaning that on average a household throws away every eighth grocery bag. Norway does not have a national policy to reduce food waste, but the country's Ministry of Climate and Environment launched a national waste management and prevention plan, From Waste to Resources, in 2013 in which food waste reduction, in addition to biogas production from organic waste material, is a key element (Fusions EU 2016b, 2). The emphasis is on food waste prevention along the value chain with particular attention paid to households. Information campaigns focus on educating consumers about food labeling, food hygiene, and optimal food storage.

However, the evidence on the impact of providing information to reduce food waste is mixed. While some programs and studies report a decrease in household food waste during information campaigns, such as ForMat in Norway, others report a limited or no impact (Hebrok and Boks 2017). The ForMat project was an initiative to reduce food waste and covered a large part of the food and beverage value chain. The aims of the project were to have an annual study of food waste, communicate research results, and develop food waste prevention strategies. The key results from the project (from 2010 to 2015) show a reduction of edible food waste of 12 percent along the supply chain (industry, wholesale, retail, and households) (Stensgård and Hannssen 2016).

Claudia Schmidt

See also: *Waste Management:* Calgary, Canada: Waste Management Is a National Effort and Calgary's Priority

Further Reading

Anon. 2017. "Oslo's Garbage Problems Pile Up." Views and News from Norway. January 19. http://www.newsinenglish.no/2017/01/19/oslos-garbage-problems-pile-up/

EU Commission. 2014. Development of Guidance on Extended Producer Responsibility (EPR). http://ec.europa.eu/environment/waste/pdf/target_review/Guidance%20on%20EPR%20-%20Final%20Report.pdf.

EU Commission. 2016a. Application Form for the European Green Capital Award 2019: Oslo. http://ec.europa.eu/environment/europeangreencapital/wp-content/uploads/2017/06/City_Introduction.pdf.

EU Commission. 2016b. Application Form for the European Green Capital Award 2019: Waste Production and Management. http://ec.europa.eu/environment/europeangreencapital/wp-content/uploads/2017/06/Indicator_7_Waste_Production_and_Management.pdf.

European Environment Agency. 2016. Municipal Waste Management across European Countries, November 14. https://www.eea.europa.eu/themes/waste/municipal-waste.

Fusions EU. 2016a. Recommendations and Guidelines for a Common European Food Waste Policy Framework. https://www.eu-fusions.org/phocadownload/Publications/D3.5%20recommendations%20and%20guidelines%20food%20waste%20policy%20FINAL.pdf.

Fusions EU. 2016b. Norway—Country Report on National Food Waste Policy. https://www.eu-fusions.org/phocadownload/country-report/NORWAY%2023.02.16.pdf.

Hebrok, M., and C. Boks. 2017. "Household Food Waste: Drivers and Potential Intervention Points for Design—an Extensive Review." *Journal of Cleaner Production* 151: 380–92.

Holmertz, S. 2015. "Oslo's Colourful Solution to Waste Management." *Waste Management World*, June 25. https://waste-management-world.com/a/oslos-colourful-solution-to-waste-management.

Millock, K. 2014. "Greening Household Behaviour and Food." OECD Environment Working Papers.

Parizeau, K., M. von Massow, and R. Martin. 2015. Household-Level Dynamics of Food Waste Production and Related Beliefs, Attitudes, and Behaviours in Guelph, Ontario. *Waste Management* 35: 207–17.

Pourramedani, A. 2016. "The Oslo Municipality Has Received over 20,000 Complaints about Garbage Collection." *Norway Today*, November 30. http://norwaytoday.info/news/oslo-municipality-received-20000-complaints-garbage-collection/.

Statistics Norway. 2014. Waste Accounts 2014. https://www.ssb.no/en/natur-og-miljo/statistikker/avfregno/aar.

Statistics Norway. 2016. Population and Population Changes. https://www.ssb.no/en/befolkning/statistikker/folkemengde/aar-berekna.

Statistics Norway. 2017. Waste from Households. https://www.ssb.no/en/natur-og-miljo/statistikker/avfkomm.

Stenmarck, Å., C. Jensen, T. Quested, and G. Moates. 2016. Estimates of European Food Waste Levels. Commissioned by the European Commission in the FUSION Project.

Stensgård, A. E., and O. J. Hannssen. 2015. Food Waste in Norway. Status and Trends (in Norwegian). http://matsvinn.no/wp-content/uploads/2016/06/ForMat-rapport-2015-translated.pdf.

Stensgård, A. E., and O. J. Hannssen. 2016. Food Waste in Norway 2010–2015. Final Report from the ForMat Project. https://ec.europa.eu/food/sites/food/files/safety/docs/fw_lib_format-rapport-2016-eng.pdf.

Port-au-Prince, Haiti: Challenges of Waste Management under Poor Governance

Solid waste management is an issue of critical importance, with both global and local implications for public health, the environment, and economies. Municipal solid waste (MSW) encompasses all waste (not a liquid or gas) that is discarded by residents and businesses with the exception of hazardous waste. Worldwide, more than 1 billion metric tons of MSW is generated, and this is expected to grow to 2.2 billion by 2025 (Vergara and Tchobanoglous 2012). While the world is rapidly urbanizing, most of this growth is occurring in small and medium-sized cities in low-income countries. In terms of geography, solid waste is largely an urban problem; city residents produce twice as much waste as those living in rural areas

(Hoornweg et al. 2013). Both the quantity and composition of waste produced vary with cultural, environmental, and socioeconomic characteristics. In Port-au-Prince, Haiti, the existing MSW problem is complicated by the geographic context: instability, poor governance, limited human and financial resources, and inadequate disposal practices. However, solutions are available that involve opportunities for the Haitian population, government, and informal sector to create an effective policy framework that aims to improve waste collection, emphasizes the reuse of waste, and considers options for reducing waste and generating renewable energy to sustain a growing population.

Port-au-Prince, the capital of Haiti and one of the poorest countries in the Caribbean, is home to over 2.5 million people. Located on the western portion of the island of Hispaniola, Port-au-Prince is situated on the south-central coast of the Gulf of Gonâve. Given its complex physical geography and environmental context, Haiti is vulnerable to several types of natural hazards, including geophysical, meteorological, and hydrological. According to geologists, Haiti is positioned on the Enriquillo Fault that runs in an east-to-west direction along the northern edge of the Caribbean tectonic plate. The country is bounded in the north by the Septentrional Fault, which crosses into the neighboring Dominican Republic. Devastating earthquakes have occurred as a result of fault slippage since the 1700s, with Port-au-Prince often in the cross hairs (Bilham 2010).

As a result of its coastal location, meteorological and hydrological hazards like tropical storms, hurricanes, and floods frequently disrupt lives in Haiti annually. Small and medium-sized cities like Port-au-Prince, where populations are expected to rise by over 32 percent between 2015 and 2030, will create conditions that increase susceptibility to harm from disasters. Cities characterized by a lack of development planning will see an explosion in slums and shantytowns, thus concentrating the poorest residents, who are often uneducated about hazards, in precarious areas (Birkmann et al. 2016). Given Haiti's poor governance and lack of disaster preparedness and response plans, escalating disaster losses are likely to occur in the future. Haiti's vulnerability to a combination of environmental hazards compromises its capacity to provide basic services and infrastructure like water, sanitation, and solid waste management to its inhabitants.

In terms of water and sanitation infrastructure, Haiti is the most inadequate nation in the Western Hemisphere; only 62 percent of the population had access to an improved water source and 24 percent had access to improved sanitation facilities in 2015 (Gelting et al. 2013; World Health Organization 2015). This lack of access contributed to the rapid spread of cholera in October 2010, and if conditions are not improved, will continue to put Haitian residents at risk. Clearly, current waste disposal practices in Haiti have consequences for both the environment and public health. The majority of households regardless of socioeconomic status in Port-au-Prince use gullies to get rid of their waste; however, almost 90 percent of poor residents prefer this method of waste elimination to others (Bras et al. 2009). Coupled with poor wastewater management and drainage networks, these activities create the potential for infectious disease as demonstrated by the October 2016 cholera outbreak from Hurricane Matthew. Ecologically, runoff from Port-au-Prince pollutes the water and adversely affects species. What's more, seasonal changes may exacerbate this environmental problem; during the rainy season in Port-au-Prince (April–November), waste that is improperly disposed of often blocks drainage channels, worsens flooding, and allows for a toxic mix of contaminants to be introduced to the bay. In addition, groundwater sources are also vulnerable to pollution from urban runoff in Port-au-Prince.

Problems associated with solid waste management are pervasive in Haiti and other low-income nations, but there are specific geographic factors that make Port-au-Prince's waste issues unique. "The current solid waste management system is not integrated; it is characterized by a high level of institutional instability, poor governance, limited human and financial resources, and improper solid waste pre-disposal practices by the urban communities. The challenge has been exacerbated by rapid and uncontrolled urbanization, political instability, social upheaval and the continuing variations in waste composition as a result of radical changes in residents' consumption patterns and lifestyles" (Noel 2010, 1). Lack of city planning and variability in waste management strategies and technologies further complicate the problem.

Although Haiti lacks any kind of national waste management plan or legislation, the Haitian government established the Metropolitan Solid Waste Collection Services (SMCRS) in 1981, thus making municipalities responsible for waste management (Riquelme et al. 2016). Since its creation, SMCRS has been responsible for the collection, transport, and disposal of solid waste generated in Port-au-Prince. Since

Haitian commuters pass by trash dumped along a street in the Port-au-Prince neighborhood of Martissant, 2013. Open dumping can lead to water pollution and the outbreak of diseases like cholera. (Thony Belizaire/AFP/Getty Images)

the 1990s, the SMCRS has suffered from budgetary constraints that have rendered their operations ineffective. For over a decade, solid waste collection and disposal in Port-au-Prince has been primarily funded by a combination of international nongovernmental organizations (NGO), the private sector, and the informal solid waste sector that include individuals who sort, collect, dispose of, and resell waste.

Compared to other world regions, Latin America and the Caribbean have the most robust and reliable data on solid waste generation. Yet experts agree that the data on solid waste production in Port-au-Prince is inconsistent. Estimates of total solid waste in the Port-au-Prince urban area range from 660 tons per day to over 1,600 tons per day. To be clear, there are no data on solid waste generation in Port-au-Prince city, which makes it difficult to assess trends in consumption patterns over time. Similarly, no data exists on solid waste collection in greater Port-au-Prince. In what is probably the most comprehensive and frequently cited data source on solid waste management, Hoornweg and Bhada-Tata (2012) put forth a snapshot of waste practices around the world, placing emphasis on production, composition, collection, and disposal by nation and by region. As shown in Table 1, total waste generation varies in cities around the globe. The population size and level of economic development certainly play a role in the amount of waste that is produced, but they do not tell the whole story. Public health and other demographic indicators would likely allow for a more in-depth understanding of these trends. However, these data should be interpreted with caution due to inconsistencies in definitions of solid waste, data collection procedures, time period, and accuracy.

Composition of solid waste is influenced by a number of factors including economic development, geographic location, and cultural norms and affects how often waste is collected and how it is disposed. Findings of the only study on

Table 1 Select Cities and Associated Waste Generation Rates

City	Data Source	Year	Population	Total Waste (Tons/Day)
Beijing, China	Hoornweg et al. 2005	2000	10,839,000	9,755
Manila, Philippines	UNSD, 2009	2007	1,660,714	4,975
Rio de Janeiro, Brazil	PAHO, 2005	2001	5,857,904	7,059
Port-au-Prince, Haiti	PAHO, 2005	2001	1,100,085	660
Kolkata, India	CPCB, 2005	2005	4,572,876	2,652
Guatemala City, Guatemala	PAHO, 2005	2001	2,541,581	2,415
Ouagadougou, Burkina Faso	UNDP, 2009	2002	876,200	693
Minsk, Belarus	UNSD, 2009	2007	1,806,200	2,182
Mexico City, Mexico	PAHO, 2005	2001	8,615,955	11,890
Tbilisi, Georgia	UNSD, 2009	2007	1,300,000	1,064

Source: World Bank. *What a Waste: A Global Review of Solid Waste Management.*

Table 2 Waste Composition in Port-au-Prince, Haiti

Organic matter	75
Sand and coal	8
Paper and cardboard	3
Glass	2
Metal	3
Plastic	7
Other	2

Source: Bras et al. 2009.

solid waste composition conducted in Port-au-Prince are summarized in Table 2 and illustrate that the majority of waste is organic matter. This may include items like food scraps, yard clippings, and wood. This finding is consistent with that of Hoornweg and Bhada-Tata (2012), which showed that low-income countries have higher rates of organic matter in their solid waste compared to their high-income counterparts. Examining common building materials, construction practices, and energy sources used for heating, lighting, and cooking in Port-au-Prince may help explain why the second-highest component in solid waste was sand and coal. Recent trends suggest that plastic waste in Haiti has grown considerably since the late 1980s when that study was undertaken in Port-au-Prince. In an effort to counter this growing pollutant, the Haitian government passed legislation banning the import of polyethylene bags and polystyrene Styrofoam containers in 2012, although some question the effectiveness given poor enforcement and monitoring of the law.

The disposal mechanisms of municipal solid waste vary geographically and much like the composition of waste, are influenced by economic growth, governance, and other cultural factors. Generally, final waste disposal options exist on a spectrum ranging from open-air dumps to sanitary landfills. Open-air dumps refer to those sites where waste is disposed of aimlessly without any consideration for public health and the environment. A sanitary landfill, essentially the opposite of an open-air dump, puts into place safeguards to minimize risks of harm to the environment and public health. Sanitary landfills are the most common form of waste disposal in the United States. Unlike open-air dumps, sanitary landfills are sites where solid waste is spread out, compacted, and covered daily with clay, foam, or other material to keep the content dry and minimize leakage of contaminated water or leachate. Because the waste is not exposed, it reduces aesthetic concerns like odor and susceptibility to pests. A controlled dump, a waste disposal option that exists somewhere between an open-air dump and a sanitary landfill, is referred to as a site that is somewhat managed. Often these controlled dumps are locations of sanitary landfills that have simply stopped being maintained over the years. Finally, unsanitary landfills, like the name suggests, are those sites where waste is not exposed; however, environmental defenses like liners are not implemented to reduce harm to people and the environment.

> **Haiti Earthquake of January 2010**
>
> Although Haiti is no stranger to seismic events, the 7.0 magnitude January 12, 2010 earthquake was the most destructive to date, resulting in over 230,000 fatalities and more than a million displaced individuals. This rupture triggered an unprecedented response by the international humanitarian aid community, generating over $13.5 billion in pledges and donations to assist with recovery efforts. The Presidential Palace, National Cathedral, and United Nations (UN) Stabilization Mission Headquarters were annihilated in the earthquake like the majority of poorly built and engineered dwellings and their remains scattered amongst the rubble in downtown Port-au-Prince. Earthquakes will continue to pose a significant risk to Haitian residents, particularly in Port-au-Prince where buildings are not constructed to be resistant to seismic hazards and no building code currently exists.

In Haiti, the main MSW disposal site is the 160-hectare Truitier open-air dump that is located 10 kilometers from downtown Port-au-Prince. Managed by SMCRS, Truitier is estimated to receive approximately 1,000 tons of waste daily (Riquelme et al. 2016). As shown in Table 3, this is not an uncommon method of waste disposal in the Caribbean, with over half of the countries utilizing it as at least one option for final removal of solid waste. Interestingly, nearly all countries with the exception of Haiti, Jamaica, and Suriname rely on more advanced methods of solid waste disposal. In fact, some countries like the Bahamas and St. Lucia tend to rely on more than one mechanism for waste disposal. Given that both of these countries attract large numbers of visitors each year due to the thriving tourism sector, solid waste disposal may be a higher priority compared to other Caribbean nations. It could also be that St. Lucia and the Bahamas receive more money from the resorts and other tourism-based industries that allow them to afford more advanced means of solid waste disposal. On a positive note, the majority of Caribbean countries favor solid waste disposal mechanisms that at least attempt to minimize contamination to the surrounding populations and environments (see Table 3). In places like Trinidad and Tobago where the primary disposal options are unsanitary landfills, although the physical infrastructure and capacity exist to convert these locations to sanitary landfills, it may be complicated because the agencies responsible for solid waste management are comprised of a combination of public and private entities.

Given the multiple challenges that Haiti faces when it comes to waste disposal, there are a number of strategies for moving forward and improving waste disposal mechanisms and quality of life for Haitian residents. First, there is a demonstrated need for standardized data collection and research on waste production and management, especially in less developed countries. Further, mechanisms of waste reuse, particularly common in cities like Port-au-Prince, should be examined and quantified. Waste management legislation and policy and a planning framework are required. Second, an MSW policy will only be successful in Haiti if it enlists the participation and cooperation of Haitian citizens, the informal sector, waste collectors, and government (Bras et al. 2009). Finally, given the composition of MSW

Table 3 Waste Disposal Methods by Country in the Caribbean

Country	Waste Disposal Mechanism
Bahamas	• Three sanitary landfills • Five unsanitary landfills • One open-air dump
Barbados	One sanitary landfill
Belize	One sanitary landfill
Guyana	One sanitary landfill
Haiti	One open-air dump
Jamaica	Eight open-air dumps
St. Lucia	• One sanitary landfill • One controlled dump
Suriname	One open-air dump
Trinidad and Tobago	6 unsanitary landfills

Source: IDB Caribbean, 2016.

in Haiti, opportunities exist in composting and anaerobic digestion, which could improve waste disposal and sanitation as well as create clean energy for a growing population (Booth et al. 2010).

Jennifer Haney

See also: Waste Management: Cairo, Egypt: The Zabaleen; Dakar, Senegal: Peri-Urban/Urban Agriculture and Urban Waste Management

Further Reading

Bilham, Roger. 2010. "Lessons from the Haiti Earthquake." *Nature* 463: 878–79.

Birkmann, Joern, Torsten Welle, William Solecki, Shuaib Lwasa, and Matthias Garschagen. 2016. "Boost Resilience of Small and Mid-sized Cities." *Nature* 537: 605–08.

Booth, Samuel, Kip Funk, and Scott Haase. 2010. *Haiti Waste-to-Energy Opportunity Analysis.* National Renewable Energy Laboratory. https://www.monroecollege.edu/uploadedFiles/_Site_Assets/PDF/Haiti_Waste-to-Energy_Final_Nov-14-2010.pdf.

Bras, Anie, Chantal Berdier, Evens Emmanuel, and M. Zimmerman. 2009. "Problems and Current Practices of Solid Waste Management in Port-au-Prince (Haiti)." *Waste Management* 29: 2707–09.

Gelting, Richard, Katherine Bliss, Molly Patrick, Gabriella Lockhart, and Thomas Handzel. 2013. "Water, Sanitation, and Hygiene in Haiti: Past, Present, and Future." *American Journal of Tropical Medicine and Hygiene* 89, 4: 665–70.

Hoornweg, Daniel, and Perinaz Bhada-Tata. 2012. *What a Waste: A Global Review of Solid Waste Management.* Washington, DC: World Bank. https://siteresources.worldbank.org/INTURBANDEVELOPMENT/Resources/336387-1334852610766/What_a_Waste2012_Final.pdf.

Hoornweg, Daniel, Perinaz Bhada-Tata, and Chris Kennedy. 2013. "Waste Production Must Peak This Century." *Nature* 502: 615–17.

Noel, Claude. 2010. "Solid Waste Workers and Livelihood Strategies in Greater Port-au-Prince, Haiti." *Waste Management* 30: 1138–48.

Riquelme, Rodrigo, Paola Mendez, and Ianthe Smith. 2016. *Solid Waste Management in the Caribbean: Proceedings from the Caribbean Solid Waste Conference.* Inter-American Development Bank. https://publications.iadb.org/bitstream/handle/11319/7650/Solid-Waste-Management-in-the-Caribbean-Proceedings-from-the-Caribbean-Solid-Waste-Conference.pdf?sequence=1.

SWANA Haiti Response Team. 2010. *Municipal Solid Waste Collection Needs in Port-au-Prince, Haiti.* Solid Waste Management Association of North America (SWANA). http://swana.org/Portals/Press_Releases/Hurricane/Haiti_Response_Team_Position_Paper_2010.pdf.

Vergara, Sintana E., and George Tchobanoglous. 2012. "Municipal Solid Waste and the Environment: A Global Perspective." *Annual Review of Environment and Resources* 37: 277–309.

World Health Organization (WHO). 2015. *Haiti: Sanitation, Drinking-Water and Hygiene Status Overview.* http://www.who.int/water_sanitation_health/glaas/2014/haiti-22-oct.pdf.

San Francisco, United States: Becoming a "Zero-Waste City"

San Francisco is an impressive example of successful waste management on a large scale in the American continent. Labeled the "Silicon Valley of recycling" by Matt Richtel from the *New York Times* (Richtel 2016) San Francisco has built on a more than 100-year tradition of recycling and on the civil-engagement culture of its citizens to address the practical challenges of day-to-day waste management. In the last 20 years, San Francisco became a leading force in the zero-waste movement, as the goal of cities looking to decrease its waste to zero (Zaman 2015), Becoming an example for other North American cities, San Francisco is now the place where zero waste can showcase its positive impacts in transforming the civil culture of communities and the ways in which city officials address waste management challenges (Cohen 2016).

Traditionally, waste management in large American cities is structured having multiple centrally located landfills to which fleets of hundreds of trucks deliver the waste collected one small load at the time from hundreds of thousands of sources during hundreds of trips a day crisscrossing the city streets. Both the landfills and the trucks are owned either by the municipalities or by one or many private contractors that compete among themselves to earn the bid to provide the service to the city. In the process of waste collection and waste management, city streets fill with gas emissions from the dump trucks, smells from the organic waste, and depressing images of trash waiting to be collected, impacting the idea that visitors have of a place and the quality of life of its residents.

In a highly touristic city such as San Francisco, with beautiful sights and a booming economy, waste management has a top priority for local officials and residents that has embraced state mandates in waste diversion, turning them into opportunities for revenue and job creation in the city. In fact, despite its lack of glamour, waste management is gaining momentum as business opportunities in American cities evolve to become a green industry with several different areas of implementation.

Some of these areas such as composting and organics that had been traditionally undervalued within the waste business are rising to participate in the generation of profits and in providing solutions to environmental issues such as greenhouse emissions (Eilperin 2013).

Waste diversion, as the amount of waste that ends in a landfill decreases, is an important element of what now is called the "circular economy" (Stahel 2016) in which nothing goes to waste; rather, materials are recovered and then reused or transformed into other materials, giving new monetary value to what traditionally has been sent to the landfill. For a city such as San Francisco, the monetary value of these elements is an important incentive, but not the only one, since by incorporating waste diversion practices, in the long term, cities became more sustainable, helping to decrease human impact over limited natural resources (Seadon 2010).

The success of San Francisco in managing waste has an important component in the relationship that local residents have with their waste. In large urban areas, most residents see their waste as a necessary by-product of their consumption habits and daily activities such as cooking and eating. Trash is an unwanted by-product that magically disappears through the building chute, or from the street curb where the trash bin is left full and many hours later is found empty. However, in San Francisco, reuse and recycle, as strategies to increase the life of a product, are not new to its residents (Recology). A set of public actions, policy changes, and aggressive education campaigns has changed the way people relate to their trash making; this is the first component of their success in waste management.

Federal, state, and municipal legislation created the legal framework for San Francisco and other California cities to set ambitious goals for waste management. Since 1970, San Francisco, with the signing of the Federal Clean Air Act and Clean Water Act, started creating community recycling centers offering residents a place to recycle material with monetary value, such as cans, glass, or newspapers (Platt et al. 2009).

In 1989, the state adopted the California Integrated Waste Management Act (State of California 1989, Chapter 1095, as amended) known as AB 939 where the State Legislature declared solid waste management as a shared responsibility between state and local governments and directed the city to create and implement a local integrated waste management plan (IWMP). Under this legislation, cities' IWMP defines the programs that, through recycling and decrease of waste, will meet solid waste diversion goals of 25 percent by 1995 and 50 percent by 2000 (CalRecycle 1997). The 1997 Sustainability Plan adopted by the Board of Supervisors included a long-term goal "to maximize sustainable uses of natural resources and to eliminate solid waste generation in the City and County of San Francisco."

In 2001, San Francisco established a commingled recycling process to make recycling easy for citizens. A large recycling facility was built at Pier 96 and opened in 2002 to sort the material into more than 16 different categories that are packed and sold to individual manufacturers using reused products such as glass, paper, cardboard, and so on (Bryant et al. 2011). Pier 96 is currently the larger recycling center in the city, sorting more than 750 tons of material every day, six days a week, and has evolved to become a key component of the strategy to achieve 75 percent diversion goals established by the Board of Supervisors in 2002 and the long-term zero-waste goals of the city.

Workers at Sunset Scavenger sort recycled construction materials in San Francisco, California, May 12, 2009. Later that week, the San Francisco Mandatory Recycling and Composting Ordinance went into effect, requiring citizens to separate their trash into recyclable, compostable, and landfill material. San Francisco plans to become the first Zero Waste city in the continental United States by the year 2020. (Justin Sullivan/Getty Images)

However, it was in 2009, that the San Francisco Board of supervisors took recycling to a higher level, passing the San Francisco Mandatory Recycling and Composting Ordinance known as No 100–09 requiring individuals to participate in recycling and composting programs by separating their trash into either recyclables, compostable, or landfill material. This law, called the toughest recycling law in the United States by the *San Francisco Chronicle*, was an aggressive attempt to cut greenhouse emissions and to stop waste going to the landfills. The law set the foundation for the three-bin system where every resident will have a blue bin for recyclables, a black bin for landfill, and a green bin for compostable material (Cote 2009).

San Francisco's geographic location and population density made it the least likely place for a success story in waste management practices. With a population of over 860,000, the city generates total waste estimates of 1.7 kg waste per capita per day for the year (San Francisco Department of the Environment 2007a). Located at the tip of a narrow peninsula and therefore surrounded by water, the city has limited spaces for waste disposal. Also, the city's hilly terrain and high concentrations of inhabitants living in apartments offer more than a challenge for trucks to do their collections and for residents to bring their waste to the bins. Yet the city has achieved nearly 80 percent of zero waste and plans to become the first zero-waste city in the American continent by the year 2020 (Sreenivasan 2013).

The challenge of waste diversion from the landfill for San Francisco is enormous, yet it has a single private contractor, Recology, with three companies that collect, transfer and process the city's waste. Recology is responsible for executing waste management policies, decreasing the negative factors of city waste, and maintaining the quality of life for its citizens.

But waste diversion and waste management are only one piece of the process toward zero waste in San Francisco. Preventing the generation of waste by buying less and reusing what a person has are key components that stop waste at its source, addressing the consumer's own behaviors. This is done through an education campaign that has consumers' and producers' responsibility as its core and looks to change the culture of waste generation at its root. The San Francisco Department of the Environment defines consumer responsibility as taking personal responsibility for the environmental cost of the products purchased, suggesting that people acquire simple habits to minimize waste generation. Some of these new habits include bringing their own bags when shopping, purchasing products that can be recycled or made from recycled material, buying local products that don't require transportation cost, and repurposing bags and packing material after purchasing an item. In the case of producer responsibility, the Bag Reduction Ordinance and the Cigarette Litter Abatement fee are two examples of policies implemented by the city to encourage responsibility by producers (SF Department of the Environment 2007). Because consumer habits in the generation of waste are similar across cultures, San Francisco's strategies in modifying their citizens' practices can be adopted by other cities in the world (C40 Cities n.d.).

The pursuit of an ambitious program such as zero waste in San Francisco has been not been without intense scrutiny. A 2014 lawsuit against Recology argued that the city has estimates of the amount of material diverted from the landfill higher than their actual values. The analysis of Samantha MacBride, an assistant professor at the City University of New York, shows that the problem was related to the way San Francisco counted the material going to the landfill that amounted to almost 20 percent less in its diversion rates claims (Minter 2014). This miscalculation may affect San Francisco's reputation as a leading city in the zero-waste movement in North America, and has renewed an old discussion within the zero-waste movement of how society understands its zero-waste goals and the choices made to manage consumption and waste.

In fact, San Francisco and other large cities embraced zero waste as a goal within their efforts to reduce, reuse, and recycle, where large percentages of waste are diverted from the landfill and recycled goods are reintroduced to the manufacturing process. But this approach is quite different from the way zero waste was originally conceptualized. In its origins in the 1970s, zero waste started as a movement to reengineer consumption habits to make the most out of the products that are manufactured. The hope was that by extending their life cycle through repurposing them, society will, in the long term, reduce the number of products needed and the stress over raw materials and natural resources. Manufactured products will have a longer life cycle, reducing the need for newer ones and decreasing the need for more manufacturing with an ultimate goal that no materials will go to landfills or incinerators (Zerowasteinstitute 2009). Taking this approach, greater responsibility rests with the designers and manufacturers of goods and with the consumers to modify their habits.

Considering the challenges to society of pursuing zero-waste goals in their original form, governments such as California and the city of San Francisco, as well as large corporations have chosen to apply a modified version of the original concept, acknowledging a progressive change in consumer habits and manufacturers' process with, nevertheless, a positive impact in the amount of material going to the landfill or used in incinerators (Townsend 2010). In this context, cities in the United States still have in San Francisco a working model of how to move forward toward the goals of zero waste and a lot of work ahead of them when considering that Americans generated nearly 35 million tons of food waste in 2010 and 97 percent of that went into landfills.

Mario A. Giraldo

See also: Pollution: Boston, United States: Cleaning Boston's Waterways—An Overview; *Waste Management:* Oslo, Norway: Prevention and Reduction, What Makes Oslo Clean

Further Reading

Bryant, Julie, Kevin Drew, Robert Haley, and Jack Macy. 2011. "The Story of Zero Waste." *Resource Recycling*: 26–28. http://www.oas.org/en/sedi/dsd/Biodiversity/Sustainable_Cities/Sustainable_Communities/Events/SC%20Course%20Jamaica%202016/Module%20IV/Resource%20Recycling%20SF%20Zero%20Waste%202011.pdf.

C40 Cities. https://www.c40.org/history.

CalRecycle. 1997. History of California Solid Waste Law, 1985–1989. https://www.calrecycle.ca.gov/laws/legislation/calhist/1985to1989.htm.

Cohen, Steven. 2016. "Zero Waste in San Francisco and New York: A Tale of Two Cities." *Huffington Post*, March 28. http://www.huffingtonpost.com/steven-cohen/zero-waste-in-san-francis_b_9556380.html.

Cote, John. 2009. "S.F. OKs Toughest Recycling Law in U.S." *San Francisco Chronicle* (SF Gate) June 10. http://www.sfgate.com/green/article/S-F-OKs-toughest-recycling-law-in-U-S-3295664.php.

Eilperin, Juliet. 2013. "Composting Efforts Gain Traction across the United States." *Washington Post*, February 3. https://www.washingtonpost.com/national/health-science/composting-efforts-gain-traction-across-the-united-states/2013/02/03/645a7024-670c-11e2-9e1b-07db1d2ccd5b_story.html.

Minter, Adam. 2014. "San Francisco's Recycling Claims Are Garbage." *Bloomberg View*, July 12. https://www.bloomberg.com/view/articles/2014-07-11/san-francisco-s-recycling-claims-are-garbage.

Platt, B., Naomi Friedman, Carolyn Grodinksy, and Margaret Suozzo. 2009. "In-Depth Studies of Recycling and Composting Programs: Designs, Costs, Results." Volume 3, Urban Areas. Institute for Local Self Reliance: 151–162. www.ilsr.org/in-depth-studies-of-recycling-and-composting-programs-designs-costs-results-volumes-i-ii-and-iii-2.

Recology. n.d. "Over 100 Years of Service." https://www.recology.com/about-us/#our-history.

Richtel, Matt. 2016. "San Francisco 'The Silicon Valley' of Recycling." *New York Times*, March 25. https://www.nytimes.com/2016/03/29/science/san-francisco-the-silicon-valley-of-recycling.html.

San Francisco Department of the Environment. 2007a. SF Achieves 69% Recycling. Press Release, April 25. http://sfenvironment.org/news/press-release/sf-acheives-69-recycling.

San Francisco Department of the Environment. 2007b. "Checkout Bag Ordinance Fact Sheet." October. https://sfenvironment.org/sites/default/files/agenda/attach/checkout_bag_ordinance_factsheet_and_information_0.pdf.

Seadon, Jeffrey K. 2010. "Sustainable Waste Management Systems." *Journal of Cleaner Production* 18: 1639–51. http://www.sciencedirect.com/science/article/pii/S0959652610002672.

Sreenivasan, Hari. 2013. "San Francisco on Track to Become Zero Waste City." National Public Radio, News Hour, January 25. https://sfenvironment.org/video/pbs-news hour-san-francisco-on-track-to-become-zero-waste-city.

Stahel, Walter R. 2016. "The Circular Economy." *Nature* 531 (March 24): 435–38. http://www.nature.com/news/the-circular-economy-1.19594.

State of California, 1989. *The Integrated Waste Management Act*: "California Integrated Waste Management Act (IWMA) of 1989." Status AB939, Chapter 1096, section 2. 1989. https://leginfo.legislature.ca.gov/faces/codes_displayText.xhtml?lawCode=PRC&division=30.&title=&part=1.&chapter=1.&article=2.

Townsend, W. K. 2010. "Zero Waste: An Aspiration or an Oxymoron?" *Waste Management & Research* 28, 1: 1–3. http://wmr.sagepub.com/content/28/1/1.

Zaman, Atiq Uz. 2015. "A Comprehensive Review of the Development of Zero Waste Management: Lessons Learned and Guidelines." *Journal of Cleaner Production* 91 (March 15): 12–25. http://www.sciencedirect.com/science/article/pii/S0959652614013018.

Zerowasteinstitute. 2009. http://zerowasteinstitute.org/.

Singapore City, Singapore: Managing Food Waste

Singapore is both a city and an island country in Southeast Asia. Located just to the north of the equator, between Malaysia and Indonesia, the city sits in the tropical zone. The climate is typically hot, humid, and rainy with two monsoon seasons all year round. Singapore is one of the most densely populated cities in the world. In a total area of 690 square kilometers, slightly larger than the city of Chicago, Illinois. It has a population of 5.6 million, more than twice as large as Chicago's 2.7 million. With virtually no natural resources, such as forests, oil deposits, or farmland, Singapore's economy depends primarily on financial services, trade, limited oil-refining industries, and a highly trained human capital. The per capita GDP is $87,885 (IMF 2016), ranking within the top 10 in the world.

The limited territorial space, densely populated communities, highly commercialized environment, and tropical climate are some of the factors that contribute to Singapore's top challenge—handling 8,559 tons of municipal solid waste (MSW) produced on a daily basis, and in a timely fashion. Moreover, 22 percent of Singapore's MSW is food waste (FW), according to the National Environment Agency (NEA 2016). In a sense, managing FW is an integral part of Singaporean households' daily occupation.

CHALLENGES OF HANDLING FOOD WASTE

What is the situation of food wastage in Singapore? A household waste study commissioned by the National Environment Agency (NEA) has found that FW accounts for about half of the waste disposed of by the typical Singapore household on a daily basis. Of this quantity, more than half could have been prevented through actions such as not over-ordering, overbuying, or overcooking. The amount of avoidable FW is equivalent to each household throwing away a 2.5 kg bag of rice every week. In addition, the study reveals that rice, noodles, and bread are the most commonly wasted food items (NEA 2017). A survey conducted in 2015 shows that 77 percent of Singaporeans regularly waste food at home, 92 percent leave leftovers in the fridge for other family members, 29 percent do not eat leftovers, and 48 percent leave leftovers in the fridge to discard later (Mendoza 2015). That being said, Singapore's FW situation is far from extraordinary.

Comparative data of 2013 shows that among the four "Asian Tigers," Singapore's daily per capita generated FW was .40 kg, lower than .51 kg in Hong Kong, and .80 kg in Taiwan, but far higher than South Korea's level in 2006 of .26 kg (Ng et al. 2015). Lower FW in South Korea is presumably due to a system known as "pay-as-you-throw," whereby consumers are electronically billed for FW they generate. The system was put in trial in South Korea in 2005 in selected cities, and was gradually implemented nationwide (Asia Today 2013). Unlike Hong Kong, Taiwan, and South Korea, however, FW reduction in Singapore is particularly difficult due to the lack of two of the common venues: 1) feeding hungry people, and 2) feeding livestock. In Singapore, high incomes and well-stocked social services have determined that the population in poverty is relatively small, and can't be a significant solution to surplus food. Reliance on the local livestock feed stream is also low, since over 90 percent of Singapore's food is imported (Agri-food & Veterinary Authority 2017). This means that FW management must primarily rely on other methods.

TREATMENT PRACTICES

Typically, FW is generated from two sources in Singapore: 1) municipal use, such as households, hotels, and restaurants; and b) by-products generated by food and beverage industries. A main difference between these two streams of FW is that industrial FW tends to be uniform and easier to treat, while municipal FW, due to its low level of purity, tends to require more work to separate the materials for recycling purposes and, hence, is more costly and time-consuming. The concept of recycling with respect to FW refers to conversion of FW to usable products, such as bioenergy, animal feeds, and organic fertilizers.

LANDFILL AND INCINERATION

Landfill had been the standard FW treatment until 1979, and multiple dump sites had been in service. In 1979, the NEA decided to adopt incineration because it allows harvesting of renewable energy. FW is considered a good candidate to be reduced through the "waste-to-energy" (WTE) process. The first WTE plant was commissioned in 1979. Today, Singapore runs four WTE plants located at Tuas and Senoko. There is one landfill offshore in operation, the Semakau Landfill. It receives non-incinerable waste and incineration ashes. The typical incineration process includes the following steps:

1. Incinerable waste is transported to the WTE plant where the transportation vehicle is weighed and its content discharged.
2. The storage temperature is reduced below atmospheric level to contain the odor of the refuse.
3. Waste material is crushed to sizes suitable for incineration, and is then incinerated in a temperature between 850–1,000 degrees Fahrenheit. Generated heat is used to produce electricity.
4. The gas cleaning system removes dust and pollutants from the flue gas before releasing it into the atmosphere through tall chimneys of 150 meters.
5. Ferrous scrap metal is collected and sent to recycling plants, and ashes are sent to the Semakau dump site. (NEA, 2017)

The WTE process contributes 2 percent of Singapore's electricity supply, according to the Ministry of the Environment and Water Resources (MEWR). Additionally, incineration yields the following benefits: it reduces waste volume by over 90 percent, which is considered effective in treating FW; and it does not produce leachate as do landfills. Leachate is known to contaminate groundwater and surface water, and has also been found to induce mosquito-borne diseases in tropical regions, such as dengue, which is considered a threat in Singapore by the NEA. However, the drawback of incineration is also obvious: it produces air-polluting gasses despite diligent efforts of control. As such, incineration typically requires intensive labor to sort out the materials, and a large portion of the work is done by hand. Moreover, incineration plants are expensive to build, costing close to $659 million per plant, compared to the Semakau landfill facilities that cost about 40 percent less. Since 1999, almost all landfills in Singapore have been shut down; FW treatment has been the job of WTE plants (Murdoch 2008).

ANAEROBIC DIGESTION AND COMPOSTING

Anaerobic digestion (AD) and composting both utilize biological processes to break down organic materials and generate renewable energy or reusable products. The anaerobic process takes place in an environment without oxygen and produces methane gas that can be captured, purified (by removing carbon dioxide, nitrogen, and oxygen), and fed through pipelines to end users. The method is broadly used in treating sewage sludge and FW. Because AD needs wet substrates for the biological reaction to sustain its process, and FW is often high in solids and requires added moisture, Singapore scientists developed the "anaerobic co-digestion" (AC) process. This process combines FW, sewage sludge, and "brown water" (feces with flush water) to synergistically produce biogas. In practice, as part of urban infrastructure design, the municipality builds co-digesters between FW and sewage collecting points (Ng et al. 2017). One advantage of AC is that it contributes to saving freshwater that is in short supply in Singapore. Every year, converting seawater to drinking water costs Singapore millions of dollars. Another benefit is that the process is capable of producing aviation fuel as a by-product. Emerging technologies have made it possible to harvest grease and cooking oil from the AC process to produce high-quality aviation fuel. Since 2016, NEA has set up experimental sites to pilot use AC technology.

COMPOSTING

Composting yields fertilizers that every garden needs. In Singapore, due to limited spaces, composting is done on a much smaller scale compared to the municipal AC systems. Because composting is manageable in the household space, it has become a hobby for some environment-loving citizens. One eye-catching activity is "vermicomposting," which uses earthworms to digest FW. Worm bins as well as worms are sold in the markets. TV stations air demo programs to help households set up the system. Worms used for vermicomposting typically include *Eisneia foetida, Lubricus rubellus* (both are red-colored worms), and *Perionyx excavates* (blue worms). For vermicomposting fans, it is a thrill to watch the process live. A blogger says, "It essentially turns trash to high-grade fertilizer with the help of composting worms. We enjoy this method as we get to interact with 'friendly crawlies' (it is quite therapeutic to watch and handle them!)" (*Straits Times* 2017).

FUTURE DEVELOPMENT

Singapore's waste management strategy will gradually shift to an integrative approach to achieve its "Zero Waste National" goal, according to the NEA. In addition to WTE, landfill, and composting, the government encourages citizens to maximally reduce (use only what you need), reuse (reuse things for the same or a new purpose), and recycle (convert waste into useful products), better known as the three "R's." In addition, hotels, schools, shopping malls, and restaurants are encouraged to use on-site food treatment systems to compost FW. More convenient recycling equipment, such as color-coded bins, will also be provided to households. Singapore is striving to push FW management forward as a social movement.

Overall, Singaporeans are highly conscious of environmental protection. Most households strive to maintain a competitive level of waste reduction. Compared with Western countries, they generate less trash per person per day than in the United States and Europe, and send very little to landfills. According to data gathered by the *Wall Street Journal*, Singaporeans send 3.8 lb per person per day, vs. 4.4 lb in the U.S. and 4.9 lb in Europe to dump sites. Moreover, out of the total solid waste, only 2 percent of the MSW is sent to landfill and 60 percent is recycled, which compares to 53 percent and 34 percent respectively in the U.S., and 31 percent and 43 percent respectively in Europe (Yep 2015). The limited land area is certainly among many factors that encourage Singaporeans to reduce MSW in every possible way.

Table 1 shows the statistics of the amount of FW generated in the past 10 years, showing the progress of a better recycling rate each year in Singapore.

Table 1 Singapore's Food Waste

Year	Food Waste Disposed of (tonne)	Food Waste Recycled (tonne)	Total Food Waste Generated (tonne)	Recycling Rate (%)
2016	679,900	111,100	791,000	14%
2015	681,400	104,100	785,500	13%
2014	687,200	101,400	788,600	13%
2013	696,000	100,000	796,000	13%
2012	618,100	85,100	703,200	12%
2011	605,800	69,700	675,500	10%
2010	538,100	102,400	640,500	16%
2009	529,400	76,700	606,100	13%
2008	500,000	68,000	568,000	12%
2007	507,700	51,200	558,900	9%

Source: NEA.

EDUCATION

Globally, approximately 1.3 billion tons of food are wasted each year, or one-third produced for human consumption, a direct economic cost of $750 billion annually. On average, per capita FW is between 95 and 115 kilograms a year in Europe and North America. By contrast, in sub-Saharan Africa, south and southeastern Asia, the per capita waste is 6–11 kg annually. If one-fourth of this waste is avoided, there would be enough to feed 870 million hungry people in the world, according to an estimate by the UN (FAO 2013). Singapore's National Environment Agency includes these data in educational programs. "Love Your Food @ Schools," for example, is one of the NEA's school programs aimed at encouraging students to cherish food and take action to reduce food wastage. The program introduces a closed-loop food waste management system on school premises. Students and staff reduce the amount of FW and use canteen stall holders to segregate FW for treatment using on-site food waste digesters. To further spread awareness of the importance of FW minimization and recycling, students join neighboring community partners in learning journeys to share information. The NEA provides detailed guidelines and tips for saving food (NEA 2016). Obviously, Singapore strives to make every citizen understand that their healthy living depends on sustaining the fragile environment they are in.

Jing Luo

See also: *Energy and Sustainability:* Singapore City, Singapore: Go Solar!; *Waste Management:* Kobe, Japan: The Cleanest City in the World

Further Reading

Agri-food & Veterinary Authority of Singapore (AVA)s. http://www.ava.gov.sg/.

Asia Today. 2013. "South Korea's Food Waste Solution: You Waste, You Pay." *Asia Today.* April 25. http://www.asiatoday.com/pressrelease/south-koreas-food-waste-solution-you-waste-you-pay.

Food and Agriculture Organization of the United Nations. n.d. "Food Waste Harms Climate, Water, Land, and Biodiversity—New FAO Report." http://www.fao.org/news/story/en/item/196220/icode/.

The International Monetary Fund. n.d. http://imf.org.

Mendoza, Don. 2015. "Singaporeans Regularly Waste Food, Survey Finds." *Today*, October 15. http://www.todayonline.com/singapore/singaporeans-regularly-waste-food-survey-finds.

Ministry of the Environment and Water Resources (MEWR). n.d. http://www.mewr.gov.sg/.

Murdoch, Gillian. 2008. "Trash and Burn: Singapore's Waste Problem." *Reuters*, May 21. http://www.reuters.com/article/us-waste-singapore-idUSSP9046620080522.

National Environmental Agency (NEA). 2016. "Love Your Food." https://www.nea.gov.sg/docs/default-source/resource/fwrguide.pdf.

National Environmental Agency (NEA). 2017. "Half of Food Waste Thrown Away by Singapore Households Can Be Prevented: NEA Household Waste Study." http://www.nea.gov.sg/corporate-functions/newsroom/news-releases/half-of-food-waste-thrown-away-by-singapore-households-can-be-prevented-nea-household-waste-study.

National Environmental Agency of Singapore (NEA). http://www.nea.gov.sg/.

Ng, Bernard Jia Han, et al. 2015. "Municipal Food Waste Management in Singapore: Practices, Challenges and Recommendations." *Journal of Material Cycles and Waste Management* Issue 1 (June 25). https://www.springerprofessional.de/en/municipal-food-waste-management-in-singapore-practices-challenge/5335868.

Sang Keon, Lee, et al. 2016. "International Case Studies of Smart Cities: Singapore, Republic of Singapore." IDB-American Development Bank. https://publications.iadb.org/handle/11319/7723.

The World Bank. 2017. "Economy Rankings." http://www.doingbusiness.org/rankings.

Yep, Eric. 2015. "Singapore's Innovative Waste-Disposal System." *Wall Street Journal*, September 13. https://www.wsj.com/articles/singapores-innovative-waste-disposal-system-1442197715.

Selected Bibliography

Al-Ali, Zaid. 2014. *The Struggle for Iraq's Future: How Corruption, Incompetence and Sectarianism Have Undermined Democracy.* New Haven, CT: Yale University Press.

Albas, Ahmet, et al. 2016. "On-Line Solution to the Bottleneck Congestion: A Case Study for Istanbul." https://www.researchgate.net/publication/242181438 _ON-LINE_SOLUTION_TO_THE_BOTTLENECK_CONGESTION_A _CASE_STUDY_FOR_ISTANBUL.

Albert, Eleanor. 2017. "The China-North Korea Relationship." *Council on Foreign Relations.* https://www.cfr.org/backgrounder/china-north-korea-relationship.

Alnajjar, Ashraf Yahya. 2015. "Waste Management in Iraq." *BioEnergy Consult*, October 1. https://www.bioenergyconsult.com/waste-iraq/.

Andersen, L. B., P. Schnohr, M. Schroll, and H. O. Hein. 2000. "All-Cause Mortality Associated with Physical Activity during Leisure Time, Work, Sports, and Cycling to Work." *PubMed.gov.* https://www.ncbi.nlm.nih.gov/pubmed /10847255.

Anderson, Jon Lee. 2013. "Slumlord—What has Hugo Chavez Wrought in Venezuela?" *New Yorker.* http://www.newyorker.com/magazine/2013/01/28/slumlord.

Arana, A. 2014. "In Mexico, a City's Scar Becomes Its Most Prized Park, La Línea Verde." *Citiscope.* January 20. http://archive.citiscope.org/story/2014/mexico -citys-scar-becomes-its-most-prized-park-la-linea-verde.

Arnold, Carrie. 2014. "Once upon a Mine: The Legacy of Uranium on the Navajo Nation." *Environmental Health Perspectives.* February. http://ehp.niehs.nih .gov/122-A44.

Asia Society. "South Korean Education Reforms." https://asiasociety.org/global -cities-education-network/south-korean-education-reforms.

Associated Press. 2016. "Smog Stays Bad; Mexico City Extends Traffic Cutback." http://www.voanews.com/content/smog-stays-heavy-mexico-city-extends -traffic-cutback/3316255.html.

Baum-Snow, Nathaniel. 2007. "Did Highways Cause Suburbanization?" *Quarterly Journal of Economics* (May). http://qje.oxfordjournals.org/content/122/2 /775.full.pdf+html.

Below, Bill. 2016. "The Case of the Shrinking Country: Japan's Demographic and Policy Challenges in 5 Charts." *OECD Insights: Debate the Issues.* http:// oecdinsights.org/2016/04/11/the-case-of-the-shrinking-country-japans -demographic-and-policy-challenges-in-5-charts.

Berlatsky, Noah. 2013. "Japan's Cutthroat School System: A Cautionary Tale for the U.S." *Atlantic*, November 22. https://www.theatlantic.com/education/archive/2013/11/japans-cutthroat-school-system-a-cautionary-tale-for-the-us/281612/.

Bhaduri, S. 2013. "Vehicular Growth and Air Quality at Major Traffic Intersection Points in Kolkata City: An Efficient Intervention Strategies." 2013. *The SIJ Transactions on Advances in Space Research & Earth Exploration (ASREE)* 1, 1 (September-October).

Biderman, Ciro. 2008. "Sao Paulo's Urban Transport Infrastructure." *LSECities*. https://lsecities.net/media/objects/articles/sao-paulo-urban-transport-infrastructure/en-gb/.

Bigon, Liora. 2009. *A History of Urban Planning in Two West African Colonial Capitals: Residential Segregation in British Lagos and French Dakar (1850–1930)*. Lewiston, NY: Edwin Mellen Press.

Bleck, Jaimie. 2015. *Education and Empowered Citizenship in Mali*. Baltimore: Johns Hopkins University Press.

Borenstein, Seth. 2015. "Syria's Civil War Linked Partly to Drought, Global Warming." *Daily Herald*. https://www.dailyherald.com/article/20150302/news/303029878.

Bury, Chris. 2015. "Is This 1917 Law Suffocating Puerto Rico's Economy?" Making Sen$e. *PBS News Hour*. http://www.pbs.org/newshour/making-sense/jones-act-holding-puerto-rico-back-debt-crisis.

Carmody, Tim. 2016. "How the Flint River Got So Toxic." *Verge*, February 26. http://www.theverge.com/2016/2/26/11117022/flint-michigan-water-crisis-lead-pollution-history.

Carter, Keith Allen. 2015. "General Motors and the City of Detroit: A Study in Urban Decline." Forum on Public Policy, February. http://forumonpublicpolicy.com/wp-content/uploads/2015/02/Carter.pdf.

Cendrowicz, Leo. 2017. "Is Belgium Fighting Hard Enough against Corruption?" *Brussels Times*, April 19. http://www.brusselstimes.com/opinion/8047/is-belgium-fighting-hard-enough-against-corruption.

Chatterjee, Rhitu. 2008. "New Delhi: Integrating Air and Climate Policies." *Environmental Science & Technology* 42, 16: 5835.

Chen Te-Ping. 2015. "China's Water Problems Are Even Worse Than You Think: Report." *Wall Street Journal*, January 13. https://blogs.wsj.com/chinarealtime/2015/01/13/chinas-water-problems-are-even-worse-than-you-think-report.

Clionadh, Raleigh, Lisa Jordan, and Idean Salehyan. 2008. "Assessing the Impact of Climate Change on Migration and Conflict." *Social Development Department, The World Bank Group*. https://environmentalmigration.iom.int/assessing-impact-climate-change-migration-and-conflict.

CNN. 2014. "On China Transcript: Urbanization." *CNN*. January 22. https://www.cnn.com/2014/01/22/world/asia/on-china-urbanization-transcript/index.html.

Cohen, Steven, Hayley Martinez, and Alix Schroder. 2015. "Waste Management Practices in New York City, Hong Kong and Beijing." http://www.columbia.edu/~sc32/documents/ALEP%20Waste%20Managent%20FINAL.pdf.

"Compulsory Nine-Year School System Kicks Off in Japan." 2016. *Japan Times*, June 10.

Coonan, Clifford. 2017. "Demise of 'Iron Rice Bowl' Brings Social Change in Chongqing." *Irish Times*. http://www.irishtimes.com/news/world/asia-pacific/demise-of-iron-rice-bowl-brings-social-change-in-chongqing-1.2626926.

Crowley-Hughes, Andrea. 2017. "New York City's Unique Urban Green Spaces." *Culture Trip*. https://theculturetrip.com/north-america/usa/new-york/articles/8-unique-urban-green-spaces-in-new-york-city.

Danish, Jamil. 2016. "Afghanistan's Corruption Epidemic Is Wasting Billions in Aid." *Guardian,* November 3. https://www.theguardian.com/global-development-professionals-network/2016/nov/03/afghanistans-corruption-epidemic-is-wasting-billions-in-aid.

Davey, Monica. 2016. "Chicago Police Try to Predict Who May Shoot or Be Shot." *New York Times*, May 23. http://www.nytimes.com/2016/05/24/us/armed-with-data-chicago-police-try-to-predict-who-may-shoot-or-be-shot.html.

De Boeck, Filip. 2015. "'Poverty' and the Politics of Syncopation: Urban Examples from Kinshasa (DR Congo)." *Current Anthropology* 56, S11: S146–58.

Denny, Elaine. 2014. "Ethnicity and Civil War." *Journal of Peace Research* 51, 2. http://journals.sagepub.com/doi/pdf/10.1177/0022343313512853.

Dolin, Eric Jay. 2004. *Political Waters: The Long, Dirty, Contentious, Incredibly Expensive but Eventually Triumphant History of Boston Harbor—A Unique Environmental Success Story.* Amherst and Boston: University of Massachusetts Press.

Economist. 2017a. "Shenzhen Is a Hothouse of Innovation." http://www.economist.com/news/special-report/21720076-copycats-are-out-innovators-are-shenzhen-hothouse-innovation.

Economist. 2017b. "What China Can Learn from the Pearl River Delta." https://www.economist.com/special-report/2017/04/08/what-china-can-learn-from-the-pearl-river-delta.

El-Hinnawi, Essam. 1985. Environmental Refugees. Nairobi, Kenya: United Nations Environmental Program. http://hdl.handle.net/20.500.11822/2651.

Environment News Service. 2013. "10 Coastal Cities at Greatest Flood Risk as Sea Levels Rise." *Environment News Service*. http://ens-newswire.com/2013/09/03/10-coastal-cities-at-greatest-flood-risk-as-sea-levels-rise/.

Fatima, Rabab, Anita Jawadurovna Wadud, and Sabira Coelho. 2014. "Human Rights, Climate Change, Environmental Degradation and Migration: A New Paradigm." Migration Policy Institute (MPI). https://www.migrationpolicy.org/research/human-rights-climate-change-environmental-degradation-and-migration-new-paradigm.

Femia, Francesco, and Caitlin E. Werrell. 2012. "Syria: Climate Change, Drought and Social Unrest." Briefing No. 11. Washington, DC: Center for Climate and Security. https://climateandsecurity.files.wordpress.com/2012/04/syria-climate-change-drought-and-social-unrest_briefer-11.pdf.

Firoozi, Ferrydoon. 1974. "Tehran: A Demographic and Economic Analysis." *Middle Eastern Studies* 10, 1: 60–76. http://www.jstor.org/stable/4282511.

Forgacs, D. 2014. *Italy's Margins: Social Exclusion and Nation Formation since 1861*. Cambridge: Cambridge University Press.

Fountain, Henry, Hiroko Tabuchi, and Somini Sengupta. 2018. "What's Different about California's Fires This Year?" *New York Times*. https://www.nytimes.com/2018/08/01/climate/california-fires-heat.html.

Fraser, Arabella. 2006. "The Cost of Climate Change: Peru Feels the Heat of Global Warming." Peru Support, November 30. http://www.perusupportgroup.org.uk/article-174.html

Freeman, Belmont. 2014. "History of the Present: Havana." *Places*. https://placesjournal.org/article/history-of-the-present-havana.

Fruen, Lauren, and Gemma Mullin. 2017. "Toxic Smog Alert—London on 'Red Alert' and Residents Warned to Stay Indoors as Toxic Air Pollution from Germany Swamps the Capital." *Sun*. https://www.thesun.co.uk/news/2651941/london-red-alert-toxic-air-pollution.

Gelting, Richard, Katherine Bliss, Molly Patrick, Gabriella Lockhart, and Thomas Handzel. 2013. "Water, Sanitation, and Hygiene in Haiti: Past, Present, and Future." *American Journal of Tropical Medicine and Hygiene* 89, 4: 665–70.

Gerston, Larry N. 2012. *Not So Golden After All: The Rise and Fall of California*. Boca Raton, FL: CRC Press.

GLA Economics. 2016. "Draft Economic Evidence Base 2016 Chapter 6: London's People 2016." *GLA Economics*. February 20. https://www.london.gov.uk/sites/default/files/chapter6-draft-eeb-2016.pdf.

Glaeser, Edward. 2005. "Urban Colossus: Why Is New York America's Largest City?" Harvard Institute of Economic Research, June. http://scholar.harvard.edu/files/glaeser/files/hier2073.pdf.

Gleick, Peter H. 2013. "Water, Drought, Climate Change, and Conflict in Syria." *Weather, Climate, and Society* 6, 3: 331–40. American Meteorological Society. https://journals.ametsoc.org/doi/abs/10.1175/WCAS-D-13-00059.1.

Global Partnership for Education. "Education in Burkina Faso." http://www.globalpartnership.org/country/burkina-faso.

Grant, Julie. "Residents Sue US Steel over Air Pollution in Western Pennsylvania." PRI (Public Radio International) "Living on Earth." https://www.pri.org/stories/2017-08-11/residents-sue-us-steel-over-air-pollution-western-pennsylvania.

Greater London Authority. 2013. "PM2.5 Map and Exposure Data." https://data.london.gov.uk/dataset/pm2-5-map-and-exposure-data.

Guirre, Itziar. 2015. "Cairo's 'Zabaleen' Garbage Collectors: Egypt's Diamond in the Rough." *Global Risk Insights*. http://globalriskinsights.com/2015/06/cairos-zabaleen-garbage-collectors-egypts-diamond-in-the-rough.

Harvey, Chelsea. 2016. "How Climate Disasters Can Drive Violent Conflict around the World." *Washington Post*, July 25. https://www.washingtonpost.com/news/energy-environment/wp/2016/07/25/how-climate-disasters-can-drive-violent-conflict-around-the-world/.

Hebrok, M., and C. Boks. 2017. "Household Food Waste: Drivers and Potential Intervention Points for Design—An Extensive Review." *Journal of Cleaner Production* 151: 380–92.

Hegre, Håvard, Joakim Karlsen, Håvard Mokleiv Nygård, Håvard Strand, and Henrik Urdal. 2013. "Predicting Armed Conflict, 2010–2050." *International Studies Quarterly* 57, 2: 250–70.

Hirst, Michael, and Kate McGeown. 2009. "Rising Sea Levels: A Tale of Two Cities." *BBC News*, November 24. http://news.bbc.co.uk/2/hi/science/nature/8369236.stm.

Holmertz, S. 2015. Oslo's Colourful Solution to Waste Management. *Waste Management World*. https://waste-management-world.com/a/oslos-colourful-solution-to-waste-management.

Istanbul Development Agency. 2014. "2014–2023 Istanbul Regional Plan." http://www.istka.org.tr/media/24723/istanbul-regional-plan-2014-2023.pdf.

Japan Times. 2015. "Sinking under Debt, Kansai Airport Privatization Will Be Test for Abe." *Japan Times,* March 14. https://www.japantimes.co.jp/news/2015/03/14/business/sinking-under-debt-kansai-airport-privatization-will-be-test-for-abe/#.W7JFg7pFxVw.

Johnson, Lisa. 2016. "Canada Wants More Chinese Workers, Students and Tourists, Says Immigration Minister." *Canadian Broadcasting Corporation (CBC) News*. http://www.cbc.ca/news/canada/british-columbia/chinese-immigration-canada-china-1.3725202.

Joshi, Mallica, and Mohit Sharma. 2016. "Landfills or Pollution Bombs? Delhi's Garbage Dumps Spewing Toxic Gases." *Hindustan Times*, May 5. http://www.hindustantimes.com/delhi/landfill-sites-or-pollution-bombs-garbage-dumps-spewing-toxic-gases/story-2abfwizFWqY5NzsFzbuFdN.html.

Juncker, Jean-Claude. 2015. "State of the Union 2015: Time for Honesty, Unity and Solidarity." European Commission Press Release Database. http://europa.eu/rapid/press-release_SPEECH-15-5614_en.htm.

"Karachi among the Five Most Polluted Cities in the World." *Express Tribune*. http://tribune.com.pk/story/1116509/lets-clear-air-karachi-among-five-polluted-cities-world.

Kart, Susan. 2009. "The Phenomenon of Récupération at the Dak'art Biennale." *African Arts* 42, 3: 8–9.

Katz, Bruce, Luise Noring, and Nantke Garrelts. 2016. "Cities and Refugees: The German Experience." https://www.brookings.edu/research/cities-and-refugees-the-german-experience.

Kelley, Colin P., Shahzad Mohtadi, Mark A. Cane, Richard Seager, and Yochanan Kushnir. 2015. "Climate Change in the Fertile Crescent and Implications of the Recent Drought." *Proceedings of the National Academy of Sciences of the United States of America (PNAS)*. http://www.pnas.org/content/112/11/3241.

Knapton, Sarah. 2017. "Air Pollution in London Passes Levels in Beijing . . . and Wood Burners Are Making Problem Worse." *Telegraph*. https://www.telegraph.co.uk/science/2017/01/24/air-pollution-london-passes-levels-beijingand-wood-burners-making.

"Koban Police Boxes Going Multilingual Ahead of 2020 Games." 2016. *Japan News* by *Yomiuri Shimbun*, November 12. https://www.questia.com/newspaper/1P4-1838521439/koban-police-boxes-going-multilingual-ahead-of-20.

Koo, Se-Woong. 2014. "An Assault upon Our Children: South Korea's Education System Hurts Students." *New York Times*, August 1. http://www.nytimes.com/2014/08/02/opinion/sunday/south-koreas-education-system-hurts-students.html.

Kumagai, Yoichi, and Robert Gibson, and Pierre Filion. 2015. "Evaluating Long-Term Urban Resilience through an Examination of the History of Green Spaces in Tokyo." *Local Environment: The International Journal of Justice and Sustainability* 20: 1018–39. https://www.tandfonline.com/doi/abs/10.1080/13549839.2014.887060.

Kumar, Ashwani. 2013. "Existing Situation of Municipal Solid Waste Management in NCT of Delhi, India." *International Journal of Social Sciences* 1, 1: 6–17.

Lamarche, Pierre, and Maud Romani. 2015. "The Assets of Self-Employed Workers." *National Institute of Statistics and Economic Studies*. https://www.insee.fr/en/statistiques/1908049?sommaire=1908062&q=paris%2C%20emploi.

Li Weimin, and Yin Bingbing. 2016. *Research on the Development of Quality Private Higher Education in Shaanxi Province*. Shaanxi: People's Publishing House.

Lukyen, Jorg. "Stuttgart Worst City for Traffic Jams." *Local*. https://www.thelocal.de/20150331/stuttgart-worst-city-for-traffic-jams.

Lutz, Ashley. 2012. "Why the 'Creative Class' Is Taking Over the World." *Business Insider*. July 28. http://www.businessinsider.com/why-the-creative-class-is-taking-over-the-world-2012-7.

Mackenzie, Tom, and Mitch Moxley. 2009. "China's 'Little Africa' Is Under Pressure." *GlobalPost*. https://www.pri.org/stories/2009-02-23/chinas-little-africa-under-pressure.

Mbacké, Khadim. 2005. *Sufism and Religious Brotherhoods in Senegal*. Translated by Eric S. Ross and edited by John Hunwick. Princeton, NJ: Markus Wiener Publishers.

Mendez-Vilas, Antonio, ed. 2006. *Modern Multidisciplinary Applied Microbiology: Exploiting Microbes and Their Interactions*. Weinheim, Germany: Wiley-VCH.

Murdoch, Gillian. 2018. "Trash and Burn: Singapore's Waste Problem." *Reuters*. http://www.reuters.com/article/us-waste-singapore-idUSSP9046620080522.

Murdock, Heather. 2016. "Saudi Arabia Seeks to Shed Dependence on Foreign Labor. *VOA News*." January 25. https://www.voanews.com/a/saudi-arabia-seeks-to-shed-dependency-on-foreign-labor/3162055.html.

Myers, Norman. 2005. "Environmental Refugees: An Emergent Security Issue." *13th Economic Forum*, Prague. https://www.osce.org/eea/14851?download=true.

National Centers for Environmental Information (NOAA). 2018. "Global Climate Report—April 2018." https://www.ncdc.noaa.gov/sotc/global/201804.

Ng, Bernard Jia Han, et al. 2015. "Municipal Food Waste Management in Singapore: Practices, Challenges and Recommendations." *Journal of Material Cycles and Waste Management*, Issue 1. https://www.springerprofessional.de/en/municipal-food-waste-management-in-singapore-practices-challenge/5335868.

Novakovic, Stefan. 2015. "An Inside Look at Toronto's New Home Energy Loan Program." *Urban Toronto,* August 27.

Oh, Hye-Ryun et al. 2015. "Long-Range Transport of Air Pollutants Originating in China: A Possible Major Cause of Multi-Day High-PM_{10} Episodes during Cold Season in Seoul, Korea." *Atmospheric Environment* 109 (May): 23–30.

Packer, George. 2015. "The Other France." *New Yorker.* http://www.newyorker.com/magazine/2015/08/31/the-other-france.

Payind, Alam. 2013. "Inside Afghanistan 23 Years after the Soviet Withdrawal." *Journal of Asian and African Studies* (April 15). https://journals.sagepub.com/doi/abs/10.1177/0021909613478394?journalCode=jasa.

Reinprecht, Christoph. 2007. "Social Housing in Austria." In C. Whitehead and K. J. Scanlon, eds. *Social Housing in Europe.* London: London School of Economics and Political Science, 35–43. http://vbn.aau.dk/files/13671493/SocialHousingInEurope.pdf.

RenminNet. 2019. "A Survey Report of Migrant Workers: 20 Million Return to Villages Due to Loss of Employment during the Global Financial Crisis" (in Chinese). http://finance.people.com.cn/GB/8889165.html.

Rigaud, Kanta Kumari, Alex de Sherbinin, Bryan Jones, Jonas Bergmann, Viviane Clement, Kayly Ober, Jacob Schewe, Susana Adamo, Brent McCusker, Silke Heuser, and Amelia Midgley. 2018. "Groundswell: Preparing for Internal Climate Migration." *World Bank Group.* https://openknowledge.worldbank.org/handle/10986/29461.

Roden, Lee. 2017. "This Map Shows Where You're Most Likely to Be Unemployed in Sweden." *Local,* February 13. https://www.thelocal.se/20170213/this-map-shows-where-youre-most-likely-to-be-unemployed-in-sweden.

Roumpani, Flora, and Polly Hudson. 2014. "The Evolution of London: The City's Near-2,000 Year History Mapped." *Guardian,* May 15. https://www.theguardian.com/cities/2014/may/15/the-evolution-of-london-the-citys-near-2000-year-history-mapped.

Saleeby, Suzanne. 2012. "Sowing the Seeds of Dissent: Economic Grievances and the Syrian Social Contract's Unraveling." http://www.jadaliyya.com/Details/25271/Sowing-the-Seeds-of-Dissent-Economic-Grievances-and-the-Syrian-Social-Contract%E2%80%99s-Unraveling.

Schleussner, Carl-Friedrich, Jonathan F. Donges, Reik V. Donner, and Hans Joachim Schellnhuber. 2016. "Armed-Conflict Risks Enhanced by Climate-Related Disasters in Ethnically Factionalized Countries." *Proceedings of the National Academy of Sciences* 113, 33: 9216–21. https://www.pnas.org/content/113/33/9216.

Sneed, Adam. 2017. "Life on the Forgotten Farm of Guangzhou." *Citylab.* https://www.citylab.com/life/2017/04/guangzhou-farms-and-urbanization/522972.

Taylor, Matthew. 2017. "Revealed: Every Londoner Breathing Dangerous Levels of Toxic Air Particle." *Guardian.* https://www.theguardian.com/environment/2017/oct/04/revealed-every-londoner-breathing-dangerous-levels-of-toxic-air-particle.

Thomson, Keegan. 2015. "What Makes Sydney Such a Great City for Students?" *Guardian*. https://www.theguardian.com/education/2015/dec/02/what-makes-sydney-great-city-for-students.

United Nations. 2014. "World's Population Increasingly Urban with More than Half Living in Urban Areas." http://www.un.org/en/development/desa/news/population/world-urbanization-prospects-2014.html.

United Nations Department of Economics and Social Affairs Population Division. 2011. "Population Distribution, Urbanization, Internal Migration and Development: An International Perspective." http://wedocs.unep.org/bitstream/handle/20.500.11822/18920/Population_Distribution_Urbanization.pdf?sequence=1&isAllowed=y.

United Nations Framework Convention on Climate Change (UNFCCC). 2017. "Climate Change Is a Key Driver of Migration and Food Insecurity." https://unfccc.int/news/climate-change-is-a-key-driver-of-migration-and-food-insecurity.

United States Department of State, Bureau of Diplomatic Security: Overseas Security Advisory Council (OSAC). 2017. "China 2017 Crime & Safety Report: Beijing." https://www.osac.gov/pages/ContentReportDetails.aspx?cid=21824.

Vilalta, Carlos, and Robert Muggah. "What Explains Criminal Violence in Mexico City? A Test of Two Theories of Crime." *Stability: International Journal of Security and Development* 5, 1: 1–22. http://dx.doi.org/10.5334/sta.433.

Westcott, Ben. 2018. "Beijing's Population Falls for First Time in 20 Years." *CNN*. January 24. http://www.cnn.com/2018/01/24/asia/beijing-shanghai-population-drop-intl/index.html.

Wiarda, Jan-Martin. 2009. "A New Class of Education." *Guardian*. https://www.theguardian.com/commentisfree/2009/sep/21/germany-now-education.

Wilczyńska-Michalik, Wanda. 2003. "Air Pollution and Damage to the Cultural Heritage in Cities: The Decay of the Cultural Heritage of Krakow." In *Sustainable Urban Patterns around the Baltic Sea: Case Studies*. Vol. 4. Uppsala: Baltic University Press, 42–53.

Wong, Olga. 2013. "The Uphill Battle for Our Green Havens—Hong Kong's Country Parks." *South China Morning Post*. http://www.scmp.com/news/hong-kong/article/1313224/uphill-battle-our-green-havens-hong-kongs-country-parks.

World Bank. 2008. "Agriculture in Syria: Towards the Social Market." http://documents.worldbank.org/curated/en/890301468304199912/Syria-Agriculture-in-Syria-towards-the-social-market.

World Bank. 2017. "Year in Review: 2017 in 12 Charts." http://www.worldbank.org/en/news/feature/2017/12/15/year-in-review-2017-in-12-charts.

World Bank. 2018. "Urban Population (% of total)." https://data.worldbank.org/indicator/SP.URB.TOTL.IN.ZS.

Xinhuanet. 2018. "Urbanization Rate of China's Agricultural Province Exceeds 50 Pct." *Xinhuanet*. http://www.xinhuanet.com/english/2018-03/05/c_137017957.htm.

Yin, Jun, Xiuqi Fang, and Yun Su. 2016. "Correlation between Climate and Grain Harvest Fluctuations and the Dynastic Transitions and Prosperity in China over the Past Two Millennia." *Holocene* 26, 12: 1914–23. http://journals.sagepub.com/doi/10.1177/0959683616646186.

Young, Bob, and Vernal Coleman. 2016. "Inside the Grim World of the Jungle: The Caves, Sleeping in Shifts, Eye-Ball-Eating Rats." *Seattle Times*, June 17, A-1. https://www.seattletimes.com/seattle-news/inside-the-grim-world-of-the-jungle-the-caves-sleeping-in-shifts-and-eyeball-eating-rats/.

Zhang, David D., C. Y. Jim, George C-S. Lin, Yuan-Qing He, James J. Wang, and Harry F. Lee. 2006. "Climatic Change, Wars and Dynastic Cycles in China over the Last Millennium." *Climatic Change* 76, 3–4: 459–77. https://link.springer.com/article/10.1007%2Fs10584-005-9024-z.

Zheng, Jinran, and Cao Yin. 2015. "Beijing to Limit Population Growth This Year." *China Daily*, January 24. http://www.chinadaily.com.cn/china/2015-01/24/content_19394117.htm.

About the Editor and Contributors

EDITOR

DR. JING LUO is a professor at Bloomsburg University in Pennsylvania. His research areas include urban studies, China's economic and political transition, and linguistics. He received a PhD from Pennsylvania State University, an MA and a BA from Peking University. He is the author of *Business and Technology in China*, ABC-CLIO, 2010; editor of *China Today: An Encyclopedia of Life in the People's Republic,* Greenwood, 2005; and author of *Over a Cup of Tea—An Introduction to Chinese Life and Culture*, University Press of America, 2004.

CONTRIBUTORS

PROFESSOR CHAD ANDREWS and his family moved to the Williamsport area in 1999, then left for Michigan in 2000, only to return to Williamsport in 2006. He owns and manages a community printmaking studio and keeps a private painting studio at the Pajama Factory. He has taught printmaking at the University of Pennsylvania, Interlochen Center for the Arts, and is currently an assistant professor of printmaking and foundations at Bloomsburg University.

DR. KERRY ARD is assistant professor of environmental sociology, Ohio State University. Her research interests are health inequality and social policy as they relate to environmental issues. She investigates how environmental risk is spatially distributed by race and class, how this affects health outcomes, and the social systems and policies that have led to these patterns.

MS. MARISOL BECERRA is a PhD candidate in environmental sociology at Ohio State University. Her research interests focus on green redevelopment in urban cities and its effects on population and neighborhood health. Ms. Becerra's research is motivated by her experiences growing up near one of Chicago's largest industrial corridors and her engagement in local community-based research to spread public health awareness of environmental hazards. Her local work in Chicago contributed to the closure of two of the oldest coal-fired power plants in the nation.

DR. LIORA BIGON has a PhD in architecture from the University of Manchester. She is a senior staff member at Holon Institute of Technology and a research fellow at the Truman Research Institute for the Advancement of Peace, Hebrew University of Jerusalem, Israel. A specialist in (post-)colonial urban history and planning cultures in sub-Saharan Africa, she has pursued fieldwork in several West African countries and published over 60 peer-reviewed articles, encyclopedia entries, and books.

DR. AIMIN CHEN holds has a PhD in economics from Pennsylvania State University. She was a tenured professor at Indiana State University (ISU), where she was awarded Distinguished Professor of the College of Arts and Sciences in 2005. Dr. Chen returned to China in 2005 and is now the President of Xi'an International University, in Xi'an, Shaanxi Province, China.

DR. NOGIN CHUNG is an associate professor in the Department of Art and Art History at Bloomsburg University of Pennsylvania. Her research interests include public art and activism in contemporary art.

DR. DINA CLARK, CPA, CIA, is an assistant professor of business at Bloomsburg University of Pennsylvania. She holds a PhD in management from Vladimir State University in Vladimir, Russia. She also holds an MBA in accounting from Pittsburg State University in Pittsburg, Kansas, and an MS degree of Engineer-Economist from the same institution. She is also a certified public accountant and a certified internal auditor. Dr. Clark specializes in international standards of accounting.

DR. CHRISTOPHER CUMO is the author of seven books and hundreds of shorter works. His eighth book is under contract with ABC-CLIO/Greenwood. He has a PhD in history, with research interests principally in the histories of science and agriculture, from the University of Akron.

MS. ASHLEE L. DAUPHINAIS CIVITELLO is a PhD student at Ohio state University in Columbus. Her area of study is Hispanic linguistics. She received an MA in linguistics from the University of Puerto Rico-Rio Piedras, San Juan, PR; and a BA in Spanish from Saint Joseph's University, Philadelphia.

CHRISTOPHER J. DONAHUE is currently an associate professor of Spanish and chairperson of the Department of Languages and Cultures at Bloomsburg University in Bloomsburg, Pennsylvania. He completed his PhD at the University of Arizona, his MA at Middlebury College and his BA at Millersville State College. His specialization is in medieval Spanish literature, with a dissertation and several publications based on the versification of the anonymous *Libro de Apolonio* (13th century) and related topics. He also teaches and researches in the areas of Spanish and Latin American cinema, in particular the cinema of Argentina of the late 20th and early 21st centuries.

About the Editor and Contributors

GABRIEL JOSÉ FORNES DUTILH holds a BS in agronomic engineering, an MBA, and a Post Graduate Certification in Special Education. He worked in agricultural businesses in Venezuela and managed two green areas contracts for the municipality of Baruta, Caracas, Venezuela. Currently he lives in Hong Kong, where he teaches Spanish and provides academic support as a learning specialist at an international school.

PROFESSOR SCOTT DUNCAN is a criminal justice instructor in the Department of Sociology, Social Work, and Criminal Justice at Bloomsburg University of Pennsylvania. Previously, he worked as a sworn supervisor with the Metropolitan Nashville Police Department, and later as a consultant with the SEDA-Council of Governments. His current research interests include criminal investigation, missing persons, criminal justice history, and policing. He holds an MBA from Belmont University, an MS from the University of Cincinnati, and is currently a doctoral student at Nova Southeastern University.

DR. MATT EVANS is associate professor of political science at Penn State in Altoona. His research and teaching interests include comparative politics, electoral politics, environmental policies, political communications, and the Middle East. His peer-reviewed articles have appeared in *International Politics, Politics & Policy, Media, War & Conflict, International Political Science Review, Local Government Studies,* the *Middle East Journal* and *Party Politics.*

DR. MARIO A. GIRALDO is an associate professor in the Geography Department at California State University, Northridge, where he teaches courses in physical and environmental geography. He is the faculty leader of the GE path Principles of Sustainability and faculty associate for the CSUN Institute of Sustainability, where he coordinates a large service-learning project with more than 500 students contributing to CSUN campus sustainability. Thanks to his work, CSUN is now composting and reusing more than 50 tons of organic waste per year in addition to reaching 60 percent of its zero-waste goals. These two projects were recognized by the CSU Chancellor's Office Award in Sustainability and by the EPA Food Challenge Achievement.

DR. JENNIFER HANEY is an assistant professor in the Department of Environmental, Geographical, and Geological Sciences at Bloomsburg University in Bloomsburg, Pennsylvania. Her primary research interests include societal vulnerability and responses to environmental hazards and geographies and drivers of terrorism. Jennifer earned her BA in geography with an emphasis on environmental planning from Bloomsburg University, an MA in geography from Binghamton University, and a PhD in geography from the University of South Carolina.

DR. BRUCE E. JOHANSEN is Frederick W. Kayser Professor of Communication and Native American Studies at the University of Nebraska at Omaha, where he has been teaching and writing since 1982. He has published 47 books, some of the most recent being *Empty Cellars, Melting Ice and Melting Tundra: Climate Change and Native American Peoples in the United States and Canada* (2016), *Up from the Ashes: Nation-Building at Muckleshoot* (2014), *and Eco-Hustle! Global Warming, Greenwashing, and Sustainability* (2015). He holds the University of Nebraska award for Outstanding Research and Creative Activity (ORCA), the state system's highest faculty recognition.

DR. SARA C. JORGENSEN is an independent scholar with a PhD in history.

DR. DOUGLAS KARSNER is an associate professor of American history at Bloomsburg University in Pennsylvania and an adjunct professor of history at Temple University, Japan Campus, in Tokyo. He teaches courses on U.S. urban history and Japanese-American relations, among others. His publications include "Aviation and Airports" in *the Journal of Urban History*, several articles on Japanese-American airline competition, and most recently "The Real Bottom Line: A History of Business Executives Move for Vietnam Peace," in *Essays in Economic and Business History*.

PROFESSOR ANASTASIA KOVALYUK has a master's in linguistics from Kuban State University of Krasnodar. She taught English in Russia. Her academic interests include psycholinguistics, applied linguistics, and intercultural communication. She was a Fulbright scholar teaching Russian language at Bloomsburg University of Pennsylvania, in 2016–2017.

DR. ELENA KRASILNIKOVA is a faculty member of the Department for Linguistics and Cross-Cultural Communication of the Vologda State University, Vologda, Russia. Her academic background includes studies of German and English at the Vologda State Pedagogical University, and European Studies at the Institute of European Cultures, Russian State University for the Humanities, Moscow. In 2017, she received Fulbright scholarship and worked as a Fulbright Language Teaching Assistant at Bloomsburg University of Pennsylvania.

DR. NAKUL KUMAR grew up in Delhi and holds a PhD in economics from George Mason University. He taught as an assistant professor of economics at Bloomsburg University of Pennsylvania. He is currently an associate professor of economics, Division of Liberal Arts and Social Sciences, Northern Virginia Community College, Alexandria, Virginia. His research focuses on the political economy of natural disaster management in South Asia.

DR. ERIC G. LESNESKIE is an associate professor in the Department of Sociology, Social Work, and Criminal Justice at Bloomsburg University. He received his PhD in criminal justice from Rutgers University. His research interests include co-offending, juvenile delinquency, and offender risk assessment.

DR. JEFF E. LONG received his PhD in history from the University of Hawaii, Manoa, where his doctoral studies focused on early Shōwa (1926–1937) militarism and the Japanese literati. Currently, he is studying the role of tenkō (ideological/political conversion) in the thought and literature of Hayashi Fusao and Shimaki Kensaku, two prominent Japanese writers during the 1930s and '40s. Long published "Songs That Cannot Be Sung: Hayashi Fusao's 'Album' and the Political Uses of Literature during the Early Showa Years" in the March 2007 issue of *Japan Forum*, and has translated Hayashi Fusao's short story "Apples" that was published in Norma Field and Heather Bowen-Struyk's edited volume *For Dignity, Justice, and Revolution: An Anthology of Japanese Proletarian Literature* in 2016. He is an associate professor in the Department of History at Bloomsburg University of Pennsylvania where he teaches lower- and upper-level courses on East Asian history.

DR. CHRISTOPHER A. MILLER is a conservation biologist with the Canadian Parks and Wilderness Society, a nongovernment organization that works to protect Canada's large natural areas. He works collaboratively with governments, indigenous communities, academics, industry, local stakeholders, and other NGOs to build support for the creation of new protected areas. Chris holds a PhD from the University of Waterloo and a BSc from Dalhousie University, and led the grassroots campaign to establish the Blue Mountain–Birch Cove Lakes Wilderness Area in Halifax, Canada.

DR. ARIAN MOGHADAM is an environmental and resource economist in the Department of Economics at Bloomsburg University. He obtained his PhD in economics from the University of Guelph, Ontario, Canada.

DR. YANHUI PANG is a professor at Bloomsburg University of Pennsylvania. Her research interest focuses on preservice teacher training, legislative support for early intervention (EI), the family's roles in EI service delivery, comparison of quality early childhood education across cultures, and ESL teaching.

DR. MYKOLA POLYUHA holds a PhD in comparative literature from Western University (Canada) and an MBA from Bloomsburg University of Pennsylvania. He works as an associate professor at Bloomsburg, where he coordinates Russian and East European Studies program. His research interests include international education, national identity, Ezra Pound's works, and modernist movements in American, German, and Slavic literatures.

DR. ERIC S. ROSS is an urban and cultural geographer whose research focuses on Muslim Africa. He has conducted research on Sufism and urbanization in Senegal as well as on cultural heritage and development in Morocco. He holds an MSc in geography from Université du Québec à Montréal and earned a PhD in Islamic studies from McGill University. Since 1998 he has been teaching geography at Al Akhawayn University in Ifrane, where he currently holds the rank of professor.

DR. ÉMILIE ROY is currently the West Africa Regional Specialist for the NGO Search for Common Ground, supervising all the research done in understanding conflicts, devising appropriate responses, and measuring the impact of projects.

Originally from Québec City, Canada, Émilie earned a PhD in Islamic Studies from McMaster University (2012), focusing on the role of *médersas* in citizenship building in Mali. She served as a professor of religious studies and anthropology and then chair of the Islamic Studies program at Al Akhawayn University. She also worked as a research consultant for various NGOs seeking to better understand cultural and religious trends in West Africa.

PROFESSOR MOUMITA ROY is an instructor of economics at Aims Community College in Northern Colorado. She holds a master of science degree in economics from Purdue University, Indiana and a master of arts degree in economics from Jadavpur University, India. She is a citizen of India and has lived and worked in Kolkata.

DR. CLAUDIA SCHMIDT is an assistant professor for marketing and local/regional food systems at Pennsylvania State University. Her research focuses on value-added agriculture and the economics of sustainability.

THELMA I. VELEZ is a PhD student at Ohio State University (USA) in the School of Environment and Natural Resources. She is currently a National Science Foundation Graduate Research Program Fellow. She holds an MS is in environmental studies and focused on the potential to sequester carbon using biochar in organic agriculture and second-generation biofuel production in India. Her work has focused on various aspects of sustainability in both social and natural sciences. Currently she is researching alternative food movements and sustainable consumption.

DR. JU XIN is a professor of physics at Bloomsburg University. His research interest is in the area of atomic, molecular optics and laser physics. He teaches Energy: Sources and Environmental Effects among other courses and has a great passion for issues related to environmental protection. Dr. Xin also enjoys Pennsylvania outdoor activities.

Index

Note: **Bold** indicates volume numbers; *italicized* page numbers indicate illustrations; page numbers followed by *t* indicate tables.

Abe, Shinzo, **1**:291; **2**:158, 232, 293
Aboriginal Australians, **1**:236
Abu Dhabi, United Arab Emirates (UAE), green spaces, **1**:130, 131–35
Adelstein, Jake, **2**:234
Afghanistan, violence, corruption, and organized crime, **2**:178, 207–11, *209*
Aggarwal, Rajiv, **2**:264
Aguascalientes, Mexico, green spaces, **1**:128–29, 135–39
Ahmed, Azam, **2**:217
Ahmedinejad, Mahmoud, **1**:287
Air pollution
   Baku, Azerbaijan, **2**:2–3, 6–10, *7*
   Karachi, Pakistan, **2**:4, 23–27, *24*
   Kolkata, India, **2**:142–43, *144*
   Krakow, Poland, **2**:3, 28–32, *29*
   New Delhi, India, **2**:4, 33–38, 34*t*
   Pittsburgh, Pennsylvania, **1**:106–10
   Rome, Italy, **2**:5–6, 39–43
   Sao Paulo, Brazil, **2**:3, 45–48
   Seoul, South Korea, **2**:2, 52–53
Air transportation, Osaka, Japan, **2**:156–58
Al-Ali, Zaid, **2**:188, 189
Alberta, Canada, waste management, **2**:240, 251–56, 253*t*, 255*t*
Aleppo, Syria, violence, corruption, and organized crime, **2**:178, 182–86, *185*
Almaki, Sarah, **2**:189–90, 192
Almaty, Kazakhstan, housing and infrastructure, **1**:188, 189–94
Almukhtar, Sarah, **2**:188, 191–92
Al-Nahyan, Crown Prince His Highness Sheikh Mohammed bin Zayed, **1**:132

Amari, Akira, **2**:233
Amazon.com, **1**:50, 51
Ambrose, Jerry, **2**:18
Amerindians, **1**:279–80
Amin, Muhammad, **2**:245
Anaerobic co-digestion (AC), **2**:295–96
Anaerobic digestion (AD), **2**:295
Anderson, Lars Bo, **1**:77
Araujo Vormittag, Evangelina da Motta Pacheco de, **2**:45
ArcelorMittal Factory, **2**:31–32
Argentina
   immigration, **1**:255–58
   migration and demographic changes, **1**:251–52, 254–58, *256*
Arnold, Carrie, **2**:57
Asahara, Shoko, **2**:232
Assad, Bashar al-, **1**:232; **2**:182
Atia, Sabah, **2**:242
Atwani, Atwan al-, **2**:243
Aum Shinrikyo, **2**:232
Australia
   energy and sustainability, **1**:66, 92–96, *94*
   housing and infrastructure, **1**:185, 233–38, *234*
   schools, **2**:65, 91–95
Austria, housing and infrastructure, **1**:186–87, 244–47
Automobile industry, **1**:213, 214–15
Azerbaijan, air and water pollution, **2**:2–3, 6–10, *7*
Azikiwe, Abayomi, **1**:218

Baden-Wuerttemberg, Germany, **2**:169
Bagasse, **1**:93

Baghdad, Iraq
  violence, corruption, and organized crime, **2:**177–78, 187–92, *190*
  waste management, **2:**237–38, 241–45, *242*
Baku, Azerbaijan, air and water pollution, **2:**2–3, 6–10, *7*
Baltic Sea, **1:**58
Bamako, Mali, schools, **2:**62–63, 67–71, *70*
Banna, Niran, **2:**190
Barrio adentro, **1:**198–99
Bastia, Tanja, **1:**255, 258
Beauchamp, Edward, **2:**101–3
Beijing, China
  energy and sustainability, **1:**65–66, 70–74, 72*t*
  traffic and transportation, **2:**119–20, 124–29, *126*
  violence, corruption, and organized crime, **2:**179, 193–97
  water shortage, **1:**65–66, 70–74, 72*t*
Belgium, violence, corruption, and organized crime, **2:**179, 197–202, *199*
Bell-Jefferson, Jackie, **2:**58
Belshaw, John Douglas, **1:**297
Bengaluru, India, **1:**21
Benz, Karl, **2:**165
Beouinde, Armand, **2:**83
Berlin, Germany
  housing and infrastructure, **1:**277
  schools, **2:**64, 72–77, *74*
Berlin Wall, **1:**228
Berlusconi, Silvio, **2:**275–76
Berman, Ethan, **2:**80
Bertolaso, Guido, **2:**275
Bhada-Tata, Perinaz, **2:**284, 285
Biking
  Casablanca, Morocco, **2:**133
  Copenhagen, Denmark, **1:**76–78, *77*
  Zurich, Switzerland, **2:**174
Biocell landfill, **2:**252–53
Biofuels, India, **1:**101
Biomass
  Frankfurt, Germany, **1:**84
  Melbourne, Australia, **1:**92–93
Bioreactor landfill, **2:**252
Black (2016), **2:**201
Black Clothes Gang, **2:**196
Bo Xilai, **1:**201, 204–5
Bonaparte, Joseph, **2:**214
Bonaparte, Napoléon, **1:**165; **2:**214
Bono, **1:**180

Boston, Massachusetts
  schools, **2:**66, 78–82, *79*
  water pollution, **2:**1–2, 11–15, *13*
Boyle, Kevin, **1:**214
Braiterman, Jared, **1:**180
Brazil
  air pollution, **2:**3, 45–48
  energy and sustainability, **1:**68, 111–15, *112*
Bremer, L. Paul, **2:**188
Brexit, **1:**4, 16–18
Brillembourg, David, **1:**197
British Columbia, Canada, migration and demographic changes, **1:**252, 294–98, *295*
Brussels, Belgium, violence, corruption, and organized crime, **2:**179, 197–202, *199*
Bryant, William Cullen, **1:**161
Buenos Aires, Argentina, migration and demographic changes, **1:**251–52, 254–58, *256*
Building insulation, Copenhagen, Denmark, **1:**78
Burkina Faso, schools, **2:**63, 83–86
Bush, George H. W., **2:**217
Byrnes, Mark, **1:**106

Cairo, Egypt, waste management, **2:**238–39, 246–50, *248*
Calderón, Felipe, **2:**217
Calgary, Alberta, Canada, waste management, **2:**240, 251–56, 253*t,* 255*t*
California
  migration and demographic changes, **1:**252, 279–83
  waste management, **2:**239–40, 288–92, *290*
Campania, **2:**275
Canada
  energy and sustainability, **1:**68–69, 120–24, *122*
  green spaces, **1:**128, 140–46, 141*t, 142*
  migration and demographic changes, **1:**252, 294–98, *295*
  waste management, **2:**240, 251–56, 253*t,* 255*t*
Caracas, Venezuela, housing and infrastructure, **1:**188, 195–99
Carbon dioxide emissions
  Copenhagen, Denmark, **1:**75–76
  London, United Kingdom, **1:**88–89
  Melbourne, Australia, **1:**66

Carbon tax, **2:**48
Carpooling, Stuttgart, Germany, **2:**168–69
Casablanca, Morocco, traffic and transportation, **2:**122, 130–33
Castro, Fidel, **1:**187, 222, 223
Castro, Raúl, **1:**223
Cathay Glory Association, **2:**98
Catholic schools, **2:**69–70
Centres d'animation pédagogiques (CAP), **2:**68
Chaebol, **2:**225
Charles I, King, **2:**15
Charles River, **2:**1–2, 11–15, *13*
Charles River Watershed Association (CRWA), **2:**13–14
Chávez, Hugo, **1:**195–96, 198
Checkley, William, **1:**271
Cheonggyecheon Stream Restoration Project, **2:**53–54
Cheung Bing-leung, Anthony, **1:**151
Chicago, Illinois, violence, corruption, and organized crime, **2:**181, 202–6
Chikan (subway groping), **2:**181, 232
China
    employment and jobs, **1:**5–6, 52–57, *54*
    energy and sustainability, **1:**65–66, 70–74, 72*t*
    green spaces, **1:**127–28, 147–52, *148,* 162
    housing and infrastructure, **1:**186, 188–89, 200–205, *203,* 206–11
    migration and demographic changes, **1:**250–51, 259–63
    schools, **2:**62, 111–16, 113*t*
    traffic and transportation, **2:**119–20, 124–29, *126*
    violence, corruption, and organized crime, **2:**179, 193–97
Choi, Jang Jip, **2:**220–21, 222
Choi Soon-sil, **2:**220, 224
Chongqing, China, housing and infrastructure, **1:**186, 200–205, *203*
Chun Doo-hwan, **2:**221–22, 223
Chung Yoo-ra, **2:**224
Chunmei, W., **2:**265
Clairton, Pennsylvania, **1:**108–9, 110
Climate change
    Peru, **1:**271–73
    Syria, **2:**184–86
Climate vs. weather, **2:**186
Coal, Singapore City, Singapore, **1:**119
Cogeneration systems, Frankfurt, Germany, **1:**83

Cohen, Sharon, **1:**215
Coleman, Vernal, **1:**49
Columbus, Christopher, **1:**41, 115
Community Energy Planning (CEP), **1:**121
Commuter rail system, Casablanca, Morocco, **2:**133
Composting
    Dakar, Senegal, **2:**258
    Singapore, **2:**295–96
Congestion, traffic. *See* Traffic and transportation
Conniff, Ruth, **1:**218
Conocarpus erectus, **2:**26
Copenhagen, Denmark, energy and sustainability, **1:**66–67, 74–79, *77*
Copernicus, Nicolaus, **2:**28
Copycat manufacturing, **1:**55–56
Corruption. *See* Violence, corruption, and organized crime
Cosa Nostra, **2:**226
Cuba, housing and infrastructure, **1:**187–88, 220–25, *221*
Cybriwsky, Roman, **2:**231

Dakar, Senegal
    landfill, **2:**260
    waste management, **2:**238, 257–61, *258*
Dak'art, **2:**261
Dandong, China, housing and infrastructure, **1:**188–89, 206–11
Danish, Jamil, **2:**210
Dawood, Qasim, **2:**243–44
Dean, Richie, **1:**270
Dearborn STEM Academy, **2:***79,* 79–80
Decentralized home power stations, Frankfurt, Germany, **1:**83
Deibert, Michael, **2:**217–18
Delhi, India
    employment and jobs, **1:**20–21
    landfills, **2:**264–65, 265–66
    waste management, **2:**239, 262–66
    See also New Delhi, India
Democratic Republic of Congo (DRC), migration and demographic changes, **1:**250, 264–68
Demographic changes. *See* Migration and demographic changes
Deng Xiaoping, **1:**53, 202, 208, 211; **2:**116
Denmark, energy and sustainability, **1:**66–67, 74–79, *77*
Detroit, Michigan, housing and infrastructure, **1:**186, 213–19, *216*

Dharavi, neighborhood (Mumbai, India), **1**:22
Díaz, Porfirio, **1**:136; **2**:215
Dipiao system, **1**:203
District energy (DE) systems, **1**:124
Diwali, **2**:38
Dixon, Roland Burrage, **1**:282
Dongan, Thomas, **1**:160
Droughts, Syria, **2**:183–84
Dry-tomb landfills, **2**:252
Duda, Andrzej, **2**:31
Duggan, Mike, **1**:216
Dumpling and skewer model of development, **1**:292
Durning, Alan, **1**:50
Dutch disease, **1**:196

Ebtkar, Masoumeh, **1**:287
Eco-villages, **1**:134
Education. *See* Schools
Eetbaar Rotterdam (Edible Rotterdam), **1**:171–72
Egan, Tim, **1**:48
Egypt, waste management, **2**:238–39, 246–50, *248*
Ehlmaier, Michael, **1**:246
Eichstaedt, Peter, **2**:58
Eiffel Tower, **1**:166
El Centro de la Raza, **1**:50
El Niño, **1**:271, 273
Electrical vehicles, **1**:84, 85
Electricity consumption
  Frankfurt, Germany, **1**:83
  Mumbai, India, **1**:98–100
Employment and jobs
  Lagos, Nigeria, **1**:1–2, 6–10, *8*
  London, United Kingdom, **1**:4, *12,* 12–18
  Mumbai, India, **1**:2–3, 19–23
  New York City, New York, **1**:24–29, 25*t*, 27*t*
  overview, **1**:1–6
  Paris, France, **1**:5, 31–35, *32,* 34*t*
  Riyadh, Saudi Arabia, **1**:3, 36–40
  San Juan, Puerto Rico, **1**:2, 41–46, *44*
  Seattle, Washington, **1**:4, 48–51
  Shenzhen, China, **1**:5–6, 52–57, *54*
  Stockholm, Sweden, **1**:3–4, 58–63, *59*
Energy and sustainability
  Beijing, China, **1**:70–74, 72*t*
  China, **1**:65–66
  Copenhagen, Denmark, **1**:66–67, 74–79, *77*
  Frankfurt, Germany, **1**:68, 79–85
  London, United Kingdom, **1**:67–68, 86–90
  Melbourne, Australia, **1**:66, 92–96, *94*
  Mumbai, India, **1**:67, 97–102
  overview, **1**:65–70
  Pittsburgh, Pennsylvania, **1**:69–70, 106–10, *107*
  Rio de Janeiro, Brazil, **1**:68, 111–15, *112*
  Singapore City, Singapore, **1**:69, 116–19
  Toronto, Ontario, Canada, **1**:68–69, 120–24, *122*
Energy-efficient buildings
  Rio de Janeiro, Brazil, **1**:111–13, *112*
  Singapore City, Singapore, **1**:116–17
Engineering is Elementary (EiE), **2**:82
Environment, New York City, New York, **1**:28–29
Erdogan, Ercep Tayyip, **2**:138
Esser, Daniel, **2**:209, 211
Ethnic enclaves, **1**:259–60, 298
European Green Capital Award (EGCA), **1**:80–81
Eye Opener Program, **2**:66, 81

Finance and construction enterprises (FCEs), **1**:204
Fish, Robert, **2**:104
Flexi-jobs, **1**:22
Flint, Michigan, water pollution, **2**:4–5, 16–21
Food waste
  Norway, **2**:279–80
  Singapore, **2**:241, 293–97, 297*t*
Ford, Henry, **1**:213
Ford, Richard, **1**:108–9
Forsberg, Carl, **2**:210–11
France
  employment and jobs, **1**:5, 31–35, *32,* 34*t*
  green spaces, **1**:130, 164–68, *167*
Franco, Francisco, **2**:214
Frankfurt, Germany
  energy and sustainability, **1**:68, 79–85
  green space, **1**:81–84
Fraser, Barbara, **1**:271, 273
Fridell, Julia, **1**:*59*
Frisch, Max, **1**:231
Fu Zhenghua, **2**:197

Gallagher, John, **1**:218
Gangs
  Beijing, China, **2**:196
  Brussels, Belgium, **2**:200–201

Chicago, Illinois, **2:**203
Sicily, Italy, **2:**228
Garbage disposal. *See* Waste management
Gardens
   Paris, France, **1:**164–68
   Tel Aviv, Israel, **1:**173–77
Garner, Jay, **2:**188
Gatbonton, Elizabeth, **1:**262
Germany
   energy and sustainability, **1:**68, 79–85
   housing and infrastructure, **1:**189, 226–32, *227*
   immigration, **1:**228–32
   schools, **2:**64, 72–77, *74*
   traffic and transportation, **2:**121, 165–69
Gilbert, Dan, **1:**217
Goto, Shinpei, **1:**180
Grand Magal, **1:**242
Grands taxis, **2:**132
Granholm, Jennifer, **2:**17
Grant, Julie, **1:**108
Green spaces
   Abu Dhabi, United Arab Emirates (UAE), **1:**130, 131–35
   Aguascalientes, Mexico, **1:**128–29, 135–39
   Beijing, China, **1:**162
   Copenhagen, Denmark, **1:**75
   Frankfurt, Germany, **1:**81–84
   Halifax, Nova Scotia, Canada, **1:**128, 140–46, 141*t*, *142*
   Hong Kong, China, **1:**127–28, 147–52, *148*
   Moscow, Russia, **1:**129–30, 154–58, *157*
   New York City, New York, **1:**128, 159–63
   overview, **1:**127–31
   Paris, France, **1:**130, 164–68, *167*
   Rotterdam, the Netherlands, **1:**129, 169–72
   Tel Aviv, Israel, **1:**130–31, 173–77
   Tokyo, Japan, **1:**129, 178–81, *181*
Greenblatt, Sharon, **1:**175
Greenhouse gas, **1:**95
Greenhouse gas emissions, Toronto, Ontario, Canada, **1:**122–24
Gropius, Walter, **2:**187
Group of Twenty (G20), **1:**39
Guangzhou, China, migration and demographic changes, **1:**250–51, 259–63
Gulabzoi, Najibullah, **2:**210

Guo Shoujing, **1:**71
Gutcher, Laine, **2:**210
Gymnasium, **2:**75–76

Hagwon, **2:**90
Haiti, waste management, **2:**238, 281–87, *283, 284t, 285t, 287t*
Haiti earthquake (2010), **2:**286
Halifax, Nova Scotia, Canada, green spaces, **1:**128, 140–46, 141*t, 142*
Hall of Princes, **2:**196
Handshake buildings, **1:**162
Hannssen, O. J., **2:**280
Hardy, Douglas R., **1:**272
Hashimoto, Toru, **2:**156
Hauptschule, **2:**74, 76
Havana, Cuba, housing and infrastructure, **1:**187–88, 220–25, *221*
Haysom, Simone, **2:**208–9
Hiebert, Daniel, **1:**297
Hinenoya, Kimiko, **1:**262
Hiroshi, Chiba, **2:**268
Hokan languages, **1:**279, 282
Home Energy Loan Program (HELP), **1:**121
Hong Kong, China
   employment and jobs, **1:**53
   green spaces, **1:**127–28, 147–52, *148*
Hoornweg, Daniel, **2:**284, 285
Household responsibility system, **1:**202
Housing and infrastructure
   Almaty, Kazakhstan, **1:**188, 189–94
   Berlin, Germany, **1:**277
   Caracas, Venezuela, **1:**188, 195–99
   China, **1:**149–52
   Chongqing, China, **1:**186, 200–205, *203*
   Dandong, China, **1:**188–89, 206–11
   Detroit, Michigan, **1:**186, 213–19, *216*
   Havana, Cuba, **1:**187–88, 220–25, *221*
   London, United Kingdom, **1:**276–77
   Munich, Germany, **1:**189, 226–32, *227*
   overview, **1:**185–89
   Sydney, Australia, **1:**185, 233–38, *234*
   Touba, Senegal, **1:**187, 239–43
   Vienna, Austria, **1:**186–87, 244–47
Huang Qifan, **1:**203–4
Huang Teng, **2:**114, 115
Huaqiangbei Electronics Market, **1:***54,* 54–56
Huffelen, Alexandra van, **1:**171
Hugo, Victor, **1:**165

Hukou system, **1:**202, 203–4
Hussein, Adnan, **2:**192
Hussein, Saddam, **2:**177, 187, 189, 191, 238, 243
Hwang, Kyung Moon, **2:**222–23
Hydroponics farming, Tel Aviv, Israel, **1:**176

Illinois, violence, corruption, and organized crime, **2:**181, 202–6
Immigration
  Argentina, **1:**255–58
  France, **1:**34–35
  Germany, **1:**228–32
  London, United Kingdom, **1:**253
  Los Angeles, California, **1:**252
  Tokyo, Japan, **1:**252
  United Kingdom, **1:**277–78
  Vancouver, British Columbia, Canada, **1:**252, 294–98
Incineration, Singapore, **2:**295
India
  air pollution, **2:**4, 33–38, 34*t*, 142–43, 244
  employment and jobs, **1:**2–3, 19–23
  energy and sustainability, **1:**67, 97–102
  traffic and transportation, **2:**122–23, 140–44
  waste management, **2:**239, 262–66
Infrastructure. *See* Housing and infrastructure
Inose, Naoki, **2:**233
Iran, migration and demographic changes, **1:**251, 283–88, *286*
Iraq
  violence, corruption, and organized crime, **2:**177–78, 187–92, *190*
  waste management, **2:**237–38, 241–45, *242*
Ishihara, Shintaro, **2:**234
Iskandar, Leila, **2:**249
Islamic Iberia, **1:**254
Islamic schools, **2:***70,* 70–71
Israel, green spaces, **1:**130–31, 173–77
Istanbul, Turkey, traffic and transportation, **2:**123, 134–38, *136*
Italy
  air pollution, **2:**5–6, 39–43
  violence, corruption, and organized crime, **2:**179–80, 226–30
  waste management, **2:**240, 272–76, *274*
Ivan the Great, **2:**105

Jachimowicz, Maia, **1:**257
Jackson, Betsy, **1:**215, 216, 218–19
Jameson, Sam, **2:**232
Jang Song-thaek, **1:**211
Japan
  green spaces, **1:**129, 178–81, *181*
  immigration, **1:**252
  migration and demographic changes, **1:**252, 289–93, *290*
  schools, **2:**66, 100–105, *104*
  traffic and transportation, **2:**121, 154–58, *155*
  violence, corruption, and organized crime, **2:**181, 230–34
  waste management, **2:**241, 267–71, *270*
Japanese Street, **1:**261–62
Jardin des Champs Élysées, **1:**164–66
Jardin du Champ de Mars, **1:**165–66
Jeanneret, Charles-Édouard (Le Corbusier), **1:**191
Jensen, Frank, **1:**75
Jiang, Chelsea, **1:**297–98
Jobs. *See* Employment and jobs
John Paul II, Pope, **2:**28
Johnson, David, **2:**233
Jones Act of 1917, **1:**42–43
The Jungle (Seattle, Washington), **1:**49
Jus sanguinis, **1:**230
Jus soli, **1:**230

Kabul, Afghanistan, violence, corruption, and organized crime, **2:**178, 207–11, *209*
Kahn, Albert, **1:**213
Kansai International Airport, **2:**157–58
Karachi, Pakistan, air pollution, **2:**4, 23–27, *24*
Karzai, Hamid, **2:**210, 211
Kato, Hoei, **2:**157
Kazakhstan, housing and infrastructure, **1:**188, 189–94
Keegan, John, **2:**189
Kelley, Colin, **2:**183, 184
Kelly, Jim, **1:**109
Khameinei, Ayatollah Ali, **1:***286*
Khan, Sadiq, **1:**17, 88
Khashoggi, Jamal, **1:**37
Khatami, Mohammad, **1:**287
Khomeini, Ayatollah Ruhollah, **1:**284, *286*
Khrushchev, Nikita, **1:**191, 192
Khrushchevkas, **1:**191
Kibbutzim Movement, **1:**177

Kim Chae-kyu, **2:**221
Kim Dae-jung, **2:**222, 223
Kim Jong-un, **1:**208, 211, 209
Kim Young-sam, **2:**223
Kingsland, A. C., **1:**161
Kingston, Jeff, **1:**181
Kinshasa, Democratic Republic of Congo (DRC), migration and demographic changes, **1:**250, 264–68
Koban, **2:**181, 231
Kobe, Japan, waste management, **2:**241, 267–71, *270*
Koike, Yuriko, **2:**233
Kokichi, Mikimoto, **1:**131
Kolbert, Elizabeth, **2:**183
Kolkata, India
   air pollution, **2:**142–43, 144
   traffic and transportation, **2:**122–23, 140–44
Korean Town, **1:**251, 260–61
Kosmowski, Daniel, **1:**217
Krakow, Poland, air pollution, **2:**3, 28–32, *29*
Krakowski Alarm Smogowy, **2:**32
Kroeber, Alfred Louis, **1:**282
Kulbachevsky, Anton, **1:**154, 156
Kumar, Ashwani, **2:**263
Kurland, Richard, **1:**296
Kurtz, Ed, **2:**17
Kwon-Hein, Jaok, **2:**223

La Linea Verde, **1:**137–39
Lagos, Nigeria, employment and jobs, **1:**1–2, 6–10, *8*
Lake Zurich, **2:**174
Landfills
   Calgary, Alberta, Canada, **2:**252–53
   Dakar, Senegal, **2:**260
   Delhi, India, **2:**264–65, 265–66
   Haiti, **2:**285
   Naples, Italy, **2:**273–76
   Singapore, **2:**294
   United States, **2:**247
Law 116: Sterilization Law, **1:**43
Le Corbusier, **1:**191
Leary, Margaret, **1:**215, 216, 218–19
Lee, Anton King-wah, **1:**150
Lee, Jay Y. (Lee Jae-yong), **2:**224, 225
Lee Myung-bak, **2:**223
Leidenfrost, Wayne, **1:**297, 298
Lem, Stanislaw, **2:**28
Leung Chun-ying, **1:**149

Li, Zhen-shan, **2:**265
Liang Ke, **2:**196
Lima, Peru, migration and demographic changes, **1:**250, 269–73, *270*
Lincicome, Mark, **2:**101
Little Africa, **1:**251, 262–63
Liu Yungang, **1:**261
London, United Kingdom
   employment and jobs, **1:**4, *12,* 12–18
   energy and sustainability, **1:**67–68, 86–90
   housing and infrastructure, **1:**16, 276–77
   migration and demographic changes, **1:**253, 274–78
London Living Wage program, **1:**15, 16
Lopez Rivera, Oscar, **1:**42
Los Angeles, California, migration and demographic changes, **1:**252, 279–83
Louis XIV, King, **1:**164, 165
Louis Philippe, **1:**165
Lu, Professor, **1:**211
Luo, Michael, **2:**237–38, 241–45, *242*

MacBride, Samantha, **2:**291
MacLehose, Murray, **1:**147
Madrigal, Alexis C., **1:**106
Maduro Moros, Nicolas, **1:**196, 199, 197
Maestas, Roberto, **1:**50
Magistris, Luigi de, **2:**276
Mali, schools, **2:**62–63, 67–71, *70*
Mamadou, Sibalo, **2:**85–86
Marco Polo, **2:**6
Martel, Lucrecia, **1:**257
Martin, Richard, **1:**98
Marzolini, Pio, **2:**170
Mass transit, Karachi, Pakistan, **2:**26–27
Massachusetts
   schools, **2:**66, 78–82, *79*
   water pollution, **2:**1–2, 11–15, *13*
Massachusetts Institute of Technology (MIT), **2:**66, 78–79
Masuzoe, Yoichi, **2:**233
Matsu, Ichiro, **2:**156
Mayeur, Yvan, **2:**201–2
Mbacké, Sheikh Ahmadu Bamba, **1:**239, 241, 242
McCallum, John, **1:**298
McChrystal, Stanley, **2:**211
Mckean, Cameron Allan, **1:**180
Médersas, **2:***70,* 70–71
Medrano, Fernando, **1:**297

Meiji years (Japan), **2:**101–2, 103
Melbourne, Australia, energy and sustainability, **1:**66, 92–96, *94*
Merkel, Angela, **1:**81, 229, 231
Metcalfe, Victoria, **2:**208–9
Mexican Revolution of 1910, **2:**214–15
Mexico
   green spaces, **1:**128–29, 135–39
   traffic and transportation, **2:**123–24, 145–49, *147*
   violence, corruption, and organized crime, **2:**180–81, 213–19, *217*
Mexico City, Mexico
   traffic and transportation, **2:**123–24, 145–49, *147*
   violence, corruption, and organized crime, **2:**180–81, 213–19, *217*
Michigan
   housing and infrastructure, **1:**186, 213–19, *216*
   water pollution, **2:**4–5, 16–21
Micro-districts, **1:**191
MicroFIT solar photovoltaic programs, **1:**124
Micro-gardening, **2:**258, 259
Migration and demographic changes
   Buenos Aires, Argentina, **1:**251–52, 254–58, *256*
   Guangzhou, China, **1:**250–51, 259–63
   Kinshasa, Democratic Republic of Congo (DRC), **1:**250, 264–68
   Lima, Peru, **1:**250, 269–73, *270*
   London, United Kingdom, **1:**253, 274–78
   Los Angeles, California, **1:**252, 279–83
   overview, **1:**249–53
   Tehran, Iran, **1:**251, 283–88, *286*
   Tokyo, Japan, **1:**252, 289–93, *290*
   Vancouver, British Columbia, Canada, **1:**252, 294–98, *295*
   Williamsport, Pennsylvania, **1:**253, 299–303, *300*
Miles, Nelson A., **1:**41
Miller, R. A., **1:**262
Ministère de l'Education Nationale (MEN), **2:**68, 70–71
Ministry of Education, Sports, Culture and Technology (MEXT), **2:**101, 103–5
Minuit, Peter, **1:**24
Mobutu Sese Seko, **1:**266
Mohammed, Abbas, **2:**245
Montesquieu, **1:**164
Moon Jae-in, **2:**225
Morocco, traffic and transportation, **2:**122, 130–33
Moscow, Russia, green spaces, **1:**129–30, 154–58, *157*
Mottainai spirit, **2:**268
Mubarak, Hosni, **2:**249
Muggah, R., **2:**218
Muhsin, Haider, **2:**245
Mumbai, India
   employment and jobs, **1:**2–3, 19–23
   energy and sustainability, **1:**67, 97–102
Munich, Germany, housing and infrastructure, **1:**189, 226–32, *227*
Munich Wall, **1:**189
Municipal solid waste (MSW). *See* Waste management
Murid Sufi order, **1:**239–43
Murray, Ed, **1:**49
Museum of Science, Boston, **2:**81–82

Naeif, Salama Dhaeia, **2:**244
Naples, Italy
   landfills, **2:**273–76
   waste management, **2:**240, 272–76, *274*
Napoléon, **1:**165; **2:**214
Navajo nation, **2:**5, 55–59
Near-urban wilderness, Halifax, Nova Scotia, Canada, **1:**141*t*, 141–46
Netherlands, green spaces, **1:**129, 169–72
Neve, Felipe de, **1:**280
New Delhi, India, air pollution, **2:**4, 33–38, 34*t*. *See also* Delhi, India
New Mexico, radioactive pollution, **2:**5, 55–59
New Yalu River Bridge, **1:**206–8, 209, 211
New York City, New York
   employment and jobs, **1:**5, 24–29, 25*t*, 27*t*
   green spaces, **1:**128, 159–63
   traffic and transportation, **2:**122, 150–53, 151*t*
Niayes, **2:**257–59
Nichols, John, **1:**218
Nigeria, employment and jobs, **1:**1–2, 6–10, *8*
Nilsson-Wright, John, **2:**223
Nixon, Richard, **2:**218
North Korea, **1:**188–89, 206–11
Norway
   food waste, **2:**279–80

waste management, **2:**240, 276–80, 278*t*
Nova Scotia, green spaces, **1:**128, 140–46, 141*t, 142*
Nuclear power
  Germany, **1:**81
  Singapore City, Singapore, **1:**118–19

Obama, Barack, **1:**42, 45; **2:**19
Oil industry, Baku, Azerbaijan, **2:**2–3, 6–10, *7*
One belt one road (OBOR) initiative, **2:**116
Ontario, Canada, energy and sustainability, **1:**68–69, 120–24, *122*
Open source philosophy, **1:**56
Open-air dumps, **2:**285
Operation Bootstrap, **1:**43
Operation CeaseFire, **2:**205–6
Organized crime. *See* Violence, corruption, and organized crime
Orr, Kevyn, **1:**215, 217
Ortega, Estela, **1:**50
Ortega Douglas, Luis, **1:**136
Osaka, Japan, traffic and transportation, **2:**121, 154–58, *155*
Oslo, Norway, waste management, **2:**240, 276–80, 278*t*
Ouagadougou, Burkina Faso, schools, **2:**63, 83–86

Pahlavi, Mohammad Reza Shah, **1:**284
Pajama Factory, **1:**299–300, *300,* 301–2, 303
Pakistan, air pollution, **2:**4, 23–27, *24*
Papachristos, Andrew, **2:**204
Paris, France
  employment and jobs, **1:**5, 31–35, *32, 34t*
  green spaces, **1:**130, 164–68, *167*
Park Chung-hee, **2:**89, 221, 223
Park Geun-hye, **2:**180, 220, 222, 223–25, *224*
Parking, Beijing, China, **2:**127
Parks, New York City, New York, **1:**160–63
Partido Revolucionario Institucional (Institutional Revolutionary Party, PRI), **2:**215–16
Passive houses, **1:**83–84
Payind, Alam, **2:**211
Pearce, Fred, **1:**273
Pearling industry, **1:**131–32

Peña Nieto, Enrique, **2:**217
Pennsylvania
  energy and sustainability, **1:**106–10, *107*
  migration and demographic changes, **1:**253, 299–303, *300*
People's Communes, **1:**201–2
Pérón, Juan, **1:**256
Persian Gulf War, **2:**187–88
Peru
  climate change, **1:**271–73
  migration and demographic changes, **1:**250, 269–73, *270*
Petits taxis, **2:**131–32
Pfiffner, James, **2:**188
Phillips, Ted, **1:**216
Photovoltaics, Frankfurt, Germany, **1:**84
Piano, Renzo, **2:**157
Pilato, Michael, **1:**301
Pittsburgh, Pennsylvania, energy and sustainability, **1:**69–70, 106–10, *107*
Plaza Roberto Maestas, **1:**50
Pohlmann, Markus, **2:**223
Poinsett, Joel Roberts, **2:**215
Poland, air pollution, **2:**3, 28–32, *29*
Pollution, **2:**1–6. *See also* Air pollution; Radioactive pollution; Water pollution
Polytechnic University of Bobo-Dioulasso (UPB), **2:**84
Port-au-Prince, Haiti, waste management, **2:**238, 281–87, *283,* 284*t,* 285*t,* 287*t*
Portland, Oregon, **1:**277
Prodi, Romano, **2:**275
Public transportation
  Casablanca, Morocco, **2:**132–33
  Copenhagen, Denmark, **1:**78
  Istanbul, Turkey, **2:**136–37
  Kolkata, India, **2:**143–44
  London, United Kingdom, **1:**88, 276
  Mexico City, Mexico, **2:**147–48
  Saint Petersburg, Russia, **2:**161–62
  Toronto, Ontario, Canada, **1:***122,* 122–23
  Zurich, Switzerland, **2:**171–74
Puerto Rico, employment and jobs, **1:**2, 41–46, *44*
Puerto Rico Oversight, Management, and Economic Stability Act (PROMESA), **1:**45
Putin, Vladimir, **1:**39

Radioactive pollution, Shiprock, New Mexico, **2:**5, 55–59
Railroads, **1:**280–81
Ramírez, Edson, **1:**272
Rashid bin Saeed Al Maktoum, Sheikh, **1:**132
Reagan, Ronald, **2:**217
Realschule, **2:**74–75, 76
Recycling, Calgary, Alberta, Canada, **2:**255–56
Reeve, James, **1:**37
Reilly, Edward, **2:**234
Reinprecht, Christoph, **1:**246
Reishauer, Edwin O., **1:**262
Renewable energy, Melbourne, Australia, **1:**93–96
Resource curse, **1:**196
Reza Shah, **1:**284
Rheault, Ludovic, **1:**296
Rhee, Syngman, **2:**221
Richtel, Matt, **2:**288
Ring roads, **2:**125–26
Rio de Janeiro, Brazil, energy and sustainability, **1:**68, 111–15, *112*
Riots, **1:**281–82
Ripley, Amanda, **2:**90
Riyadh, Saudi Arabia, employment and jobs, **1:**3, 36–40
Rodriguez Castillo, Juan, **1:**280
Roh Moo-hyun, **2:**223
Roh Tae-woo, **2:**223
Rohani, Farid, **1:**296
Rome, Italy, air pollution, **2:**5–6, 39–43
Roosevelt, Franklin D., **1:**161
Rotterdam, the Netherlands, green spaces, **1:**129, 169–72
Roxbury Latin School, **2:**66, 80–81
Ruiz Cortines, Adolfo, **1:**136
Rumpshakers, **1:**213
Russia
 green spaces, **1:**129–30, 154–58, *157*
 schools, **2:**63–64, 105–10
 traffic and transportation, **2:**120, 160–65, *161*
Russian Federation Transport Strategy 2030, **2:**164

Sadek, Wathek, **2:**243
Sadr, Moqtada al-, **2:**192, 243
Saint Petersburg, Russia, traffic and transportation, **2:**120, 160–65, *161*
Sale, Murray, **2:**232
Salinas de Gortari, Carlos, **1:**136
Sall, Khalifa, **2:**259
Sami, Ola, **2:**243
Sami, Sabah, **2:**244
San Francisco, California, waste management, **2:**239–40, 288–92, *290*
San Juan, Puerto Rico, employment and jobs, **1:**2, 41–46, *44*
Sanitary landfill, **2:**285
Santa Anna, Antonio López de, **2:**214–15
Sao Paulo, Brazil, air pollution, **2:**3, 45–48
Saudi Arabia, employment and jobs, **1:**3, 36–40
S-Bahn, **2:**173–74
Schellnhuber, Hans Joachim, **2:**184–85
Schmitt, Eric, **2:**217
Schools
 Bamako, Mali, **2:**62–63, 67–71, *70*
 Berlin, Germany, **2:**64, 72–77, *74*
 Boston, Massachusetts, **2:**66, 78–82, *79*
 Ouagadougou, Burkina Faso, **2:**63, 83–86
 overview, **2:**61–66
 Seoul, South Korea, **2:**65–66, 87–90
 Sydney, Australia, **2:**65, 91–95
 Taipei, Taiwan, **2:**64–65, *96,* 96–100
 Tokyo, Japan, **2:**66, 100–105, *104*
 Vologda, Russia, **2:**63–64, 105–10
 Xi'an, China, **2:**62, 111–16, 113*t*
Schulz, Sebastian, **2:**190
Science, technology, engineering, and math (STEM), **2:**66, 78–82
Sea Forest, **1:**179–80
Seager, Richard, **2:**183–84
Seattle, Washington, employment and jobs, **1:**4, 48–51
Seine Valley, France, **1:**31–32
Sekundarschule, **2:**76
Senegal
 housing and infrastructure, **1:**187, 239–43
 waste management, **2:**238, 257–61, *258*
Seoul, South Korea
 air pollution, **2:**2, 52–53
 schools, **2:**65–66, 87–90
 violence, corruption, and organized crime, **2:**180, 220–25, *224*
 water pollution, **2:**2, 50–52, *51,* 53–54
Seth, Michael, **2:**87–88, 222
Set-Setal movement, **2:**261
Sewage treatment plants, Kobe, Japan, **2:**269

Shah, Agha Muhammed, **1:**283
Shah, Nassar Ed-Din, **1:**284
Shakespeare, William, **2:**182
Shanghai, China, **1:**21
Shanzhai industry, **1:**55–56
Shen Baozhen, **2:**96
Shenango Coke Works, **1:**108
Shenzhen, China, employment and jobs, **1:**5–6, 52–57, *54*
Shiprock, New Mexico, radioactive pollution, **2:**5, 55–59
Shuey, Chris, **2:**56
Sicily, Italy, violence, corruption, and organized crime, **2:**179–80, 226–30
Singapore City, Singapore
  energy and sustainability, **1:**69, 116–19
  waste management, **2:**241, 293–97, 297*t*
Six-party talks, **1:**210
Skyline alleys, **1:**162
Slums, **1:**197–98
Small and medium-sized enterprises (SMEs), **1:**9–10
Smith, John, **2:**15
Smith, Stephen J., **2:**156
Snyder, Rick, **1:**215; **2:**16–17, 19
Social housing, Australia, **1:**236–37
Solar panels
  Melbourne, Australia, **1:***94,* 95
  Rio de Janiero, Brazil, **1:**113–14
  Singapore City, Singapore, **1:**117–18
South Korea
  air pollution, **2:**2, 52–53
  schools, **2:**65–66, 87–90
  violence, corruption, and organized crime, **2:**180, 220–25, *224*
  water pollution, **2:**2, 50–52, *51,* 53–54
Soviet-Afghan war, **2:**207–8
Spanish colonization of the Americas, **2:**213–14
Special economic zone (SEZ), **1:**208–9
Special education, Taiwan, **2:**98–99
Spencer, John, **2:**189
Stadtbahn, **2:**167–68
Steel, Pittsburgh, Pennsylvania, **1:**106
Steele, Jonathan, **2:**207
Stensgård, A. E., **2:**280
Stephens, Kathleen, **2:**225
Sterilization program (Puerto Rico), **1:**43–44
Stockholm, Sweden, employment and jobs, **1:**3–4, 58–63, *59*
Strategic Subject List, **2:**204–5, 206

Streetcars, Zurich, Switzerland, **2:**172–73
Stuttgart, Germany, traffic and transportation, **2:**121, 165–69
Subways, New York City, New York, **2:**122, 150–53, 151*t*
Sugarcane, **1:**115
Sugrue, Thomas, **1:**214, 215, 218
Sullivan, Tim, **2:**210–11
Summer Olympics (Mexico City, 1968), **2:**216
Sustainability. *See* Energy and sustainability
Sweden, employment and jobs, **1:**3–4, 58–63, *59*
Switzerland, traffic and transportation, **2:**121–22, 170–74, *171*
Sydney, Australia
  housing and infrastructure, **1:**185, 233–38, *234*
  schools, **2:**65, 91–95
Syria, violence, corruption, and organized crime, **2:**178, 182–86, *185*
Syrian War, **1:**232
Szymborska, Wislawa, **2:**28

Taipei, Taiwan, schools, **2:**64–65, *96,* 96–100
Taiwan, schools, **2:**64–65, *96,* 96–100
Talbot, Margaret, **1:**110
Taliban, **2:**208, 209–10
Talyan, V., **2:**263
Tanaka, H., **1:**262
Tanaka, Kakuei, **2:**233
Tanaka, S., **1:**262
Tang, Bo-Sin, **1:**150
Taxis, **2:**131–32
Tehran, Iran, migration and demographic changes, **1:**251, 283–88, *286*
Tel Aviv, Israel, green spaces, **1:**130–31, 173–77
Terán Market, **1:**138
3D printing, **1:**27–28
Three R's (reduce, reuse, and recycle), **2:**240, 252, 269
Todd, Douglas, **1:**294
Tokyo, Japan
  green spaces, **1:**129, 178–81, *181*
  migration and demographic changes, **1:**252, 289–93, *290*
  schools, **2:**66, 100–105, *104*
  violence, corruption, and organized crime, **2:**181, 230–34

Tongva Amerindians, **1:**279
Too Good to Waste Strategy, **2:**254
Toronto, Ontario, Canada, energy and sustainability, **1:**68–69, 120–24, *122*
Toronto Green Standard, **1:**120–21
Total trihalomethanes (TTHM), **2:**19, 20
Touba, Senegal, housing and infrastructure, **1:**187, 239–43
Tower of David, **1:**197–98
Traffic and transportation
    Beijing, China, **2:**119–20, 124–29, *126*
    Casablanca, Morocco, **2:**122, 130–33
    Istanbul, Turkey, **2:**123, 134–38, *136*
    Kolkata, India, **2:**122–23, 140–44
    Mexico City, Mexico, **2:**123–24, 145–49, *147*
    Mumbai, India, **1:**100
    New York City, New York, **1:**28–29; **2:**122, 150–53, 151*t*
    Osaka, Japan, **2:**121, 154–58, *155*
    overview, **2:**119–24
    Saint Petersburg, Russia, **2:**120, 160–65, *161*
    Stuttgart, Germany, **2:**121, 165–69
    Zurich, Switzerland, **2:**121–22, 170–74, *171*
Tramlines
    Casablanca, Morocco, **2:**133
    Istanbul, Turkey, **2:**136
Transportation. *See* Traffic and transportation
Trees
    Karachi, Pakistan, **2:**25–26
    Moscow, Russia, **1:**154–55, 156–58, *157*
    Tokyo, Japan, **1:**179
Trittin, Jürgen, **1:**81
Trolleybuses, Zurich, Switzerland, **2:**173
Trotsky, Leon, **1:**191
Trump, Donald, **1:**39, 218, 232, 294
Tung Chee-hwa, **1:**149
Tunnels, Istanbul, Turkey, **2:**136–37
Turkey, traffic and transportation, **2:**123, 134–38, *136*
Turner, Duncan, **1:**56

Uber, **2:**128–29, 132
Umi no Mori (Sea Forest), **1:**179–80
United Arab Emirates (UAE), green spaces, **1:**130, 131–35

United Kingdom
    Brexit, **1:**4, 16–18
    employment and jobs, **1:**4, *12,* 12–18
    energy and sustainability, **1:**67–68, 86–90
    migration and demographic changes, **1:**253, 274–78
United States
    employment and jobs, **1:**4, 5, 48–51
    energy and sustainability, **1:**69–70, 106–10, *107*
    green spaces, **1:**128, 159–63
    housing and infrastructure, **1:**186, 213–19, *216*
    migration and demographic changes, **1:**252, 253, 279–83, 299–303, *300*
    radioactive pollution, **2:**5, 55–59
    schools, **2:**66, 78–82, *79*
    violence, corruption, and organized crime, **2:**181, 202–6
    waste management, **2:**239–40, 247, 288–92, *290*
    water pollution, **2:**1–2, 4–5, 11–15, *13,* 16–21
University of Koudougou (UK), **2:**84
University of New South Wales (UNSW), **2:**92, 93–94
University of Ouagadougou (UO), **2:**84
University of Technology's Sydney (UTS) Institute for Public Policy and Governance, **2:**94–95
Uranium mines, **2:**5, 55–59
Urban forestry, Karachi, Pakistan, **2:**25–26

Vahid-Dastjerdi, Marzieh, **1:**287
Vancouver, British Columbia, Canada, migration and demographic changes, **1:**252, 294–98, *295*
Veisten, Knut, **1:**77
Venezuela, housing and infrastructure, **1:**188, 195–99
Verkehrsbetriebe Zurich (VBZ), **2:**172
Verkehrs-und Tarifverbund Stuttgart (VVS), **2:**167
Vermicomposting, **2:**296
Viberg, Rebecka, **1:***59*
Vienna, Austria, housing and infrastructure, **1:**186–87, 244–47
Vilalta, C., **2:**218
Violence, corruption, and organized crime
    Aleppo, Syria, **2:**178, 182–86, *185*

Baghdad, Iraq, **2:**177–78, 187–92, *190*
Beijing, China, **2:**179, 193–97
Brussels, Belgium, **2:**179, 197–202, *199*
Chicago, Illinois, **2:**181, 202–6
Kabul, Afghanistan, **2:**178, 207–11, *209*
Mexico City, Mexico, **2:**180–81, 213–19, *217*
overview, **2:**177–81
Seoul, South Korea, **2:**180, 220–25, *224*
Sicily, Italy, **2:**179–80, 226–30
Tokyo, Japan, **2:**181, 230–34
Vologda, Russia, schools, **2:**63–64, 105–10
Vologda Multidisciplinary Lyceum, **2:**108–9
Vologda State University, **2:**109–10
Voltaire, **1:**164
Vom Hau, Matthias, **1:**255, 258

Wade, Abdoulaye, **2:**259
Wang, Hao, **2:**265
Wang Yi, **1:**210
Washington, George, **1:**24, 160
Washington (state), employment and jobs, **1:**4, 48–51
Waste management
    Baghdad, Iraq, **2:**237–38, 241–45, *242*
    Cairo, Egypt, **2:**238–39, 246–50, *248*
    Calgary, Alberta, Canada, **2:**240, 251–56, 253*t*, 255*t*
    Dakar, Senegal, **2:**238, 257–61, *258*
    Delhi, India, **2:**239, 262–66
    Kobe, Japan, **2:**241, 267–71, *270*
    Naples, Italy, **2:**240, 272–76, *274*
    Oslo, Norway, **2:**240, 276–80, 278*t*
    overview, **2:**237–41
    Port-au-Prince, Haiti, **2:**238, 281–87, *283,* 284*t,* 285*t,* 287*t*
    San Francisco, California, **2:**239–40, 288–92, *290*
    Singapore City, Singapore, **2:**241, 293–97, 297*t*
    United States, **2:**247
Watanabe, Teresa, **2:**232
Water pollution
    Baku, Azerbaijan, **2:**2–3, 6–10, *7*
    Boston, Massachusetts, **2:**1–2, 11–15, *13*
    Flint, Michigan, **2:**4–5, 16–21

Seoul, South Korea, **2:**2, 50–52, *51, 53*–54
Water shortage, Beijing, China, **1:**65–66, 70–74, 72*t*
Weather vs. climate, **2:**186
Wen Jiabao, **1:**207
Wiarda, Jan-Martin, **2:**75
Williams, Brian Glyn, **2:**208
Williams, Phil, **2:**191
Williamsport, Pennsylvania, migration and demographic changes, **1:**253, 299–303, *300*
Wilson, Mary, **1:**271
Wing, Paul, **2:**189
Women
    Iran, **1:**285–87
    Japan, **1:**291
    Saudi Arabia workforce, **1:**38
Wong, Siu-Wai, **1:**150
Woodhull, C. S., **1:**161
Worms, **2:**296
Wowereit, Klaus, **2:**77
Wright, Frank Lloyd, **2:**187
Wyant, Dan, **2:**17, 19

Xi Jinping, **1:**209, 262; **2:**116, 193, 196
Xi'an, China, schools, **2:**62, 111–16, 113*t*
Xi'an International University, **2:**114, 115
Xiaobei Road, **1:**262

Yakuza, **2:**233–34
Young, Bob, **1:**49
Young, Ian, **1:**297
Yutori, **2:**66, 101, 103–4

Zabaleen, **2:**249–50
Zagorin, Edmund, **1:**216
Zayed bin Sultan Al Nahyan, Sheikh, **1:**132
Zero waste, **2:**288–92
Zero Waste Building Program, **1:**123–24
Zero Waste National (Singapore), **2:**296
Zhao, Yan, **2:**265
Zhou Yongkang, **2:**196–97
Zones touristiques internationales (ZTI), **1:***32,* 32–34, 34*t*
Zoot Suit Riots, **1:**281
Zurich, Switzerland, traffic and transportation, **2:**121–22, 170–74, *171*